Secret Agents

TIME LINE

1945 Truman takes office

Atomic bombs dropped on Hiroshima and
Nagasaki

1946 Surge in first mass–produced televisions on
market

J. Edgar Hoover decries "red fascism"

Atomic Energy Commission takes over
Manhattan Project

1947 Beginning of UFO sightings

House Un–American Activities Committee
(HUAC) begins hearings on
Communism in the film industry

1948 Communists take control of
Czechoslovakia

Marshall Plan

Term "Cold War" is coined by Barnard
Baruch

Israel declares independence

Scientists begin to study health of uranium
miners

1949 First modern computer (EDSAC at
Cambridge) completes first automatic
computation

USSR explodes an atomic bomb

Mao declares People's Republic of China

1950 Klaus Fuchs charged with giving information about the atomic bomb to USSR

FBI arrests David Greenglass

Korean War begins

Julius and Ethel Rosenberg arrested

Diner's Club credit cards first issued—
beginnings of credit card culture

1951 Rosenberg trial and conviction

I Love Lucy first airs

First nuclear power station

"Rock 'n' roll" named

1952 Popular films: *It Came From Beneath the
Sea* and *Red Planet Mars*

First television broadcast of elections:
Eisenhower wins

1953 Rosenbergs executed

Death of Stalin

First *Playboy* on the newsstands

Armistice signed in Korea

Roy Cohn becomes chief counsel to
Senator Joe McCarthy

James Bond introduced in *Casino Royale*

1954 Army–McCarthy hearings televised for 36
continuous days

McCarthy censured

Televisions in one half of U.S. homes

Brown v. Board of Education

1955 Disneyland opens

Rosa Parks arrested

Montgomery Bus Boycott begins

Albert Einstein dies

1956 Martin Luther King, Jr.'s house is bombed

Federal district court rules bus segregation
unconstitutional

Soviet Union in Hungary

Florida begins to investigate National
Association for the Advancement of
Colored People (NAACP) for
Communist infiltration

1957 Death of McCarthy

Riots in Little Rock, Arkansas; Eisenhower
sends in federal troops

King founds Southern Christian Leadership
Conference

Sputnik

1958 U.S. *Explorer I*

Many Southern schools close rather than
desegregate

Khrushchev comes to power in Soviet
Union

1959 Eisenhower on peace tours of Europe

Martin Luther King, Jr., goes to India to
study with Ghandi

Culture Work
A Book Series from the Center for Literary and Cultural Studies at Harvard
edited by Marjorie Garber

Media Spectacles
Marjorie Garber, Jann Matlock, and Rebecca L. Walkowitz, editors

Secret Agents

The Rosenberg Case, McCarthyism, and Fifties America

Edited by
Marjorie Garber
and
Rebecca L. Walkowitz

Routledge » New York & London

Published in 1995 by
Routledge
29 West 35th Street
New York, NY 10001

Published in Great Britain by
Routledge
11 New Fetter Lane
London EC4P 4EE

The editors gratefully acknowledge the permission of the following publishers to
reprint for this volume these essays: Cultural Forecast: Shutesbury, MA, for "The
Rosenbergs and the Crime of the Century" by Blanche Wiesen Cook, from *The
Rosenbergs: Collected Visions of Artists and Writers* edited by Rob A. Okun,
copyright © 1993 by Rob A. Okun; BasicBooks, a division of HarperCollins
Publishers, Inc., for "Censorship of Uranium Mining in the 1950's," from *Cancer
Wars* by Robert N. Proctor, copyright © 1995 by Robert N. Proctor; Verso: New
York and London, for "The Work of the State," from *The Chicago Gangster
Theory of Life: Nature's Debt to Society* by Andrew Ross, copyright © 1994 by
Andrew Ross.

Design: David Thorne
Printed in the United States of America on acid-free paper.

Library of Congress Cataloging-in-Publication Data
Secret Agents: the Rosenberg case, McCarthyism, and fifties America /
edited by Marjorie Garber and Rebecca L. Walkowitz.
    p.   cm.   —(Culture work)
Includes bibliographical references and index.
ISBN 0-415-91119-2 (cl) — ISBN 0-415-91120-6 (pb)

    1. Rosenberg, Ethel, 1915–1953.   2. Rosenberg, Julius, 1918–1953.
    3. Communists—United States—Biography.   4. Spies—United States—
    Biography.   5. Trials (Espionage)—United States.   6. McCarthy, Joseph,
    1908–1957.   7. Cold War.   8. United States—Politics and government—
    1945–1953.   I. Garber, Marjorie B.   II. Walkowitz, Rebecca L.   III. Series.

HX84.R578S43   1995   95-22436
364.1'31'097309045—dc20   CIP

Contents

PART THREE
Testimonies

Acknowledgments

The editors wish to thank the many friends and colleagues whose insights and labor were essential to the production of this book. In particular, we are indebted to Alice Jardine, who was instrumental in conceiving this project and who early recognized its importance. Our thanks also to Carol Forney and Jenn Meeropol for their crucial work at the early stages of the volume.

Helpful conversations with K. Anthony Appiah, Virginia Carmichael, Dan Danielsen, Ellen Fitzpatrick, Diana Fuss, Bonnie Honig, Barbara Johnson, D. A. Miller, Londa Schiebinger, and Andrea Walsh extended our thinking about the questions addressed here. Barbara Akiba, Christina Carlson, Karen Friedland, and Herrick Wales at the Center for Literary and Cultural Studies at Harvard provided generous assistance throughout the production of the volume. Robert Meeropol, Michael Meeropol, and Rob A. Okun made possible the reproduction of several important images in this book. We are grateful to the Walter J. Minton Fund, Radcliffe College, and Time Warner Inc. for their financial support. Our warm thanks to William Germano and Eric Zinner at Routledge for their wise advice and their close attention to this project.

(Courtesy of Michael and Robert Meeropol)

Introduction

Secret Agents

Rebecca L. Walkowitz

> The sacrosanct fetish of today is science.... Since bombs are your means of expression, it would be really telling if one could throw a bomb into pure mathematics. But that is impossible.
>
> —Joseph Conrad, *The Secret Agent*

In the trial of Julius and Ethel Rosenberg—perhaps the most famous bomb scandal of this century—Conrad's "impossible" vision became a real conspiracy and media spectacle: the Rosenbergs were convicted and executed not for throwing a bomb but for stealing its secrets. Conrad's *The Secret Agent*, loosely based on a bomb scandal of the 1890s, imagines what our own fin de siècle might call "virtual" terrorism: a direct attack on knowledge and cultural icons, on the metaphors of the modern world. The deep irony of the "impossible" bombing extends in Conrad's novel beyond practical difficulties to a paradox of intent: breaking the law, the Secret Agent actually aims to provoke punishment and police action. Moreover, the Secret Agent exists in a world where government detectives and political spies are one and the same, where criminals and constables share activities and functions.

As many of the essays in this volume demonstrate, the Rosenberg case turned on similar ironies of narrative and agency. Indeed, the trial exploded "pure science" in its most technical and figurative manifestations, destroying any conviction that technology might be, or could be, insulated from cultural or political life. The Rosenberg story, like the event that inspired Conrad's novel, has been reenacted as fiction in a variety of media and contexts. Most recently, on the fortieth anniversary of the execution, the American Bar Association held a "mock trial" to reconsider the evidence; a jury acquitted the "mock Rosenbergs," finding that in today's courts they would not have been convicted of espionage.

In the 1950s, the trial of the Rosenbergs on charges of "Atomic Spying" and "stealing the secrets of the Atomic bomb" galvanized America, provoking public debate on all sides. Even American Jewish groups and the American Left, communities in which the Rosenbergs worked and lived, were deeply divided by the case. Had the Rosenbergs passed "atomic secrets" on to the Russians, secrets so vital that they enabled the Soviet Union to build its own atomic bomb? Or were they set up by a government eager for scapegoats in an era of military competition and nationalist anxiety? The trial in many minds came to stand for the paranoia of the Cold War.

Today, many of the issues that aroused fierce partisanship in the 1950s are still with us. Roy Cohn, one of the most fervent prosecutors of the Rosenbergs, reappears powerfully in Tony Kushner's prize-winning *Angels in America*, as indeed does the quietly confident figure of Ethel Rosenberg. New revelations about the dangers of bomb testing, and secret government-sponsored "experiments" involving radiation in children's milk, are among the public concerns of the nineties. A new biography of J. Edgar Hoover, and a remarkable number of sensational, televised trials and congressional hearings, calls attention to an earlier era in which hearings, trials, and alleged government cover-ups tested the practice of democracy. Feminism, civil rights, the death penalty, due process, homosexuality, immigration—all of these issues came into focus in and around the Rosenberg case and the McCarthy era, with its blacklisting of many artists, writers, filmmakers, and intellectuals.

Through the lens of the Rosenberg case, contributors to *Secret Agents* refract a cultural history of the 1950s. Several authors in this volume interpret the 1950s as a culmination of political and social anxieties about espionage, patriotism, racial integration, and technology, while others look back on the earlier decade as a seminal moment in the controversies of the 1990s. For instance, Ellen Schrecker scrutinizes a long tradition of anti-communist investigations and hysteria in her eloquent account of the early Cold War of the 1930s and 1940s, while Andrew Ross describes the recent World Trade Center bombing in the context of the Rosenberg trial—as another test case "in what was to be considered 'American' and what was not." Turning to the Civil Rights movement, to advertising, to early situation comedy, to biography and physics, contributors elaborate the rich cultural landscape in which the Rosenberg case unfolded and intervened. Contributors address competing interpretations of this history and consider the effects of interpretation and historical perspective on the scientific, technological, and legal concerns of today. The world of the 1950s, critics demonstrate, informs recent studies of the causes of cancer, academic controversies in the humanities, and legal debates over capital punishment.

Whether they look backward or forward, many essays in this collection describe how McCarthyism placed intellectuals at risk for their political lives; they describe a time when congressional committees and university governors deemed political commitment grounds for professional dismissal. As they describe McCarthyism, many contributors here court its specter to the extent that they make visible the political or personal stakes of their scholarly arguments. For several authors, this visibility is not incidental but critically imperative. In the McCarthy era, the public spectacle of intellectuals and politics in close proximity mobilized two related questions: To what extent can political statements be intellectual statements? Can the true intellectual, even a "public intellectual," be political? These questions are no less pertinent today.

Scholars and journalists alike have renewed attempts to locate the place from which intellectuals speak; in the academy this concern infuses work on biography and identity politics, and in the media it recurs in recent articles about scholars who comment on—and "make"—the news. In this volume, essays by Alice Jardine, Bruce Robbins, and David Suchoff track this contemporary interest as well as its roots in McCarthyism and debates among the New York intellectuals. The political and media focus on "intellectuals" in both epochs—now and then—not only raises the question "For whom do intellectuals speak?" but adds the following gloss: "What is an intellectual? Who decides? What is at stake in such exclusions?"

Public commentators in the 1950s contested the literary and intellectual merits of the *Death House Letters*—the personal correspondence between Julius and Ethel Rosenberg in the few years before their execution. These letters became a crucial factor in the political legacy of the Rosenberg executions. In this volume David Thorburn exposes the multiple agents behind these letters: a recent complete edition collected by Michael Meeropol, the Rosenberg's elder son, indicates that the couple's correspondence was severely edited and at times rewritten after their death. Over the past several decades, critics have used the letters to assess the Rosenbergs' authenticity as political and intellectual subjects. Yet the editing process poses two important questions about this demand for authenticity and, more broadly, about the production and reception of literary texts: What was imagined to be political, intellectual, or even socially palatable in the 1950s? And if the letters weren't themselves "authentic," what happens to the contest over political or intellectual truth for which they were the battleground?

In the 1990s, the right to claim intellectual authenticity, and the political authority that goes with it, often depends on claims to victimization—now frequently invoked in the "political correctness" debates. The analogy between McCarthyism and "political correctness" is a common one, if somewhat complicated by the two-way traffic in epithets: pundits on the Right cry "McCarthyism" in response to critiques of conservative tradition, critiques which they vilify as "politically correct"; pundits on the Left who offer these critiques argue that the term "politically correct" works to reproduce institutional divisions and intellectual caricatures reminiscent of the 1950s, and thus they cry "McCarthyism" as well.

The resolution of the "political correctness" stalemate, like the "secret" of the Rosenberg case, depends on the evidence: it depends on what is admitted to evidence, either as marginal or canonical, as pertinent or impertinent. Is politics part of academia or a force projected into it? Given the extent to which higher education has become a platform issue at every level of electoral politics, is it possible (or desirable) for scholars to insulate their academic inquiries from the national debates that address them? Gayatri Chakravorty Spivak argues persuasively on this matter that "radical teachers at universities—an important apparatus of upward class mobility—should attend to the nature of the institution that is their contractual space—and not ignore their obligation by claiming a spurious marginality, and declare the desire for revolution as its accomplishment. I believe the teacher, *while operating within the institution*, can foster the emergence of a committed collectivity by not making her institutional commitment invisible."[1]

Spivak's position troubles traditional accounts of the public intellectual as well as some recent demands for a more narrowly-defined literary practice. Spivak understands the academic institution, with its pedagogy and research, as a social space that is both distinct and permeable: it is a site of exchange within the circulation of public life. This argument disputes the very grounds on which some have demanded, and so implied, a fundamental distinction between "literary and educational terms" and the "gender, racial and class politics" invoked to discuss them.[2] The literary scholar Harold Bloom, in *The Western Canon*, has advanced such a demand, arguing that intellectual and aesthetic standards in the humanities and social sciences are being destoyed "in the name of social justice." By publishing in the trade press and expounding in the media, however, Bloom himself tests the boundaries of these distinctions and of the category "public intellectual."[3] On the one hand, perhaps an *intellectual* cannot really *be* "public," if the former category is reserved for those who shun "social justice" or who claim political neutrality for their work. On the other hand, as Bruce Robbins has written, "public" for some means "hovering somewhere above the messy melee of actual collective and overlapping identities that is society."[4] This "public," Robbins sharply explains, can only *be* public as it does not announce itself, or its authority, *as* public, in terms of institutions or specific social spaces.

Other recent discussions of the public intellectual also associate the scholar's authority with a position of marginality and distanced critique, even though they often acknowledge the fundamental necessity of critical intervention. Edward Said has characterized the intellectual as "exile and marginal, as amateur, and as the author of a language that tries to speak the truth to power."[5] Embracing the position of "the amateur," Said offers a gesture of self-deprecation that is at the same time accompanied by a claim to relative objectivity. Exile or not, Said rigorously separates his "rank amateur" opinions on "broader matters" from his professional presentation of literature inside a classroom.[6] At a time when literature has so often become the focus of international dispute and censorship, it seems doubtful that literary critics such as Said could be "amateurs" in the affairs of public policy. Scholars in this volume negotiate this debate in readings of trial narratives, advertisements, or contemporary drama and in historical studies of uranium or espionage; they bring their expertise and disciplinary training to bear on topics that at times cross, perhaps extend, the boundaries of academic discourse.

The Rosenberg case and the McCarthy era have much to instruct about the roles of intellectual "exile" and political "amateur." As Carol Hurd Green, Joyce Antler, Marie Ashe, and Robert Meeropol document in this collection, prosecuting attorneys used Ethel Rosenberg's refusal to act "like a victim," and her refusal to separate motherhood and political activism, to vilify her as an unnatural, unsympathetic woman. Attorneys cast Ethel Rosenberg as a contradiction in terms, since motherhood was presumed to be outside or above politics whereas activism was most engaged in it. This contradiction was incompatible with conventional femininity and with the sympathy owed to "proper" victims. Ethel Rosenberg's fate in the hands of the writers, the news media, and the film industry is suggestive of the power and constraints of claimed victimization. Today, one might claim the political authority of anti-McCarthyism—perhaps in Ethel Rosenberg's name—but, as this volume suggests, this legacy is framed by competing agendas and stereotypes.

The contributors to this volume "question authority"—and ethical authority, in particular—in the most fundamental way: they demonstrate the making of authority as a process, showing how the New York intellectuals, J. Edgar Hoover, the Rosenberg prosecutors, and government scientists alike constructed a fiction of coherence from contradictory facts. Contributors address these fictions as they were promoted as fact in the Rosenberg trial and in the

McCarthy era, and also as they have continued to influence today's cultural politics. In their backward and forward glances, these essays incorporate new facts and new fictions in their analysis. Michael Cadden, for example, considers how today's critics on the Left have mobilized a homophobic rhetoric in their attacks on McCarthy attorney Roy Cohn, who died of AIDS in 1986. Although Cadden fully condemns Cohn's efforts to prosecute the Rosenbergs, he nevertheless argues that much contemporary writing about Cohn's life has recycled the hypocrisy of Cohn's homophobia by refusing to mention the gay sexual practices of the back room or bedroom that, by insinuation, come to substitute for the openly discussed and condemned political practices of the courtroom. What Cadden perceptively shows, and what many other essays in this volume also suggest, is the contiguity between back room, bedroom, courtroom, even boardroom, and classroom.

Recognizing this contiguity, our contributors examine multiple sites of midcentury American culture, from spy novels and situation comedy to trials and scientific research, seeking to challenge the traditional perspectives through which these artifacts have been seen. These essays return to Roy Cohn or the Jell-O box or the Rosenberg letters to resituate them, and, moreover, to estrange them from the symbolic positions that they have occupied. In this estrangement it is not so much that the authority of political figures, such as Roy Cohn, or of political narratives, such as those about gender and espionage, is undermined by new vulnerabilities and critiques but, rather, that authority emerges here as a performance subject to interventions and internal contradiction.

Secret Agents has been organized into sections that, by their titles, are meant to defamiliarize what we know about the Rosenberg case, McCarthyism, and fifties America. *Secrets*: What were "the secrets," and what is the secret about secrets? *Agents*: Who were the agents? Where did the spies, or the stories about spies, or the stories about the Rosenbergs as spies, come from? *Testimonies*: What, or who, was on trial in the 1950s? What can today's testimonies to "that time" tell us about trials, memory, and historical transformation?

Many of the individuals or objects discussed in the *Secrets* essays are famous, if not infamous, characters in the Rosenberg drama: Roy Cohn, J. Edgar Hoover, the FBI, Julius and Ethel Rosenberg, David Greenglass, uranium, the Jell-O box. For most Cold War spectators, these characters *were* the secrets—of the atomic bomb, of Soviet conspiracy, of American strength. Yet what Stanley Goldberg writes of the atomic bomb secrets proves similarly true for a host of others addressed here: there wasn't a single, consistent "secret." Moreover, the term, "secret," is not an empty or objective category but a political maneuver. As Marjorie Garber and Blanche Wiesen Cook explain in the collection's opening essays, political conspiracies need secrets, and so the Rosenberg trial and its McCarthyist logic required a covert story to reveal.

The editors understand *Secrets* to include gaps in trial testimony, unacknowledged agendas, closeted sexualities, unknown scientific data, censored information, and other condensed rhetoric of 1950s culture. The first section of this volume includes contributions from a very wide range of disciplines; literary critics, historians of science, political theorists, and social historians collectively explore the underexplained mythologies of a watershed event in this century. In a close reading of trial narratives and cultural intertexts, Marjorie Garber examines the missing pieces to the famous Jell-O box, which was a telling clue in the Rosenberg prosecution. The Jell-O box, Garber persuasively argues, was the "evidence" whose proof lay in the patriotic values of its pudding. Turning to several shocking, classified CIA memos from the 1950s, released only recently through Freedom of Information Act litigation, Blanche Wiesen Cook shows how the U.S. Government hoped to use the Rosenbergs as pawns in sophisticated political warfare.

The Rosenbergs were executed for stealing the production secrets of the atomic bomb, but anxiety about bomb-related information touched scientific knowledge far beyond the putative how-to-do-it instructions: as Joyce Nelson and Robert N. Proctor explain, corporation laboratories and government bureaucrats transformed discoveries about uranium, the effects of radiation, and atomic fallout into additional secrets to be patrolled and censored. Power brokers such as J. Edgar Hoover and Roy Cohn enforced this broad secrecy through a Cold War rhetoric that often tied Communist conspiracy to homosexuality, lack of patriotism, bad motherhood, and other accusations framed as social pathology. In their essays on Hoover and Cohn, Thomas L. Dumm and Michael Cadden provide a new context for this rhetoric in the light of Hoover's and Cohn's own sexual secrets, revealed and pathologized by biographers in the last few years. Engaging similar themes, Alice Jardine recounts the transformation of Cold War technologies in the decades since the 1950s.

The secrets about secrets in the first group of essays recast the agents, and relocate the agency, in narratives about the 1950s. In the essays grouped under the heading *Agents*, contributors show that the conspiracy theories that produced the "real," accused spies also produced powerful "fictional" characters, such as James Bond, who helped fashion the nationalism and professionalism of the Cold War marketplace. Thus Ellen Schrecker's history of early Cold War espionage prosecutions sets the stage for the literary and intellectual trials discussed by Bruce Robbins, David Suchoff, David

Thorburn, Carol Hurd Green, Joyce Antler, and Marie Ashe. Essays in this section extend the range of presumed participants in the contests of 1950s political culture: cultural critics, historians, and legal scholars here read the social texts of the period, from essays and letters to novels, films, and television.

In the final section, *Testimonies*, contributors consider the Rosenberg trial in the legal context of the Civil Rights movement, death penalty legislation, and the recent, high-profile World Trade Center bombing trials. Contributors also take personal contexts into account: five lawyers, including the Rosenberg's younger son, Robert Meeropol, place the Rosenberg case in terms of their own perspectives on, or from, the period. David Kennedy, Morton J. Horwitz, Randall Kennedy, and Karl E. Klare testify to the broad effects of the Rosenberg trial on their own convictions and in the tradition of legal convictions since the 1950s. Finally, Andrew Ross suggests what the Rosenberg case can teach us about public trials, xenophobia, and conspiracy theories in the 1990s. Reading accounts of the "terrorist threat" to American government and economy, Ross brings the underlying rhetoric of national and ethnic purity into sharp focus.

National purity, ethnic purity, and "pure" mathematics. As Conrad's provocateur understood, an attack on scientific knowledge—the crime for which the Rosenbergs were executed—was seen as a threat against "the whole social creation."[7] The contributors to *Secret Agents* elaborate the "telling" consequences of such an "impossible" crime.

NOTES

Epigraph from Joseph Conrad, *The Secret Agent* (1907; reprint, London: Penguin, 1984), 66–67.

1 Gayatri Chakravorty Spivak, *Outside in the Teaching Machine* (New York and London: Routledge, 1993), 294, her emphasis.

2 Norman Fruman makes this argument in "Bloom at Thermopylae," *New York Times Book Review*, October 9, 1994, 9.

3 Harold Bloom, *The Western Canon: The Books and School of the Ages* (New York: Harcourt, 1994), 35.

4 Bruce Robbins describes Russell Jacoby's figure of the public intellectual in *Intellectuals: Aesthetics, Politics, Academics* ed. Bruce Robbins (Minneapolis: University of Minnesota Press, 1990), xiv–xv.

5 Edward Said, *Representations of the Intellectual* (New York: Pantheon, 1994), xvi.

6 Ibid., 88.

7 Conrad, *The Secret Agent*, 66.

PART ONE

Secrets

(Courtesy of Kraft General Foods, Inc.)

1

Jell-O

Marjorie Garber

And this may help to thicken other proofs
That do demonstrate thinly.

—*Othello*

The infamous "Jell-O box." In the trial of Julius and Ethel
Rosenberg it would come to be regarded as the key piece of prosecution
evidence, the "necessary link" tying the Rosenbergs to a purported conspiracy to steal the secret of the atomic bomb. As Judge Irving Kaufman put
it in his charge to the jury, "the Government contends that you have a right
to infer that there existed a link between Julius Rosenberg and Yakovlev [the
Soviet agent] in that Julius Rosenberg in some way transmitted...the Jell-O
box-side to Yakovlev."[1] And Irving Saypol, the prosecutor, claimed that
Harry Gold's testimony about the Jell-O box "forged the necessary link in
the chain that points indisputably to the guilt of the Rosenbergs."[2]

The Jell-O box, the government contended, was a sign, a password from
one conspirator to another. Ruth Greenglass testified that in January 1945
her brother-in-law Julius took her into the kitchen of his apartment and cut
the side of a Jell-O box into two odd-shaped pieces, giving one to Ruth and
keeping the other for himself. "This half," she said he told her, "will be
brought to you by another party and he will bear the greetings from me and
you will know that I have sent him."[3]

With the Jell-O box the government produced the damning code phrase—

"the greetings"—uttered by self-proclaimed courier Harry Gold. As the conspirators met and matched their Jell-O box halves, Gold (it was said) intoned the surprisingly uncryptic words, "I come from Julius." Without this primal scenario, the government had no evidence to present, nothing to link the Rosenbergs to David Greenglass and the atomic secrets.

Of course, the actual Jell-O box used in this transaction, as Roy Cohn and Myles Lane matter-of-factly admitted to the jury, had not been preserved. But since all Jell-O boxes look more or less alike (differing only as to which of the six delicious flavors then available—strawberry, raspberry, cherry, orange, lemon, and lime—had been favored on the crucial occasion), the prosecution helpfully produced, as an aide-mémoire in the courtroom, a fac-simile of the Jell-O box panel in question, a simulacrum of the Jell-O box side that Harry Gold had, he said, presented to David Greenglass on that fateful morning in June 1945 in Albuquerque, New Mexico.

"The history of this Jello box side," said chief prosecutor Saypol in his summation to the jury, presumably holding up the object in question, "the history of this Jello box side, the greetings from Julius, and Greenglass's whereabouts in Albuquerque come to us not only from Ruth and David, but from Harry Gold, ...a man concerning whom there cannot be a suggestion of motive... [since] he has been sentenced to thirty years."[4] Much has been written about Harry Gold's active fantasy life, his spectacular history of untruthfulness: the wife and twin children he invented and described to his coworkers, his reasons for suddenly claiming to be Klaus Fuchs's courier, his opportunity, in the course of their adjacent incarceration in the Tombs, to concoct a story that concurred with that of David Greenglass. "Re-creating" in testimony an event that may never have occurred in life, Gold recalled an ambiguous, opaque transaction for which the Jell-O box was the chief clue, the clarifying agent. In a masterpiece of defamiliarization he described for the court the item he had received from Yakovlev as "a piece of cardboard, which appeared to have been cut from a packaged food of some sort. It was cut in an odd shape, and Yakovlev told me that the man Greenglass, whom I would meet in Albuquerque, would have the matching piece of cardboard."[5] On the witness stand he peered forward earnestly to examine the two cut halves of a Jell-O box and indicate for prosecutor Myles Lane which half more closely resembled the one he supposedly had received from Yakovlev and later matched with the half possessed by David Greenglass.

Yet in pretrial testimony, as is frequently noted, Gold had been much less specific about the occurrence, and the signifying details, of this meeting. It was David Greenglass who first mentioned, in a statement to the FBI the day after his arrest on June 16, 1950, that his visitor carried "a torn or cut piece of card," not at that time identified as a Jell-O box. Greenglass supple-

David Greenglass (right), with a U.S. Marshal (left), on his way into court for sentencing as a convicted atom spy in 1951. (AP/Wide World Photos)

Harry Gold (right), testifying before the U.S. Senate. (AP/Wide World Photos)

mented this oral testimony with a memo to his attorney dated the following day.[6] Only belatedly did Gold "remember" Greenglass's name, and address, and the fact that he himself had been in Albuquerque at all.[7]

As for Gold's coded message, the disarmingly direct "I come from Julius," it had emerged, over the course of Gold's depositions, from a welter of other possibilities. In a recorded interview on June 14, asked explicitly by his attorney, John D. M. Hamilton, whether the conspirators had some agreed-upon recognition sign, Gold replied, "Yes, we did, and while this is not the exact recognition sign I believe that it involved the name of a man and was something on the order of Bob sent me or Benny sent me or John sent me or something like that."[8] The phrase was "Benny sent me," say Miriam and Walter Schneir in their book *Invitation to an Inquest*;[9] Virginia Carmichael cites the phrase "Benny from New York sent me"[10] as one of Gold's versions of the message. In the documentary film *The Unquiet Death of Julius and Ethel Rosenberg* former FBI agent Richard Brennan testified that when he first interrogated Harry Gold, "he used the expression Benny sent me, which was the best that he could recall at the time. Subsequently, when the trial of Greenglass led to Rosenberg, we asked him…could it have been Julie sent me or Julius sent me. And immediately he brightened with a great light— yes, that is it. It wasn't Benny, it was Julius sent me."[11]

"Benny sent me." And then, "It wasn't Benny, it was Julius sent me." Like the elusive MacIntosh in Joyce's *Ulysses*, "Benny" here appears—and then disappears—out of nowhere, an apparent artifact. If we resist the suggestion that there was a real spymaster in New York and that it was he, the sinister Benny, and not the innocent (and framed) Julius Rosenberg who cut in pieces the mysterious Jell-O box, we are left with this supplement: "Benny sent me." What, if anything, does Benny—rather, than, say, Bob, or John, or Julius—have to do with the story Harry Gold told on the witness stand, the story, which evolved over the period of his incarceration, of the Jell-O box, the coded password, and espionage?

Joyce's joke about "MacIntosh," you may recall, is based on a comic mechanism of association and slippage. Leopold Bloom has seen a man *in* a macintosh—a British term for raincoat, after Scottish inventor Charles Macintosh—and, through a series of aural misunderstandings, the man is hypostasized into someone *named* MacIntosh, who then makes cameo appearances throughout the novel. Bloom is talking to a newspaper reporter:

—And tell us, Hynes said, do you know that fellow in the, fellow was over there in the…

He looked around.

—Macintosh. Yes, I saw him, Mr Bloom said. Where is he now?

—M'Intosh, Hynes said, scribbling. I don't know who he is. Is that his name?"[12]

"I don't know who he is—is that his name?" Consider now the case of Benny Kubelsky, better known as Jack Benny, a Jewish comic, entertainer, and radio personality, the most popular radio host of his time. Jack Benny ruled the air waves in the early days of radio. And for seven years, from 1934 to 1941, each Sunday night, Jack Benny's immensely successful radio program was brought to you by General Foods, and was called "The Jell-O Program."[13]

"Jell-O again!" Benny would salute his audience each evening. During the program, Benny's patter included a constant joking with announcer Don Wilson about the product, so that soon "even pre-school-age children could rattle off Jell-O's 'six delicious flavors.'"[14] Benny and his wife, Mary Livingstone (born Sadie Marks), appeared (suitably refitted with WASP noses and profiles) in print Jell-O ads for magazines like *Country Gentleman*. So closely did American audiences link Benny and Jell-O that in a poll taken in 1973 of middle-aged listeners asked to name his radio sponsor, most answered "Jell-O," although in fact Benny was subsequently sponsored by Lucky Strike cigarettes for almost twice as long as he had been by Jell-O.[15]

"Benny sent me." When Harry Gold, fantasist and storyteller supreme, named to the FBI the supposititious man who gave him the Jell-O box half to deliver, he may well have been right the first time. It *was* in a way Benny who sent him, insofar as anyone did. "Benny" and "Jell-O" were themselves two halves of a single code phrase for American popular culture of the thirties and forties, and, for many listeners, for at least three decades after that. "Jell-O again!"

Moreover, it is not, I think, insignificant that Jack Benny, born Benny Kubelsky, was a *Jewish* comedian, and one whose most famous comic turns came from an emphasis on his stereotypically "Jewish" signature qualities (stinginess; the violin), despite the fact that he never used a Jewish accent in his act. For, as it happens, gelatin as a product, and Jell-O as a brand, was much in debate among Jewish leaders in the period from 1933 to 1952.

Here is the opening sentence of a book entitled *Gelatin in Jewish Law*, by Rabbi David I. Sheinkopf: "Can a substance of non-kosher origin undergo physical transformations that render it permissible according to Jewish Law?"[16] At issue was the question of gelatin's origin, from the collageneous tissues of nonkosher animals. Some types of gelatin derive from bones and cowhides, others from pigskins. An extended tradition of rabbinic commentary from Maimonides down to the present day has debated the kosher status of animal by-products that at one time in the course of their treatment

Jack Benny, rehearsing his radio
show in 1954. (AP/Wide World Photos)

Benny, with his
signature violin.
(AP/Wide World Photos)

are rendered inedible for canine consumption and then are completely reconfigured, through chemical changes, so that they become, in effect, new substances.

"Forbidden substances," as Rabbi Sheinkopf points out, can "lose their prohibition once they become unsuitable for normal eating purposes." Or, as a flyer sent out by Kraft General Foods in the spring of 1993 under the heading "Jell-O Brand Gelatin Dessert" insists, "During manufacture of gelatin, chemical changes take place so that, in the final gelatin product, the composition and identity of the original material is completely eliminated." "Because of this," the flyer continues,

> gelatin is not considered a meat food product by the United States government. The plant is under supervision of the Federal Food and Drug Administration. If the government considered gelatin a meat food product, the plant would operate under the Meat Inspection Branch of the Department of Agriculture.
>
> Jell-O Brand Gelatin is certified as Kosher by a recognized orthodox Rabbi as per enclosed RESPONSUM.

And the Responsum, six pages in Hebrew, is indeed enclosed in the same mailing.

I have to admit that as a young Jewish girl growing up on Long Island in the fifties in a secularized family and eating Jell-O brand gelatin dessert on the average of three times a week, in all of its six delicious flavors, it never occurred to me to worry about whether what I was eating was kosher, much less whether it was a highly disguised kind of meat. But for the observant Orthodox community this was and is a real question, made more crucial by the emergence in the thirties and forties of commercial products like *Junket* (a dessert mix containing rennet from the dried stomach lining of a calf) and, especially, Jell-O. Two Orthodox rabbis, Samuel Baskin and Simeon Winograd, originally gave a *hekhsher*, or kosher certification, to Jell-O brand gelatin but were persuaded to withdraw it in November 1951, because Jell-O's manufacturers used pigskins as well as cowhides and cattle bones as a gelatin source.[17] Since that time the disputes appear to have been resolved, although a footnote in Sheinkopf's book alleges that Jell-O is still made from pigskins, and expresses astonishment that supervising rabbis from Atlantic Gelatin could possibly endorse Jell-O.[18] The marketing of conspicuously kosher products like Kojel, a gelatin dessert manufactured in Brooklyn and available in Jewish food stores since the 1930s, emphasizes the point: not every jel(lo) is ko(sher). In any case, the sheer amount of printed material that General Foods mails out when asked about its Jell-O brand bespeaks a certain concern about this question.

Nonetheless, the product is today clearly stamped and declared not only kosher but kosher for Passover. The period of significant debate about its status, from the first written decision of acceptance handed down by Rabbi Hayyim Ozen Grodzienski of Vilna in 1935 to the controversies of 1950–51,[19] coincides with the period from Jack Benny's first identification with "The Jell-O Program" (in 1934–35) to the date of the Rosenbergs' trial and execution, in 1950–51—a trial that hinged directly on the question of whether or not Julius Rosenberg cut a Jell-O box in half in his New York kitchen and sent it as a sign and a password to his brother-in-law. ("Benny from New York sent me.")

But if the hidden marketing anxieties of General Foods converged in part around the kosher controversy, the public advertising campaign had much more to do with patriotism. Jell-O, like Lucky Strike and a host of other products, was eager to help America win the war. Print ads from 1940 present Jack Benny and Mary Livingstone as WASP Americans showing Farmer and Mrs. Gill how to make a Jell-O Plum Pudding, a traditional Christmas dessert. By 1944 the company was urging its consumers to "Keep a Waste Chart Like the Army's" and offering a coupon that, together with six cents in stamps, would get you Jell-O's "Bright Spots for Wartime Meals." By 1944 Jell-O itself was apparently a scarce commodity, as several ads acknowledged, even patriotically forgoing a competitive edge to urge that if grocers run out of Jell-O, consumers "make these useful wartime dishes with some other brand of gelatin dessert."

In 1946, with the war over and jobs scarce, somber ads run in magazines like *Capper's Farmer* and *Country Gentleman* urged Americans to give up their nest eggs to make more jobs, identifying the product with the quintessential American spirit of free trade and business expansion, and concluding, in large type at the bottom of the page, "Jell-O is a Product of General Foods and American Enterprise." The word "America" or "American" appears seven times in the printed text, and the word "freedom" five times. No picture of the product, in its box or in its prepared form, appears anywhere in this broadsheetlike ad, which signals its own selflessness and generosity through this omission. By 1948 the crisis was apparently over, for the Jack Benny salutation "Jell-O Again!" was triumphantly displayed above the Benny mantra of "six delicious flavors."

Considered in the frame of the Rosenberg case, there is a certain inadvertent irony in some of these ads, like the one for Jell-O's "locked-in flavor" or the light-hearted query from 1944 run in *McCall's*, *Women's Home Companion*, and *Life* magazines, "Is there a Party hiding in your Ice-box?" But the keynote of all of the subsequent advertising campaigns has been to universalize Jell-O as a quintessentially American (and even Christian) food, closely tied to mainstream culture: voting, scouting, the Fourth of July, children, grandparents, weight watching, and, again, plum pudding. Considered in the context of the Rosenberg case, there is a sense in which the use of a Jell-O box as the supposed clue to a Communist conspiracy to deliver America and its free enterprise system into the hands of the Soviet Union ranks as the ultimate, if trivial, outrage. A Communist Jewish man is in the kitchen, cutting up Jell-O boxes, while his neglected children listen to the radio ("Jell-O Again"), and his wife, who *should* be in the kitchen making kosher Jell-O molds, is masterminding the theft of atomic secrets. Is this any way to rebuild America?

Harry Gold, himself a Jew like virtually all the key players (on both sides) in the Rosenberg trial, artlessly reported to his attorneys in pretrial testimony that the chief topic in his initial conversations with the Greenglasses was the absence of familiar food products in the deserts of New Mexico: "I think that their principal talk concerned the difficulty of getting Jewish food, delicatessen, in a place like Albuquerque and a mention by the man that his family or possibly her family regularly sent them packages including salami."[20] As the Schneirs note, there is no mention in this recorded interview of the "Julius" password or the cut Jell-O box. The scene, real or fantasized, is familiar to any urban Jew who has spent time in "a place like Albuquerque," or even to fans of Calvin Trillin and his pilgrimages to Arthur Bryant's Kansas City barbecue. What does linger in the air here, however, stronger than the smell of salami or barbecue, is the question of what is kosher.

Kosher. From the Hebrew for "fit," "proper," "permissible." Now adopted into American slang and present in most American dictionaries. Here are some of the things expert Leo Rosten, the author of *The Joys of Yinglish*, has to say today about the American usages of this common and complex word.

> —Legitimate, legal, lawful. "Is this deal *kosher*?" "Is this deal on the up-and-up?" "Everything is *kosher*" means "Everything is proper."
> —"The real McCoy," trustworthy, reliable. "Is he *kosher*?" which once meant, "Is he Jewish?" is now taken to mean, "Can I trust him?" or "Is he part of the group?" or (as I heard it used in the Pentagon) "Has he been cleared for classified information?"
> —Approved by a higher source; bearing the stamp of approval. "It's *kosher*," when uttered by a company V.P., can mean that his president has approved.[21]

Notice the degree to which "kosher," in America, has now become a political term. A person who is deemed "kosher" is "cleared for classified information," "part of the group," "approved by a higher source," and even, in a triumph of transethnic transmogrification, "the real McCoy" (or, perhaps, the real MacIntosh). The new *American Heritage Dictionary* goes out of its

Magazine advertisements for Jell-O from the 1940s.
(Courtesy of Kraft General Foods, Inc.)

way, or so it seems to me, to give a usage citation under "kosher" from the *Christian Science Monitor*, of all places.[22] Kosher, like lox and bagels, has gone mainstream (indeed, since lox is smoked salmon, I suppose we could say *up*stream).

But Rosten's book was published in 1989, and my dictionary is the 1992 Third Edition, with a usage panel that includes Harold Bloom, Justin Kaplan, Cynthia Ozick, Elaine Showalter, and numerous other Jewish intellectuals who have themselves been koshered by mainstream success. Forty years ago it was another story.

The place of Jell-O in the American Jewish mythology of the 1940s and '50s was both fascinating and complex. At a politically progressive summer camp held on the grounds of Kutsher's Catskill resort campers were served an American flag made of Jell-O on the Fourth of July.[23] Philip Roth's brash autobiographical hero Alex Portnoy (b. 1933) contrasts his childhood idealization of his mother with the pity and contempt he felt for his father. "It was my mother who could accomplish anything," Portnoy tells his analyst. "She could make jello, for instance, with sliced peaches *hanging* in it, peaches just *suspended* there, in defiance of the law of gravity." And Portnoy's father? His son remembers him chiefly as a martyr to constipation: "I remember that when they announced over the radio the explosion of the first atom bomb, he said aloud, 'Maybe that would do the job.'"[24] Yet even Portnoy's father was proud of his wife's Jell-O, not least for its "real Jewish" character, as he explains to a gentile coworker he has brought home to dinner: "that's right, Anne, the jello is kosher too, sure, of course, has to be."[25]

Like Benny Kubelsky, koshered by General Foods into Jack Benny, with a seemly nose and an appetite for Jell-O plum pudding, Jell-O itself both marked and crossed the borderline between Jewish and Christian, American and foreign, kosher and *trafe*. As such, and embodied in the split or bifurcated box, it was the perfect sign for the politics of the Rosenberg case.

I return then to my epigraph, spoken of course by Iago, the master plotter and master opportunist, the man who seized on another overdetermined domestic object, a woman's handkerchief, and made it the sign of calumny. "This may help to thicken other proofs / That do demonstrate thinly." The Jell-O box is not a random signifier, however it made its way into the evidence submitted in the trial of Julius and Ethel Rosenberg. Overdetermined by both its relationship to the Jewish community and its much more highly visible status as the quintessentially American middle-class and patriotic food, America's just dessert, Jell-O was already a culturally loaded term, "the necessary link," when Roy Cohn or one of his colleagues cut a facsimile of a Jell-O box into pieces and displayed it to the court.

NOTES

1   Walter Schneir and Miriam Schneir, *Invitation to an Inquest: A New Look at the Rosenberg-Sobell Case* (New York: Dell, 1968), 374.

2   Ibid., 401.

3   Ibid., 372–73.

4   Ibid., 155.

5   Ibid., 402.

6   Ibid., 418.

7   Ibid., 368, 423.

8   Ibid., 401–2.

9   Ibid., 418.

10 Virginia Carmichael, *Framing History: The Rosenberg Story and the Cold War* (Minneapolis: University of Minnesota press, 1993), 79.

11 Alvin H. Goldstein, (producer), *The Unquiet Death of Julius and Ethel Rosenberg.* (Chicago: Facets Multimedia, 1989); script version (New York: Lawrence Hill, 1975).

12 James Joyce, *Ulysses* (New York: Vintage, 1962), 112.

13 Mary Livingstone Benny and Hilliard Marks with Marcia Borie, *Jack Benny* (Garden City, NY: Doubleday, 1978), 61.

14 Milt Josefsberg, *The Jack Benny Show* (New Rochelle, NY: Arlington House, 1977), 470.

15 Josefsberg, *The Jack Benny Show*, 360.

16 David I. Sheinkopf, *Gelatin in Jewish Law* (New York: Bloch, 1982), 7.

17 Ibid., 12–13.

18 Ibid., 13n.

19 Ibid., 10, 95–96.

20 Schneir and Schneir, *Invitation to an Inquest*, 401.

21 Leo Rosten, *The Joys of Yinglish: An Exuberant Dictionary of Yiddish Words, Phrases, and Locutions....* (New York: McGraw-Hill, 1989), 304–5.

22 *The American Heritage Dictionary of the English Language*, 3rd ed. (Boston: Houghton Mifflin, 1992). *kosher*, 2a. "Legitimate; permissible: '*consolidating noneditorial functions of the papers, which is kosher*' (*Christian Science Monitor*)."

23 This is the recollection of historian Ellen Schrecker, who attended the camp.

24 Philip Roth, *Portnoy's Complaint* (New York: Bantam, 1970), 2, 3, 10.

25 Ibid., 93.

2

The Rosenbergs and the Crimes of a Century

Blanche Wiesen Cook

When all the ashes of the twentieth century settle and all the lies are laid to rest, the assassination of Julius and Ethel Rosenberg will continue to loom enormous. The sacrifice of the Rosenbergs will forever be a monument to a century of violence, holocaust, and hatred; a ceremonial slaughter in a vastly wicked time. Seen in full light, and from a distance of forty years, the contest seems bizarre: The Rosenbergs and the Bomb. Two proud Jews confronted by a bloated, brutal, twisted state. The crime of the century sketched on a Jell-O box, or exploded upon Hiroshima, Nagasaki, Nevada, the Pacific Islands; countless deaths in Guatemala, Lebanon, Korea, Vietnam, Chile, Grenada, Panama, El Salvador, Iraq....

The trial of the Rosenbergs was the occasion for an extraordinary outpouring of haunting, provocative, galvanizing words and images: paintings, photographs, poster art, poetry, essays, letters. Rob Okun's *The Rosenbergs: Collected Visions of Artists and Writers*, recently reissued to commemorate the 40th year of their sentence, includes photographs and visuals from around the world, poems and essays by W.E.B. Du Bois, Louise Bernikow, Allen Ginsberg, Margaret Randall, Adrienne Rich, Walter and Miriam Schneir, among many others. These splendid works do more than chronicle the series

Fernand Léger, *Liberty, Peace, Solidarity*, 1952.
(Courtesy of Robert Meeropol)

of events that culminated in the Rosenberg "case" and its aftermath. They enable us to pause and reconsider our own lives, our own dedication to truth and hope and justice. Who were we then? Who are we now? What kind of world can we imagine? How can we participate?

Who were Julius and Ethel Rosenberg? What did they read, what did they sing? What did they believe? Who did they champion? Why were they targeted? What was their crime? Two ordinary Jewish New Yorkers who believed in a nonfascist future; who believed a new day might dawn—without pogroms or racism or poverty or war. Communists probably; Communists believed those things after and during the depression and the great antifascist war.

The thing is, the Cold War froze all reality, froze information, froze our hearts and minds. Communists were demonized; demons had no souls; no love in their hearts. The state that targeted the Rosenbergs insisted that the twentieth century was to be neither Nazi nor Communist; it was to be the American Century. After 1945 it became the century of total war. And the Rosenbergs refused to bow or grovel; they never went supine. Eisenhower said: "See, they love their ideology more than their children. In the face of power unbridled, arrogant, obscene, they rejected a deal, a cynical and crass propaganda deal that would have set them free, made them rich, and transformed their future."[1]

Because of the Freedom of Information Act, the CIA released an astounding memo on January 22, 1953, detailing a modest proposal: If the Rosenbergs would agree to "appeal to Jews in all countries to get out of the communist movement and seek to destroy it," their sentences could be commuted. The "advantages" of this scheme could "scarcely be overstated from a psychological warfare standpoint."

"The couple is ideally situated to serve as leading instruments of a psychological warfare campaign designed to split world communism on the Jewish issue, to create disaffected groups within the membership of the Parties, to utilize these groups for further infiltration and for intelligence work."

The Rosenbergs should be handled tactfully: People "of the sort of the Rosenbergs can be swayed by duty where they cannot be swayed by considerations of self-interest. They should not be asked to trade their principles for their lives—for one thing, such an appeal to cowardice would almost certainly fail." They should instead be "offered two things psychologically: (1) an opportunity to recant while preserving their self-respect and honor; (2) a new purpose in life."

The psychological strategists of the CIA thought the "ideal emissaries" to introduce this proposal "would be highly intelligent rabbis, representing reformed Judaism, with a radical background or sympathetic understanding of radicalism, and with psychiatric knowledge.... Should the operation succeed, generous commutation appears indicated—both to encourage others to defect and to utilize the Rosenbergs as figures in an effective international psychological warfare campaign against communism primarily on the Jewish question."

This political warfare deal coincided with qualms expressed by members of the State Department who were concerned that the Rosenbergs' execution would harm America's interests throughout Europe, a continent seething with protests and almost unanimous opposition. From France (where posters of a smiling Ike featured a mouthful of his perfectly white teeth, each one an electric chair), U.S. ambassador C. Douglas Dillon urged Eisenhower to stay the execution: It would be a public relations disaster. The "great majority of French people of all political leanings feel that the death sentence is completely unjustified" and due entirely to the "political climate peculiar to the United States." Even those who considered the Rosenbergs guilty of something believed the death sentence absurd when "compared with the prison terms meted to British scientists Allan Nunn May and Klaus Fuchs." In addition, there were all the "latest doubts" about David Greenglass's reliability, his undenied "perjury charges," his wife's awareness that her husband was "an hysteric," and a liar. This is a story about love and hate. This is a morality play. The premier passion killing of the Cold War, this is an epic that will never die.

For all the CIA's psychological enthusiasm, did nobody pause to consider this family's dance of death? Who was David Greenglass, Ethel's baby brother? The family baby, his mother loved him best. "My baby brother. I loved him very much." What had he stolen? A tool? Was it irradiated? Was his mind fried? His heart dried? His soul emptied? What was his deal? With whom did he make it? Where is he hiding now? Where do they hide when they kill their sisters? Sacrifice their daughters? Drop bombs on humanity? Create Death in a test tube?

Then there were the children, and the world's reaction to ten-year-old Michael's letter, a plea to Eisenhower on behalf of himself and his six-year-old brother Robert: "Please let Mommy and Daddy go and not let anything happen to them."

But Eisenhower was unmoved. He feared to appear "weak and fearful" in the face of subversion. "The action of these people has exposed to greater danger of death literally millions of our citizens." And now, Ike concluded, "they have even stooped to dragging in young and innocent children in order to serve their own purposes."

The crime of the century. Just who was it who overthrew the enlightened

President Dwight D. Eisenhower.
(AP/Wide World Photos)

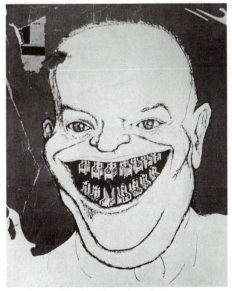

Outraged French citizens plastered a
poster portrait of President Eisenhower all
over Paris. Louis Mittelberg, *His Famous
Smile*, 1952.
(From *The Rosenbergs: Collected Visions of Artists and
Writers*. Courtesy Rob A. Okun / Cultural Forecast)

and democratic government of Iran in 1953 and dropped those bombs on Guatemala City in 1954 and unleashed COINTELPRO (the FBI's vast and dirty Counter-Intelligence Program) in 1956, and accepted the extravagant insanities of MK-ULTRA (code-word for the CIA's most repellent dirty tricks)? Psychological warfare. Mind control. LSD. Death-dealing experiments in laboratories. Fallout. Radiation. Cancer. Leukemia. AIDS. Repentance. Hope.

The Rosenbergs: two Jews from Seward Park High School and City College, betrayed by their siblings, sacrificed by the state, at first abandoned by the Communist Party USA and large segments of the organized political "Left," which fled into silence and fear; supported nonetheless by radical individuals who remained independent and determined: journalists and activists around the original *Guardian*—Jim Aronson, Cedric Belfrage, Bill Reuben—who were later joined by Virginia Gardner, Helen Sobell, Emily Altman; they wrote and organized and would not let the story settle.

And they have sons who love them still.

Ethel Rosenberg would be almost eighty now. On January 24, 1953, she wrote, IF WE DIE:

> You shall know, my sons…
> Why we leave the song unsung,
> the book unread, the work undone…
>
> Work and build my sons, and build
> a monument to love and joy,
> to human worth, to faith we kept
> for you, my sons….

All over the world there are and will always be children of the Rosenbergs—individuals with courage, eager to carry on, to resist tyranny, to challenge authority, to make it better, to contemplate the possibilities of creating a caring, concerned society with security and justice for all.

The poetry, the images, the history, the deeply emotive works their assassination evoked, collected in Rob Okun's book, refortify and challenge us all: How do we live authentic lives? How do we see and understand our world? Why do we need art and activism? Why does the state work so hard to control our minds, fetter our consciousness? How can we regroup, go on, be bold? What does it take to think deeply, feel profoundly, agitate. Not since the 1930s have so many people been so organized in so many causes. The needs are urgent, and every one of us faces the renewed challenge: Make a poster, write a letter, read a book, make a difference, ACT UP.

NOTES

1 All of the quotes from the CIA and FBI documents released through the Freedom of Information Act (FOIA) relating to the Rosenbergs, are discussed in full in Blanche Wiesen Cook's *Declassified Eisenhower: A Divided Legacy of Peace and Political Warfare* (Doubleday, 1981; Penguin, 1984).

   See also: Cook and Gerald Markowitz, "History in Shreds: The Fate of the Freedom of Information Act," *Radical History Review* No. 26 (October 1982); Gerald Markowitz and Michael Meeropol, "The Crime of the Century Revisited: David Greenglass' Scientific Evidence in the Rosenberg Case," *Science and Society*, Vol. 44 (Spring 1980); and Gerald Markowitz, "How Not to Write History: A Critique of The Rosenberg File," *Science and Society*, Vol. 48 (Spring 1984).

Atomic bomb smoke column over Nagasaki.
(AP/Wide World Photos)

3

TV, the Bomb, and the Body
Other Cold War Secrets

Joyce Nelson

There are whole disciplines, institutions, rubrics in our culture which
serve as categories of denial.
—Susan Griffin, *A Chorus of Stones*

The two mass media that have dominated the second half of the
twentieth century are television and the atomic bomb. The intricate relationships between these two mass media have been explored at length elsewhere,[1] but here I want to recapitulate and expand on some of the
connections between them in order to link them more closely to the events
surrounding the trial of the Rosenbergs. In so doing, I hope to shed light on
some of the "categories of denial" still at work in our society forty years
after the Rosenbergs' trial and execution.

TURNING THE SWITCH

In 1937 NBC had a mobile TV unit traveling throughout New York City
transmitting live coverage to a tower atop the Empire State Building for
rebroadcast by a central transmitter.[2] Although this mobile unit was intended to spark popular interest in the potential of the new broadcast medium,
corporate manufacturers such as General Electric, Westinghouse, and RCA
(NBC's parent company) had not yet decided to invest in mass production of
TV sets. The outbreak of war in Europe in 1939 further impeded TV's marketing development, as U.S. corporations eyed the lucrative possibilities of

military contracts rather than the risks of investment in new consumer technologies.

But the delay in TV's launch as a mass medium did not mean that television as a technology went into abeyance during World War II. In fact, TV was important to the building of the bomb and has remained intertwined with the nuclear industry ever since. Atomic physicist Leo Szilard, at whose urgings the Manhattan Project was instigated, has written of an important research breakthrough in 1939 during which he and Enrico Fermi were working on the still uncertain possibilities of an atomic chain reaction. According to Szilard:

> Everyone was ready. All we had to do was turn a switch, lean back, and watch the screen of a television tube. If flashes of light appeared on the screen it would mean that large-scale liberation of atomic energy was just around the corner. We just turned the switch and saw the flashes. We watched for a little while and then we went home. That night there was very little doubt in my mind that the world was headed for grief.[3]

We have here an indication of the technical interdependence of the two media. The "screen of a television tube" was necessary to indicate the flashes heralding the "large-scale liberation of atomic energy." At the turn of the switch the screen conveyed the hoped-for sign to the assembled scientific audience. Szilard's description of this moment is oddly suggestive of the typical TV viewer: turning on the switch, leaning back, gazing at the screen, seeing the flashes, then watching for a little while. Szilard idly observes a spectacle that has no emotional connection to the "grief" he foresees as a result of his work.

GE, TV, THE BOMB

The second level of intersection between TV and the bomb occurs in their similar corporate sponsorship. RCA, General Electric, and Westinghouse—the first corporations to market TV sets in 1946—had been involved in the nuclear industry since its inception, and at least one of these companies, GE, was an adviser in the Manhattan Project.[4] Moreover, representatives from both General Electric and Westinghouse played a crucial role in the top-secret 1941 decision to undertake the building of the atomic bomb.

According to the author Stanley Goldberg, William Coolidge, director of research at General Electric Research Laboratories, and L. W. Chubb, chief scientist at Westinghouse, were both appointed in 1941 to a "special blue-ribbon committee" of scientists reviewing the nascent work of the U.S. Uranium Committee for the purpose of making recommendations about future activities.[5] The committee's final report, submitted to Vannevar Bush on November 24, 1941, concluded favorably that "a fission bomb of superlatively destructive power will result from bringing quickly together a sufficient mass of element U235. This seems to be as sure as any untried prediction based upon theory and experiment can be."[6]

Goldberg notes: "The report estimated that the project would cost $133 million. (The amount actually spent between June 1942 and August 1945 exceeded $2 billion.) Among the appendixes there was supposed to be an estimate of the cost of a full-blown program, to be drawn up by Chubb and Coolidge. They agreed to suppress such an appendix because, in Coolidge's words, 'such a statement might be decidedly prejudicial to the active prosecution of the research work which is so clearly indicated.'"[7] At the time, no one seems to have questioned whether it was "decidedly prejudicial" to have GE and Westinghouse represented on such a committee—given the corporations' vested interests in proceeding with the research. As one commentator has noted, "GE entered World War II doing $340 million of business a year and emerged doing $1.3 billion."[8]

Much of that surge in GE's fortunes was the result of the company's involvement in the Manhattan Project, with GE an important supplier of process equipment and power supply apparatus.[9] GE also provided the principal electrical apparatus for the Hanford Engineer Works in Washington State, which produced plutonium for the bomb dropped on Nagasaki.[10] Arthur Compton, a physicist and a GE consultant for the seventeen years prior to the building of the bomb, convinced General Leslie Groves, head of the Manhattan Project, to award more of the project's contracts to GE.[11]

In addition, GE president Charles E. Wilson was appointed in September 1942 as vice-chair of the War Production Board, which had full authority over all war production. In this role Wilson helped ensure that all necessary materials were allocated for the Manhattan Project.[12] Wilson's immediate predecessor at GE, Gerald Swope, was appointed in 1942 as assistant U.S. secretary of the treasury, member of the executive committee of the National War Fund, and chair of the National War Fund budget committee.[13] With such considerable tie-ins to the Manhattan Project, "GE's role in the development and ultimate use of the bomb was substantial."[14]

MANHATTAN PROJECT AS MODEL

In many ways the Manhattan Project is the most appropriate model for the transnational business operations that would come to characterize the postwar world. An absolutely secret endeavor, hidden from the U.S. Congress—its escalating costs buried in the annual budget of the U.S. Army Corps of Engineers[15]—this massive project involved thirty-seven installations in nineteen states and Canada, more than forty-three thousand employees, the first fully automated factories, and a mushrooming budget at a time of heavy restrictions on spending.[16] A quantum leap beyond any previous business arrangement, this multinational marshaling of expertise from the fields of science, business, engineering, the military, government, and public relations ultimately demonstrated the phenomenal efficiency with which such a complex could function.

The hiding of this behemoth seems an impossible feat. Yet, until its spectacular bursts of achievement in the summer of 1945, the Manhattan Project operated in a kind of secret, invisible void. The majority of its thousands of employees had no real idea of the true nature of the project. Only a highly select few knew its actual goal, and even fewer were allowed to grasp the overall complexity of interconnections within the entire project.

As head of the project, General Leslie R. Groves of the Army Corps of Engineers instituted two significant working principles to ensure absolute secrecy: the compartmentalization of information inside the project, and strict press censorship outside it.[17] While the latter precaution is not surprising, the former needs an explanation, provided by Groves himself seventeen years after the war: "Compartmentalization of knowledge, to me, was the very heart of security. My rule was simple and not capable of misinterpretation— each man should know everything he needed to know to do his job and nothing else."[18]

In the new world of the postwar era, ushered in by the mushroom clouds over Hiroshima and Nagasaki, these two operating principles would remain the structuring framework for the smooth advancement of the military-industrial complex. Secrecy—resulting from the censorship/manipulation of the press, and the purposeful fragmentation and compartment-alization of information—would become crucial to the creation and maintenance or the nuclear new world order. As that new world congealed around the Manhattan Project's atomic bomb, U.S. corporate hegemony influenced even the decision to drop the bomb.

THE PERMANENT WAR ECONOMY

The historian Charles L. Mee, Jr., has observed that President Truman's advisers "were in conflict about the use of the bomb. Some military men said it would save a million American lives. Others simply assumed that, since the bomb had been developed at great expense, it would be used. Momentum was on its side."[19] Truman had been advised by the U.S. army, Air Force, and Navy, however, "that the bomb was not militarily necessary to defeat Japan, or to save millions of American soldiers' lives."[20] The Japanese were, in fact, already attempting to surrender through diplomatic channels, but "Truman made the decision to use it (the bomb), and having made the decision, let it be known that he never lost a moment's sleep over it."[21]

Perhaps one reason for Truman's decision, and for his lack of regret afterward, is that the U.S. business community, led by General Electric, not only was in favor of the bomb's use on Japan but collectively agreed on the "necessity" of a permanent war economy for the postwar years.[22] Reluctant to downscale industrial production to prewar levels, the corporate sector also perceived the lucrative benefits of continuing military contracts.

In January 1944 GE's Wilson, vice-chair of the War Production Board—which oversaw the efforts of five hundred business executives involved in industrial war production—gave a speech to the Army Ordnance association in which he characterized disarmament as a "thoroughly discredited doctrine" and advocated that the United States "Should henceforth mount a national policy upon the solid fact of an industrial capacity for war, and a research capacity for war."[23] Many authorities point to this speech and the concepts Wilson advocated as the beginning of the postwar U.S. policy of an unprecedented permanent military economy.[24]

Just months after Wilson's speech, GE consultant and prominent Manhattan Project physicist Arthur Compton recruited GE's vice president Zay Jeffries to help on planning for postwar nuclear research.[25] Jeffries headed a scientific committee that concluded that it was "vitally important" for the United States to "keep the lead in nuclear research and its industrial applications."[26] Compton's plan, based on private industry's continuing involvement in nuclear development, advocated that "the job was to produce not just one weapon but weapons in quantity in assembly-line fashion."[27] Around the same time, in August 1944, Wilson resigned his post at the War Production Board and returned to GE for his second term as the company's president.[28]

With GE and the larger business community already planning a postwar future based on increased "assembly-line" nuclear capacity for war, Arthur Compton played a significant role in Truman's decision to use the bomb:

> Compton served on an interim committee formed by Secretary of War Henry Stimson in March 1945 to advise on whether and how to use the atomic bomb against Japan. Many of the scientists who had developed the bomb vigorously opposed using it on population centers. Compton discredited the scientists' appeals and convinced the committee to recommend dropping the bomb on Japanese cities. Newly inaugurated President Truman followed the committee's recommendation and ordered two bombs dropped on Hiroshima and Nagasaki.[29]

CENSORED VISION

During the weeks immediately following the surrender of Japan, U.S. occupation forces shot more than eighty-five thousand feet of 16-mm film documenting the extensive bodily suffering of the irradiated survivors—footage that was not declassified until 1980.[30] Similarly, the U.S. military confiscated some forty-five thousand feet of documentary film footage shot by Japanese producer Akira Iwasaki during the immediate aftermath of the Hiroshima bombing.[31] This footage also remained classified for decades. In 1946, when Japanese doctors attempted to release their own detailed documentation on radiation-related diseases, their information was also censored by the U.S. occupation forces.[32]

Thus documentary material that might have alerted the North American public not only to the tremendous bodily suffering caused by the atomic bomb, but also to the real dangers of radiation itself was effectively hidden from an unknowing public. The timing of this suppression of evidence coincided with another important series of events that took place in 1946.

In that year RCA brought its first mass-produced televisions onto the market, followed quickly by GE, Westinghouse, and other set manufacturers. At the same time, the U.S. military began atomic testing on the Bikini Atoll in the Pacific. Part of this massive experimentation was a series of bomb tests staged for the world press in order to dispel rumors about the harmful effects of radiation through atmospheric testing. This 1946 series of tests, code-named "Operation Crossroads," was a massive public relations campaign waged by Joint Task Force One—made up of the U.S. Army, Navy, and Air Force.

According to Stephen Hilgartner, Richard Bell and Rory O'Conner, authors of *Nukespeak*, Joint Task Force One involved "41,963 men, 37 women, 242 ships, 156 airplanes, 4 television transmitters, 750 cameras, 5,000 pressure gauges, 25,000 radiation recorders, 204 goats, 200 pigs, 5,000 rats and the atomic bombs."[33] A media event staged for 114 U.S. news correspondents, as well as observers and press representatives from several other countries, Operation Crossroads was intended to be "the best-reported as well as the most-reported technical experiment of all time"—as its official history claims.[34] Downplaying the hazards of nuclear fallout, Operation Crossroads went to elaborate lengths to show that there were "no visible effects" on living beings exposed to the atomic tests."[35]

It is significant that this nuclear PR event in 1946 incorporated "4 television transmitters" in its publicity entourage. With set sales barely beginning, there would have been only a few thousand TV owners capable of receiving a transmission at the time, aside from that fact that, without any relay stations, the signal could not have reached the U.S. mainland. Thus Operation Crossroads actually served a dual PR purpose: to dispel rumors about radioactive fallout and to display the new medium of television to the eyes of the press, and through them, to the world.

This staged "technical experiment," designed to show that there were "no visible effects" from radiation and thus no danger, replaced what might have been shown to the immediate postwar public: the censored footage of irradiated Japanese victims. This footage, which revealed the all too horribly visible effects of radiation on the body, was not a sight in keeping with the goals of the U.S. military-industrial complex emerging at that time. By substituting the 1946 PR imagery of Operation Crossroads for the suppressed and censored Japanese film footage and documentation, the U.S. nuclear powers-that-be were able to proceed with their plans.

In this sense television transmitters *had* to be present at Operation Crossroads, regardless of whether there was any mainland U.S. audience for their transmissions. For a society in which "seeing is believing," the presence on Bikini Atoll of this latest techno-visual marvel signified that the most scientific and up-to-date "eye" was being brought to bear on those disturbing rumors about fallout and radiation's dangers. When this "technical experiment" revealed "no visible effects" on living beings placed at a so-called safe distance from the blasts' epicenters, an unknowing public was reassured. But at the time, there was an even deeper irony at work.

TV AS BOMB

At the same time that Operation Crossroads was downplaying the hazards of radiation, and using television to do so, TV set manufacturers discovered in 1946 that their new consumer technology, for which great marketing plans were already under way, was emitting detectable low-level radiation from three sources: the cathode-ray tube, the high-voltage shunt regulator tube, and the high-voltage rectifier tube.[36] Without alerting the public, RCA, GE, Westinghouse and other set manufacturers decided not to redesign the TV sets in order to eliminate their radiating properties.[37]

Two years later, in 1948, the Victorian Company invented a diode that could replace the high-voltage shunt regulator tube—thereby eliminating at least one of the sources of radiation in the TV set—but corporate heads decided that costs of design alteration would be too high.[38] The U.S. military, however, immediately adopted the diode for use in its radar display circuits and geiger tube circuits.[39]

From 1946 until 1962 nothing appeared in the U.S. print media that would in any way alert the public that their TV sets had certain bomb-like radiating features—which brings us to the third level of intersection between these two mass media.[40] TV set radiation did not become a public issue until the late 1960s. This seeming nonchalance toward the public as a mass viewing body can be contrasted with the care taken of the cameras set up to record the first test of the atomic bomb, an event code-named "Trinity" and triggered at 5:30 a.m., July 16, 1945, in the New Mexican desert. According to the official Trinity photographer Berlyn Brixner, the fifty cameras used to record the first nuclear explosion were "completely enclosed in special steel and lead bunkers that I designed, and they looked out through lead-glass windows eight to ten inches thick."[41]

NAMING THE MENACE

A year after TV's presence at Operation Crossroads, where it was both a sign of a new technological "eye" and an ironic diversion from radioactive fallout issues, the medium played witness to another historic event: "In October 1947, the House Committee on Un-American Activities, chaired by Representative J. Parnell Thomas of New Jersey, opened public hearings on 'communism' in the film industry. NBC, CBS, and ABC television cameras and microphones were on hand in a caucus room of the House office building in Washington as scores of celebrities assembled under banks of floodlights hung among crystal chandeliers."[42] In retrospect it is arguable that the anti-Communist hysteria sweeping the continent in the late 1940s was a corollary of the sanitized publicity campaign simultaneously being conducted around the burgeoning nuclear industry. Under the guidance of House Un-American Activities Committee (HUAC) members John McDowell of Pennsylvania, Richard M. Nixon of California, Richard B. Vail of Illinois, John S. Wood of Georgia, and Chairman Thomas, the North American public would be encouraged to deflect serious attention from the real (if unperceived) dangers of nuclear radiation to the perceived (if not entirely real) dangers of communist infiltration throughout the land. If, in the first instance, TV could reveal "no visible effects," in the second it was able to show the scores of celebrities affected by the "red menace." The deflection was, of course, entirely useful to an expanding U.S. nuclear coterie.

The broadcasting historian Erik Barnouw has argued that this witch-hunt atmosphere, coinciding with the formative years of television, made the TV industry "learn caution and cowardice."[43] But the powers within the industry—especially RCA, GE, Westinghouse, Du Pont—also had much to gain from such a political climate, given their direct involvement in nuclear expansion and their "need" for a permanent war economy.

On March 12, 1947, President Truman, having already followed corporate wishes in bombing Japan, gave his Truman Doctrine speech declaring that henceforth United States hegemony was no longer limited to the Americas, that the U.S. recognized no geopolitical limitations to its interests and would henceforth protect those interests everywhere in the world.[44] Nine days after his speech, Truman announced that he was setting up, by executive order, an Employee Loyalty Review Board that would ensure against "infiltration of disloyal persons" into the government.[45]

In retrospect, Truman's latter announcement can be understood in the larger context defined here by the nuclear critic Brian Easlea: "The necessity of a 'permanent war economy' which had been first argued as early as 1944 by leading industrialists and military chiefs, was now being vociferously advocated. The survival of capitalism in the United States demanded increased arms expenditure and that in turn necessitated the manufacture of a major enemy."[46] Although U.S. intelligence had reported in November 1945 that Russia would be incapable of war for at least fifteen years and in 1946 had intercepted communiqués regarding Russian demobilization on a massive scale,[47] disarmament, as GE's Charles Wilson had asserted, was a "thoroughly discredited doctrine" for an emerging superpower based on "industrial capacity for war." In 1947 the United States possessed thirteen atomic bombs; by 1948 the figure had risen to fifty, and thereafter, as GE consultant Arthur Compton had advocated, atomic bombs were mass-produced in the United States.[48]

BOMBING THE MAINLAND

By 1951 the United States instituted a new phase of atomic-weapons testing. No longer would the bomb tests occur only on some remote "elsewhere" seemingly removed from daily North American life. Rather the new program of bombing was to take place in the continental USA, in the Nevada desert. Although the Bikini Atoll and nearby Eniwetok in the South Pacific were still used as testing-grounds throughout the new phase—receiving a total of sixty-six nuclear blasts during the period 1948–1958 —for security reasons these areas were deemed unsuitable for the new series of experiments and research planned.

The new program called for the purposeful, systematic exposure of American and Canadian servicemen and personnel to the direct effects of atomic bombs. The army's newly formed Human Resources and Research Office needed to gather detailed data on motivation, morale, psychology, and training methods most useful for troops engaging in a nuclear war.[49] From 1951 and on through the decade between two hundred fifty thousand and five hundred thousand servicemen were exposed to the effects of atomic bombs in the more than one hundred tests conducted.[50] Countless civilians located in the path of the fallout were also exposed, but apparently the collecting of data on them was of less interest to the needs of the military.

This whole new phase of nuclear testing obviously called for a renewed PR campaign to deal with two new dimensions: 1) bombing the continental USA itself and 2) exposing servicemen to the blasts. Unlike Operation Crossroads, staged for the press in 1946 at far-off Bikini Atoll, this new PR campaign would have to be pitched directly to the American public in whose backyard the bombs were exploding.

Given these factors it is no surprise that TV was the primary means through which this PR effort was conducted. A popular mass medium already installed in millions of North American homes by 1951 and expanding exponentially across the continent every month during the early 1950s, television was the obvious site on which to build a society unified around the bomb. The very popularity of this mass medium, with its pleasurable entertainment function in the home, could ideologically manage and contain the spectacle of bomb blasts imaged on its screen.

As the tests proceeded throughout 1951 and into the spring of 1952, the Atomic Energy Commission invited selected members of the U.S. print and broadcast media to observe and play witness to this new development in nuclear experimentation. On April 22, 1952, during the Tumbler-Snapper series of bomb tests, the commission permitted the first TV coverage of the blasts to be transmitted to American homes.[51] This is the fourth level of conjunction between TV and the bomb: with the nuclear flashes first witnessed by Szilard on a TV tube now become the full-blown mushroom cloud imaged on TV screens across the land. The U.S. Advertising Council also stepped in to assist with the PR effort in 1952, sponsoring a telecast of one of the bomb tests at Yucca Flat and using the occasion to emphasize the "safe threshold" of radioactive fallout, the wisdom of erecting bomb shelters in backyards, the need for a Ground Observer Corps, and the ever-present Communist menace.[52]

By the time of Eisenhower's election, the United States had already stockpiled one thousand nuclear warheads.[53] According to Carole Gallagher, photographer and author of the text *American Ground Zero*, "when confronted with the dangers that atmospheric bomb tests imposed on citizens living near the Test Site, Eisenhower is alleged to have said, 'we can afford to sacrifice a few thousand people out there in the interest of national security.'"[54]

Had the real dangers of radiation, documented in Japan from 1946 onward, not been suppressed and censored by the United States, it is doubtful whether the nuclear juggernaut could have advanced as it did. Keeping the secret of radiation's deadliness was of crucial importance in the immediate postwar years. In such a context of nuclear secrecy, it was entirely useful to deflect the focus onto not only the dangers of the "Communist menace" but also the seeming treason of the Rosenbergs. It is this theme of treason, almost a fetish in the rhetoric surrounding their trial and execution, that deserves some scrutiny, for there was another, very closely guarded secret being kept at the time by the powers-that-be—a secret not widely known almost fifty years after World War II.

ANOTHER ENEMIES LIST

In 1983 Charles Higham's book, *Trading with the Enemy*, documented the existence of what he called "the Fraternity"—a group of U.S. and British corporations and financiers who had secretly traded with the Nazis throughout World War II.[55] Higham was by no means the first writer to investigate such corporate connections to the Nazis, but his book (now out of print) was the first to reveal the extent of such treasonous dealings on the part of Fraternity members, whose U.S. corporate names include Standard Oil of New Jersey (now Exxon), Ford Motor Company, ITT, General Motors, Du Pont, General Electric, and RCA.[56] According to Higham, all the Fraternity members "were represented internationally by the National City Bank or by the Chase National Bank."[57]

At the time of Pearl Harbor, U.S. business had some $475 million invested in Nazi Germany, with Standard Oil ($210 million), General Motors ($35 million), ITT ($30 million), and Ford ($17.5 million) each concerned to ensure their German holdings against the specter of Soviet Communism.[58] As Bertram Gross notes in *Friendly Fascism*, "top business circles sincerely believed 'Better Hitler than Stalin.'"[59] Despite the presence of the Soviet ally during the war, multinational business's fear of Communism outflanked even its aversion to the specter of the Third Reich and the horror of Nazi atrocities—which, after all, were no real threat to business as business.

At least two of these Fraternity arrangements had come under investigation in the early 1940s: GE's collaboration with the German industrialist and munitions maker Alfred Krupp[60] and Standard Oil's arrangement with the German petrochemical giant I. G. Farben.[61] GE was brought to trial on August 30, 1940, by the Anti-trust Division of the Justice Department.[62] As the trial proceeded,

> John Henry Lewin, Assistant to the Attorney General in the Anti-trust Division, said GE's agreement with Krupp was "directly responsible for the disadvantage at which this country finds itself in comparison with its enemies" in the use and production of hard metals. Krupp was later convicted of using slave labor in his Nazi armaments factories. For its collaboration with Nazi war criminal Krupp, GE was found guilty of price fixing with the Nazis during World War II. For this crime, GE, its two subsidiaries, and three company officers were fined a mere $36,000.[63]

The arrangement between Standard Oil of New Jersey and I.G. Farben came under investigation by a U.S. Senate committee in 1941.[64] I. G. Farben was known to have built its own concentration camp adjacent to Auschwitz—I. G. Auschwitz, as it was called by its directors—where camp labor was literally worked to death in the production of artificial rubber for the Reich's military needs.[65] Though some members of the U.S. Senate committee were appalled by the Standard Oil-I. G. Farben arrangement, so "lacking in patriotic concern," nothing seems to have come of the investigation.[66] As Peter Collier and David Horowitz write, John D. Rockefeller—the major shareholder in both Standard Oil and the Chase Bank—"had become a citizen above suspicion."[67]

A better explanation is provided by Higham. Writing about Standard Oil's transactions with Nazi Germany, he quotes from a December 26, 1941, message from the U.S. ambassador to Britain, John G. Winant: "Embassy concurs with British view that on balance there is no reason for taking action which would at most be only minor irritant to Germans and which might complicate an already difficult situation or lead to unfortunate consequences as regards future operations of American and British oil companies."[68]

The Fraternity members were poised to benefit economically no matter which side won the war. Higham writes that their dealings with the Nazis "were known about in Washington and either sanctioned or deliberately ignored."[69] Thus, Exxon, the Chase Bank, Ford, ITT, GM, Du Pont, GE, and RCA were able to avoid "unfortunate consequences as regards future operations" and rapidly expand during the postwar era into the global powers that they are today.

Obviously, this is the list of enemies that should have been made public after the war. These are the names that should have been named. But just as obviously, such exposure would have greatly interfered with their corporate postwar agenda. The involvement of Fraternity members General Electric, RCA, and Du Pont in the nascent nuclear/television industries of the 1940s raises huge questions about their roles in creating the witch-hunt atmosphere of the early Cold War and later, in hyping what came to be called "the sunny side of the atom." In this sense, the Rosenbergs were a useful foil in keeping the spotlight from focusing on another form of treason.

Similarly, to my knowledge no one has fully explored the role that Fraternity members may have had in the early days of the United Nations, especially regarding nuclear issues at the time. As the late William L. Shirer has informed us in his memoirs, on December 14, 1946, the U.N. Assembly cast a unanimous vote, fifty-four to zero, "to press forward for general disarmament, including the abolition of the atom bomb and the establishment of an on-the-scene inspection to see that no one cheated. At the time, of course, only the U.S.A. had the bomb and it was not willing to give up its monopoly and put the bomb under the control of the U.N."[70] With uncharacteristic reticence Shirer concludes this section of his analysts by saying merely, "If this had happened, we might not face such a grim nuclear future as we do today."[71]

But as Collier and Horowitz have documented, one of the key driving forces behind the formation of the U.N. was the Rockefeller family, who donated the land, helped decide (through the State Department's Nelson Rockefeller) which countries were to be included as founding members, and tended to view this new world body as primarily the result of Rockefeller initiative.[72] The U.N. involvement of one of the Fraternity members, combined with GE, RCA, and Du Pont corporate lobbying for a nuclear future in the 1940s, clearly raises another area of a research inquiry for scholars interested in unraveling the early history of the Cold War.

Nonetheless, the Rosenberg rial and executions were arguably part of an intricate web of deflections away from two other secrets that, had they become fully public at the time, likely would have dramatically altered the postwar world. No doubt it is for this very reason that the two secrets—the corporate Fraternity that traded with the Nazis and the true dangers of radiation—remain for the most part unknown to the general public. As Carole Gallagher has observed with regard to the latter danger: "Deadened by fifty years of nuclearism, we may have mutated into a nation of 'good Germans' unwilling to see."[73] Tragically and ironically, it is our own bodies that are subject to this globalized, slow-motion holocaust.

NOTES

Epigraph from Susan Griffin, *A Chorus of Stones: The Private Life of War* (New York: Doubleday, 1992), 162.

1 Joyce Nelson, *The Perfect Machine: TV in the Nuclear Age* (Toronto: Between the Lines, 1987); reprinted in the United States as *The Perfect Machine: TV & the Bomb* (Philadelphia: New Society, 1992).

2 Erik Barnouw, *Tube of Plenty* (New York: Oxford University Press, 1975), 85.

3 Leo Szilard quoted in Peter Pringle and James Spigelman, *The Nuclear Barons* (London: Sphere, 1983), 8.

4 INFACT, *Bringing GE to Light* (Philadelphia: New Society, 1990), 95.

5 Stanley Goldberg, "Creating a Climate of Opinion: Vannevar Bush and the Decision to Build the Bomb," *Isis*, Spring 1992, 438 and 440.

6 Quoted in ibid., 446.

7 *Ibid.*, 446–47.

8 INFACT, *Bringing GE to Light*, 94.

9 *Ibid.*, 95.

10 *Ibid.*

11 *Ibid.*

12 *Ibid.*

13 *Ibid.*

14 *Ibid.*

15 Goldberg, "Creating a Climate of Opinion," 449.

16 Stephen Hilgartner, Richard C. Bell, and Rory O'Conner, *Nukespeak: The Selling of Nuclear Technology in America* (New York: Penguin, 1983), 22.

17 *Ibid.*, 25.

18 Leslie Groves quoted in *ibid.*, 26.

19 Charles L. Mee, Jr., *The Marshall Plan: The Launching of the Pax Americana* (New York: Simon and Schuster, 1984), 34.

20 *Ibid.*

21 *Ibid.*

22 Brian Easlea, *Fathering the Unthinkable: Masculinity, Scientists and the Nuclear Arms Race* (London: Pluto Press, 1983), 120.

23 Charles Wilson quoted in INFACT, *Bringing GE to Light*, 95.

24 INFACT, *Bringing GE to Light*, 95.

25 *Ibid.*, 94.

26 *Ibid.*

27 Arthur Compton quoted in *ibid.*

28 INFACT, *Bringing GE to Light*, 96.

29 *Ibid.*, 95.

30 Rosalie Bertell, *No Immediate Danger?* (London: Women's Press, 1985), 138.

31 Peter Wyden, *Day One: Before Hiroshima and After* (New York: Warner, 1985), 327.

32 Bertrell, *No Immediate Danger?*, 137.

33 Hilgartner, Bell and O'Conner, *Nukespeak,* 72.

34 William A. Shurcliff, *Bombs at Bikini: The Official Report of Operation Crossroads* (New York: W. H. Wise, 1947), 38.

35 Bertell, *No Immediate Danger?*, 74.

36 J. G. Ello, "Measuring Color-TV Generated X-Rays," *Electronic World*, Vol. 86, July 1971, 37.

37 Don Ward, "TV X-Rays," *Radio-Electronics*, Vol. 41, April 1970, 55.

38 *Ibid.*

39 *Ibid.*

40 Nelson, *The Perfect Machine*, 129–43.

41 Berlyn Brixner quoted in Robert Del Tredici (photographs and text), *At Work in the Fields of the Bomb* (Vancouver: Douglas and McIntyre, 1987), 185.

42 Barnouw, *Tube of Plenty*, 108.

43 *Ibid.*, 112.

44 Lee, *The Marshall Plan*, 50.

45 Harry Truman quoted in *ibid.*, 71.

46 Easlea, *Fathering the Unthinkable*, 120.

47 Lee, *The Marshall Plan*, 57.

48 Robert W. Malcolmson, *Beyond Nuclear Thinking* (Montreal: McGill-Queen's University Press, 1990), 13.

49 Thomas H. Saffer and Orville E. Kelly, *Countdown Zero* (Harmondsworth: Penguin, 1982), 43–44.

50 *Ibid.*

51 Erik Barnouw, *The Sponsor* (New York: Oxford University Press, 1978), 162.

52 *Ibid.*, 162–63.

53 Malcolmson, *Beyond Nuclear Thinking*, 13.

54 Carole Gagllagher (Photographs and text), *American Ground Zero: The Secret Nuclear War* (Cambridge: MIT Press, 1993), xxviii.

55 Charles Higham, *Trading with the Enemy: An Exposé of the Nazi-American Money Plot, 1933–1949* (New York: Delacorte Press, 1983), xvi.

56 *Ibid.*, xiv.

57 *Ibid.*

58 *Ibid*, xvi.

59 Bertram Gross, *Friendly Fascism: The New Face of Power in America* (Montreal: Black Rose Books, 1980), 20.

60 INFACT, *Bringing GE to Light*, 94.

61 Peter Collier and David Horowitz, *The Rockefellers: An American Dynasty* (New York: Holt, 1976), 225.

62 INFACT, *Bringing GE to Light*, 94.

63 *Ibid.*

64 Collier and Horowitz, *The Rockefellers*, 225.

65 Tom Brower, *Blind Eye to Murder: Britain, America and the Purging of Nazi Germany—A Place Betrayed* (London: Andre Deutsch, 1981), 18.

66 Collier and Horowitz, *The Rockefellers*, 225.

67 *Ibid.*

68 John Winant quoted in Higham, *Trading with the Enemy*, 57.

69 *Ibid.*, xv.

70 William L. Shirer, *20th Century Journey: A Native's Return* (New York: Bantam, 1992), 100.

71 *Ibid.*

72 Collier and Horowitz, *The Rockefellers*, 234–48.

73 Gallagher, *American Ground Zero*, xxxiii.

British scientist Klaus Fuchs, returning from prison
after serving sentence for atomic espionage.
(AP/Wide World Photos)

4

The Secret about Secrets

Stanley Goldberg

INTRODUCTION

When the Rosenbergs were arrested and tried, I was just a kid—sixteen years old—on the fringes of the political Left in Cleveland. I was in the proper frame of mind to be convinced, knowing virtually nothing about the case, that the Rosenbergs were totally innocent. In 1953, when the Rosenbergs were executed, I was not only out of high school, I was out of the country—cocooned on an aircraft carrier. I had lost track of more than the fate of the Rosenbergs.

My own education with regard to the Rosenberg case began in earnest in 1957 when I discovered John Wexley's *The Judgment of Julius and Ethel Rosenberg*.[1] At the time, the popular consensus was that the Rosenbergs had been spies, that they had given the Soviets the vital secret or secrets necessary to understand how to build an atomic bomb. In fact, most Americans probably accepted Judge Irving Kaufman's final harangue that the Rosenbergs' perfidy had resulted in the deaths of tens of thousands:

> I consider your crime worse than murder. Plain deliberate contemplated murder is dwarfed in magnitude by comparison with the crime you have committed. In

committing the act of murder, the criminal kills only his victim. The immediate family is brought to grief and when justice is meted out the chapter is closed. But in your case, I believe your conduct in putting into the hands of the Russians the A-bomb years before our best scientists predicted Russia would perfect the bomb has already caused, in my opinion, the Communist aggression in Korea, with the resultant casualties exceeding fifty thousand and who knows but that millions more of innocent people may pay the price [of] your treason.... You are hereby sentenced to the punishment of death and it is ordered...you shall be executed according to the law.[2]

The Wexley book was written from a point of view that is sympathetic to the Rosenbergs and written from the perspective of the political sector in which they participated. In reading it, however, I was engaged less in these political views and the question of the Rosenbergs' guilt than in the course of the trial itself. Whether or not the Rosenbergs had actually participated with others in providing the Soviets with information about the atomic bomb was moot. The government had not made its case. For example, Wexley could point out with ease a number of contradictions and gaps in government testimony. The bias of the judge seemed to me painfully obvious. Since that time other observers have corroborated and strengthened and further documented Wexley's contentions on the lack of definitive evidence and Judge Kaufman's improprieties.[3]

The fact that the Rosenbergs, along with Morton Sobell, had been convicted on such insufficient evidence was confounding. I finally rationalized it by recognizing that the conviction of the Rosenbergs had taken place within the semihysterical ambience of 1949–50. It was widely believed, as is represented in the quote from Judge Kaufman above, that the Soviets would have required many years to discover the secret of the atomic bomb. Since the Soviets now had their own atomic bomb, they must have been given the secret through traitorous acts of espionage. Now the world was in mortal danger. In such an atmosphere, the civil rights of Morton Sobell and the Rosenbergs, including their right to a just trial, had been trampled in the stampede to explain away the fact of the Soviet bomb.[4]

Even though I was only a third-year physics major, it was already clear to me, on the basis of the little technical testimony that had been released, that had the Soviets relied on the information Ethel Rosenberg's brother admitted to providing, they would still be trying to build their first bomb. It was also clear to me that, unfortunately, the strategy that Emmanuel Bloch had pursued in defense of the Rosenbergs had been poorly thought out and executed. With the best of intentions, Bloch's fumbling had allowed the government, literally, to get away with murder.

Now, more than forty years after the fact, though I am less convinced than before that the Rosenbergs were not in some way complicit in passing information to the Soviets, I still do not believe that they gave the Soviets *the* secret of the atomic bomb or that information provided by them advanced Soviet progress toward completion of their first atomic bomb. My judgment about Bloch's efforts has not changed, but given what we know about collusion between the judge and the prosecution,[5] and the degree to which the testimony of key witnesses was manipulated by the prosecution,[6] there is probably nothing that anyone could have done to change the outcome.

We may soon be able to show, definitively, whether the Rosenbergs worked for the Soviets in any espionage capacity. One of the happy consequences of the disintegration of the Soviet Union has been the opening of a number of Soviet archival sources, including KGB files. Thus far access has been spotty. To date, no document implicating the Rosenbergs has emerged. No former Soviet agents known to have controlled aspects of espionage operations in the United States have named the Rosenbergs as part of their network of informants. Unless some definitive piece of paper emerges from the Russian archives, the question of the technical guilt of the Rosenbergs will remain, forever, an unanswered question.

MANHATTAN PROJECT SECURITY
In September 1942, General Leslie R. Groves took command of the Manhattan Project. One of his first tasks was to ensure the security and secrecy of the project. There were three major aspects to that program: hiding the budget for the project within the very large appropriations requests for the Army Corps of Engineers and thereby keeping the project secret not only from the public but from the Congress as well;[7] counterintelligence; and compartmentalization of information.[8] The key premise underpinning the compartmentalization program was that if a person knew only that which was required for him or her to complete the tasks to which the person was assigned, the seriousness of security breaches would be limited. No one would have an overall picture of the nature of the project. This scheme worked extremely well on an industrial level—so well that on the day Hiroshima was bombed the fact that the United States possessed an atomic bomb came as a total surprise to most of the people who had helped to produce it, as well as to the country as a whole. Even though a half-million American citizens worked for the Manhattan Project at some point during the war (peak employment, in the summer of 1944, was one hundred sixty thousand people working in various factories and laboratories located in thirty-nine states and Canada), only a handful of people actually understood the purpose of their labor.[9]

Compartmentalization of information, however, could not be strictly enforced in the Manhattan Project laboratories at the University of California at Berkeley, the University of Chicago, or Columbia University, where scientists and engineers were trying to work out the plans for the factories where nuclear fuels were to be produced. In the laboratories at Los Alamos there was no compartmentalization of information at all among those who were responsible for designing and fabricating the weapons that utilized those fuels. Laboratory director J. Robert Oppenheimer had convinced Groves that in order to carry out their responsibilities intelligently, Los Alamos scientists and engineers, regardless of their specific assignments, had to understand all aspects of the design problem. Oppenheimer also told Groves that it would be much more difficult to recruit the talent he needed if conditions within the laboratory did not come close to emulating those in civilian laboratories with respect to the free flow of information. That is one of the reasons that the laboratory was placed in such a remote location. Rather than fencing off each part of the work from all other parts of the work, the entire laboratory was fenced off.

It was Groves's counterintelligence group that was primarily responsible for making industrial compartmentalization a success. The strategy used can best be described as "tactics of terror." At each industrial site undercover counterintelligence personnel worked in all phases of the production process. Lapses in the enforcement of compartmentalization or evidence of curiosity about the significance of an operation on the part of employees led to immediate dismissal. There was no appeal, no second chance. It did not take too many such dismissals for word to get around. Counterintelligence agents also worked undercover at Manhattan Project university-based laboratories. At Los Alamos there was no point in having undercover counterintelligence employees. There Groves relied on the isolation of the site, reinforced by a barbed wire fence and guards at the two gates. In addition, towns in the vicinity, the largest being Santa Fe, were flooded with Manhattan Project counterintelligence undercover agents as well as anonymous agents of the FBI.[10]

SPIES GALORE

The recently opened Russian archives may not have revealed anything about the alleged spy activities of the Rosenbergs, but those archives have already disgorged a number of remarkable documents showing that despite the best efforts of Groves and his counterintelligence group, a flood of information and data on the American bomb project was being delivered to the Soviets all during and after the war. Not just from Klaus Fuchs either, but from other American and/or British physicists as well—just how many and who they all were is not yet known and may never be completely discovered. The motivation of these people seems to have been the same. They wanted to ensure that there would be a level playing field between the powers after the war. My own assessment of the willingness of these scientists to *act* on such an analysis is that in doing so, they arrogated to themselves the duties of the Department of State and the Department of Defense. Such usurpations, even as a matter of conscience, are sadly and fundamentally out of step with shared principles I consider to be at the heart of a participatory democratic community. At the same time, I recognize that acts of conscience are part of living a life and living a life is not a matter of logic.[11]

These people need not have worried. The Soviets had been working on the development of their own bomb since 1943. Apparently, even before Groves was appointed head of the Manhattan Project, even before the Manhattan Project itself had come into existence, even before Klaus Fuchs had come to America, a large cache of documents from the American uranium program had been delivered to the Soviets, documenting research on the various techniques of isotope separation, on reactor physics and engineering, and on initial investigations into bomb design. In mid-1943, acting on Joseph Stalin's order, the Soviets began in earnest their own atomic bomb program. Information updating American progress on the bomb continued to be made available to the director of the program, a brilliant nuclear physicist, Igor Kurchatov. By the end of 1945 the Soviets had an excellent perspective on the American program and had seen some interesting ways of leapfrogging to a more sophisticated design. Their enthusiasm for attempting such innovations, however, was tempered by the certain knowledge that should the program fail, the minister overseeing the project, the notorious Lavrenti P. Beria, would see to it that the leaders of the program, at the very least, would pay with their lives. Knowing that the American bomb worked, Kurchatov decided, understandably, that it would be in his own best interest, and that of his associates, to make the first bomb an exact duplicate of the American one. Once they got Beria off their backs, then they would be free to explore their own ideas.[12] We now know that, at best, the information the Soviet scientists received from the Manhattan Project saved them a little time and money, but most important, it guaranteed their lives.

THE ORE BOTTLENECK

What really convicted the Rosenbergs and what really made it possible for Judge Kaufman to mete out that monstrous sentence was the widely held belief that there had been *a* secret, some deep hidden principle of nature that had been discovered during the war by physicists in America and that no one else could possibly discover in the short term without assistance from those in the know. In fact, there was no such secret. This myth was largely the result of General Leslie Groves's insistent claim, supported by the hubris of some scientists, that it would take the Soviets twenty years to build their own bomb. For public consumption Groves trumpeted the belief that the Soviets did not have the scientific talent and technical infrastructure to figure out the secret. What he *really* believed was that they would not be able to get high-grade ore. No ore, no bomb. Groves was not a stupid man. If anyone knew the difficulties in wresting uranium from its ores, it was Leslie R. Groves.

Early in his tenure as head of the Manhattan Project, Groves had set up a special office in New York staffed with mining and geological experts. The office was dubbed the Manhattan Project's "Murray Hill Area office." The existence of this office was so secret that the name, which came from the region of Manhattan in which the office was physically located, did not appear on any report not marked "Top Secret" until long after the war.[13] The first task of this office was to make a worldwide survey of potential sources of uranium and thorium ores, the two elements from which fissionable material can be obtained with relative ease. Groves's experience in the Manhattan Project had quickly taught him an important lesson. Given the difficulty in extracting uranium metal from its ore, not just any ore would do; one had to have a relatively rich source of ore to be able to quickly amass sufficient amounts of uranium metal from which one might either separate out the rare fissionable isotope or manufacture fissionable plutonium. The Manhattan Project had been lucky to have available ore from the Shinkolobwe Mine located in the Belgian Congo's Katanga province, by far the richest known source of uranium in the world. Based on the preliminary 1943 surveys of the Murray Hill office, Shinkolobwe ore together with known sources of uranium on the North American continent constituted over 90 percent of the world's potential supply of uranium. This estimate was based largely on published reports. The Murray Hill Area office did do considerable field work from near the end of the war through 1946 but for understandable reasons had little information on the situation in those countries which fell under Soviet control.[14]

Nevertheless, Groves's confident estimate that it would take the Soviets twenty years to produce an atomic bomb was based on his belief that they did not have available to them mineral deposits rich in uranium. His argument was so powerful and so persuasive that he convinced his civilian superiors, Vannevar Bush and James Conant. Earlier, in 1944, Bush and Conant had argued that it should take the Soviets about as long as it took us to build their first bomb.[15] Groves apparently convinced them otherwise.[16] Unknown to Groves, the Soviets had available to them fairly rich ores in Southeast Germany.[17] And, more important, he had not counted on Soviet ingenuity with regard to techniques for refining uranium—techniques that we ourselves did not begin to examine until after 1948.

PROTECTING THE SECRETS OF THE BOMB

What made it possible for Groves and others to successfully propagate the secrets story was that it fit with long-held misconceptions and confusions on the part of Americans about the relationship between science and technology. The prevailing view in the United States, since the last quarter of the nineteenth century, has been that something called "pure research," by which is meant "the search for truth for its own sake," is a prerequisite for effective technological innovation. This ubiquitous claim was especially precious to some of the principal innovators working within an industrial research setting.[18] The evidence pointed to by those who advertised the notion of a necessary connection between science and technology were such technological triumphs as the chemical dye industry and the (then) recent eruption of electrical technologies as represented by the telephone, telegraph, lamp, and electrical power industries. But close examination of all of these cases shows that their emergence depended, almost entirely, on the clever manipulation of materials. The individuals responsible for these accomplishments, such as Alexander Graham Bell or Thomas Alva Edison, had relatively little idea of, or interest in, the significance of the phenomena being exploited in terms of what they could elucidate about the basic laws of nature and their operation. What science does contribute to the process is to draw attention to particular *phenomena*: for example, the motion of a piece of iron when a coil of wire is energized or the fact that the flow of current in an electrical circuit can be modified by changing the pressure on a group of confined carbon granules that are part of the circuit in question and that also serve as the mouthpiece of a telephone. But newly discovered phenomena are not the exclusive province of science. Technological activities themselves often draw attention to hitherto undetected effects. The claim that "pure" or "fundamental" or "basic" research is the only route to the successful exploitation of physical phenomena is a self-serving myth perpetuated by those who apparently worry that without such justification, the kind of research we call "pure" or "basic" or "fundamental" will no longer be perceived to be worthy of support by cost-conscious stockholders or taxpayers.[19]

This myth has been reified in law—in the original Atomic Energy Act of 1946 and its successor, the Atomic Energy Act of 1954. Regulations based on the act specify two categories of classified nuclear information: Restricted Data (RD) and Formerly Restricted Data (FRD). The RD category contains detailed information on the various components that make up a nuclear device—their composition, physical characteristics, and geometric relation to each other. FRD includes such information as the size and location of the nuclear arsenal. All Restricted Data for all nuclear devices the United States has ever produced, including the very first—the bomb tested in the desert in New Mexico in July 1945—as well as those dropped on Japan in August of 1945, are still classified as top secret. Restricted Data is sometimes referred to as "born secret." It is the view of those committed to protection of that information that it is the only thing that has thus far prevented so-called potentially "proliferant" nations such as Iraq and Pakistan from acquiring nuclear arsenals—in short, this information contains the secrets of the atomic bomb. Presumably, it is those secrets which the Rosenbergs transmitted to the Soviets.

THE SECRET ABOUT SECRETS

The core scientific idea underpinning nuclear technology is the evidence that uranium and a few other heavy atomic nuclei undergo fission and in doing so, release, atom for atom, unprecedented amounts of energy. This phenomenon was discovered at the end of 1938, and news of its discovery was widely propagated. Physicists in America, the British Empire, Germany, Japan, the Soviet Union, and other places immediately understood the implications. The question was, could one engineer an environment that would exploit this phenomenon for a weapon or for the production of power? The answer to *that* question was announced to the world on August 6, 1945, in the most dramatic way possible.

As Groves and most of the scientists who worked on the project understood, given the availability of ores, all that was required was a cadre of reasonably trained scientists and engineers and the will necessary to devote large amounts of money and human energy to run down the limited number of possibilities for exploiting the phenomenon. It is not a trivial job, but it is not the secret of the ages. As has been demonstrated by the former USSR, by Israel, Iraq, Pakistan, India, China, South Africa, perhaps North Korea, and God knows who else, any other nation willing to commit resources that might otherwise be used to better the lot of its citizenry can figure out the tricks of the trade, that is, can make a functioning atomic bomb.

Slowly, ever so slowly, those countries with substantial nuclear arsenals have come to recognize that these weapons are worthless. Their only value lies in the threat of unbearable destruction. What makes them worthless is that the havoc they wreak recognizes no national boundary or political demarcation. To destroy your enemy is to destroy yourself. It is this recognition more than any other that has, I believe, fueled the enthusiasm of the major nuclear powers to begin dismantling the bulk of the sixty thousand nuclear warheads that now dot the landscapes of the world. But meanwhile, in spite of government attempts to protect restricted data, the information required to manufacture fission and fusion bombs is readily available. For example, though still strictly classified by the Department of Energy, the fact that the first plutonium bombs contained 6.1 kilograms of plutonium was first published in 1975. Data on the geometry of the first uranium bomb along with the precise dimensions and the precise weight of the hollow and solid cylinders of uranium contained in the weapon—though still considered highly secret—have been out in public view for quite a long time. Even when precise information about one or another aspect of the design is not available, enough of the principles of operation are known to ensure that any determined bomb builder can figure it out—even someone who does not have a Ph.D. in physics. The idea that RD and FRD have been the roadblock keeping potentially proliferative nations from building atomic bombs is foolish. As I have already suggested, roadblocks, if they exist, are the discipline, the money, and the raw materials.

THE IRRELEVANCE OF SECRETS

In the summer of 1973 a student at Hampshire College, where I was teaching, found, in a local used bookstore, what amounted to a terrorist manual for making bombs of all sorts. The last in the series was a crude plutonium bomb constructed within a short length of sewer pipe. I showed this recipe to a physicist acquaintance of mine.

"Won't work," he intoned.

"Why not?" I asked.

"Not a very elegant implosion," he replied.

"Wait a minute," I said, "would it take down the Empire State Building?"

"I don't know about taking it down," he answered, "but it certainly would destroy it."

"Might it contaminate a ten-square-block area of New York City for several years?" I continued.

"More like thousands of years," was his reply.

"Well?" I inquired.

"It is just not an elegant solution to the problem," he repeated.

So much for elegance. So much for secrets.

NOTES

A version of this paper was read at "Forty Years After: The Rosenberg Case and the McCarthy Era," a conference organized by the Harvard Center for Literary and Cultural Studies, Cambridge, Massachusetts, May 8–9, 1993.

1 John Wexley, *The Judgment of Julius and Ethel Rosenberg* (New York: Cameron and Kahn, 1955).

2 Irving Kaufman quoted in Walter Schneir and Miriam Schneir, *Invitation to an Inquest: A New Look at the Rosenberg-Sobell Case* (Garden City, N.Y.: Doubleday, 1965), 170–71.

3 See, e.g., Wexley, *Judgment*, Chap. 16, 372–413. See also Schneir and Schneir, *Invitation to an Inquest*, 119–21, 261–64, 371–73; Robert Meeropol and Michael Meeropol, *We Are Your Sons: The Legacy of Ethel and Julius Rosenberg*, 2d ed., (Urbana: University of Illinois Press, 1986), Part 3, 341–438.

4 Contemporary newspaper and news magazine accounts of the arrest, trial, and execution of the Rosenbergs read today have a surreal, Kafkaesque quality about them. The Rosenberg case also spawned the publication of many hysterical, shrill anti-Communist tracts. See, e.g., Solomon A. Fineberg, *The Rosenberg Case: Fact and Fiction* (New York: Oceana, 1953).

5 Meeropol and Meeropol, *We Are Your Children*, 369–75. One should rightfully approach the claims of the Rosenberg children cautiously and with initial skepticism, but they provide clear and unequivocal documentation of gross misconduct on the part of Judge Kaufman, prosecutor Saypol, and Saypol's assistants.

6 See, e.g., Schneir and Schneir, *Invitation to an Inquest*, 374–77, 397–403; Meeropol and Meeropol, *We Are Your Children*, 187–90, 354.

7 The strategy of keeping the Congress in the dark had been devised by Vannevar Bush, who oversaw research on "the uranium problem" between 1940 and 1942. Bush had served, essentially, as Franklin D. Roosevelt's science adviser. One of the reasons that Bush decided to turn the project over to the Army Corps of Engineers when the project's demands for resources began to outstrip Bush's ability to provide for those demands from presidential discretionary funds was because it would be possible to continue funding without having to tell the Congress the nature of the project. See Stanley Goldberg, "Creating a Climate of Opinion: Vannevar Bush and the Decision to Build the Bomb," *Isis* 83 (1992): 429–52.

8 Groves's security system is described in detail in Stanley Goldberg, *Fighting to Build the Bomb: The Private Wars of Leslie R. Groves* (South Royalton, VT: Steerforth Press, forthcoming).

9 See, e.g., Stanley Goldberg, Manhattan Project Video History Interviews, Collection Division 2: Oak Ridge, Session 5, Smithsonian Institute Archives. Transcripts of the sound track of these video histories are available from the Smithsonian Archives.

10 Groves and his chief of counterintelligence, Lt. Col. John Lansdale, had a deep distrust of the FBI and of the tactics of FBI director J. Edgar Hoover. Though the FBI was used to handle routine security checks, FBI agents were not

allowed within any Manhattan Project facility. Their presence in Santa Fe was tolerated but had no formal relationship to Manhattan Project counterintelligence. See John Lansdale, *John Lansdale Jr. Military Service* (unpublished ms.), 33–34.

11 If Klaus Fuchs and Soviet agents are to be believed, money was never an issue. In fact, Fuchs, who was insulted by the gesture, refused money when it was proffered. See Robert C. Williams, *Klaus Fuchs: Atom Spy* (Cambridge: Harvard University Press, 1987); Norman Moss, *Klaus Fuchs: The Man Who Stole the Atom Bomb* (New York: St. Martin's Press, 1987). See also excerpts from an interview with Fuchs in "The Red Bomb," a three-part Discovery Channel mini-series that was broadcast Sept. 12–14, 1994. This mini-series also contains remarks by Fuch's mentor, physicist Rudolph Peierls, who describes Fuchs as "naive" and "arrogant."

12 Yuli Khariton and Yuri Smirnov, "The Soviet Bomb: The Khariton Version," *Bulletin of the Atomic Scientists* 49, no. 4 (May 1993): 20–31.

13 For example, the name "Murray Hill" appears nowhere in the first volume of the official history of the Atomic Energy Commission. See Richard G. Hewlett and Oscar E. Anderson, Jr., *The New World: A History of the United States Atomic Energy Commission, Volume I, 1939–1946* (University Park: Pennsylvania State University Press, 1962).

14 The story of the Murray Hill Area office is discussed in Gregg Herken, *The Winning Weapon: The Atomic Bomb in the Cold War, 1945–1950* (New York: Knopf, 1980); in Jonathan E. Helmreich, *Gathering Rare Ores: The Diplomacy of Uranium Acquisition, 1943–1954* (Princeton: Princeton University Press, 1986) and in Stanley Goldberg and Charles Ziegler, "General Groves and the Atomic Monopoly: The Second Myth" (forthcoming).

15 James B. Conant and Vannevar Bush, memo to the Post War Policy Commission, September 19, 1944, National Archives and Record Administration, Record Group 77, Army Corps of Engineers, Papers of the Manhattan Engineer District, the Harrison Bundy Files, Folder 76.

16 Vannevar Bush published *Modern Arms and Free Men* in October 1949. In the body of the book, Bush's rationale for why the Soviets would require at least ten to fifteen years to develop nuclear weapons was that only an environment that adhered to democratic forms, such as is found in the United States, could easily foster scientific and engineering innovation. The book was being printed when President Harry S. Truman announced, in October 1949, the fact that the Soviets had detonated an atomic bomb. Bush was forced to add a hurriedly prepared preface acknowledging the Soviet feat. See Vannevar Bush, *Modern Arms and Free Men: A Discussion of the Role of Science in Preserving Democracy* (New York: Simon and Schuster, 1949).

17 Helmreich, *Gathering Rare Ores*, 247–50.

18 See for example, Arthur D. Little, *The Relation of Research to Industrial Development* (Boston, 1917); J. J. Carty, "Relation of Pure Science to Industrial Research," *Science*, 44 (1916): 511–18. Little, who taught at MIT near the turn of the century, was the founder of the Arthur D. Little Company. Carty was the chief engineer of the Western Electric Company laboratories and, as such, was the director of one of the precursors to the Bell Telephone Laboratories. See Stanley Goldberg, "American Attitudes toward Basic Research and the Rise of the Industrial Research Laboratory" (forthcoming).

19 In recent years the issues surrounding the justification of scientific research have been further muddied by the military's enthusiastic support of abstract scientific work immediately following World War II, support that was sustained, during the period we refer to as the "Cold War." It should be pointed out that such support assured the military of access to some very clever people. At the same time, scientists were known to brag among themselves about their cleverness in writing research proposals that gave the appearance of providing practical applications to potential military funders but that in reality provided a cover for allowing the scientists to pursue their own interests in "pure," abstract science. See, e.g., Paul Forman, "Behind Quantum Electronics: National Security as Basis for Physical Research in the United States, 1940–1960," *Historical Studies in Physical and Biological Science* 18 (1987): 149–229.

The ultimate rationale for public or private support of scientific work has to be the same as the rationale for support of artistic or humanistic work: It is one of the things that separates us from other species. We are driven to pursue such questions. We cannot turn those drives off. They are defining features of humanity and of civilization.

5

Censorship of American Uranium Mine Epidemiology in the 1950s

Robert N. Proctor

Danger is foremost in our minds when we think of atomic radiation.
—Heinz Haber, *The Walt Disney Story of Our Friend the Atom*

A great deal of attention has focused on the radiation experiments that the U.S. Army, the Atomic Energy Commission, the Public Health Service, and other branches of government conducted on unsuspecting American citizens in the 1950s. The timing of the revelations is, as one might imagine, political: much has to do with the appointment of a new Department of Energy secretary, Hazel O'Leary, who has promised an open look at this darker side of history. Much also has to do with the end of the Cold War: it is perhaps not entirely accidental that the most celebrated revelations coincided with the joint decision, in December 1993, of the governments of Russia and the United States no longer to point their missiles at one another. There is also the levity of distance: the same forces that have allowed a younger generation of German scholars to explore the Nazi past now allow a younger generation of historian-critics to unearth this seamy side of American history.[1]

I have recently published a book on what causes cancer—what cancer has to do with not just bad habits but also bad business, bad government, and even bad science. Radiation occupies a special place in the history of the human body. Radiation causes cancer, though how and to what extent have been controversial since radiation cancers were first observed in the early years of this century. The adventurous use of X-rays produced some of the first such cancers,[2] and the tragic outcome of the 1920s radium craze[3] alerted a formerly guileless public to the danger—especially after hundreds of radium dial painters contracted cancer of the jaw from ingesting radioactive paint.[4] The Manhattan Project vastly increased the scale of nuclear exposures, and the postwar nuclear boom allowed cancers to be planted in the lungs of thousands of uranium miners and millers.

The story I want to tell here, however, is about deception. The politics of knowledge often lies in the structure of our ignorance: not just who knows what, why, when, and where, but also who keeps quiet about—or fails to investigate—this, that, or another thing. Ignorance, like knowledge, is a manufactured product: it is important to ask why "we" know certain things, and don't know others. In the 1950s, McCarthyites argued that the secrets of the atom bomb had fallen into enemy hands, with the help of domestic traitorous agents such as Ethel and Julius Rosenberg. As it turns out, there were other nuclear secrets governments were eager to protect—deadly secrets concerning the magnitude of the hazards of nuclear-related work, especially uranium mining.

EARLY EPIDEMIOLOGY

It is important to realize that uranium mining is unlike most other kinds of mining in that during the course of blasting and digging for ore, radioactive radon-222 gas is released. Radon-222 is a natural decay product of uranium, with a half-life of about three and one-half days. Radon gas by itself poses no real danger: as a noble gas, it is chemically inert and is simply exhaled. But its radioactive "daughter products"[5] can settle in the lungs and injure those tissues. The primary hazard comes from polonium-218 and 214, alpha-emitting radionuclides that lodge in the lining of the lung. Uranium miners are also bombarded by gamma radiation, but the primary danger, again, stems from the ingestion and inhalation of alpha emitters. Smoking in combination with uranium mining can prove especially dangerous: Geno Saccamano, a resident of Grand Junction, Colorado, and an internationally known pathologist, showed in the 1960s that uranium mining in combination with cigarette smoking could increase one's odds of getting lung cancer by as much as thirty times. More recent studies have shown that nonsmokers are also at risk: Robert J. Roscoe of the National Institute for Occupational Safety and Health has shown that nonsmoking uranium miners followed from 1950 to 1984 were thirteen times more likely to die from lung cancer than a comparable group of nonsmoking U.S. veterans.[6]

Knowledge of the health hazards of uranium mining, however, dates back to long before the time that Americans became involved in the enterprise.

Indeed, the hazards were appreciated prior even to the discovery of X-rays, primarily through epidemiological studies of the silver and uranium miners in the *Erzgebirge* (ore mountains) of Germany and northern Czechoslovakia, near the towns of Schneeberg in Saxony and Joachimsthal in Bohemia. These mines had been worked since the sixteenth century, first as a source of silver (the word "dollar" is derived from *thaler*, a shortened form of *Joachimsthaler*, a coin made from the very pure silver of this region) and later as a source of nickel, cobalt, bismuth, uranium and arsenic. Miners from this region had long been known to suffer from a painful and "consumptive" lung disease locally known as *Bergkrankheit* (mountain sickness),[7] correctly identified by F. H. Härting and W. Hesse in 1879 as lung cancer. Härting and Hesse found that miners lived only about twenty years after entering the mines and that about three-quarters of all miners in this region were dying from lung cancer. This latter figure would be even higher, they suggested, were miners not also dying prematurely from other causes, such as accidents.[8]

For most of the nineteenth century the uranium miners' *Bergkrankheit* was most commonly attributed to foul air, "consumption," or "miner's phthisis" (probably silicosis or silico-tuberculosis). The ailment was correctly diagnosed as cancer in the 1870s, but it was not until the 1920s that the specific cause was identified as the inhalation of radioactive gases. Even after the disease was recognized as cancer, scientific belief commonly blamed the inhalation of arsenic (Härting and Hesse's view), fungal spores on wooden mine supports, or "genetic predispositions" fostered by inbreeding in these remote mountain regions.[9] The first measurements of radioactivity in the air of the Schneeberg mines were published in 1924 in one of Germany's leading physics journals by P. Ludewig and S. Lorenser.[10] Subsequent studies confirmed that the radioactivity in any given mine could vary by several orders of magnitude but was generally highest, as one would expect, near the drill holes where new ores were ripped from the rock face. According to one calculation, workers were inhaling an average of 12.4 mg of radium per year, an extremely toxic dose. Wilhelm Hueper, author of the pathbreaking *Occupational Tumors and Allied Diseases*, pointed out in 1942 that mine workers had long been aware that certain shafts were more hazardous than others: the shaft found to have the highest radioactivity, for example, was popularly known as the *Todesschacht*, or "death mine."[11] Ludewig and Lorenser's 1924 survey had found between two thousand and nine thousand picocuries per liter in this mine; this was convincing evidence, in their view, that radon inhalation was the primary cause of the miners' cancer.

THE AMERICAN EXPERIENCE

In the United States, concern about the health effects of exposure to radon emerged largely after World War II in response to the rapid growth of the U.S. military's demand for uranium. U.S. bomb production, driven at a frenetic pace by Cold War fears and military-industrial enthusiasm, required the extraction of huge quantities of ore,[12] all of which—by law—had to be sold to the Atomic Energy Commission (AEC). Ores were eventually found throughout the world, but the most important U.S. source for many years was the arid "four-corner" region best known as the Colorado Plateau stretching across Utah, Colorado, New Mexico, and Arizona. Skyrocketing demand set off a uranium rush, though smaller investors were soon driven out by larger companies, and by the end of the 1950s five or six large corporations—notably Kerr-McGee, Union Carbide, Anaconda, United Nuclear, and Homestake Mining—dominated the industry. After the Arab oil embargo of 1973 oil companies joined in the search for uranium, including Exxon, Gulf, Mobil, Conoco, Getty Oil, Atlantic Richfield, and Standard Oil of Ohio. In 1966 there were six hundred uranium mines in the United States (all on the Colorado Plateau) employing twenty-five thousand miners, 90 percent of whom worked underground.[13] Many of these were Navajos, the long-standing native residents of this part of the world.

Given the European experience, the emergence of a radon hazard in U.S. uranium mines should not have been difficult to predict. Gaseous emissions from radium had been recognized as a potential health hazard since early in the century, and by the end of the 1930s efforts had already been made to establish a "tolerance concentration" for inhaled radon.[14] Wilhelm Hueper in 1942 presented an elaborate historical review of the discovery of the radon-lung cancer link in European mines along with a convincing refutation of efforts to attribute the disease to other factors, like inbreeding.[15] A 1944 review by Egon Lorenz for the *Journal of the National Cancer Institute* concluded that "the radioactivity of the ore and the radon content of the air in the mines are generally considered to be the primary cause" of the European *Bergkrankheit*.[16] In 1947 an expert on occupational cancer predicted that "one will see cases of cancer and of leukemia in our newest group of industrialists, workers in the field of fissionable materials."[17]

Knowledge, however, does not necessarily result in action. In the late 1940s, several scientists tried to alert the federal government of the uranium mining hazard, but without success. Bernard Wolf and Merril Eisenbud, the first and second directors of the AEC's Medical Division, traveled to Colorado in April of 1948 to inspect the mines and recommend protections for the workers but were rebuffed when they tried to alert their superiors to the problem: "Much to our surprise, we were told by Washington that the health problems of the mines were not the responsibility of the AEC, and that they should be left to the jurisdiction of the local authorities." The AEC had been assigned by Congress the responsibility for radiation safety in the nuclear program but, according to a bizarre interpretation of the 1946 Atomic Energy Act, the commission was bound only to regulate radiation exposures *after* the ore had been mined. Responsibility for the health and safety of uranium miners was left up to individual states, a situation that Merril Eisenbud rightly recognized as "absurd," given their lack of equipment and expertise to deal with the expected health problems.[18]

This was not a good time to cross the AEC on matters of radiation safety. The radiologist William F. Bale in 1949, for example, was ignored by the AEC when he presented evidence that U.S. miners were being exposed to levels of radioactivity high enough to cause lung cancer. H.J. Muller, the Nobel laureate celebrated as both the "founder of radiation genetics" and (later) the first president of the American Society of Human Genetics, was barred from speaking at the International Conference on the Peaceful Uses of Atomic Energy at Geneva in 1955. Muller had been involved in publicizing the threat posed by radiation to the genetic integrity of the species and for that reason was feared by the commission, which twisted his ideas and sought to present a more benign view of the health effects of radiation.[19]

The most dramatic case of censorship, however, is that of Wilhelm C. Hueper, founding director of the National Cancer Institute's Environmental Cancer Section (1948–64). Hueper had begun an investigation of the health of uranium miners in the spring of 1948, only to see his research blocked when the AEC heard about his plans to publicize the work. The case is interesting, so if the reader will indulge me, I shall go into some detail.

Paul Starr's well-known book *The Social Transformation of American Medicine* states that American scientists in the early postwar years "enjoyed autonomy within the constraints of professional competition." This was indeed the position of officials in charge of the NIH Division of Research Grants, Hueper's superior, who in 1951 wrote: "The investigator works on problems of his own choosing and is not obliged to adhere to a preconceived plan. He is free to publish as he sees fit and to change his research without clearance if he finds new and more promising leads. He has almost complete budget freedom as long as he uses the funds for research purposes and expends them in accordance with local institutional rules."[20] Hueper's own experience shows, though, that political pressures were not entirely foreign to the setting. The German émigré and former Du Pont employee had already made many enemies for his efforts to track down industrial carcinogens: shortly after joining the NCI in 1948, for example, he had received a letter from the Federal Loyalty Commission informing him that he was under investigation for disloyalty to the United States. Du Pont's medical director had denounced him as a Nazi, a trumped-up charge that was dismissed when

Hueper was able to show that it had come from a colleague jealous of the acclaim he had won for his work on occupational bladder cancer. Hueper was later accused of harboring "communistic tendencies," though this, too, was shown to have no more substance than the Nazi charge.

In April of 1948 Hueper had begun a project to study the health of uranium miners, well aware of the fact that European uranium miners had long suffered from very high rates of lung cancer. His efforts in this area were stymied, however, by the fact that all NIH papers dealing with radiation had to be cleared by the Atomic Energy Commission. When Hueper sought to present evidence of the threat at a 1952 meeting of the Colorado State Medical Society, the AEC's Director of Biology and Medicine, Shields Warren, ordered the head of the NCI to instruct Hueper to delete all references in his paper to the hazards of uranium mining. Hueper initially refused on the grounds that he had not joined the institute to become a "scientific liar"; pressed with the demand, though, he felt he had no alternative but to withdraw from the conference. He did send a copy of his paper to the society's president, explaining his decision. When word got around that he was not silently accepting his censorship, Warren again wrote the director of the NCI, this time asking for Hueper's dismissal. Hueper stayed on at the institute but was soon thereafter barred from all epidemiological work on occupational cancer. The order came from the surgeon general. Hueper was henceforth allowed to do only experimental work on animals, and was prohibited from further investigations into "the causation of cancer in man related to environmental exposure to carcinogenic chemical, physical, and parasitic agents."[21] As Victor Archer recalls the incident, Hueper was essentially barred from research travel west of the Mississippi.[22] Hueper later complained that government censorship of studies on the health effects of uranium mining had delayed measures to remedy the situation, leaving countless men to die who otherwise could have been saved. It would be ten years before a comprehensive report identified lung cancer as a hazard for this occupation, and this only after the governor of the state of Colorado had urged its writing.[23]

The U.S. Public Health Service (PHS) began to study the environmental hazards of the mines and the health of underground miners in 1949 and 1950, but this agency, too, was hamstrung by apathy, bureaucratic conservatism, and government censorship. In the early 1950s the service launched an educational program to inform mining companies and state agencies of the health risks posed by uranium mining but—incredibly—the miners themselves were never informed of the hazard.[24] The service recommended improved ventilation and the wearing of masks, though none of these recommendations was mandatory and the effort was therefore of little consequence. In the summer of 1952 a PHS team measured radon levels in 157 mines in Colorado, Utah, Arizona, and New Mexico and found median concentrations ranging from 8 pCi/l (at Eastern Slope) to 9,000 pCi/l (at Bull Canyon). The highest levels recorded were at Bull Canyon and Marysvale, where peak readings of 59,000 pCi/l and 48,700 pCi/l were obtained.[25] In 1957 the service proposed a standard of one "working level" (WL)—equivalent to 100 picocuries of radon daughters per liter of air—as the maximum safe level of radioactivity in a working mine; by its own admission, 64 percent of all workers were exposed to levels at least ten times this high, levels that were predicted to cause lung cancers.[26] As late as 1961, nearly a third of all U.S. uranium miners were still breathing more than 1,000 pCi/l at work.[27]

Victor Archer and three of his colleagues at the Public Health Service published the first major study of U.S. uranium miner epidemiology in 1962. The miners had now been followed for over a decade, and the first excess cancers were beginning to appear. Accidents and heart disease were still the primary hazards, but five of 907 miners with more than three years experience underground had already died from lung cancer, when only one such death was expected.[28] These preliminary results were confirmed a year later, when an updated analysis of the PHS date showed that uranium mine workers were more than five times as likely to die from respiratory cancer than the normal population, and that men who had been exposed to the highest levels of radiation showed lung cancer rates up to forty times higher than expected. These and subsequent studies confirmed what had been known to European physicians for the better part of a century—that improperly ventilated uranium mining causes cancer.[29]

THE "DEAD BODY APPROACH"

It is sometimes said that firm proof of a radiation hazard in U.S. mines emerged only in the 1960s,[30] and it is true that published reports of American cancer deaths did not appear until this time. But, as we have seen, good evidence that such deaths would occur was available much earlier and was ignored or even suppressed by the Public Health Service acting on orders of the Atomic Energy Commission. European journals were filled with warnings, and Americans familiar with this literature had amply warned the agencies who should have acted to lessen the exposures. The Public Health Service Report of 1957 called for "the immediate application of corrective measures,"[31] and half a dozen scientists had warned—since the late 1940s—of an impending public health disaster.[32] But nuclear authorities were reluctant to push for anything that might impede the flow of uranium from mines to mills to weapons. Duncan A. Holaday, the PHS's health physicist responsible for monitoring the radiation in U.S. uranium mines, became frustrated by the failure of the AEC to warn the miners or to force the industry to clean up its act: in 1953 he complained that "the only way we can ever get anything done is to collect [dead] bodies and lay them on somebody's doorstep." Victor Archer, the epidemiologist who from 1956 to 1968 supervised the PHS's study of cancer among the uranium miners, used similar language to express his own frustration. In the mid-1970s, at the trial of former Navajo miners and their families suing the federal government for compensation, Archer testified that he and his colleagues had caved in to AEC and PHS pressures not to publicize the hazard: "We did not want to rock the boat.... [W]e had to take the position that we were neutral scientists trying to find out what the facts were, that we were not going to make any pubic announcements until the results of our scientific study were completed."[33] Official pressures to "monitor" the disaster without informing those at risk or forcing the companies to reduce the hazard led PHS scientists to characterize their study as a "death watch" or "dead body approach." A federal judge involved in the Navajo case charged that U.S. atomic authorities had failed to warn the miners in order to guarantee "a constant, uninterrupted and reliable flow" of uranium ore "for national security purposes."[34]

Local physicians were certainly not unaware that something was amiss. Lung cancer had always been rare among the Navajos as it still is, relatively speaking, today. By the mid-1950s physicians on the plateau began to see increasing numbers of Navajos with the disease: "It got so I didn't need to wait for the tests. They would come in—the wife and the six kids were always there, too—and they would say they had been spitting blood. I would ask and they would answer that they had been in the mines. Then I didn't need to wait to make the diagnosis, really, I already knew." Of course, not everyone knew, or wanted to admit they knew: as late as 1979, Kerr-McGee spokesmen were still denying that Navajos who had worked in the mines had contracted cancer from their work.[35]

The Atomic Energy Commission and Public Health Service were not the only agencies unwilling or unable to tackle the problem. The Bureau of Mines had long regulated health and safety standards in the nation's coal mines, but it was not until 1966 that it was authorized to regulate health and safety in uranium mines. The Labor Department was equally negligent, despite the powers granted its secretary under the Walsh-Healy Act of the 1930s to stop government purchases from hazardous mines. During the years of federal neglect, responsibility for monitoring and regulating the radiation hazard in mines was left up to individual states. Utah state officials in 1959 tried to have one company, Vanadium, install ventilation equipment, but without success.[36] Colorado was the only state to recognize radon-induced lung cancer as a compensable disease: an actuarial firm hired by the state in the mid-1960s calculated that by 1985, 1,150 cases of lung cancer would have arisen from radiation exposure in the mines. These figures assumed, rather optimistically, that exposures would cease after 1966.

Federal action finally came on May 5, 1967, when President Johnson's secretary of labor, W. Willard Wirtz, announced that the U.S. government would purchase no more uranium from mines in which there was more than 0.3 WL of radiation. Wirtz's decision immediately ran afoul of the government's Joint Committee on Atomic Energy, a Senate body charged with both supervision and promotion of the nuclear industry—a relationship labor union critics characterized as "the fox guarding the henhouse." The committee, siding with the AEC, made it clear it wanted to retain the Public Health Service's standard of 1.0 WL. At hearings before the Joint Committee on Atomic Energy, Paul C. Tomkins, executive director of the Federal Radiation Council, testified that the labor secretary's recommendation of 0.3 WL "could do nothing but close up the [nuclear] industry." A Kerr-McGee physicist testified that miners could sustain up to three working levels of radiation without harm. Wirtz was ultimately forced to accept the AEC/PHS standard; critics of the sequence of events observed that miners, the weakest of all the participants in the drama, would have to continue "their deadly love affair with the daughters of radon."[37]

It is strange that miners were treated so shabbily by government health, labor, and atomic authorities. An indoor occupational radon standard of ten picocuries per liter had been established by the National Bureau of Standards in 1941; the National Council on Radiation Protection in 1953 recommended that this same standard be extended to mines.[38] The International Council on Radiation Protection adopted the PHS's standard of one hundred picocuries per liter (equal to one working level) in 1959, but a subsequent survey showed that the average for U.S. uranium mines remained as high as 2.0 WL in 1966 (down from about 7.0 WL in 1957). In 1971 the newly created Environmental Protection Agency reduced the maximum allowable level of ambient radon to one-third of a working level, or four working-level months (WLMs) per year. Exposures at the mines dropped significantly, but in 1975, a monitoring blitz by the Mine Safety and Health Administration (MSHA) found that miners were still being exposed to 4.6 WLMs per year on average, slightly above the EPA limit and several times higher than what was being claimed by the companies. Risk assessments later showed that even the EPA's standard of 4.0 WLM/year more than doubled one's risk of lung cancer after thirty years of exposure.[39]

Controversies continue to ebb and flow over the precise shape of the dose-response curve, but no one doubts that miners are still dying. By 1978, 205 of the thirty-four hundred white miners followed by the Public Health Service since the early 1960s had died of lung cancer; by 1990 this number had grown to nearly twice that figure. Given that thirty to forty thousand men have worked in the U.S. uranium mines since the 1940s, it is probable that four or five thousand Americans have died, or will eventually die, from lung cancer caused by that line of work. Hundreds of others have had a lung removed or been otherwise debilitated.[40]

CRIME AND PUNISHMENT

Why were systematic efforts to monitor the hazard not even set up until the 1960s? Why, even after this time, were miners allowed to suffer ten to thirty times the legal levels? Why were the miners never warned? Many of these mines were on Navajo lands and many miners were Native Americans; some have suggested that racism may have played a role in the failure to establish effective standards early on. The fact that the thirty-four hundred miners originally studied by the PHS were all white lends credence to such a theory, as does the fact that Navajo miners were not studied until the 1960s.[41] Fear of losing a reliable labor source, though, was probably also a factor. In 1985, in a case brought by non-Indian miners against the federal government, Judge Aldon Anderson of the U.S. district court in Utah ruled that the AEC failed to warn uranium miners out of a misguided sense of national security: "The AEC feared that informed miners would flee the mines and thereby threaten the nation's uranium supply."[42]

The problem, in other words, was not simply one of ignorance. Duncan A. Holaday, a Public Health Service scientist who warned federal officials about the danger early on, has testified that "by the late 1940s, there was no question in anybody's mind that radiation in the mines was a real problem.... But nobody in the Atomic Energy Commission wanted to pay attention." Holaday calculated in 1954 that mine operators could install ventilation equipment at a cost of only five or six cents per pound of processed uranium—a cost that easily could have been passed on to the AEC. (The AEC bought more than three million pounds of the metal that year at about twelve dollars per pound.) Holaday's advice was ignored by the AEC and mine operators, however, on the grounds that ventilating the mines was "unnecessary and too expensive."[43] The AEC and the commercial nuclear establishment wanted uranium on the cheap. Security was given a much higher value than safety, and the end result was the loss of workers' lives. Wayne Owens (D-Utah), one of the congressional sponsors of the 1991 Radiation Exposure Compensation Act (and whose own brother-in-law died from lung cancer caused by uranium mining) has put the matter rather simply: "These people were used as guinea pigs...in the life-and-death struggle with 'godless communism.'"[44]

Efforts to obtain compensation for the injured miners or their families have been made since the 1970s. Compensation, though, has been slow in coming—when it has come at all. (Ironically, compensation has been easier to obtain in certain former East bloc countries—such as Czechoslovakia—where uranium mining abuses were far more severe than in the United States.)[45] In 1991, after decades of unsuccessful efforts to obtain federal compensation for injured miners, Congress finally passed the Radiation Exposure Compensation Act, setting up a $30 million trust fund to compensate uranium miners along with other victims of radiation exposure—notably "downwinders" of southern Utah, participants in nuclear tests, and certain workers at atomic plants. The text of the act included a formal apology: "The Congress apologizes on behalf of the Nation to the individuals...and their families for the hardships they have endured."[46] Congress in 1991 and 1992 voted to increase the total fund to $200 million. Miners who suffered from lung cancer are now, theoretically, entitled to $100,000 compensation from the fund. Families may be compensated if the victim is no longer living. Bureaucratic red tape has thus far made it difficult, however, to obtain compensation. The forms one must fill out are daunting, running to more than one hundred pages. Written proof must be provided that one was exposed and got cancer from that exposure. Only lung cancers are compensable, and smokers must prove that their exposure was "excessive." Most of those who worked in the so-called dog holes (very small mines with little or no ventilation) have no way of proving they worked in such places, and medical records may be even harder to come by. The Indian Health Service, to whom many Navajo miners turned for treatment, generally destroyed records after twenty-five years, and elderly widows of victims may not even have written evidence of their marriage. As a result of these and other problems, it has been difficult for families to obtain compensation. By mid-1992 only half a dozen claims had been successfully paid out, though the rate has increased since then. By May of 1993 compensation claims had been approved for 328 miners and 348 Nevada Test Site participants. Many claims have been denied, and many more are pending.

Money has finally begun to trickle into the communities where lung cancers were bred, but the process has been slow. Stewart L. Udall, the former interior secretary who has served as a lawyer for many victims, recently characterized the administration of the process as "a bureaucratic legal maze designed to prevent compensation to Navajo miners. There's no pity for what happened to these people. No understanding. You have a compassionate program administered in an utterly uncompassionate manner." Jim John, a Navajo man who lost his father to lung cancer in 1971 when his father was only thirty-four, put the matter bluntly: "It's a bad thing that happened here.

It's a bad thing for anybody to do. It destroyed lives. It took the beauty away from this mountain."[47]

CODA

In February 1950 FBI agents questioned David Greenglass about the disappearance of some uranium from Los Alamos when he was stationed there. Greenglass later admitted that he had taken a piece of uranium as a souvenir but had thrown it into the East River when he became frightened of discovery. On June 15, 1950, two FBI agents came to his apartment and renewed their questioning. At some point in the twelve-hour period during which they spoke, emphasis apparently shifted from the stolen uranium to a supposed visit by Harry Gold and, ultimately, to the suggestion that David's sister Ethel and her husband Julius Rosenberg were guilty of passing on bomb secrets to the Russians.[48]

Nowhere in the trial record does the theft of the uranium appear, even though it arguably gave David Greenglass a motive for incriminating another person instead of himself in the business of espionage. Greenglass's brother Bernard signed an affidavit attesting to the stolen uranium on May 31, 1953, a document contained in the record of the Rosenbergs' final appeal.[49] Clearly, more than one kind of censorship, and more than one kind of health hazard, attached to close contact with uranium in the decade of the fifties.

NOTES

A more extensive discussion of uranium mine epidemiology can be found in my book, *Cancer Wars: How Politics Shapes What We Know and Don't Know About Cancer* (New York: Basic Books, 1995), from which parts of the present essay have been taken.

1 Eileen Welsome, "The Plutonium Experiment," *Albuquerque Tribune*, Nov. 15–17, 1993; Geoffrey Sea, "The Radiation Story No One Would Touch," *Columbia Journalism Review*, Mar./Apr. 1994, 37–40.

2 The first German report of a radiation-induced cancer concerned a 33-year-old worker at a roentgen tube manufacturing plant; see Albert Frieben, "Cancroid des rechten Handrückens," *Deutsche medicinische Wochenschrift, Vereins-Beilage* 28(1902):335. His arm was amputated at the shoulder in 1902, and he died from a recurrence of the disease in 1906. In the United States, Clarence Dally, Thomas A. Edison's assistant, became the first American known to have died from exposure to X-rays. He had developed cancers in his arms and hands, both of which were amputated shortly before his death in 1904 (he also received X-ray treatments for the disease in the hope "of undoing what

the ray itself had done"). See Catherine Caufield, *Multiple Exposures: Chronicles of the Radiation Age* (New York: Harper, 1989), 13. In 1911 two German reviews documented fifty-four separate cases of radiation-caused cancers (mostly among physicians and their assistants), and a French review three years later listed more than a hundred cases. See Otto Hesse, *Symptomologie, Pathogenese und Therapie des Röntgenkarzinoms* (Leipzig: J. A. Barth, 1911); Paul Krause, "Zur Kenntnis der Schädigung der menschlichen Haut durch Röntgenkunde und Radiumforschung," *Zeitschrift für Röntgenkunde und Radiumforschung* 13(1911): 256–64; Sophie Feygin, *Du cancer radiologique* (Paris, 1914).

3   An expensive radium tonic sold under the brand name "Radiothor" was marketed in the 1920s; a well-known Pittsburgh industrialist, Eben Byers, drank a bottle a day from 1926 until 1931, when he contracted cancer of the jaw. His death in 1932 took much of the wind out of the radium-cure sails, though treatments of this sort continued on a smaller scale into the post-World War II era and, to a limited extent, even today. In certain Montana mines, for example, you can still breathe radon gas as an arthritis "therapy"; radon therapy also remains very popular in certain resort areas of the former Soviet Union. The Pyatigorsk Superior Radon Center in Georgia still prepares radon drinks, baths, enemas, and vaginal and nasal irrigations for more than one thousand patients per day. See David J. Brenner, *Radon: Risk and Remedy* (New York: W.H. Freeman, 1989), 76.

4   Angela Nugent, "The Power to Define a New Disease: Epidemiological Politics and Radium Poisoning," in *Dying for Work*, ed. David Rosner and Gerald Markowitz (Bloomington: Indiana University Press, 1986), 177–91; William D. Sharpe, "The New Jersey Radium Dial Painters: A Classic in Occupational Carcinogenesis," *Bulletin of the History of Medicine* 52 (1979): 560–70.

5   The equation of females and sexual danger in the 1950s is exposed in Elaine May, *Homeward Bound: American Families in the Cold War Era* (New York: Basic Books, 1988). For a critique of the use of the term "radon daughters" by "macho photon-jocks" see K.J. Kearfott, "Health Physics Language and Professionalism," *Health Physics* 66 (1994): 235–36.

6   Robert J. Roscoe et al., "Lung Cancer Mortality among Nonsmoking Uranium Miners Exposed to Radon Daughters," *JAMA* 262 (1989): 629–33.

7   Georgius Agricola was a physician in Joachimsthal from 1527 to 1533; his famous *De Re Metallica* (1556) described the health effects of silver mining in this region, where miners inhaled a corrosive dust that "eats away the lungs, and implants consumption in the body; hence in the mines of the Carpathian mountains women are found who have married seven husbands, all of whom this terrible consumption has carried off to a premature death" (trans. H.H. Hoover and L.H. Hoover [London: Dover, 1912], 214).

8 F.H. Härting and W. Hesse, "Der Lungenkrebs, die Bergkrankheit in den Schneeberger Gruben," *Vierteljahrsschrift für gerichtliche Medizin* 30 (1879): 300, and 31 (1879): 109–12, 325. Lung cancer was recognized as a compensable occupational disease for miners in 1926 in Schneeberg (Germany) and in 1932 in Joachimsthal (Czechoslovakia). See Wilhelm C. Hueper, *Occupational Tumors and Allied Diseases* (Springfield, Ill.: Charles C. Thomas, 1942), 435–59.

9 On the inbreeding hypothesis, see M.-S. Vesin, "Cancer pulmonaire provoqué par les émanations radioactives," *Archives des maladies professionnelles* 9 (1948): 280–83; M.T. Macklin and C.C. Macklin, "Does Chronic Irritation Cause Primary Tumor of the Human Lung?" *Archives of Pathology* 30 (1940): 924–55; Egon Lorenz, "Radioactivity and Lung Cancer: A Critical Review of Lung Cancer in the Miners of Schneeberg and Joachimsthal," *Journal of the National Cancer Institute* 5 (1944): 13.

10 P. Ludewig and S. Lorenser, "Untersuchung der Grubenluft in den Schneeberger Gruben auf den Gehalt an Radiumemanation," *Zeitschrift für Physik* 22 (1924): 178–85.

11 Hueper, *Occupational Tumors*, 441.

12 Uranium-235 is the fissile isotope required for bomb production; extraction of U-235 from the more common U-238 requires a formidable separation process involving industria facilities of unprecedented size and expense. The Piketon uranium enrichment facility north of Portsmouth, Ohio, for example, at one mile long and more than ten stories tall, is still today the largest building in the world. In the early 1980s, its enormous magnets, used to accelerate ionized uranium atoms to separate the lighter and more fissionable U-235, consumed about one percent of all U.S. electricity—roughly the amount consumed by the entire city of Los Angeles. Two other enrichment facilities—the "Y-12" facility at Oak Ridge, Tennessee, and the facility at Paducah, Kentucky—were of comparable dimensions. See Geoffrey Bernstein's extraordinary "Cascade: Worker Resistance at the Portsmouth Uranium Plant," senior thesis, Harvard University, 1981.

13 Milton Viorst and J.V. Reistrup, "Radon Daughters and the Federal Government," *Bulletin of the Atomic Scientists*, Oct. 1967, 25–29.

14 E. S. London, "Über die physiologischen Wirkungen der Emanation des Radiums," *Zentralblatt für Physiologie* 18 (1904): 185–88; John Read and J.C. Mottram, "The 'Tolerance Concentration' of Radon in the Atmosphere," *British Journal of Radiology* 12 (1939): 54–60.

15 Hueper, *Occupational Tumors*, 435–59.

16 Lorenz, "Radioactivity and Lung Cancer," 5, 13.

17 Fred W. Stewart, "Occupational and Post-Traumatic Cancer," *Bulletin of the New York Academy of Medicine* 23 (1947): 146.

18 Merril Eisenbud, *An Environmental Odyssey* (Seattle: University of

Washington Press, 1990), 60–62.

19 Elof A. Carlson, *Genes, Radiation, and Society* (Ithaca: Cornell University Press, 1981), 6, 356–67.

20 Paul Starr, *The Social Transformation of American Medicine* (New York: Basic Books, 1982), 343–44.

21 Wilhelm C. Hueper, "Adventures of a Physician in Occupational Cancer: A Medical Cassandra's Tale (1976), unpublished autobiography, Hueper papers, National Library of Medicine, 174–79 and 264–65.

22 Telephone interview with Victor E. Archer, April 10, 1992.

23 Hueper, "Adventures," 245–47.

24 Keith Schneider, "Uranium Miners Inherit Dispute's Sad Legacy," *New York Times,* January 9, 1990.

25 Duncan A. Holaday et al., *Control of Radon and Daughters in Uranium Mines and Calculations on Biologic Effects* (Washington, D.C.: U.S. Public Health Service, 1957), ix–x and 2–4.

26 Ibid. Holaday had first proposed a "working level" equal to 100 picocuries per liter in his *Interim Report: Health Study of the Uranium Mines and Mills* (Washington, D.C.: U.S. Public Health Service, 1952), coauthored with W. David and H. N. Doyle.

27 Duncan A. Holaday, "History of the Exposure of Miners to Radon," *Health Physics* 16 (1969): 547–52, esp. 551.

28 Victor E. Archer, Harold J. Magnuson, Duncan A. Holaday, and Pope A. Lawrence, "Hazards to Health in Uranium Mining and Milling," *Journal of Occupational Medicine* 4 (1962): 55–60. This paper dealt with deaths through 1959.

29 Joseph K. Wagoner et al., "Unusual Cancer Mortality among a Group of Underground Metal Miners," *New England Journal of Medicine* 269 (1963): 284–89; Victor E. Archer, Joseph K. Wagoner, and Frank E. Lundin, "Lung Cancer among Uranium Miners in the United States," *Health Physics* 25 (1973):351–71.

30 An official history of U.S. radiation safety asserts that "it took eleven years in a single experiment to establish some of the really long-term effects of inhaled uranium"; see J. Newell Stannard, *Radioactivity and Health* (Springfield, VA: Batelle, 1989), 409.

31 Holaday et al., *Control of Radon*, 4.

32 Holaday had concluded as early as 1951 that a human health tragedy was unfolding in consequence of the failure of the AEC and the mining companies to mechanically ventilate the mines; see Howard Ball, *Cancer Factories: America's Tragic Quest for Uranium Self-Sufficiency* (Westport, CT: Greenwood, 1993), 49–51.

33 Holaday is cited in Raye C. Ringholz, *Uranium Frenzy: Boom and Bust on*

the Colorado Plateau (Albuquerque: University of New Mexico Press, 1989), 148; Archer is cited in Ball, *Cancer Factories*, 46 and 59–60. Ball's book is the best history of the efforts of uranium miners to obtain compensation for lung cancers caused by mining for the AEC.

34 Ball, *Cancer Factories*, 11–12, 49. See also the insightful legal analysis in George J. Annas, "The Nuremberg Code in U.S. Courts: Ethics vs. Expediency," in *The Nazi Doctors and the Nuremberg Code* (New York: Oxford University Press, 1992), ed. George J. Annas and Michael A. Grodin, 209–10.

35 Molly Ivins, "Uranium Mines in West Leave Deadly Legacy," *New York Times*, May 20, 1979; compare also Ringholz, *Uranium Frenzy*, 166–222.

36 Ball, *Cancer Factories*, 49.

37 Viorst and Reistrup, "Radon Daughters," 26–27; Miller.

38 The Public Health Service in 1952 had proposed a temporary standard of 100 pCi/l, ten times higher than the 1941 NCRP figure. See Holaday, David, and Doyle, *Interim Report*.

39 Richard W. Hornung and Theodore J. Meinhardt, "Quantitative Risk Assessment of Lung Cancer in U.S. Uranium Miners," *Health Physics* 52 (1987): 417–30.

40 Caufield, *Multiple Exposures*, 84–86; Schneider, "Uranium Miners."

41 Rosalie Bertell, *No Immediate Danger?* (London: Women's Press, 1985), 83–88; Ball, *Cancer Factories*, 50. Joseph Wagoner in 1979 suggested a possible racial bias in the government's dealings with Navajos: "In 1978, the government started notifying all shipyard workers and others who had been exposed to asbestos, but nothing like that has been done for the miners. Is it because they are Westerners with little power in their Congressional representation, because they are Indians so no one needs to care?" (Ivins, "Uranium Mines"). Native Americans in the early 1980s owned about half of the nation's privately owned uranium reserves; see Sandra E. Bergman, "Uranium Mining on Indian Lands," *Environment*, Sept. 1982, 6–35.

42 Ball, *Cancer Factories*, 12.

43 Schneider, "Uranium Miners."

44 Sandra D. Atchison, "'These People Were Used as Guinea Pigs,'" *Business Week*, Oct. 15, 1990, 98. Compare also the statement of a Colorado health inspector concerning the 1950s that "anybody that said a thing against uranium mining was suspected of being a communist"; cited in Harvey Wasserman and Norman Solomon, *Killing Our Own: The Disaster of America's Experience with Atomic Radiation* (New York: Delacorte, 1982), 149.

45 In the Soviet Union and in other parts of Eastern Europe, prisoners were literally worked to death in mines, apparently as part of a deliberate plan to kill them. Outside North America, the largest single producer of uranium in the world was the German Democratic Republic, where, from 1945 to the end of

the 1980s half a million workers produced some two hundred thousand tons of enriched uranium for Soviet atomic bombs and reactors. The authority responsible for coordinating the East German effort was code-named *Wismut* (literally "bismuth") to disguise the fact that uranium was the primary object of interest. With its own Communist Party organization, hospitals, secret police, and propaganda apparatus, Wismut was, as a 1993 *Science* news feature put it, "an all-powerful state within a state," shrouded in secrecy. See Patricia Kahn, "A Grisly Archive of Key Cancer Date," *Science* 259 (1993): 448–51; "The Legacy of Schneeberg," *Nuclear Engineering*, Feb. 1991, 7; also Werner Schüttmann, "Deutsche Opfer für Moskaus Atombombe," *Der Tagesspiegel*, Jan. 13, 1991. A somewhat smaller program existed in Czechoslovakia, on the southern slopes of the *Erzgebirge*. Tens of thousands of political prisoners were forced to work in seventeen uranium "concentration camps" from the late 1940s through the early 1960s; epidemiological studies were conducted, but the State Security Police barred their publication. See my letter, "The Oberrothenbach Catastrophe," in *Science* 260 (1993): 1676–77. Czechoslovakian scientists in the 1970s published several reports on the hazards of uranium mining but never mentioned the fact that forced labor had been used.

46 U.S. Congress, Senate Committee on Labor and Human Resources, "Radiation Exposure Compensation Act," 101st Congress, 2d session (1990), 2. On the "downwinders," see Howard Ball, *Justice Downwind: America's Atomic Testing Program in the 1950s* (New York: Oxford University Press, 1988); Carole Gallagher, *American Ground Zero: The Secret Nuclear War* (Cambridge, MA: MIT Press, 1993).

47 Keith Schneider, "Valley of Death: Late Rewards for Navajo Miners," *New York Times, May 3, 1993*.

48 Walter Schneir and Miriam Schneir, *Invitation to an Inquest: A New Look at the Rosenberg-Sobell Case*. (Garden City, NY: Doubleday, 1965), 359–61; John Wexley, *The Judgment of Julius and Ethel Rosenberg* (New York: Cameron and Kahn, 1955), 85.

49 The confidential interoffice memos of the Greenglasses' attorney, O. John Rogge, did contain both a mention of the "sample of uranium" and the information that he had thrown it into the East River. But the details of this petty theft were omitted from the trial record. See Wexley, *Judgment*, 100.

FBI Director J. Edgar Hoover.
(AP/Wide World Photos)

6

The Trial of J. Edgar Hoover

Thomas L. Dumm

Could the facts be separated from the incomprehensible lightning storm of the possible?

—Georges Bataille, *The Trial of Gilles de Rais*

Have you no sense of decency, sir, at long last?

—Joseph Welch to Joseph McCarthy, Army–McCarthy Hearings

MATERIAL EVIDENCE

In what sense do we seek the facts? We might ask this not only of the historical tribunals sifting through the records of the trials of Ethel and Julius Rosenberg but also of those who have taken up the task of judging the Rosenberg's most famous tormentor. Georges Bataille's metaphorical use of lightning has an American parallel, I think. We live in the society of electricity—the captured, though never domesticated form of lightning. Electricity imbues our collective life and death with their own peculiar meanings. Electrocution as a means of death is quite modern, but it also connects us to the most mysterious elements of life, the alternating charges that shape our not-so-collective consciousness.[1] Bataille's incomprehensible lightning storm might gravitate to the level of electrocution, perhaps even to the electrical grids that traverse our united states.[2] For instance, the electricity that riveted Ethel and Julius and burned them to death, in turn hot-froze the musculature of J. Edgar Hoover, apotheosis of American fascism. The flash of its contact with their lives illuminates, if only in grotesque profile, one of our alternative united states, a space of connection still desired by many of us, a crossroad where some of us still hope to meet, at large somewhere in the late twentieth century. Hoover is revealed in the incomprehensible lightning storm of the possible. Its light freezes his image before us. Yet the image may not be comprehended in the darkness that follows. Hence it might be absorbed and, perhaps less likely, forgotten. The lightning melds the possible to the factual. Hence, the incomprehensible lightning storm of the possible is the matrix of our facts, and our facts cannot be appreciated, that is to say, known as more than facts, in any light less vivid than that provided by the electricity coursing through our bodies.

What do we see in Hoover? American abundance or American absence? Hoover both overflows and is a void. Joseph Welch's famous question to McCarthy would have been better targeted to Hoover, but no one then was both brave enough *and* powerful enough. In retrospect, all of us can know that McCarthy was the buffoon, that Cohn was the proxy for Hoover, and that Hoover was the Big Enchilada of the anti-Communist Right. (Oh, sure, there was Nixon. He was no slouch, Nixon, but he was also too anxious to please, too concerned with being elected, or as Garry Wills once described him, fundamentally anxious to be whatever we wanted him to be, a cipher of a different sort than Hoover.)[3] It is of Hoover we must ask, have you no decency? And when we ask, we must be attuned to the deep ambiguity of this question. What does it mean to *have no sense of decency*?

We need to distinguish between indecency and a *lack* of decency. Our question seeks to separate the latter from the former. A lack of decency is special, distinguishing, and hence more troubling than indecency. There are many among us who are eager to grant Hoover his indecency, to define him as a bad man. Bad, because he was a (closet) homosexual, bad because he was a bigot, bad because he was a hypocrite, bad because he was corrupt, bad because he was a blackmailer, bad because he abused his considerable power. But who among us has not been bad in these ways? To have no decency, by contrast, is to be set apart, to be both more and less than indecent. This condition necessarily precedes indecency, but most of us, having once lacked decency, learn how to fill the lack in ways that enable us to become decent and indecent in turn. It is called growing up. Hoover was someone more distinctive, a person able to live without filling his lack. To do this in a land of abundance, and to achieve the power that he did, is worthy of examination if only because it might provide yet another register for assessing the extent of the trouble that afflicted this country during the forty years of the Cold War and that trouble's persistence in our current dreams of united states.

I want to dwell on Hoover's lack, and his incapacity to fill it, either through decency or indecency. Imagine this essay as notes taken from his posthumous trial. It could serve as a fictive companion to Khrushchev's Stalin speech, in which he attempted to assess the damage done to the USSR by Stalinism. Since it is unlikely that any agent of our government would do so, and since the traditional New Left of this country is ill-equipped to render judgments on those who have judged them, suffering from their own moralistic hangover, the task of both defining and interring Hooverism seems left for those of us less under the shadow of his influence, whose predominant connections to the FBI were formed from watching television.

CHARACTER WITNESSES

J. Edgar Hoover's necessarily posthumous trial is conducted in the same two forums through which he once gained so much of his power: that of public relations and that of private rumor. Hoover was among the first to see how Hollywood movies and publicists could solidify his Washington power base.[4] He used the power base afforded him by his popularity to fight in the realm of private rumor (not so private now as it once was) the exposures threatening his power. Hoover, Walter Winchell, Joe McCarthy, and the younger players, William F. Buckley, Robert Kennedy, Roy Cohn, were all denizens of this world of publicity and gossip in the early 1950s.

Political operatives, professional fixers, men known to be reactionary in their views and shallow in their political commitments still inhabit the middle ground of the political culture of united states. They rule through connections and exclusions. They form temporary and permanent alliances with each other, and they *turn on* each other (in all the senses that term implies). We might know better how such operators work if we briefly examine Roy Cohn, who was Hoover's protégé, and whose participation in the Rosenberg trial as a prosecutor marked his emergence as a national figure. Cohn is often understood to be an exemplary figure from this subculture, and he was indeed able to use the connections he developed during this period to become a successful lawyer long after his public reputation was tarnished during the Army-McCarthy hearings.

When Cohn died of AIDS in 1986 a minor furor erupted. Because he had built his reputation accusing others of harboring secret desires against the government of the United States, and because, Cohn having sometimes worked on the "problem" of homosexuals in government, his closeted character seemed deeply wrong. Despite his own sexual relations with men, he had maintained a lifelong public posture against homosexuality and gay rights, never shifting his public view concerning the immorality of homosexuality. His relationship with another member of McCarthy's staff in the early 1950s, David Schine, was the subject of much rumor and speculation.[5] In the years that followed his mother's death, Cohn became less "discreet" about his sexual activities; but even then he claimed not to be homosexual.[6]

In short, Cohn circulated in the higher circles of New York and national politics on the assumption that he was part of a homosocial, as distinct from homosexual, network of "power players."[7] He was remarkably disingenuous as a political actor, chronically under indictment for shady legal practices, often under investigation by the Internal Revenue Service for failure to pay taxes, known as a "mob" lawyer. But his connections and his energy enabled him to "fix" things, that is, to trade favors with those in positions of power.

This trading of favors had a distinctly sexual edge to it for him. Politics was his primary source of sexual pleasure, in the most unmediated ways possible. For instance, we might note his description of how he did his homework as a boy. "When I finished my homework I would lie in bed without any clothes on and I would just think. I would think about politics. I had already met Roosevelt. I would think about the law, because sometimes later in the evening I would go down to my father's chambers or I would sit in court and I would think.... Sometimes I'd jerk off...."[8] Or this depiction of a social evening in Provincetown. "A friend recalled going home early one summer evening, and inquiring the next morning how the rest of the night had gone, being told that, 'We all stood around the piano. Roy sang three choruses of 'God Bless America,' got a hard-on, and went home to bed.'"[9] Well, why not find the very *idea* of American politics sexually stimulating? After all, politics can easily be explained as being no more and no less than the immediate exercise of desire. In this reading it finds its most salient expression in the play of exchange, in one hand washing the other, in the winning and losing that occurs between men. Cohn operated under a code that Sidney Zion, his authorized biographer, describes as favors given and favors received.[10]

Within the matrix of that game, one seeks protectors as well as protagonists. And while Joe McCarthy was a major sponsor of Cohn, more important, behind Cohn and McCarthy stood J. Edgar Hoover. Hoover guided Cohn through his earliest incursions into the world of Communists, providing him with information and advice during the course of Cohn's prosecution of the Rosenbergs. Hoover protected Cohn from his enemies, giving him inside knowledge that helped him escape conviction after he was indicted for tax evasion.[11] He seemed to do so in exchange for a particular kind of fealty, the willingness of Cohn to adopt an obsequious attitude. Cohn was adept at this posture toward older men, and Hoover tolerated nothing less from his subordinates. Moreover, Cohn shared a common enemy with Hoover in Robert Kennedy, whose own hatred of Cohn led him to abuse the office of Attorney General of the United States in order to prosecute him. Hoover aided Cohn and attempted to damage Kennedy because the Kennedy brothers, John but especially Robert, represented two commitments that both Cohn and Hoover feared and loathed.

John Kennedy's compulsive philandering seemed to disturb Hoover great-ly, even as it gave him an edge in his dealings with the Kennedy administra-tion.[12] Was Hoover disturbed because JFK's sexual promiscuity signaled a lack of self-discipline or because of its compulsory heterosexual character? Probably both, but to the extent that Hoover worried about the assertion of compulsory heterosexuality reflected in Kennedy's behavior, his ambivalence and shame regarding his own desires would have been intensified. Every time Hoover learned of JFK's secretly having intercourse with a woman, Kennedy's behavior could have seemed an implicit rebuke against him for his secret activities. Robert Kennedy's commitment to civil rights for African Americans was possibly even more disturbing to Hoover. Hoover was a racist, a not uncommon flaw among Washingtonians of his generation. But Hoover was also the object of racist rumors to the effect that he himself was of black ancestry, passing as a white man. Anthony Summers presents evi-dence of the rumors surrounding Hoover's ancestry in attempting to explain his virulent hatred of Martin Luther King.[13] Hoover's relationship with Robert Kennedy, which was widely known to have been filled with conflict, was especially so in regard to the FBI's lackluster performance in the area of civil rights law enforcement and in regard to Hoover's constant harassment of King (though Kennedy was not above using some of the information the FBI director was able to obtain from his wiretaps).

Hatred and self-loathing operated in tandem for Hoover. In a sense, he resisted the compulsory heterosexuality dominant in Washington social life. If one took that argument seriously, though, one would also have to say that he was a pioneer in the movement for civil rights for African Americans. But in both cases the closeted character of his resistance had damaging effects that redounded far beyond Hoover himself.

That Hoover's ambivalences were reflected in the policies of the FBI is not only obvious but also worth noting. The national police agency of the United States was under the control of a single person, a reflection of his personali-ty. The translation of personal desire into public power was direct. In this sense, Hoover was quite different from Roy Cohn. Cohn's desire could be characterized not simply as polymorphous but as objectless. He desired. To say that his object of desire was power, or that politics turned him on, is only to note the identity of power with desire. Desire for power is but the most general term one can use to describe objectless desire. Cohn's failure was that he did not understand power in terms that would make its higher plea-sures, its higher exercise, fully accessible to him. Following his early rise to prominence, he became a pariah in the halls of power. Admittedly, Cohn operated well from his marginal position, but his failure to organize his desire, to discipline it by creating an order over it, by subordinating it by lending it to an objective control, made those in the highest position of power wary of him. His failure of discipline differentiates him from Hoover, even as it makes him Hoover's perfect foil.

Adapting the techniques of the organizers of Bible schools to the bureaucracy of justice,[14] understanding the importance of the development of the cult of personality and using it to his fullest advantage, absolute in his moral fervor, yet never moving beyond the sanctioned approval of those presidents whom he hated (absolute in fervor but when the crunch came, always willing to compromise), Hoover created the field of "Americanism" that informed right and wrong in the prosecution and punishment of law offenders for half a century. His power was coupled to the decency he lacked. He insisted that criminals were animals and developed the policing tactics that would ensure that they were treated as such. He condemned those who failed to present themselves as good. He carefully projected the image of the moralist, fastidious in his dress and deportment. He insisted that the men he recruited for the FBI be of impeccable moral credentials, recruiting them not from the Ivy League universities but from southern and midwestern colleges. In his range of activities his moral discourse established the matrix for shaping and ordering his own objectless desire.

Richard Powers writes that sometime after 1935, when his image as a superhero had been solidified by Hollywood, Hoover started talking like a "tough guy."[15] His rhetoric concerning the "nature" of the criminal began to resound with the passion of the purist. And yet there was also another edge to it, the inevitable pornographic trace left by the closeted moralist. For instance, in a speech to the Hi-Y clubs of America in 1936, he said, "John Dillinger was nothing but a beer-drinking plug-ugly, who bought his way from hideout to hideout, being brave only when he had a machine-gun trained upon a victim and the victim was at his mercy. When Dillinger finally was brought to bay, he was not a romantic motion picture figure but only a coward who did not know how to shoot, except from ambush."[16] These comments harbor the experienced knowledge of an under-cover operator. Dillinger could not shoot, except from ambush—he needed to sneak up on people in order to discharge his weapon. But how could Hoover know? Perhaps the appropriate formula is the simple one: It takes one to know one.[17]

Against the filthiness and the hidden dangers presented by such criminal aspirations, Hoover counterposed a world of decency.

> There is no romance in crime and there is no romance in criminals. We have passed through an era in which ill-advised persons and sentimental sob-sisters have attempted to paint the desperate law violators of America as men and women

of romance. They are the absolute opposite. They are rats, vermin, regurgitating their filth to despoil the clean picture of American manhood and womanhood. They sink deeper and deeper into a mire of viciousness which inevitably leads to filth in mind, filth in living, filth in morals and bodily health. They travel steadily downward until at last they are no more than craven beasts.[18]

The dirty story will be covered up by the cleansing image of decent people battling evil. This opposition between clean and dirty governs Hoover's moral discourse. Moral filth is closely associated with bodily filth, and the filthy are linked to the romance of "sob-sisters." It is an old discourse, initiated, perhaps, during the American Enlightenment, but Hoover's moral hygiene has roots as well in the great crucible of twentieth century American experience generated by the opposition between the demands of security and the quest for freedom. If Hoover had sex with men while despising homosexuality, his drive to degrade the criminal and ridicule the "sob-sisters" who refuse to do so becomes understandable as more than a police practice. When one realizes that Hoover had a special personal relationship with one of his agents, Clyde Tolson, that lasted from 1928 until Hoover's death in 1972, his moralistic fervor, bodily metaphors, absolutist rectitude, and gendered discourse begin to fit together.

EXPERT TESTIMONY

One way to understand the tensions at work in the closeted homosexual desires of powerful men is by thinking about the demands imposed on men in charge to appear to be masculine. In a famous aphorism (entitled "Tough Baby"), Theodor Adorno has suggested that there is a relationship between hidden homosexual desire and violence, and that the creation of the "tough guy" as a cultural archetype is deeply tied to that relationship. Adorno's model is cinematic, quite possibly based on Humphrey Bogart or, even more likely, given the high bourgeois patina he puts on it, Cary Grant (especially in his role in Alfred Hitchcock's *North by Northwest*). These men are surrounded by masculine, tactile objects: "smoke, leather, shaving cream." "The pleasures of such men," Adorno wrote,

> have about them a latent violence. This violence seems a threat directed against others, of whom such a one, sprawling in his easy chair, has long since ceased to have a need. In fact it is past violence against himself. If all pleasure has, preserved within it, earlier pain, then here pain, as pride in bearing it, is raised directly, untransformed, as a stereotype, to pleasure: unlike wine, each glass of whiskey, each inhalation of smoke, still recalls the repugnance that it cost the organism to become attuned to such strong stimuli, and this alone is registered as pleasure.[19]

By elevating the hedonistic calculus to the psychodynamic of a "named" neurosis, sadomasochism, Adorno succeeds in naturalizing the phenomenon he describes, suggesting that the "he-man" is the "true" effeminate.[20] But we need not follow Adorno and reduce matters in such a misogynist—and ultimately homophobic—manner. Instead, we can think about the description itself.

That description places a male body at risk in the continuous reinscription of a code of desire. Small acts of violence shape, scar, addict the male body. The strong stimulation of whiskey (an "acquired taste") is but one example of the damage done to the body as it pursues pleasure by resisting itself. So while Adorno suggests that "He-men are thus, in their own constitution, what film plots usually present them to be, masochists," their masochism can only be read as such if one ignores the ambiguity of the term "constitution." That the constitution of the tough guy's masochism is culturally specific is suggested by the very specificity of Adorno's title for this aphorism, "Tough Baby," which contains several oxymoronic paradoxes: infantile and violent, feminine and hard, unlucky and patronized.

Adorno's assertion of the "truth" of homosexuality as a form of sadomasochism obscures the political problem underlying his dialectic. His final shift, which reverses the poles of analysis—totalitarianism shifts from being an aggressive principle to being a passive one, and the intellectual becomes the "real" man—enables him, to his own satisfaction at least, to escape a fixed judgment concerning homosexuality as such. But rather than inhabit the bifurcated space that separates men into intellectuals and tough guys, he attempts to dispense with them both in an act of dismissive transcendence, throwing away the tough baby with the bathwater. Homosexual desire simply becomes the shadow of fascism.

Jacques Lacan provides another, perhaps more fruitful approach to the problem of masculine desire and reactionary politics in his famous essay on the mirror stage. There Lacan introduces the idea of the body-in-pieces.[21] For him the fantasy of the body-in-pieces is an anxiety retrofitted onto the male child's assumption of his completeness, a completeness that is achieved representationally when he first recognizes himself in a mirror. The male child identifies his ego, or "Ideal-I," with his body. The male subject thus anticipates a wholeness and completion not directly available through subjective experience. For Lacan, this infantile assumption presents a primary paradox for the adult. With the fantasy of completeness comes the anxiety of and perception of fragmentation.[22]

Reflecting on the relationship of the concept of the body-in-pieces to Hitler's fascism, Susan Buck-Morss has emphasized the concept's connection to war trauma.[23] She notes that the importance of the mirror stage lies in its retroactive apprehension. That is, it is triggered in memory by the contemporary experience of the adult. "Thus," she argues, "the significance of Lacan's theory emerges only in the historical context of modernity as precisely the experience of the fragile body and the dangers to it of fragmentation that replicates the trauma of the original infantile event (the fantasy of the *corps morcelé*)."[24]

The experience of this fragile body, while situated by Buck-Morss in Germany, can also be situated in the united states of homosocial desire that dominate the American polity. Fear of the body-in-pieces by those who hold power continues to haunt all of us as we seek to break through the fear that consumed Hoover. We are haunted because we have not faced his heritage, a heritage of secrecy and power. Can we break with the reflexive relationship national security has with itself, only being a nation when whole, only being secure when a nation?

HEARSAY

Hoover believed that his absolute duty was to protect us from social change. Changes from the status quo of his parochial Washington, D.C. upbringing, whether they had to do with race relations and shifts in the extent of rights enjoyed by people, the evolution of family structure, or even the appearance of organized crime, were disturbances that cluttered up the world of right and wrong. The incoherence he perceived in the very idea of civil disobedience allowed him to understand the civil rights movement to be, in some ways, worse than Communism, in that it presented a challenge to law that was explicit and graphically enacted. The sexual peccadilloes of Martin Luther King, Jr., represented for him the general moral degeneracy of the entire civil rights movement, because they showed someone who was more than willing to live out ambivalent desires. For Hoover, in the face of the double ambivalences shaped in the twin closets of race and gender identity, such inconsistency was reduced to being a sign of filth.

Hoover's persona fits the political profile of the narcissistic fascist characterized in Buck-Morss's reading of Lacan. A primary expression of such anxiety is fear of contamination. Klaus Theweleit's *Male Fantasies* suggests an even more troubling link. For Theweleit the link between homosocial culture and misogyny in Weimar culture was rooted in the fear of dirt, and that fear was associated in a variety of ways with bodily fluids.

> At some point, his [the soldier male's] bodily fluids must have been negativized to such an extent that they became the physical manifestations of all that was terrifying. Included in this category were all of the hybrid substances that were produced by the body and flowed on, in, over, and out of the body: the floods and

stickiness of sucking kisses; the swamps of the vagina, with their slime and mire; the pap and slime of male semen; the film of sweat that settles on the stomach, thighs and anal crevice, and that turns two pelvic regions into a subtropical land-scape; the slimy stream of menstruation; the damp spots wherever bodies touch; the warmth that dissolves physical boundaries (meaning not that it makes *one* body out of a man and woman, but that it transgresses boundaries; the infinite body; the body as flow).[25]

Theweleit notes that during the Weimar period, boys were raised to cut off these flows.

One thing is certain: as part of the boys' very early training to be soldier males (and what Wilhemine bourgeois—or, indeed, what social-democratic—educa-tion didn't have that as its goal?), harsh punishments were meted out if any of the wet substances in question turned up other than in its specifically designated place or situation. One after another, the streams were cut off or banished to the back of beyond. A social dam and drainage system captured every stream—even beer-laden streams of vomit, which had to vanish into a particular basin of the club-house before any of the "old boys" caught sight of them. As far as I can see, only three streams were permissible: streams of sweat; streams of speech; and the inex-haustible streams of alcohol. Under specific conditions (toward which the entire system steered), a fourth stream was added: the stream of blood from murdered victims, or the stream of your own "raging blood."[26]

This frantic concern with corruption, particularly linked with female bod-ies and flows, this regimentation, suppression and control of flows as a sign of masculine control of the body, this terror constituted the hatred and anger of the German *Freicorps*. But what does it have to do with the campaigns of Hoover?

In his biography of Hoover, Richard Powers notes the historical connec-tions in question:

In both Europe and the United States, veterans who felt threatened by revolu-tionary ideology organized themselves to defend against the revolution. The most violent was the German *Freicorps*, which put down the German revolution and killed Karl Liebnecht and Rosa Luxemburg. In the U.S., the leaders and mem-bers of the wartime American Protective League, disbanded after the armistice by order of the Justice Department, begged to be allowed to regroup to oppose bolshevism and, in isolated instances, this offer was informally accepted. In an uncomfortably close parallel to the *Freicorps*, the American Legion was founded on May 15, 1919. In November 1919, there was a pitched battle between mem-bers of the IWW and the American Legion in Centralia, Washington, in which one of the IWW members, Wesley Everest, himself a World War I veteran, was castrated, hanged, and shot to death by a mob of Legionnaires.[27]

Powers notes that Hoover had to concern himself with the excessive enthusiasm of the Legion, because its members too often went beyond the law in their campaigns. But the existence of such a group marked an American constituency similar to these German men, a constituency that shared a common concern. The morass, the muck, the swamp, or as Hoover put it, the filth, that would "despoil the clean picture of American manhood and womanhood" had to be destroyed in order to keep things clean, to keep America pure.

Anthony Summers's study of Hoover's private life enables us to understand how the struggle for purity shapes the closeted operative's identity.[28] Summers documents charges made by others that Hoover engaged in crossdressing as a prelude to group sex with younger men. According to several witnesses, at least once he dressed in a fluffy black dress and stockings and another time wore a red dress. He would wear makeup. Significantly, Summers's primary informant notes that he didn't participate in anal intercourse. According to Susan Rosenthiel, who was at the time married to one of Hoover's sexual partners, "[H]oover had a Bible. He wanted one of the boys to read from the Bible. And he read, I forget which passage, and the other boy played with him, wearing the rubber gloves. And then Hoover grabbed the Bible, threw it down and told the second boy to join in the sex."[29] In other words, Hoover allowed himself to be played with, but he avoided that dirty orifice.

For Hoover cross-dressing seems to have operated as a gesture of absolute appropriation and absorption of the flows of the female into the body of the misogynist-homophobic male. In what is only a slight irony, cross-dressing for Hoover seems to have been a homophobic strategy. His hatred of women, particularly women who he thought denied the role of the traditional mother, might speculatively be connected to his cross-dressing if we imaginatively reconstruct his (non)relationship with Ethel Rosenberg.

The alleged incidents of cross-dressing Summers reports would have occurred in 1958, about five years after the Rosenberg electrocutions. Hoover despised Ethel Rosenberg, not least because when in prison, Ethel Rosenberg refused to see her mother (who took the side of Ethel's brother, urging her to betray her husband Julius).[30] Rosenberg's rejection of her mother was unimaginable to Hoover. As Virginia Carmichael suggests, "Hoover's relationship to his own mother served a defensive function in his obsession with the enemy within."[31] The threat Ethel Rosenberg posed was that of overturning the man in the superior position, dominating him by evading her natural function as a mother. As one report on Ethel and Julius's relationship suggested, "Julius is the slave, and his wife, Ethel, is the master."[32] Ethel was sentenced to death in an attempt to get Julius to confess to his crimes; that he never did became for Hoover retroactive evidence of the disorder of their relationship.

Five years later Hoover puts on a red dress. Roy Cohn introduces him as "Mary" to Susan Rosenthiel: perhaps this is but a reflection of the commonplace name given to older homosexual men.[33] But "Mary" is also the name of the mother of Christ, he who in the eyes of the conservative Christian from Washington, D.C., was killed by the Jews only to rise again. Hoover as Mary, Mother of God obliterates the ambiguities represented by that other woman, the Jew who fails to be a good mother, who fails to make the conversion to Christianity, who fails, in fact, even to be a good criminal, Ethel Rosenberg. The battle of American democracy against Communism is a continuation of the battle of Christian and Jew. Brandishing his Bible as he is prepared by his helpers to discharge his weapon, putting on a red dress, Hoover armors himself against his fear of the body-in-pieces. He thus turns the tables on the vermin criminals with his own ambush.

INSTRUCTIONS TO THE JURY

The celebration of flows reflected in the desire for and celebration of ambiguity, the readiness to open oneself up emotionally, physically, and politically, and the experimental cast to one's bodily arrangements that characterize some of the most wondrous elements of gay culture has a darker double in the closeted practices of J. Edgar Hoover. But the pleasures of open celebration contrast strongly with the terrors of corruption and fear of flows underlying the cultural discourse of the superior position cover-up, the open secrets held by powerful political operators. Are the pleasures of the closet to be confined to the hatred of the Right? Of course not. But the closet is where one is likely to find, as a historical artifact and as a potential site of corruption, the exercise of power in the name of exclusion and security.

The fear of infection has raised its controversial head again with the rise of AIDS, tightening its grip on the collective imagination of the American polity and, as an almost predictable consequence, being used by those who would demonize queer culture. Being a man in a superior position in this culture, it seems, means to define oneself against queerness. But men in a superior position cannot stop sharing in queerness, it is our compulsion, and hence we must purify our selves to avoid its debilitating effects, its threat to our power. How much more effort will it take to purify our selves, what political bargains are we men in power willing to make as the epidemic spreads? What repressions will we tolerate and condone? The queer politics of AIDS is thus confronted with the united state of national *insecurity*.

The trial of J. Edgar Hoover is in the end the trial of the national insecurity state. Women must be put back in the home, children must protected from the unnatural disorder of things, and all of us must obey the law of nature, in public.[34] But in secret places the pleasure of public moralism is most fully realized in the intensity of its violation. The closet serves its highest purpose for the reactionary Right precisely to the extent that it enables right-wingers to put criminals on trial even as they themselves commit the worst crimes of which they accuse others, namely, the subversion of democracy and freedom. Such games are not played in the name of ethics, or pleasure, but in the name of nothing more than the lack that cannot be overcome. Unable to relax for long enough to cultivate a caring relationship to the world, they cannot see the damage they do to themselves and to those they condemn to death. J. Edgar Hoover remains their role model, even if they can no longer speak his name.

NOTES

1 The electric chair has its origins as a humane reform of capital punishment. Its invention by Thomas Edison in the mid-1880s, however, was inspired by Edison's competition with Westinghouse over the form of electricity that would power the country. Edison favored direct current. Westinghouse favored alternating current. In trying to show that AC was dangerous, Edison sent one of his employees around the country electrocuting dogs and cats in public demonstrations. When New York State passed a law establishing electrocution as the means of death (The Electrical Death Act, June 4, 1888), prison officials attempted to acquire a Westinghouse dynamo to supply the AC power to kill the first man condemned to die by this new method. Westinghouse, an opponent of capital punishment, refused to supply the dynamo (and noted that DC would do the job every bit as thoroughly). Edison then arranged the purchase of one of Westinghouse's dynamos (by way of a South American dealer controlled by the Edison company) and had it shipped to New York, where it was used to electrocute one William Kemmler on August 6, 1890. When word of the feud between Edison and Westinghouse became public, public backlash against Edison was so strong that it contributed to the wiring of American utilities in AC mode. For details concerning these events, see Ron Wikberg, "The Horror Show," in *Life Sentences: Rage and Survival behind Bars*, ed. Wilbert Rideau and Ron Wikberg (New York: Times, 1992), 286–88.

That the format of the electrical grid so crucial to the development of twentieth century American life was influenced by a struggle over the death penalty is perhaps irrelevant to the discussion of Hoover's relationship to the Rosenbergs. But I seek a common level, a connection between them, a way in which they link to form a united state of attraction.

2 For a further exploration of the theme of united states, see Thomas L. Dumm, *united states* (Ithaca: Cornell University Press, 1994), especially Chapter 1, "Dear Laurie Anderson." My use of the term in lowercase is designed to distinguish the condition of united states as a field of the political unconscious from the field of state power and governmental organization known as the United States. Yet it also refers to the way in which "the state," as an entity, is constantly infiltrated, resisted, challenged, undermined, and corrupted by the expression of private desires.

3 Garry Wills, *Nixon Agonistes: The Crisis of the Self-Made Man* (New York: Houghton Mifflin, 1970).

4 See Richard Gid Powers, *Secrecy and Power: The Life of J. Edgar Hoover* (New York: Free Press, 1987), 196–209.

5 See Nicholas von Hoffman, *Citizen Cohn* (New York: Doubleday, 1988) for a thorough examination of Cohn's career and private life. On Cohn's relationship to Schine, see 188–93.

6 This denial is fabulously expressed by Tony Kushner in his play *Angels in America, a Gay Fantasia on National Themes: Part One, Millennium Approaches* (New York: Theatre Communications Group, 1993). Kushner's Cohn says this in response to his doctor, while denying that he is homosexual: "Homosexuals are not men who sleep with other men. Homosexuals are men who in fifteen years of trying cannot get a pissant antidiscrimination bill through City Council.... I have sex with men. But unlike nearly every other man of whom this is true, I bring the guy I'm screwing to the White House and Ronald Reagan smiles at us and shakes his hand. Because *what* I am is defined entirely by *who* I am. Roy Cohn is not a homosexual. Roy Cohn is a heterosexual man, Henry, who fucks around with guys" (45–46).

7 Von Hoffman discusses at length the evolution of social attitudes toward homosexuality in Washington and New York political circles. See *Citizen Cohn*, 228–33.

8 Ibid., 63–64.

9 Ibid., 120–21.

10 See Sidney Zion's *The Autobiography of Roy Cohn* (Seacaucus, NJ: Lyle Stuart, 1988). Zion collaborated with Cohn and then finished the book after his death. For reasons having to do as much with Cohn's tax liability as anything else, Zion is listed as the sole author of the work, which he compiled from taped remembrances of Cohn as Cohn was dying.

11 Von Hoffman, *Citizen Cohn*, 283.

12 Richard Powers notes that "in John Kennedy Hoover saw a man who lacked

sexual self-discipline, which Hoover interpreted as weakness of character.... Hoover, to whom self-control was everything, had in his files tapes of the youthful John F. Kennedy in bed, discussing government and military matters with a woman [Inga Avrad, during World War II] under suspicion as an enemy agent" (*Secrecy and Power*, 358–59).

13 See Anthony Summers, *Official and Confidential: The Secret Life of J. Edgar Hoover* (New York: Putnam, 1993), 349–50.

14 Powers, *Secrecy and Power*, 19–20.

15 Ibid., 210.

16 Ibid.

17 This simple phrase has been an extraordinarily productive starting point for much of the recent work of Eve Kosofsky Sedgwick. It deeply informs her project in her book *Epistemology of the Closet* (Berkeley: University of California Press, 1990) and in her recent collection of essays entitled *Tendencies* (Durham: Duke University Press, 1993). For a discussion of Sedgwick in relation to the larger issue of right-wing homosociality, see Dumm, *united states*, Chapter 3, "George Bush, or Sex in the Superior Position."

18 Powers, *Secrecy and Power*, 210.

19 The aphorism under discussion is from Theodor Adorno, *Minima Moralia: Reflections from Damaged Life*, translated by E. J. N. Jephcott (London: Verso, 1974), 45–46.

20 For a directly contrasting view of the *practice* of sadomasochism, see Michel Foucault, "Sexual Choice, Sexual Act," in *Politics, Philosophy, Culture*, ed. Lawrence D. Kritzman (New York: Routledge, 1989), 299.

21 See Jacques Lacan, "The Mirror Stage as Formative of the Function of the I as Revealed in Psychoanalytical Experience," in *Ecrits, a Selection*, trans. Alan Sheridan (New York: Norton, 1977), 1–7.

22 Ibid., 2–3.

23 Susan Buck-Morss, "Aesthetics and Anaesthetics: Walter Benjamin's Artwork Essay Reconsidered," *October* 62 (fall, 1992): 3–41. This section of Buck-Morss's analysis rests heavily on Hal Foster's essay "Armor Fou," *October* 57 (spring, 1991): 65–81.

24 Ibid., 37.

25 See Klaus Theweleit, *Male Fantasies: Volume One, Women, Floods, Bodies, Histories*, trans. by Stephen Conway (Minneapolis: University of Minnesota Press, 1987), 410–411.

26 Ibid., 412.

27 Powers, *Secrecy and Power*, 59.

28 Summers, *Official and Confidential*.

29 Susan Rosenthiel quoted in ibid., 255.

30 For a discussion of Hoover's antipathy to Ethel Rosenberg on the grounds of

her disrespect for her mother, see Ronald Radosh and Joyce Milton, *The Rosenberg File: A Search for the Truth* (New York: Holt, 1983), 376. For an excellent discussion of the relationship between Hoover and Ethel Rosenberg, see Virginia Carmichael, *Framing History: The Rosenberg Story and the Cold War* (Minneapolis: University of Minnesota Press, 1993), 102–103.

31 Carmichael, *Framing History*, 102.

32 Ibid., 103. Carmichael notes that the psychological profile suggesting Julius's domination by Ethel was used repeatedly in various accounts and official reports on the Rosenberg case.

33 Summers, *Official and Confidential*, 254.

34 For an explicit and powerful manifesto of this movement to put gays back in the closet, see "Morality and Homosexuality," by the Ramsey Colloquium, *Wall Street Journal*, Feb. 24, 1994.

7

Strange Angel
The Pinklisting of Roy Cohn

Michael Cadden

When Ned Weeks, the thinly disguised autobiographical hero of Larry Kramer's *The Normal Heart*, learns from a friend that he has been removed from the board of directors of the play's fictional version of the Gay Men's Health Crisis (GMHC), he responds defensively by naming names—the members of a group even more important to him than the one he founded:

> I belong to a culture that includes Proust, Henry James, Tchaikovsky, Cole Porter, Plato, Socrates, Aristotle, Alexander the Great, Michelangelo, Leonardo da Vinci, Christopher Marlowe, Walt Whitman, Herman Melville, Tennessee Williams, Byron, E. M. Forster, Lorca, Auden, Francis Bacon, James Baldwin, Harry Stack Sullivan, John Maynard Keynes, Dag Hammarskjold.... These are not invisible men.... The only way we'll have real pride is when we demand recognition of a culture that isn't just sexual. It's all there—all through history we've been there.[1]

Without stopping to argue cases with a fictional character, I want to label the mode of performance Ned engages in as "pinklisting." The subtitle of Martin Greif's *The Gay Book of Days* defines my genre wittily if not succinctly: *An Evocatively Illustrated Who's Who of Who Is, Was, May Have Been,*

Roy Cohn (right) consults with Senator Joseph McCarthy.
(AP/Wide World Photos)

Roy Cohn, at Army–McCarthy Hearings, 1954.
(AP/Wide World Photos)

Probably Was, and Almost Certainly Seems to Have Been Gay during the Past 5,000 Years.[2]

For the most part, pinklisting in the hands of gay and lesbian writers is as celebratory as it is speculative. Perhaps especially for a person of my generation and those older than I (I'm forty-something), books like *The Gay Book of Lists*, *Lavender Lists*, *Lesbian Lists*, and *The Big Gay Book* serve the function of collecting in print all the dish that went into the epic catalogs of our oral tradition in the years before Stonewall. Their subject headings suggest the hope that sheer numbers will end centuries of heterosexist lies, secrets, and silence: "19 Famous Gay and Lesbian Relationships," "14 Men Who Loved Boys," "17 Lovers of Natalie Barney," "50 Gay and Lesbian Authors Who Have Won Major Mainstream Awards," "22 People Who Confronted the Military." Gay and lesbian pinklisting sees itself as providing role models and suggests, however problematically, the continuity of a gay and lesbian presence (and usually struggle) across the borderlines of time and place.

In *The Gay Book of Lists*, Leigh W. Rutledge extends the genre into more dangerous terrain, listing "3 Men the Gay Movement Doesn't Want to Claim"[3]—Francis Cardinal Spellman, J. Edgar Hoover and Joseph R. McCarthy. None of these men, you will note, make Larry Kramer's Hall of Fame. Nor does a gay man who was friends with all three and is the subject of this article, Roy Cohn. As a rule, when Cohn is subjected to the phenomenon of pinklisting, the performance is not produced by gay writers interested in community pride. The standard pinklisting of Roy Cohn appears in what passes for the liberal press in the United States. Both homophobic and heterosexist, liberal pinklisting usually has far more to do with blacklisting, a genre Cohn understood well, than with the celebration of a gay presence in history. Take, for example, these poisonous lines from Robert Sherrill's review of Nicholas von Hoffman's biography *Citizen Cohn*,[4] a review that appeared in the *Nation*: "Cohn was rumored to have humped, or been humped by, [David] Schine, his colleague of the McCarthy days, but von Hoffman says there is no evidence of such a relationship. Ditto the rumors that he humped, or was humped by, his dirt-supplying pal J. Edgar Hoover. Ditto the rumors that he humped, or was humped by, Cardinal Spellman (who reputedly was hot for choirboys)—all very, very close friends of Cohn, to be sure, but by von Hoffman's reckoning they serviced one another only in political ways."[5]

Sherrill's over-the-top review is a classic example of the homophobic pinklisting of Roy Cohn that has characterized much of the liberal press since Cohn's death from AIDS in 1986. Proscribed by both their own journalistic code of ethics and Cohn's legendary litigiousness from yelling "fag" in

print while he was still alive, reporters have taken every postmortem oppor-
tunity to avenge themselves against this right-wing icon and his cronies, often
in the same inquisitorial style that they helped make infamous. Here's
Sherrill, in the role of latter-day Joe McCarthy, on the fact that Cohn had
ties to a so-called "lavender Mafia," a group of closeted gay men in the
Reagan administration: "This seems to be a line of investigation that von
Hoffman was too lazy to pursue. Roughly how many men does he mean?
How close to the White House do these rumors take us? How high do they
go?" One almost expects Sherrill to insist that von Hoffman "name names."

Sherrill caps his performance with a moralizing literary gloss on von
Hoffman's description of Cohn's deathbed, pinklisting Cohn as a victim less
of AIDS than of another fin-de-siècle syndrome first identified by Oscar
Wilde—DGS: "To his death he denied that he was homosexual, but the
Dorian Gray scene of his dying of AIDS said it all: 'Roy…lay in bed,
unheeding, his flesh cracking open, sores on his body, his faculties waning'
and with a one inch 'slit-like wound above [his] anus.'" (No doubt it was not
till they had examined the rings that they recognized who he was!) It is all
too easy to assume what the unspoken "all" that Sherrill assumes this scene
"says" actually is; his narrative forges the links between closeted cause and
corporeal effect. I can only respond to Sherrill's use of Cohn's hideous death
as the fitting narrative closure to a life he disapproved of with the words that
Joseph Welch, Cohn's chief adversary at the Army-McCarthy hearings, once
aimed at Cohn's employer: "Have you no sense of decency, sir, at long last?
Have you left no sense of decency?"

Decency is in low supply when the subject is Roy Cohn and the venue is
the mainstream press. In the weeks before his death, he was the subject of
both a *60 Minutes* report that focused on the illness he insisted was liver cancer and a Jack Anderson–Dale Van Atta column that published both the real
nature of his disease and the details of his treatment. Of course, neither of
these pieces flaunted the conventions of doctor-patient and governmental
confidentiality because they were interested in Cohn's illness; they did so,
rather, because of what that illness might allow them to say about the sexuality Cohn had chosen to keep hidden. AIDS gave them a final opportunity
to out Cohn and thus shatter his immunity from journalistic gossipmonger-
ing. As Andy Rooney succinctly put it, Cohn "denied he was a homosexual
suffering from AIDS. Death was an effective rebuttal to that last denial."[6]

Before the body was cold, the *New York Times* weighed in with headlines
whose tongue-in-cheek campiness barely contained a hysterical glee: on the
front page, "Roy Cohn, Aide to McCarthy and Fiery Lawyer, Dies at 59";
and inside, "Roy Cohn, McCarthy Aide and Flamboyant Lawyer, Is Dead."[7]
"Fiery"? "Flamboyant"? As Eve Kosofsky Sedgwick has remarked, "why

not say 'flaming' and be done with it?"[8] The obituary itself moves quickly to the causes of death—one primary, "cardio-pulmonary arrest," and two secondary, "dementia" and "underlying HTLV-3 infections," in order to establish its real interest in the infected body of Roy Cohn: "Most scientists believe the HTLV-3 virus is the cause of AIDS, or acquired immune deficiency syndrome, the fatal disease that cripples the body's immune system and is statistically most common among homosexual men and intravenous drug users." One can almost hear the entire editorial board in the background gloating, "Got 'im."

The obituary goes on to sketch what the *Times* obviously means to be the profile of an archetypal gay man but one whose sexuality their own house ethics enjoined them from disclosing. Alvin Krebs, the writer, helpfully informs us that "[Cohn's] parents, particularly his mother, doted on their only child, bragging about how clever he was"—the kind of detail presumably so generic that it goes missing from obituaries of "normal" men but retained here to evoke a very fifties notion of the dire consequence of doting motherhood. Another woman, in this case a political enemy of Cohn's, is again called in to do the dirty work when the obituary finally turns to the articulation of its homosexual subtext:

> There were sneering suggestions that [Cohn, Schine, and McCarthy] were homosexuals, and attacks such as that by the playwright Lillian Hellman, who called them "Bonnie and Bonnie and Clyde."
>
> Years later, Mr. Cohn denied that he was "ever gay inclined" and pointed out that Mr. McCarthy got married and had a son, and that "David Schine married a former Miss Universe and had a bunch of kids."

A killer transition oozing with cheap irony indicates that nobody at the *Times* was taken in by Cohn's denial: "Nonetheless, it was Mr. Cohn's intense devotion to Mr. Schine at the time they were working for the McCarthy committee that got them both into serious trouble." Finally, just in case the reader has failed to get the unspeakable point of this obituary, a few well-chosen "lifestyle" items are added to complete the picture of Roy C: "Mr. Cohn was a short, ungainly man with thinning hair and blue eyes, which were often bloodshot, perhaps because he kept late yours at fashionable discotheques such as Studio 54 and the Palladium, although he said he 'adored' the sun. He also admired animals, chiefly dogs, and his office contained an extensive collection of stuffed animals." Here even Cohn's verbs require the quarantine of quotation marks. A *Times* man dares risk nothing more stylistically bold than the decidedly less theatrical "admired" for fear of contamination by this gay, conservative, nocturnal life.

Let me make it clear at this point that I am no fan of Roy Cohn. I have no

problem with the way he is memorialized in the AIDS quilt, for example—
"Bully. Coward. Victim."—especially if that last noun is allowed to resonate
as fully as possible. I have no problem with the demonization of Roy Cohn;
as a liberal in good standing, I consider Cohn as something like evil incarnate, but for his politics, not for his sexual identity. Krebs's *Times* obituary,
like Sherrill's review, paints Cohn as a pathological freak—a latter-day version of the Robert Walker character in Hitchcock's *Strangers on a Train*.
Instead of an ideological critique of a very ideological man, they luridly suggest, but never logically argue for, the connections between Cohn's sexual
identity, right-wing politics, and death from AIDS. They rejoice in the fact
that as a diseased member of the American body politic, Roy Cohn has been
lopped off.

A number of works by contemporary gay male artists have attempted to
reclaim Roy Cohn from a homophobic discourse that parades itself as political analysis—pinklisting as a form of blacklisting. Instead of dismissing
Cohn as the enemy, these artists see him as a figure who can be valuably
deployed to raise important questions about definitions of gay identity and
gay community. Robert Mapplethorpe's portrait of Cohn, for example, shows
a disembodied head floating in blackness, more death mask than record of
a living human being. This is John the Baptist as imaged and imagined by
Samuel Beckett, though of course it is Mapplethorpe himself who has played
the role of Salome and beheaded Cohn with a single queer photographic gaze.
Uncharacteristically, however, Mapplethorpe does not in any way fetishize
the queerness of this particular queer subject, choosing to emphasize instead
Cohn's isolation not only from the body politic he might have identified with
but also from his body itself. Divorced from either corporeal or community
context, Cohn is simply seen, as it were, "giving good head."

In another gay appropriation of Cohn, Ron Vawter's two-part performance piece *Roy Cohn/Jack Smith* (1992) juxtaposes the performance
artist's re-creation of an outrageously campy, Salomelike solo by avant-garde
cult figure Jack Smith with Gary Indiana's version of what a pro-family,
antigay dinner speech by Roy Cohn might have sounded like. In his introduction to the evening, Vawter explained why, as a gay New Yorker who
was HIV-positive, he was drawn to these two men who shared with him a
city, a sexual orientation, and a probable cause of death. As he later explained
in an interview, "I thought the two placed together would make for an interesting spectrum of male homosexuality…. I was interested in how these two
very different people reacted and responded to a society that set out to
repress their sexuality…. In my mind they were the farthest extremes one
could be, and I was afraid of both of them. Quite frankly, I was afraid that
behaving homosexually required one either to be like a Jack Smith or like a

Roy Cohn, and both positions were scary."[9]

It is this same variety of subject positions within male homosexuality in the United States that informs the work I want to focus on next, Tony Kushner's two-part epic *Angels in America: A Gay Fantasia on National Themes*. Like Vawter, Kushner places Cohn at the center of his examination of gay identity and community. But while Vawter investigates two ends of a discrete spectrum, Kushner works from the assumption that Cohn's identity, and gay identity in general, is at the center of contemporary American life. Kushner's Cohn also raises questions about the nature and purpose of pinklisting and about its value for a new queer politics.

In his program notes for the Royal National Theatre of Great Britain's production, Kushner notes how his own multiple identifications during a southern boyhood led him to Cohn: "Cohn was homosexual, and so am I. He was also Jewish, but there were lots of great Jews to read about, and nearly no gay men (this was Louisiana, 1968); when one came along, my attention was fixed."[10] Kushner later took a "grim satisfaction" in Cohn's death from AIDS, but according to an interview with Arthur Lubrow in the *New Yorker*, he was "jolted out of his enjoyment" by the aforementioned *Nation* article written by Robert Sherrill, which, in Kushner's eyes, "equated Cohn's corrupt political life with his sleazy sex life." Kushner was fascinated by the fact that it was Cohn, not McCarthy, who was the usual target of anticonservative venom: "People didn't hate McCarthy so much—they thought he was a scoundrel who didn't believe in anything. But there was a venal little monster by his side, a Jew and a queer, and this was the real object of detestation."[11] In the program note for the National, Kushner indicates what, for him, the case of Roy Cohn might mean: "AIDS is what finally outed Roy Cohn. The ironies surrounding his death engendered a great deal of homophobic commentary, and among gay men and lesbians considerable introspection. How broad, how embracing was our sense of community? Did it encompass an implacable foe like Roy? Was he one of us?"

Kushner's play answers with what I take to be an uncomfortable yes—and that yes marks out precisely the distance between a first-generation AIDS play like *The Normal Heart* and a second-generation work like *Angels in America*. If Kramer's play is about how the health problems of a relatively homogeneous minority have been ignored or dismissed by American majoritarian culture, Kushner's play reflects a new gay self-recognition about the ways in which the oppression of gays and lesbians, like the oppression of other minority groups, has been integral to majoritarian self-recognition, especially during the Reaganite eighties when antihomosexuality served many of the same proposes that anti-Communism did in the fifties. In *The Normal Heart*, when Ned Weeks complains about the silence of his associates at the fictional version of the GMHC, he is complaining about the lack of big mouths at the margins of American life. The silence and denial of Roy Cohn took place center stage in American power politics and takes center stage in Kushner's refiguration of the American political landscape. For Kramer AIDS is about the fate of the gay community; for Kushner AIDS, while retaining a gay-specific identity, is about the fate of the country.

Like all discourse surrounding AIDS, *Angels in America* is about definitions of identity. Part One of the play, *Millennium Approaches*, begins with many definitions at least superficially in place. A rabbi eulogizes the values brought from the old country and laments the passing of a generation of Russian Jewish immigrants to America: "How we struggled, and how we fought, for the family, for the Jewish home, so that you would not grow up *here*, in this strange place, in the melting pot where nothing melted." Indeed, nothing is melting in the opening scenes; conservatives stick with conservatives; gay men with gay men; Mormons with Mormons. The society of the play is fractured into groups with their own labeled identities. The label no one claims is "American"; as the rabbi puts it to his community, "You do not live in America. No such place exists. Your clay is the clay of some Litvak shtetl, your air the air of the steppes."[12] Kushner's plot focuses on the plight of two couples, one that appears to be straight, the other gay. No sooner have these identities been established, however, than they begin to break down, as systems of identification prove to be as vulnerable as immune systems. As Kushner explained in an interview, "It is all neatly set up, but then it doesn't work out because of all sorts of internal stresses. The Mormon who is married is also gay, and one of the gay characters has AIDS and the other one can't deal with it. So within that seemingly homogeneous unit there is enormous conflict and potential for eruption."[13]

Cohn acts as the satanic catalyst of the piece, forcing crises of identity and identification in many of the men who surround him. In part, these crises are forced by Roy's insistence on his personal brand of social Darwinism, the primacy of the individual in the struggle for an existence. Demanding loyalty to himself, he nonetheless paradoxically preaches a gospel of self-sufficiency. He counsels Joe, the Mormon husband and a potential "Roytoy," in the tones of the Great Tempter: "Love; that's a trap. Responsibility; that's a trap too. Like a father to a son I tell you this: Life is full of horror; nobody escapes, nobody; save yourself." Roy advises Joe against identifying with any other person or group; the Cohnian self must be created ex nihilo: "Don't be afraid; people are so afraid; don't be afraid to live in the raw wind, naked, alone" (*Angels 1*: 58).

For his characterization of Cohn's sense of his own sexuality, Kushner seems to have taken his cue from an unpublished fragment of a 1978 interview Cohn gave to Ken Auletta for *Esquire*. When asked about the rumors of his homosexuality, Cohn responded, "Anybody who knows anything about me or who knows the way I function in active life, would have an awfully hard time reconciling that with any kind of homosexuality. Every facet of my personality, of my aggressiveness, my toughness and everything along those lines is just totally, I suppose, incompatible with anything like that."[14] In Kushner's play, Roy's parallel denial of his homosexuality takes place after his doctor has informed him that he has AIDS. Roy forces the physician to admit that he considers Roy a homosexual, then gives the doctor a lesson in gender definitions:

> Your problem, Henry, is that you are hung up on words, on labels, that you believe they mean what they seem to mean. AIDS. Homosexual. Gay. Lesbian. You think these are names that tell you who someone sleeps with, but they don't tell you that…. Like all labels they tell you one thing and one thing only: where does an individual stand in the pecking order? Not ideology, or sexual taste, but something much simpler: clout. Not who I fuck or who fucks me, but who will pick up the phone when I call, who owes me favors. This is what a label refers to. Now to someone who does not understand this, homosexual is what I am because I have sex with men. But really this is wrong. Homosexuals are not men who sleep with other men. Homosexuals are men who in fifteen years of trying cannot get a pissant antidiscrimination bill through City Council. Homosexuals are men who know nobody and who nobody knows. Who have zero clout. Does this sound like me, Henry? (*Angels 1*: 45).

Cohn's sophistry embodies the intellectual, moral, and spiritual stagnation from which most of Kushner's characters and the nation itself are seen to suffer in *Angels in America*. Incapable of reconciling "homosexuality" and "clout," Roy chooses to remain in fundamental contradiction with himself. As he explains to his doctor, "Roy Cohn is not a homosexual. Roy Cohn is a heterosexual man, Henry, who fucks around with guys…. AIDS is what homosexuals have. I have liver cancer" (*Angels 1*: 46). In refusing to allow corporeal information to shake his hegemonic power over what words mean, Cohn is this play's Angel of Death. It is his collapse at the end of Part One that harbingers the messageless annunciation of a new angel that concludes the first half of *Angels in America*. While Roy insists to the ghost of Ethel Rosenberg that he is immortal ("I have *forced* my way into history. I ain't never gonna die"), Ethel, in her role as the play's prophet of liminality, responds that a new world order is about to be established: "History is about to crack wide open. Millennium approaches" (*Angels 1*: 112).

The title of Part Two of Kushner's epic, *Perestroika*, acknowledges one of the many extraordinary challenges to the Cohnian worldview provided by the social and political changes of the mideighties at home and abroad. Indeed, Cohn's series of deathbed scenes serves as a metaphor for the collapse of the Manichean paradigms upon which he built his life and career. But Roy refuses to go gentle into that good millennium. Indeed, the message the angel has arrived to deliver is finally revealed and, ironically, echoes Roy's own constant telephonic injunction to "hold." In Kushner's comic take on the interpretation of AIDS as divine instruction, he provides his angel with a negative message, a new gospel of stasis. All creation is to stop moving. God, it seems, has been missing from the heavens since 1911; because the angels know God loves movement, especially human movement, they hope that by putting an end to human travel, thought, and imagination, they might force his reappearance. The message is refused by its human prophet, however, and with it the ethos of Roy Cohn. Roy begins *Millennium Approaches* with a bark into the phone—"Hold"—and he ends his human journey, some six and a half hours later in *Perestroika*, with the same word.

Like that of Kushner's angel, Roy's horror in the face of movement and change, his desire to keep everyone and everything on hold, evokes the image of Walter Benjamin's "angel of history":

A Klee painting named "Angelus Novus" shows an angel looking as though he is about to move away from something he is fixedly contemplating. His eyes are staring, his mouth wide open, his wings are spread. This is how one pictures the angel of history. His face is turned towards the past. Where we perceive a chain of events, he sees one single catastrophe which keeps piling wreckage upon wreckage and hurls it in front of his feet. The angel would like to stay, awaken the dead, and make whole what has been smashed. But a storm is blowing from Paradise; it has got caught in his wings with such violence that the angel can no longer close them. This storm irresistibly propels him into the future to which his back is turned, while the pile of debris before him grows skyward. This storm is what we call progress.[15]

Not even Roy Cohn can resist the storm of progress; the world refuses to hold and, at his hospital bedside, it begins its movement toward a new community based on a solidarity across both new and old lines of group identification as a queer assortment of mourners gathers to say Kaddish. Belize, a black ex-drag queen and Roy's former nurse, has come at least in part out of a sense of gay solidarity: "A queen can forgive her vanquished foe." Louis, an out gay Jewish liberal who views Cohn as "the polestar of human evil," has come to steal his supply of AZT for his former lover, a tacit acknowledgment of the lessons in power Cohn might have to teach the gay community; he stays to confront, for the first time, the reality of death—a reality that caused him to abandon his lover and that is as horrible in an enemy as it is in a friend. Even Ethel Rosenberg is there; in her previous scene with Roy, she confessed to hoping he'd die a more terrible death than hers, but she went on to sing him a Yiddish lullaby. As she returns to say Kaddish over his dead body, we are invited to speculate that she does so as a Jewish mother. Louis and Ethel have not forgotten all that divides them from Roy Cohn, however; they end the prayer with their own contribution—"You sonofabitch" (*Angels 2*, 124, 95, 126).

When Roy returns to earth for a final interview with his Mormon protégé, Kushner teases us with the possibility that Roy has been transformed by his final illness. After kissing the young man softly on the mouth, he offers a prophecy of his own: "You'll find, my friend, that what you love will take you places you never dreamed you'd go" (*Angels 2*, 127). However, in Roy's final appearance in the play, at a location in the next world characterized by "volcanic, pulsating red light" and "a basso profundo roar, like a thousand Bessemer furnaces," we learn that Roy has not changed; indeed, he has engaged a new client. He will defend God in a cosmic family court against angelic charges of abandonment—the apotheosis of his career as a lawyer for the rich and famous: "I'm an absolute fucking demon with Family Law. Just tell me who the judge is, and what kind of jewelry does he like" (*Angels 2*, 138).

In Kushner's epilogue, those left on earth crystalize into the new society they have struggled toward throughout the play. Male, female; straight, gay; black, white; agnostic, Mormon, Jew—they have survived the breakdown of families and relationships; the collapse of the Soviet Union, the ozone layer, and the immune system; the opportunistic diseases associated with AIDS; the messages of angels; and the mania of Roy Cohn. Roy was right; what they have loved has taken them places they never dreamed they'd go. But unlike Roy, they look forward; they have come to accept not only that movement is essential to life, but that it is good. Like the character whose Benjaminian lines conclude the play proper, they share the belief that "nothing's lost forever. In this world, there is a kind of painful progress. Longing for what we've left behind, and dreaming ahead" (*Angels 2*, 144).

The new community of the Epilogue is not, of course, based on the conventional union of happy couples; the play is ruthless in its assertion that two plus two is not a stable enough equation to base a life on, much less a progressive political vision. Neither has this community bought into the individualistic ethos of Cohn; the politics of one plus one doesn't add up fast enough, if it ever adds up at all. Instead, Kushner leaves us with the image of four individuals who, despite their very real differences, have chosen, on the basis of their collective experience, to think about themselves as a community working for change. It is Prior, the AIDS patient who has rejected his role as prophet of stagnation, who offers the play's valedictory blessing—both on those gathered onstage, beneath the Angel of Bethesda Fountain in Central Park, and on those gathered offstage in the audience: "You are fabulous creatures, each and every one" (*Angels 2*, 148). His campy and powerful benediction suggests a third term that might mediate between the two Roy Cohn could not hold together—a quintessentially fifties term recycled for nineties resistance. What *do* you call a homosexual with clout? Just what Roy always feared. Queer.

NOTES

1 Larry Kramer, *The Normal Heart* (New York: New American Library, 1985), 114.

2 Martin Greif, *An Evocatively Illustrated Who's Who of Who Is, Was, May Have Been, Probably Was, and Almost Certainly Seems to Have Been Gay during the Past 5,000 Years* (New York: Carol Publishing Group, 1982).

3 Leigh W. Rutledge, *The Gay Book of Lists* (Boston: Alyson, 1987), 46.

4 Nicholas von Hoffman, *Citizen Cohn* (New York: Doubleday, 1988).

5 Robert Sherrill, "King Cohn," *Nation*, May 21, 1988), 720. All Sherrill quotations are from this article.

6 Andy Rooney statement reported by Eve Kosofsky Sedgwick in *Epistemology of the Closet* (Berkeley: University of California Press, 1990), 243.

7 Alvin Krebs, "Roy Cohn, Aide to McCarthy and Fiery Lawyer, Dies at 59," *New York Times*, Aug. 3, 1986. Subsequent quotations are from this article.

8 Sedgwick, *Epistemology*, 243.

9 Ron Vawter quoted in Jessica Hagedorn, "Ron Vawter," *BOMB*, fall 1992, 46.

10 Program of the Royal National Theatre of Great Britain for *Angels in America, A Gay Fantasia on National Themes: Part One: Millennium Approaches* (British premiere at the Cottesloe Theatre, Jan. 1992).

11 Arthur Lubrow, "Tony Kushner's Paradise Lost," *New Yorker*, Nov. 30, 1992, 60.

12 Tony Kushner, *Angels in America, A Gay Fantasia on National Themes: Part One: Millennium Approaches* (New York: Theatre Communications Group, 1993), 10, 111. Subsequent references to the play shall appear in the body of my text as *Angels 1*. References to the second part of Kushner's play, *Perestroika* (New York: Theatre Communications Group, 1994), shall appear as *Angels 2*.

13 Tony Kushner interviewed in Hilary de Vries, "A Playwright Spreads his Wings," *Los Angeles Times*, Oct. 25, 1992.

14 Roy Cohn's remarks reported by Sidney Zion in *The Autobiography of Roy Cohn* (Secaucus, NJ: Lyle Stuart, 1988), 240.

15 Walter Benjamin, "Theses on the Philosophy of History" in *Illuminations*, trans. Harry Zohn (New York: Schocken, 1968), 257–58. For another artistic appropriation of this passage, see Laurie Anderson's "The Dream Before" on her album *Strange Angels* (Warner Brothers Records, 1989).

8

Flash Back, Flash Forward

The Fifties, the Nineties, and the Transformed Politics of Remote Control

Alice Jardine

LOOKING FORWARD TO THE PAST

Around 1990, when I first started thinking about the strange relationship between the American 1950s and 1990s, I depended on the metaphor of "repression."[1] I would talk about the cultural and political return of the repressed 1950s into the 1990s, producing uncanny effects of déjà-vu. Or I would joke about the possibility that Dennis Hopper's famous line from the 1990 film *Flashback*—"The nineties are going to make the sixties look like the fifties"—was backwards: the nineties are both so out of and into control, they might actually make the fifties look like the sixties.[2] But I soon realized that the connections between the fifties and the nineties that interest me are not those of depth or irony but rather those of surface and access. That what I think an increasing number of people have been experiencing as a "haunting" of the nineties by the fifties is not about the resurgence of memory but about flashes of recall and reruns. I decided that this realization was not being overdetermined by my interest in "the postmodern," but rather that "the postmodern" had finally overdetermined our social capacity to *realize things* in the world. I also began to think about the 1950s fear that someone "Outside" was in control from some remote place, as opposed to the 1990s fear that No One is in control of the remote at all.

It was from within the context of these haunting ruminations that the importance of "the Trial of the Century" became clearer to me, and I shall return to it shortly. The Rosenberg Event was, after all, the dark hole of what I have termed the First American Fifties, 1945–55, and that period's burning question: *how did this country get from Hiroshima and Nagasaki to Disneyland in ten years?* More directly, what has been the psychohistorical significance of that particular ten-year configuration of clockworked, lock-stepped simultaneity, which brought us nuclear testing, Cold War rhetoric, the massification of television, the emergence of science fiction film, and the almost frantic domestic containment of women, homosexuals, and racial and ethnic minorities?[3] While the Second Fifties (1955–65) are just as fascinating, it is the First Fifties that I think are most urgently in need of attention from progressive cultural and political theorists worried about the deep structures of the 1990s. Why?

Well, there are the obvious reasons: like the fact that elder U.S. baby boomers are moving into major positions of power, into national and international government, industry, and education. What makes us click? Are the first products of postwar American culture more psychically imprinted by Roy Rogers, Howdy Doody, Fury, and Captain Kangaroo than by, say, the history of the Korean War and McCarthyism? Or was that the moment when mass culture and mainstream history became psychotelevisually inseparable? Is it possible that this inseparability produced a generation for whom simulation is fundamentally more "real" than "reality," while the question of who is in control depends on which channel you watch?[4]

These questions lead us quickly to another reason: the genesis of "the postmodern era" in the First 1950s. That period is as close as postmodern theorists have been able to get to pinpointing a semblance of an origin for that strange unanchoring of reality from the real that was then not yet called virtual and that has today permeated both domestic and public space. I think that most of the important questions facing us in the nineties can be traced right back to the beginnings of our last great epistemological rupture in the early fifties. For example, from within the contemporary sphere of our American postmodern sense of loss of bearings, the question of control seems to me paramount. If we look back at the early 1950s, control was a major issue then as well. Then, the object was to persuade, to produce a consensus that, say, it was the Kremlin controlling all of us from various remote positions. This consensus could be achieved through the combined resources of a still early-1940s propaganda machine and the best show business had to offer. Whether the threat was located on the inside or the outside, among local university teachers or on Mars, First Fifties containment could be effected through sustained counter*images* of pure and clean human decency and genuine American goodness at work, at home, close up, for a better consumerist future. In the technologically sophisticated, mediatized 1990s, however, goodness and truth are in trouble, the image can no longer be believed: consensus is out and access is in, with speed, efficiency, and performance at the touch of a button.[5] It seems to me that the 1990s are, in fact, less about the image than about the flash: flashes on a screen, bursting forth, giving off light, with great speed, as with rapid news transmission. The word "flash" also connotes something showy, even indecent...(like the fast-moving consumer items on home shopping channels?).[6] Whenever and wherever one feels threatened, at that moment, the object is to hit the remote control fast and, above all, don't relinquish it until every possible aspect of every possible angle of the threat has flashed before your eyes. By then, hopefully, it will be time to go to sleep.

But if for me and other theorists of the postmodern these technoetiological, difference and sameness connections between the two eras are fascinating, even more so are their current temporal and spatial interactions. For at this very moment in the process of beginning to understand the postmodern, it seems to me that the absolutely most compelling reason for looking carefully at the First 1950s is their flash resurfacing—politically, culturally, and psychologically—in the 1990s. Producing something like an "anniversary effect" of the era of McCarthyism, important elements of the First Fifties (evoking the beginnings of postmodernism) are strangely resurfacing during the moment of dramatic endings we are currently living through: the endings of a century, of a millennium, most particularly for us here, the endings of the Cold War symbolic apparatus that has shaped political reality for most of the world for forty-something years. Of course, we are also perhaps experiencing something else just as dramatic if not more so: the endings of at least this phase of the postmodern era that we are just beginning to be able to describe, endings that will lead us toward something more "transmodern"—the term I have adopted to describe our most current moment, one signaled acutely by the endings of first-world, bipolar, industrial, mass culture hegemony and heading us toward something based in a more global, polycentric, particularized, informational network of cultures in which geopolitical determinants give way progressively to more techno-symbolic configurations.[7]

Some of the ways in which what we might call "the virtual fifties" have flashed across our nineties screens, from the midst of these endings, have been obvious, even funny: like when George Bush practically called Bill Clinton a Communist during the 1992 presidential campaign[8] or when sentimental nostalgia for the cultural fifties (for example, through recent filmic remakes of such fifties children's TV shows as *Lassie*, *Maverick*, and *Wyatt Earp*) becomes comedy in spite of itself.

Most such flashes, however, have not been so funny. Some have involved news items surfacing *about* the early 1950s: for example, reports of widespread secret radiation testing on orphans, mental patients, prisoners, and so forth,[9] or of how the government has hidden the extent to which everyone in the country has been a "downwinder" of the fifties nuclear tests carried out in Arizona and Utah.[10] But most flashes are more of the "haunting" kind, flashes *from*, rather than about, the fifties, as if caught up in a kind of citational repetition: for example, the bizarre mimesis between the Korean and the Gulf Wars (not to mention recent discussions about North Korea); or white cops beating up blacks in L.A. and shooting them in Detroit; or a resurgence of fundamentalist Christian inspired anti-Semitism. Old fifties characters have reappeared on our screens: Alger Hiss, finally cleared of conspiracy charges in 1992; Rock Hudson and Liberace, dead from AIDS; Roy Cohn, as creator of Donald Trump; or those two immortal infants Marilyn (claimed by Madonna as her spirit) and Elvis (who seems to haunt most movies and plays these days). Then there are the truly ghostly reruns, like pregnant comic TV actresses getting the attention of the White House (when Lucy got higher ratings than Eisenhower, and Murphy Brown took on Dan Quayle). Or, as pointed out by Beth Katzoff, the way the fifties have returned within the semiotic terms of such pop culture icons as the "Teenage" (a major category in the fifties) "Mutant" (evoking fifties fears of radiation contamination), "Ninja" (evoking a preinformation-age Japan) "Turtles" (direct from the duck-and-cover films I saw as a child).[11] Or, on a more sociological plane, there are the ways in which David Riesman's gender-blind rhetoric of the "Outer-Directed Man" has resurfaced to describe Deborah Tannen's essentialized woman and the "Inner-Directed Man" has resurfaced as Robert Bly's "Real Man," while the greatest 1950s danger for men—conformity—and for women—ambition—are writ large on our nineties movie screens.[12] And, perhaps as the most bizarre flash effect of all, there is the way in which the most widely watched and long-running TV trial in television history—the Army-McCarthy hearings—seems to have prefigured the uninterrupted sequence of TV trials over the past few years, including the Iran-Contra hearings, the Anita Hill hearings, the Kennedy-Smith trial, the L.A. Police trials, and now O. J. Simpson and soon, no doubt, the World Trade Center and/or Oklahoma bombing trials.[13]

LOOKING BACK TO THE FUTURE

Most important, we must also consider here the flashy resurgence of the political and cultural right wing in the nineties, a right wing as well funded and fully organized as ever it was in the fifties. Many progressives find themselves asking, but when did they all get back together!? Ellen Messer-Davidow, in her recent article "Manufacturing the Attack on Liberalized Higher Education," answers this question in detail, linking the Old Right of the fifties and the New Right of the nineties very directly: "After the triumph of Roosevelt and the New Deal, conservatives described themselves as 'the Remnant'; they were, in the words of one, 'obscure, unorganized, inarticulate.' The establishment of the *National Review* by William F. Buckley, Jr., in 1955 'laid the foundations for everything that followed.'"[14] Conservatives henceforth had a forum for organizing and intervening. Messer-Davidow traces their interventions through the founding of Young Americans for Freedom in 1960; the Goldwater campaign in 1964; the conservative direct-mail campaigns of the seventies; the founding of PACS; the rise of the Christian Right, culminating with the founding of the Heritage Foundation in 1973, the Committee for the Survival of a Free Congress in 1974, and the Leadership Institute and the Moral Majority in 1979.

> Thus, between 1955 and 1980, the Right became a powerful political movement. It had built a coalition of conservative strains (Old Right, neoconservative, New Right, Christian Right, libertarian, free-market and supply-side economics, etc.) and an infrastructure of national organizations, interest groups, churches, and corporate councils.... Today the conservative movement, the term now preferred by many of its members, is intent on strengthening the coalition by training the "Third Generation" and organizing the grass roots. During these same decades, the Right also enlarged its infrastructure with foundations, think tanks, media, training institutes, and legal centers that began to focus their resources on cultural change.[15]

It was finally Ronald Reagan, the actor-president who used cue cards when meeting with foreign dignitaries,[16] who, during the 1980s, put in place the apparatus and policies that would eventually shape the American nineties. As Messer-Davidow explains, "With the election of President Reagan in 1980, conservatives were finally in a position to use the government to make national cultural change, and they began with education."[17] The "education campaign" got under way in earnest at the beginning of the nineties. I have written elsewhere, for example, about how the 1990–92 political-correctness media campaign was in part a maneuver to test historical, print-based as well as newer, electronic-based forms of intellectual and political surveillance for broader introduction into the general electronic marketplace of the nineties.[18] Just as McCarthy's fifties apparatus depended heavily on old-fashioned "informers" and "publicity"—with the general battle cry being "Convince The Public"[19]—so too has the nineties right-wing apparatus understood just what newfangled mechanisms it would take to be convincing enough both within and without university walls. The PC media blitz was invented and orchestrated by groups of well-organized conservative organizations, funded from the "outside" by the Bradley, Coors, Olin, Scaife, and Heritage Foundations and reinforced by members of their "inside" organizations such as the Madison Group and the National Association of Scholars. This campaign directly echoed fifties McCarthyism, with its key rhetorical devices, conceptual definitions, and institutional legacies directly and explicitly inherited from battles previously fought: the terms of these early nineties battles were transparently set in the early fifties. And yet, as with so many of these political flashes and hauntings from the past, there are almost always mysterious transformations. For example, it is progressive scholarship and art that are now labeled the "New McCarthyism" by the these old McCarthylike campaigns.[20]

Dennis H. Wrong once pointed out that for Hannah Arendt in 1951, "organization is the *sine qua non* of totalitarian movements. It is the power of organization, both openly flaunted and working in the darkness, that lends reality to the 'ideological fictions' of the movement."[21] It is extraordinary to note the degree to which the right wing of the nineties has copied the organizational history and structure of the fifties Communist Party whose totalitarian history it once so detested, developing broad conspiratorial strategies miming the very same ones it could only fulminate against forty years ago. Faced with this huge apparatus, progressive intellectuals in the nineties have thus far been able to accomplish little beyond bemoaning their own total lack of organization and laughing at the Right's absurdist accusations of orchestrated, conspiratorial attacks on Western civilization by hyperorganized hoards of left-wing feminists, poststructuralists, and multiculturalists.[22]

I think, in fact, that progressive intellectuals in general have been taken by surprise that the university has been one of the first major targets of the nineties right wing. But it is not all that surprising when one considers that it was in the fifties that generally liberal institutions began to anticipate outside pressures by moving away from the university's historical role as a site of intellectual ferment and advocacy for social reform toward a new role as a self-policing bastion of neutral nonadvocacy and apolitical scholarship. Intellectuals were instructed to divorce themselves and their scholarship from all politics, and those who didn't suffered. Academic freedom was redefined as the preservation of the professionalism and autonomy of the institution—the definition many still use today, even as intellectual ferment has returned to the academy in new and often progressive ways.[23] It is this ferment that the Right wants to bring to an end once again in order to break what conservatives believe is a liberal monopoly on higher education.

According to Messer-Davidow, "the immediate goal is to transform the higher-education system into a free-market economy by weakening liberal institutions and strengthening conservative ones."[24]

Mobilized from within these refracted fifties-nineties connections is an unceasing attack on the intellectual. Andrew Ross has written on how emergent mass culture in the fifties blocked the integration of intellectuals, who slowly became charged with containing mass culture within certain boundaries—eventually becoming "inspectors" of the nation's cultural health. This led to the ascendancy of postwar "experts"—the psychiatrists, psychotherapists, and sociologists and other doctors of society.[25] If "intellectuals" became the "experts" of the fifties, in the nineties, they are being sucked into the media vacuum of the everyday ridiculing of what they do. Those who stubbornly cling to their self-image as "important intellectuals" are most often being kept busy as academic bureaucrats, while *everyone else* but them becomes an expert on radio talk shows where a *Larry King Live* can lead the electronic nation in a simulated conversation about the latest media-produced reality event. In this context, at this point, the flash of difference between progressives and conservatives is that the former continue to struggle to regain control of their image (how very fifties of them) while the latter have figured out how to get people to pass around the remote (very nineties indeed).

FLASH BACK

What does all of this have to do with "the Trial of the Century"? June 19, 1993 marked the fortieth anniversary of Ethel and Julius Rosenberg's electrocution, and many of us die-hard intellectuals are still deeply troubled and moved by that execution no matter how much time and transformation goes by the way. But why? There have been many tragic and unjust executions in this country. Yet there was something about this one that was momentous. In fact, our historical, cultural, and political memory leaves little doubt that the Rosenberg Event was in many ways the central event of the American 1950s, even perhaps of the American twentieth century. But also and just as importantly, it remains central today as well because of something the last forty years have driven home mercilessly: it does matter how stories get told,[26] and it also matters that the cultural and political right wing in this country has finally noticed that those of us who specialize in narrative and discourse analysis may actually understand something they do not understand about public policy, history, and politics. As Virginia Carmichael has pointed out so well, it was the Rosenberg *story* that "played a crucial explanatory and justifying role in the formulation of the cold war," and the case's now "embedded stories"—the official story, the media story, the human story, the legal story— continue to provide high social drama, in *history* as well as in novels, plays, the visual arts, cinema, and music. Carmichael shows how, among other things, the Rosenberg Event highlights the *function* of storytelling in history and how the close study of that function in terms of this particular story provides an "occasion for acknowledging and coming to terms with an unresolved breach in the national narrative of moral purpose."[27] I would just add that, at least for the near future, the now powerful baby boomer's both conscious and unconscious politics may stand to gain a great deal from a better understanding of that breach.

But I think there's more. I think the Rosenberg Event is also of crucial importance as perhaps *the* initiatory postmodern event of the American fifties, along the way marking the right wing's first flashy—and successful—manipulations of the just then initializing mediascape.[28] It just has to remain fundamentally amazing, *unbelievable*, to anyone who has studied the trial carefully—the evidence, the events, the testimony—that what happened at that trial *really* happened. Life as stranger than fiction indeed, but in very new ways. For it was with the Rosenberg Event that the right wing was first able to *simulate* the logic of conspiracy (seeing it everywhere and engaging in it all the while) in order to create a virtual (legal) fiction of a materially impossible reality. The "unreal" quality of the 1950s trial of the Rosenbergs directly announced the simulationist hauntings of the postmodern, if not eventually transmodern 1990s.

The Rosenberg case (July 17, 1950–June 19, 1953) almost exactly paralleled the high points of both McCarthyism (February 9, 1950–December 2, 1954) and the Korean War (June 25, 1950–July 27, 1953). In fact, I wonder often about what would have happened to Julius and Ethel Rosenberg if they had managed to live one more month—until July 27, 1953, the end of the Korean War.... Or if they had managed to live another year—until June 1954 and the end of the televised Army-McCarthy hearings.... I have to wonder about what would have happened if the Rosenberg trial had itself been televised....

Julius and Ethel Rosenberg grew up in the depression thirties questioning the system that laid waste to so many lives. They believed in the necessity of working-class solidarity. They believed in the fight against Franco, against fascism. They wanted justice; they wanted socialism; and the American Communist Party was the vehicle for both. They were Jewish, intellectual, pro-union, living on the Lower East Side. They were also fighting anti-Semitism, which was at an all-time high in prewar America; as Ilene Philipson notes, "about one-third of all Americans thought Jews were less patriotic than other Americans; almost half felt there was good reason for anti-Jewish feeling; about half thought Jewish businessmen were less honest than others; and almost two-thirds found Jews to have some objectionable qualities."[29] By the 1950s, this anti-Semitism would provide bizarre background noise for the trial itself, an event in which almost all of the major actors—except for the jury—were Jewish.

In the atmosphere of McCarthy's America, the Rosenberg case soon became bigger than Sacco and Vanzetti in the twenties; bigger than the Dreyfus case in France. For, suddenly, there it was, what had to be the flashiest fiction of the immediate post-war period: the Secret of the Atomic Bomb. And the Rosenbergs—bad guys bigger than life—were accused of having stolen it and turned it over to the Soviet Union. Judge Kaufman considered their crime worse than murder. They were, in his opinion, the cause of both the Korean War and the threat of atomic annihilation. This was not what they were accused or convicted of. But he ordered them killed anyway.[30]

On February 3, 1950, Klaus Emil *Julius* Fuchs, a German-born scientist living in Britain, confessed to having given atomic information to the Soviet Union. He was convicted and sentenced to fourteen years in prison, this result based on the only evidence there was: his own confession. Fuchs was supposed to have named someone called Harry Gold as the main courier from the United States. He actually never named Gold, himself a pathological liar also convicted on the sole basis of his own confession. (In fact, Fuchs failed twice to identify Gold from photographs.) As the FBI and the CIA continued to question Gold, however, he claimed to have been passed a very big secret from a young army sergeant in Albuquerque, New Mexico, named David Greenglass. The password was "I come from Julius." Well, not exactly. Gold continued to assert that he didn't remember the exact password: "I believe that it involved the name of a man and was something on the order of Bob sent me or Benny sent me or John sent me or something like that."[31] You can almost hear the rest—FBI: "Could it have been Julie or Julius?" Gold: "Yes! Yes! That's it." Suddenly David Greenglass's and Harry Gold's Jell-O box halves—supposedly used as a sign of recognition—were a perfect fit.[32]

The famous Jell-O box in this case is only the most bizarre—and the most postmodern—of a series of material objects presented as evidence but that in one way or another just weren't *real*. It is, of course, already hard to decide whether Jell-O in and of itself is real. On the box, it always says "imitation." The Jell-O box used at the trial was, at the very least, a double imitation, however, since it wasn't the *real* box used by "the spies." The story goes that Roy Cohn bought it at a local store, selecting "imitation raspberry flavored" Jell-O whereas no one knows what the imitation flavor might have been of the box being imitated, assuming it ever existed, which it probably never did. This unreality, this sense of constantly reiterated, simulated, imitated reality pervades all of the "evidence" in the trial: a "Russian console table" that was actually from Macy's (with no secret compartment at all); a fraudulent and forged hotel card; a passport photo not for passports; bomb sketches for kids....

But the problem continued to be posed *as if it were real: someone* must have given "the Secret of the Atomic Bomb" to the Russians—and that particular someone had to be found. And so on June 15, 1950, the FBI obtained the confession from Ethel Rosenberg's brother, David Greenglass, that he had been actively involved in a "conspiracy to commit espionage." Here we are at the postmodern heart of this event: none of these people were actually charged with espionage, but, rather, they were charged with *conspiracy* to commit espionage. That way, the only evidence required was *the uncorroborated testimony of co-conspirators*. It seems the FBI kept David Greenglass and Harry Gold in the same cell for a long time so that they could figure out how the story should be told....

Julius Rosenberg was then arrested on July 17, 1950. Ethel was picked up on August 11 for having *typed* "the secret." (She had left her two sons, Michael and Robert, with some neighbors, thus beginning for them a long, painful struggle in the bizarre borderlands of fiction and reality that has made them no doubt honorary citizens of the postmodern era.)[33] The Rosenberg trial began on March 6, 1951. On March 29, 1951, Ethel and Julius Rosenberg were found guilty of conspiracy to commit espionage. This verdict was rendered by a homogeneous, all-male-but-one jury of no Jews, no liberals, and "nobody who read anything but the conservative press" as it says in the court record. On April 5, 1951, Ethel and Julius were sentenced to die on May 21, 1951.

We know now that it was not only the evidence in this trial that seemed to radiate simulationist postmodernism but many of the people involved as well. Especially those members of the fifties Right who colluded unashamedly, behind the scenes, to make this story turn out the way they wanted. Head prosecutor Saypol, assistant prosecutor Cohn, and Judge Kaufman were thoroughly in touch—it has been reported by Cohn's biographers that he would even call Kaufman at the courthouse from pay phones all through the period of the trial, even from the Stork Club, where he would sit and talk about the case with his good friends Walter Winchell and J. Edgar Hoover over drinks. Roy Cohn may, in fact, have been the first truly postmodern character of the last forty years, one whose capacity for negotiating and indeed creating never ending chains of flashy and purely performative "realities" was amazing. After making his reputation in the fifties, he would go on to become one of the last forty years' principal realitymakers and breakers, whether it was with City Hall, the press, Hollywood, the jet set, the archdiocese, the unions, the media, or both major political parties at once. He would people his quite unreal life with leaders of industry, politics, the judiciary, real estate, the arts, the unions, and the mob. He would be on a first-name basis with most governors, senators, mayors, political bosses, mafia leaders, mobsters, builders, gamblers, labor magnates, movie and TV stars, lawyers, publishers, reporters, columnists, and tycoons. He would be a close friend of Ronald Reagan (one of his major fund-raisers, in fact), Donald Trump's adviser, lawyer, and friend; and a long time co-conspirator of Jesse Helms. Roy Cohn would finally get caught in a real *flesh and blood body* contradiction though: after actively and maliciously campaigning against homosexuality in general and gay and lesbian individuals in particular throughout America—all the while leading a flamboyantly nonmonogamous gay life—he died of AIDS in 1986. It seems strange that he didn't quite make it to the nineties.[34]

Simulated objects as evidence; uncorroborated conspiracy as charge; networked and protean right-wingers in control of their fate—it does not seem to me that the Rosenbergs had much of a chance to present what they no doubt experienced as the simple, authentic reality of their seemingly pre-postmodern lives. The unreality of the postmodern condition was taking them over (a different kind of body snatching perhaps). The appeal process was endless, and when that was finally over, not one single court, including the Supreme Court, had ever deigned even to review the case. It was too hot. The country was too hot. The Korean War was too hot. McCarthy was too hot. The Cold War was too hot. Reality had gone cold.

The execution was scheduled for Thursday, June 18, 1953, at 11 P.M.—Ethel and Julius's fourteenth wedding anniversary. It was later rescheduled for Friday night, June 19, 1953, at 11 P.M. Protests against this trumped-up reality had begun all over the nation—all over the world. Hundreds of thousands of people gathered in great swarms of *utter disbelief*. In answer to the defense attorneys' objection to the execution being carried out on the Jewish Sabbath, Attorney General Brownell—or was it some combination of Roy Cohn and Judge Kaufman?—decided against postponing the execution until Monday. After all, that would have given the defense more time. No, he moved it up. The Rosenbergs would be killed earlier, at eight o'clock on Friday night—a few minutes before sunset, a few minutes before the Jewish Sabbath.

The night of the execution, all over the world, there were massive demonstrations demanding mercy for both of the Rosenbergs, but especially for Ethel. In Union Square, there was a huge multifaith prayer meeting. In Paris, at the Place de la Concorde, people were killed rushing the American Embassy...in London...in Rome...Everyone was commenting on how unreal it all was. *You just couldn't believe it*, people have said looking back. The Rosenbergs' lawyer, Manny Bloch, ran frantically all over the Supreme Court, the White House, all over Washington trying to see the judges, the president, to get a stay, a reprieve, some clemency, some hearing for the facts, for the truth.... Outside Sing Sing, state troop reinforcements were called in to surround the place while patrol boats cruised the Hudson. Julius Rosenberg was killed first—at 8:06 P.M. He quietly murmured the twenty-third psalm up until the very last second. Ethel died less peacefully, a few minutes later, having to be jolted three times over the space of five full minutes.

FLASH FORWARD

As if to hyperemphasize the postmodern aura of the fifties Rosenberg Event— there has already been a nineties rerun:

> A mock trial jury yesterday [August 10, 1993] found Julius and Ethel Rosenberg not guilty of plotting to give US atomic secrets to the Soviet Union, in a colorful restaging of the "espionage trial" of the century that sent both to the electric chair.
>
> The American Bar Association used real lawyers, a judge, and a jury of ordinary citizens to recreate the 1951 trial, updated to today's legal standards.
>
> The mock Rosenbergs said they were members of the Communist Party—the real ones took the Fifth Amendment on that question—but emphatically denied spying.[35]

"Real lawyers"; "updated to today's legal standards"; "the mock Rosenbergs": these are the phrases—marking the assumption of a previous reality being "overwritten" with a new one—that lock this doubled Rosenberg Event into the logic of postmodern simulation. Located within both the 1950s beginnings and 1990s endings of the postmodern era, it is perhaps the most instructive and transformative case we have for thinking about the transmodern future, a future where *real flesh and blood bodies* will continue to be what is at stake in the struggle for the public and its members' ideas, money, and votes by remote.

Back in 1983 Hal Foster posited a now famous distinction between two kinds of postmodernism: a postmodernism of resistance and a postmodernism of reaction.[36] While this distinction was put forward in the context of a discussion of periodization and aesthetics, it remains helpful in a more general way—but is it still relevant? Is there still a difference in kind and degree between an intellectual, aesthetic, and political postmodernism that questions and resists—even attempts to deconstruct—the status quo and one that simply simulates and enhances it by going with the quo's flow? To the extent that the advent of the postmodern condition has been most directly connected to the far-ranging and fast-moving technological innovations of the past forty years, what has been (and what is today) the historical link between the new technologies and reactionary, indeed fascist impulses and incarnations? Does it not seem that innovative technologies have, at least in the twentieth century, tended to aggregate, even herd people toward reaction, toward fascism rather than toward solidarity and resistance? One thinks of the Nuremberg rallies staged only to be filmed.[37] And while one can always point to the resistance of individuals within the simulationist landscapes of advanced postmodernism—hackers on the nets, artists in the videoscape—most, if not all, of the cyber, virtual, and video technologies they are using can be traced back to origins in one of the most reactionary sectors of American culture: United States Defense Department-funded research and development.

At the very least, I think it is safe to say that today, in the midnineties, the cultural, economic, and political "status quo" in this country can be described as a fully virtualized postmodernism. Almost every aspect of the culture is or soon will be electronically touched by technologies no longer belonging only to the national security state as in the fifties, but owned now by the multi-national high-tech conglomerates of the 1990s. And within this current electronic culture of simulation, to "go with the flow" is to capitalize on it and enlarge it to include one's own goals. It is this that I think the right wing in this country has understood better than most: theirs is an extremely successful postmodernism of reaction. For example, just in the realm of education, their new "consciousness-raising high technology" is in the works: a national television network with signed affiliates in major metropolitan areas and with programming targeted most directly at college campuses, national media-training workshops, a private national computer-network database of progressive intellectuals and artists, and so on. Or, for example, there are forthcoming systemwide pressures on all kinds of educational institutions to introduce to students their "commercially produced" interactive and on-line computer and media technologies, not to mention the ultimate simulation machines, the virtual-reality technologies themselves. In fact, if in fifties education it finally became a question of who could resist intimidation, in the nineties it will be a question of who can resist commercialization. On this front those of us in higher education could learn a lot from our colleagues in K through twelve who are already in the battle with such for-profit initiatives as the Whittle Corporation's Channel One and Benno Schmidt's Edison Project and their plans for broadening the impact of commercial media on children while they are in school.[38]

What is it that the Left has understood about or done with postmodernism and its technological mediascapes beyond the now familiar, vague, and probably utopian promises of a mass democratization of information? Could any of the simulationist tactics of the Right's reactionary postmodernism be useful to the Left's postmodernism of resistance? Or does the Right have such a monopoly at this point on postmodern tactics of political manipulation and technologies of simulation that the Left has been stuck with a "reality" that

119

can, in fact, no longer be resisted because its "realness" is so remote? Or perhaps it is true that the notions of Right and Left themselves have become hopelessly unreal within fully virtualized, mainstreamed postmodernism.

Or perhaps—in short—some of us have been *talking about* resistant postmodernism while others have been *doing* reactionary postmodernism for far too long and now it is time to move on. Paying attention to the current hauntings of the nineties by the First American Fifties could certainly be instructive in this regard, helping to short-circuit a perhaps worn-out choice. In particular, I think that our attention should include some sustained focus on the Rosenberg Event—on the depths of its surfaces, on how extensively it was produced and processed by the Right, on the cautionary tales of its simulationist manipulations, on how easy it was, finally, for two real, flesh and blood people to be killed by an electronic machine.

Of course, today, it is hard to pay sustained attention to such complicated matters, to think them through, indeed, to get one's bearings at all. It is not the First American Fifties: the struggle for control of the American heart and mind has apparently shifted from remote lands to the remotes in our hands.... But here's a flash: in a country soon to have five hundred TV channels, can cultural critics who still desire to remain progressive intellectuals and citizens of the world become transmodernists fast enough to avoid being relegated to mere noise, static—the snow on a dead channel?[39] Don't touch that dial!

NOTES

1 For the purposes of this essay, "the fifties" and "the nineties" are but usefully provocative temporal bookends for the emergence and spread of postmodernism and now its transformation.

2 The Hopper line represents just one pop-cultural example of the new kind of attention focused on the complicated relationships between the fifties and the sixties over the past few years. I think this new level of attention derives in part from the fact that the classic fifties—the closest this country has ever come to embracing outright fascism as opposed to so-called friendly fascism—is a largely untheorized and unself-analyzed period, very often still today represented nostalgically and apolitically, sandwiched between the endlessly commentated and ever politicized 1940s and 1960s. For example, it has recently been suggested that, in fact, most of what we attribute to the 1960s actually happened in the 1950s and only became conscious and widely popularized in the sixties. In Molly Haskell's words, "It was as if the whole period of the fifties was a front, the topsoil that protected the seed of rebellion that was germinating

below. The cultural disorientation had begun, but it had yet to be acknowledged." As quoted in Wini Breines, *Young, White, and Miserable: Growing Up Female in the Fifties* (Boston: Beacon Press, 1992), 1.

3 I use the word "psychohistorical" here in a way not unrelated to Fredric Jameson's notion of the political unconscious (see Fredric Jameson, *The Political Unconscious* [Ithaca: Cornell University Press, 1981]), although psychohistory has actually existed as a discipline since the fifties. Psychohistorians attempt to trace the links between individual psychologies and concurrent historical events. See, for example, Saul Friedlander, *History and Psychoanalysis: An Inquiry into the Possibilities and Limits of Psychohistory* (New York: Holmes and Meier, 1978).

4 I would hope here to evoke all possible associative resonances of both "real" and "reality," from those attached to the theories of Jacques Lacan (certainly a thinker of the fifties for the nineties) through Disneyworld to cyberspace and new forms of "virtuality."

5 See Jean-François Francois Lyotard's *The Postmodern Condition* (Minneapolis: University of Minnesota Press, 1984) for one of the earliest and best accounts of this process. See also, of course, the work of Jean Baudrillard, especially *Amérique* (Paris: Grasset, 1986).

6 See the entry for "flash" in *The American Heritage Dictionary*, 3d ed.

7 I have adopted and adapted the term "transmodern" as well as its incipient descriptive apparatus from Clive Smith, who points also to the "trans/trance modern" framing and release of the subjectivities shaped by modernism and postmodernism. My thanks to him for this timely and suggestive concept.

8 "President Bush tonight accused Gov. Bill Clinton of not telling the truth about his visit to Moscow as a student in the 1960s.... 'I don't want to tell you what I really think, because I don't have the facts,' he said. 'But to go to Moscow one year after Russia crushed Czechoslovakia, not remember who you saw? I really think the answer is, level with the American people." *New York Times*, Oct. 8, 1992.

9 See, for example, *US News and World Report*, Jan. 24, 1994.

10 See, for example, Carole Gallagher, *American Ground Zero: The Secret Nuclear War*, (Cambridge: MIT Press, 1993; publication funded by the Nevada Humanities Committee et al).

11 Beth Katzoff was a student in my fall 1992 seminar at Harvard, "I Like Ike, but I Love Lucy: Women, Popular Culture, and the 1950s." E.g.: "The word 'teenage' had first appeared in the popular press in the 1920s, but the idea that there was a time of life between childhood and adulthood that could be isolated, and that had its own peculiar characteristics, belongs largely to the 1950s." Richard Maltby, ed., *Passing Parade: A History of Popular Culture in the Twentieth Century* (Oxford: Oxford University Press, 1989), 140.

12 See David Riesman, *The Lonely Crowd* (New Haven: Yale University Press, 1961); Deborah Tannen, *You Just Don't Understand* (New York: Ballantine, 1991); Robert Bly, *Iron John: A Book about Men* (Reading, MA: Addison-Wesley, 1990).

13 See Andrew Ross's essay in this collection for thoughts on the obligatory nature of these TV trials.

14 Ellen Messer-Davidow, "Manufacturing the Attack on Liberalized Higher Education," *Social Text* 36 (1993): 43.

15 Messer-Davidow, "Manufacturing the Attack," 44.

16 America on Line (Reuters), Aug. 13, 1994.

17 Messer-Davidow, "Manufacturing the Attack," 44.

18 On the question of the PC campaign, see, for example, my "Illiberal Reporting," in *After Political Correctness: The Humanities and Society in the 1990s*, eds. Christopher Newfield and Ronald Strickland (Boulder, CO: Westview Press, 1995). In France the link is often made between le P(arti) C(ommuniste) and le P(olitically) C(orrect).

19 Earl Latham, ed., *The Meaning of McCarthyism* (New York: Heath, 1973).

20 On the "New McCarthyism," see Bruce Shapiro, "McSniglet," in *Nation*, Feb. 14, 1994. The author suggests that "obsession with sexual conspiracy in the 1990s has replaced the Communist conspiracy mongering of the 1950s." This is an interesting observation, but it risks the implication that the containment of female sexuality was not intimately linked to other forms of containment in the fifties. See, for example, Breines, *Young, White, and Miserable*; Joyce Nelson, *The Perfect Machine: TV in the Nuclear Age* (Toronto: Between the Lines, 1987); or Carol A. B. Warren, *Madwives: Schizophrenic Women in the 1950s* (New Brunswick, NJ: Rutgers University Press, 1987).

21 Hannah Arendt summarized by Dennis H. Wrong, "McCarthyism as Totalitarianism," in Latham, *The Meaning of McCarthyism*, 35.

22 One of the few exceptions to this general inability to respond to attacks from the Right has been the good work of the small but vocal group of academics, a group founded by Professor Gerald Graff, Teachers for a Democratic Culture.

23 See, for example, Ellen Schrecker's excellent *No Ivory Tower: McCarthyism and the Universities* (New York: Oxford University Press, 1986).

24 Messer-Davidow, "Manufacturing the Attack," 49.

25 See Andrew Ross, "Containing Culture in the Cold War," in *No Respect: Intellectuals and Popular Culture* (New York: Routledge, 1989).

26 I wish to acknowledge here Nancy Miller's formulation, one shared many years ago with me in a conversation, and one that has sustained me well during long battles with the right wing over the past couple of years.

27 Virginia Carmichael, *Framing History: The Rosenberg Story and the Cold War* (Minneapolis: University of Minnesota Press, 1993), xi–xiii.

28 I owe many of my first insights into the connections between postmodernism and the Rosenberg Event to conversations with Jenn Meeropol, whose Harvard senior honors thesis remains the most up-to-date and succinctly accurate account of the Rosenberg trial I have seen: see Jennifer Meeropol, "The Framings of Ethel Rosenberg: Gender, Law, Politics, and Culture in Cold War America," (senior essay, Harvard University, 1994).

29 A public opinion survey quoted by Ilene Philipson, *Ethel Rosenberg: Beyond the Myths* (New York: Franklin Watts, 1988), 69.

30 What follows is a compilation and summation of what has been verified according to many different sources on the trial. See, for example (in order of publication): John Wexley, *The Judgment of Julius and Ethel Rosenberg* (New York: Cameron and Kahn, 1955); Walter Schneir and Miriam Schneir, *Invitation to an Inquest: A New Look at the Rosenberg-Sobell Case* (Garden City, NY: Doubleday, 1965); Robert Meeropol and Michael Meeropol, *We Are Your Sons: The Legacy of Ethel and Julius Rosenberg* (Boston: Houghton Mifflin, 1975); and Ronald Radosh and Joyce Milton, *The Rosenberg File: A Search for the Truth* (New York: Holt, 1983). See also Meeropol, "Framings."

31 Schneir and Schneir, *Invitation to an Inquest*, 402.

32 For the definitive analysis of the most famous piece of evidence in the Rosenberg trial—the Jell-O box—see Marjorie Garber's essay in this volume.

33 One of the more bizarre instances of this "borderlanding" would have to be E. L. Doctorow's *The Book of Daniel* (New York: Vintage, 1971).

34 The Broadway smash hit *Angels in America* brought some of the more postmodern aspects of Roy Cohn's persona to life. For the details, see, for example, Sidney Zion, *The Autobiography of Roy Cohn* (Secaucus, NJ: Lyle Stuart, 1988), and Nicholas von Hoffman, *Citizen Cohn* (New York: Doubleday, 1988).

35 See the *Boston Globe*, Aug. 11, 1993, 65, and the *Wall Street Journal*, Aug. 26, 1993.

36 Hal Foster, "Postmodernism: A Preface," in *The Anti-Aesthetic: Essays on Postmodern Culture* (Port Townsend, WA: Bay Press, 1983), xii.

37 For this insight into the relationship between technology and fascism, I am once again indebted to Clive Smith.

38 See, e.g., Messer-Davidow, "Manufacturing the Attack."

39 "The sky above the port was the color of television, tuned to a dead channel" is the first line of William Gibson's cyberpunk classic *Neuromancer* (New York: Ace, 1984), 3.

PART TWO

Agents

Senator Joseph McCarthy.
(AP/Wide World Photos)

9

Before the Rosenbergs

Espionage Scenarios
in the Early Cold War

Ellen Schrecker

Julius and Ethel Rosenberg were typical victims of the McCarthy era, unique only in the severity of the sentence imposed on them. They were or had been Communists and their trial and execution were the culmination of an intensive five-year campaign to root Communism and all the individuals, ideas, and organizations associated with it out of American life. Whether or not the Rosenbergs were spies, most of their fellow citizens thought they were and assumed that their punishment, though extreme, was justified.

That consensus has long since disappeared. Instead of having perpetrated the so-called crime of the century, the Rosenbergs became its victims—convicted on rather meager evidence and sentenced to death by a judge who colluded with the prosecution. No one, not even the most vocal advocates of the couple's guilt, believes that their trial was fair. It was, as Ronald Radosh and Joyce Milton put it, "a grave miscarriage of justice."[1] Among the leading culprits were J. Edgar Hoover, Roy Cohn, Judge Irving Kaufman, and an anti-Communist consensus that allowed the Rosenbergs to be killed and thousands of other political undesirables to be fired, jailed, deported, or otherwise punished.

That consensus did not evolve spontaneously. It had been carefully nurtured and orchestrated by a network of anti-Communist activists. The most important member of that network was, of course, Hoover. Whatever his sexual orientation, there was nothing closeted about J. Edgar Hoover's commitment to anti-Communism. It was his lifelong mission. And he pursued his crusade against Communism with the same passion and brilliance that he devoted to building up the FBI and his and its reputation.[2] But Hoover was not alone. Although the most powerful and certainly most highly regarded witch-hunter in Cold War America, he functioned as part of a broader network of militant anti-Communists who had been peddling their ideological wares for years until the Cold War made it possible for them to impose their view of the Communist menace on the rest of the nation.

They were able to do this because they were able to propagate the notion that members of the Communist Party (CP) threatened America's security. The threat was greatly exaggerated, but in the late 1940s, as relations between the United States and the Soviet Union deteriorated rapidly, previously innocuous activities came to seem increasingly ominous. Moreover, there was enough plausibility in the scenario that Hoover and his allies constructed to convince all but a tiny handful of independent radicals that Communists were dangerous. The party facilitated the process. While it certainly did not *cause* McCarthyism, many of the CP's policies and practices—its secrecy, lack of internal democracy, and above all its loyalty to the Soviet Union—made it possible for most Americans to believe that the Communist Party, though formerly viewed as an unpopular political sect, now endangered the nation.

The Communist threat was quite specific: subversion, sabotage, and espionage. Moreover, by the late 1940s enough evidence had accumulated about the CP's involvement in such activities to convince federal officials and then the rest of the nation that the danger was real—that Communist soldiers might undermine military morale, Communist-led unions might cripple crucial defense industries with strikes, and Communists in sensitive positions might give vital secrets to the Soviet Union. These scenarios were persuasive because they were bolstered by commonly held stereotypes about the nature of Communism and by a few actual cases that seemingly revealed that Communists were, in fact, Soviet agents. Because Hoover and his allies had access to the machinery of the state, at both the local and national levels, they were able to intensify the anxieties surrounding Communism by criminalizing it. Political trials, like that of the Rosenbergs, transformed dissent into felony and portrayed the Communist Party as an illegal conspiracy. They also disseminated the demonized image of Communism by exploiting the individual cases of subversion, sabotage, and espionage that seemed to confirm the existence of a Communist threat.

By the time the Rosenbergs were arrested in the summer of 1950, most Americans probably believed that, as Hoover repeatedly insisted, "any member of the Communist Party is an active or potential Soviet espionage agent."[3] This wildly distorted stereotype, which Hoover and his anti-Communist allies successfully purveyed to the rest of the nation, rested on a highly selective study of the Communist classics, bolstered by the testimony of embittered and/or opportunistic former reds. It dehumanized Communists by perpetrating a highly exaggerated and oversimplified image of American party members—rigid, doctrinaire automatons who unhesitatingly obeyed every order that their party superiors transmitted from Moscow. As Hoover's ghostwriter graphically put it, "The trained member is one on whom the party depends to commit espionage, derail a speeding train, and organize riots. If asked, gun in hand, to assault the Capitol of the United States, he will be expected to obey."[4]

Such a stereotype provided the intellectual underpinning for the anti-Communist crusade. Most important, it contributed to the criminalization of American Communism by supplying an implicit motivation for whatever offense an individual Communist had presumably committed. No defense was possible. Whenever accused Communists tried to present themselves in a favorable light, they would be met by the widely quoted words of Lenin that a Communist must "agree to any and every sacrifice, and even—if need be —resort to all sorts of stratagems, maneuvers and illegal methods, to evasions and subterfuges."[5] No wonder, then, that during the 1950s most Communists relied on the Fifth Amendment; whatever they said in their own defense would be discounted. By the time the Rosenbergs got to court, the notion that Communists were guilty by definition had become so widely accepted that it would have been a surprise if they had escaped conviction.

But such dubious verdicts had not always been the rule. In 1946, for example, it is doubtful that federal prosecutors could have gotten a conviction on the kind of evidence that they brought into Judge Kaufman's courtroom in the spring of 1951. (And, in fact, an attempt to prosecute a Seattle-based Soviet naval officer for espionage early in 1946 ended in acquittal.)[6] It took several years for the automatic assumption of Communist guilt to take hold. The process through which that occurred is important; in the rest of the paper I will try to give a brief overview of the way in which the most damaging scenario of the Communist threat, the notion that Communists were Soviet spies, developed and was disseminated throughout the United States.

The story begins in Berkeley—in the 1930s as well as the '60s a hotbed of radical politics. Berkeley students and teachers supported the unionization drives of Harry Bridges's longshoremen, raised money for the Spanish

Loyalists, and a few even joined the CP. One of the most visible figures in the Berkeley Left was the charismatic physicist and future scientific leader of the atomic bomb project, J. Robert Oppenheimer. His girlfriend, brother, and sister-in-law were in the party, and his wife, whose first husband had been killed in the Spanish Civil War, was a close friend of Steve Nelson, the party's local organizer. Many of Oppenheimer's friends and students were also in or near the CP. Though Oppenheimer had abandoned all his left-wing activities by 1942 when he became the Manhattan Project's scientific director, his previous connections, as well as his later admission that he had been approached to give information to the Russians, aroused the suspicions of the project's security officers who feared (not without reason, it should be noted) that Communist sympathizers might spy for the Soviet Union, at that time, of course, an American ally. The FBI was also concerned about Oppenheimer. It had been collecting information about him even before the war; and in 1941 it had put him on its list of potential subversives to be picked up for custodial detention. In the years that followed, Hoover continued to warn the military authorities and the Truman administration about the distinguished physicist's "Communist affiliations." Nonetheless, because of Oppenheimer's value to the Manhattan Project and his later prominence as the "father of the bomb," he was protected from reprisals until 1953.[7]

His ex-students were not so fortunate. A few of them, David Bohm, David Fox, Max Friedman, Giovanni Rossi Lomanitz, and Joseph Weinberg, worked for the Manhattan Project at the Berkeley Radiation Laboratory during the war. Their political background and activities made them suspect to begin with. Bohm and Fox had been in the party and Lomanitz, though never a card-carrying member, was just as radical. When they tried to organize a union at the Radiation Lab the project's security officers became even more suspicious. The union, the Federation of Architects, Engineers, Chemists, and Technicians, or FAECT, had been established in 1934 by a group of left-wing technicians and civil servants mainly in New York City.[8] Its organizational efforts in navy yards and military depots as well as the obvious presence of Communists like Julius Rosenberg within its ranks convinced military intelligence officials that its activities, in the words of a May 1941 report, "are subversive in intent and definitely interfere with military efficiency and National Defense effort."[9]

Thus, when Lomanitz, Fox, and the other former Oppenheimer students at Berkeley began to organize a FAECT local in the Radiation Laboratory, red lights began to flash throughout the military and intelligence community. In a September 9, 1943 memorandum alerting President Roosevelt to the "very alarming" dangers of FAECT at Berkeley, secretary of war Henry Stimson noted that "it is unquestionable that the union organization will be used to further espionage activity of agents of a foreign power" and asked Roosevelt to have the CIO disband the local.[10] The FBI was also concerned. "The Bureau's attention is directed to the above organization," the local FBI agent in San Francisco wrote his superiors in November 1943, "as one which is believed to constitute a very definite menace to the internal security of this country and one which provides a well-nigh perfect avenue for either Russian-inspired or voluntary espionage for Russian benefit by the Communist Party of the United States."[11]

In fact, as far as the intelligence community was concerned, the Radiation Laboratory's security had already been compromised. Besides organizing a FAECT local, some of the scientists there had been in contact with Steve Nelson, who had been in touch with members of the Soviet consulate. The FBI picked up these contacts from its electronic surveillance of Nelson. Military intelligence officers who had climbed a tree outside of Nelson's house one night claimed that they had seen the young physicist Joseph Weinberg dictate a secret formula to the Communist leader. They had also helped FBI agents eavesdrop on a dinner conversation between Martin Kamen, another Manhattan Project scientist, and a Russian diplomat at a San Francisco restaurant. What further proof was needed? The security people swung into action and forced the main offenders from the project. Lomanitz's draft deferment was canceled; Kamen lost his security clearance and had to work in a shipyard. The FAECT local, of course, disappeared.[12] The case did not, even though there was no concrete evidence that any spying had ever taken place. Nelson, Weinberg, and Kamen insisted that they had never done anything wrong and offered plausible explanations for their alleged espionage activities, but the intelligence officers and FBI agents involved remained convinced that the left-wing Radiation Laboratory scientists had been Soviet agents.[13]

Throughout the late 1940s, the FBI which took over the case from military intelligence continued to press the investigation. It questioned these scientists repeatedly, but to no avail. By then a new political agenda lent urgency to the quest for spies within the Manhattan Project, for the espionage issue now became involved with the controversy about the peacetime uses of atomic energy. Should the United States try to avoid an arms race by offering to share the results of its scientific research? Or should it retain its monopoly over the development of atomic energy and guard the secret of the bomb as vigilantly as it had during the war? Most of the scientists involved with the bomb project realized that the so-called "secret" of the bomb did not exist and that it would be only a matter of time before the other major industrial nations, in particular the Soviet Union, would be able to build their own atomic weapons. The military establishment disagreed. Its members could not believe that any other power—especially one as allegedly backward and barbaric as the Soviet Union—could replicate the American feat. To share scientific knowledge was to weaken the United States and lessen, not increase, the chances of world peace.[14]

The battle was joined over the issue of civilian control of atomic energy. When they discovered that Congress was about to pass a measure putting nuclear matters entirely in the hands of the armed services, the Manhattan Project scientists organized a massive lobbying effort.[15] The military and its allies fought back. One of their main weapons was an attempt to discredit the scientific community, to portray its members as soft-headed and even disloyal. The FBI supported these efforts. As early as the fall of 1945, just as the Senate was debating the matter, Hoover began sending the White House reports on some of the scientists and others who were trying to ensure civilian control over the development of atomic energy. Oppenheimer was probably the most well known of these people, but the bureau seemed to be equally as concerned about Edward U. Condon, a former Manhattan Project physicist who had just been named to head the Bureau of Standards within the Department of Commerce. Hoover noted Condon's "pro-Soviet attitude" and commented at length on his contacts with other people on the Left.[16] These attacks escalated over the next few years and eventually became public in the spring of 1948, when Parnell Thomas, chairman of the House Un-American Activities Committee (HUAC), accused Condon of being "one of the weakest links in our atomic security."[17]

The accusations and investigations soon spread to the other left-wing scientists in the Manhattan Project. California's Un-American Activities Committee called up some of the Berkeley Radiation Laboratory people in 1946, and HUAC subpoenaed them two years later, when it began to investigate Robert Oppenheimer, his physicist brother Frank, and the alleged Communist infiltration of the atomic bomb project. The committee's efforts proved no more successful than the FBI's. It could find no espionage, though some of the scientists it questioned over the next few years did admit that they had been in the party. Others denied HUAC's charges and a few, Lomanitz, Bohm, and Fox among them, took the Fifth Amendment and refused to answer any questions about their politics.[18]

HUAC's failure to uncover any real atom spies was irrelevant. The inquiry served other functions. At the time it began its investigation of the Berkeley Radiation Laboratory, the committee was just coming into its own as a vehicle for publicizing the threat of Communist espionage. It collaborated closely with the FBI and offered the bureau an invaluable forum for airing charges in cases that could never be prosecuted. In the specific case of Oppenheimer's left-wing students, the HUAC hearings were crucial for disseminating the notion that, as the committee's spokesmen repeatedly alleged, these scientists "did deliver to the Soviet government every piece of scientific information they had from the Radiation Laboratory." The hearings also served more partisan purposes. They gave the political opponents of the Truman administration an opportunity to attack it as unconcerned about national security, and they reinforced the unfavorable image of scientists, thus helping the military regain control of the atomic energy program.[19]

In many respects, HUAC and the other committees were an even more useful mechanism for disseminating the anti-Communist message than criminal prosecutions, for they were unconstrained by legal procedures and rules of evidence. They could punish political undesirables by exposure and the threat of a contempt citation. Among the committees' other contributions to the process of demonizing Communism that made the Rosenberg case possible was the wide publicity they gave to the Fifth Amendment and to the notion that people who refused to answer questions about Communism were actually admitting their guilt—a notion that was to prove particularly lethal to the Rosenbergs. The Radiation Laboratory hearings were an early instance in which the committee followed up on the refusal of some of its witnesses to cooperate with it by trying to prosecute them—though not, it should be noted, for espionage. The men who had taken the Fifth were indicted for contempt of Congress. And Joseph Weinberg, whom the committee had sensationally labeled in its reports as "Scientist X," was prosecuted for perjury. He had denied knowing Steve Nelson, not to mention handing over atomic secrets to him. Ultimately all the former Berkeley scientists were acquitted. But the damage had been done. Most of them lost their jobs, and, more important, the publicity that accompanied their cases reinforced the connection between Communism and atomic espionage in the public mind.[20]

Exaggerated as that perception became, it was nonetheless true that there had been spies on the Manhattan Project. And it was also true that many people who were in or near the Communist Party, whether in the Manhattan Project or elsewhere, had given secret information to the Soviet Union. And as evidence about all these activities began to accumulate in the late 1940s, the notion that Communists were Soviet agents became increasingly widespread.

The first solid evidence of such espionage surfaced in Ottawa, Canada, on the evening of September 5, 1945, only a few weeks after the war had ended, when Igor Gouzenko, a cipher clerk in the Soviet Embassy defected from his post, taking with him a sheaf of documents indicating that over twenty pseudonymously identified British and Canadian citizens had been giving information to the Soviet Union. One, the British physicist Alan Nunn May, had been involved in the Manhattan Project and had given a few samples of enriched uranium to his Russian contacts. The other agents were Canadian scientists and bureaucrats who handed over technical and political data of varying value. Most of them belonged to a secret Communist Party unit of middle-class intellectuals and had been recruited as spies by party officials at Moscow's request. Though some of these people denied Gouzenko's charges, others admitted them and were fairly open about their activities, for they did not feel that they had done anything seriously wrong. The Soviet Union was an ally and they believed that they had been furthering the war effort.[21]

Since the allies were still hoping to maintain amicable relations with the Soviet Union, the Canadian government did not immediately act on Gouzenko's revelations beyond informing the British and American authorities about them. Gouzenko also claimed that similar espionage had taken place in the United States, though he had no proof to back up the charge. Nonetheless, in his reports to the White House about the case, Hoover passed on Gouzenko's allegation that he had heard that "an assistant to an Assistant Secretary of State under Mr. Stettinius, was a paid Soviet spy."[22] The Truman administration, however, seemed unconcerned about the matter and the Gouzenko case remained buried until March 1946, when information about it was leaked to the Washington columnist Drew Person, probably by military officials who hoped that revelations about espionage would scuttle plans for civilian control of atomic energy.[23]

In the meantime, the FBI had found another spy ring to reinforce its conviction that American Communists were Soviet agents. The spies in question were a group of middle-level federal officials who, Elizabeth Bentley told the bureau, had been giving her material for transmission to the Soviet Union. Dubbed "the Red Spy Queen" by the media, Bentley was a thirty-seven-year-old Vassar graduate who approached the FBI's New York field office in early November 1945 to talk about her experiences in the Soviet underground. Her lover, a high-level party functionary, had recruited her, so Bentley claimed, and had given her the task of ferrying government secrets from a group of secret Communists in Washington to her Russian handlers in New York City.

She named about eighty people—Alger Hiss (whom she first identified as Eugene) and an assistant secretary of the treasury, Harry Dexter White, among them. Her most valuable agents, Bentley claimed, worked under the direction of a Treasury Department employee named Nathan Gregory Silvermaster. Hoover immediately informed the White House of Bentley's charges and then set about trying to prove them.[24] The bureau gave the case top priority and assigned 250 agents to it. But despite the intensive surveillance and wiretapping of the main suspects, the only solid evidence the FBI could find was the photographic darkroom that Silvermaster had in his basement and the fact that he and Bentley's other agents seemed to be friends.[25]

These people were not unknown to the bureau. Most of them were the kind of politically active New Dealers who supported left-wing causes or gave money to the Spanish Republicans. And it is quite likely that some of them were in the Communist Party. Many of them had already been investigated by the FBI in accordance with the Roosevelt administration's attempt to rebut HUAC's early charges that there were Communists in official posts. The main investigations took place in 1942 after the committee's chairman sent a list of 1,124 allegedly disloyal employees to the attorney general in October 1941.[26] The bureau interviewed most of the people on the list and sent reports on them to the agencies they worked for. It also compiled five volumes of detailed findings that Hoover wanted to submit to Congress. But, since Roosevelt was more interested in discrediting HUAC than in exposing Communists, the administration muffled the investigation and few of the people under suspicion lost their jobs. The abortive inquiry festered in the FBI's institutional memory, however, for Hoover and his agents were sure that many of the people they had investigated should have been dismissed. Bentley's charges only confirmed their suspicions and heightened Hoover's growing conviction that the Democratic administration was soft on Communism.[27]

But despite its all-out efforts to corroborate Bentley's allegations, the bureau had not unearthed enough evidence for a successful criminal prosecution. Accordingly, Hoover did not want to take the case to court. He doubted that a prosecution would succeed, and he looked for other ways to punish the alleged conspirators and publicize Bentley's story. The Justice Department, then under enormous pressure to prove that it was alert to the dangers of Communism, ignored Hoover's advice and convened a special grand jury. As the FBI director had suspected, the evidence was too weak even for an indictment. All the people Bentley had fingered either insisted on their innocence or took the Fifth, and the federal prosecutors had to drop the case.[28]

But other venues existed. And although Bentley's alleged agents could not be prosecuted for espionage, the charges against them could still be aired by friendly journalists and congressional committees. By the summer of 1948, when Bentley went before HUAC, the committee was still in the process of working out its role in the anti-Communist crusade. As we have already noted with regard to the Berkeley Radiation Laboratory scientists, congressional investigations were crucial in disseminating the ideological scenarios about the Communist menace. The hearings that HUAC held in August 1948 to showcase Bentley's charges were the most important of the Cold War, for they produced the Hiss case. In order to bolster Bentley's testimony, the committee called up a *Time* magazine editor named Whittaker Chambers, who claimed that he had preceded Bentley as the courier servicing the Communist underground in Washington. He named many of the same people Bentley had, including Alger Hiss. Over the next few months Chambers and HUAC (and especially HUAC's most ambitious and effective member, the first-term California congressman Richard M. Nixon) pursued the case against Hiss and ultimately produced what appeared to be documentary evidence that Hiss and other federal officials had been giving information to the Russians. Though the Hiss case did not involve *atomic* espionage, it certainly reinforced the notion that Communists spied.[29]

In March 1949 the FBI found yet another spy. She was Judith Coplon, a twenty-eight-year-old Justice Department employee who was arrested on a downtown street in New York City in the company of Valentin Gubitchev, a Soviet engineer who worked for the United Nations. In Coplon's pocketbook was a handwritten memorandum containing allegedly top secret information about American counterintelligence work and the efforts of Amtorg, the Soviet Union's trading company, to obtain a scientific instrument used in making an atomic bomb. There was also a sealed package that had once contained a pair of stockings that held about thirty so-called data slips, little pieces of paper with information from the FBI reports that Coplon read during the course of her work as a political analyst in the Justice Department's Foreign Agents Registration section. The bureau had had Coplon under surveillance for several months and had observed two earlier rendezvous between her and Gubitchev in which the two had acted as if they were trying to avoid being followed. They wandered around the streets of Washington Heights, jumped in and out of subway cars, and once simply passed each other walking in different directions on the sidewalk.[30]

Coplon had two trials: one in Washington for taking the documents and a second in New York for trying to pass them to the Russians. Though she certainly seemed to have been sympathetic to the Left, her political proclivities never became important to her case. No doubt because the physical evidence against Coplon was so strong, the prosecution did not even try to show that she had Communist connections. Coplon and her attorney insisted that she had been framed and that her trysts with Gubitchev were purely romantic. Her explanations were not particularly convincing and she was speedily convicted. However, because the FBI had illegally wiretapped Coplon's conversations with her attorney, she was eventually freed on appeal. Still, her legal victory did not erase the evidence of her apparent espionage from the mind of the public. Her apprehension ostensibly proved that as late as the spring of 1949 there were Soviet spies within the federal government.

As a result, by the time the Soviet Union detonated an atomic bomb in August 1949, it was not hard to believe that espionage agents were responsible for the Soviet feat. The proponents of the American atomic monopoly had been so successful in propagating the notion of the "secret" of atomic energy and the anti-Communist network had been so successful in disseminating the notion that Communists spied that the Rosenberg case seemed almost inevitable.

What led the FBI via Fuchs, Gold, and Greenglass to the Rosenbergs remains unclear. In a 1986 memoir the former FBI agent Robert J. Lamphere claims that the bureau was alerted to Fuchs's identity in September 1949 when government cryptologists deciphered a 1944 cable from the Soviet consulate in New York to the KGB in Moscow that indicated the presence of an agent within the British delegation at Los Alamos. Lamphere also claims that other deciphered messages led the bureau to Coplon and even gave clues about the Rosenbergs themselves.[31] The problem here is that we have only Lamphere's word to go on. Code breaking is such delicate business that, as I was told by an FBI employee, we won't see any materials from such an operation in our lifetime.

Even without the decoded cables, the FBI could have stumbled on the Rosenbergs during the course of its frenzied search for Fuchs's collaborators, for some of the principals had connections to the other espionage cases of the period. Fuchs's name had been in the address book of one of Gouzenko's alleged agents. Harry Gold had been fingered by Bentley. And Julius Rosenberg was a member of FAECT whose CP connections had long been known to the FBI.[32] Were he and his wife Soviet agents? I'm not sure that we'll ever know. But certainly by the summer of 1950 it had become all too easy for the FBI to make the case that a Communist engineer who could have had an opportunity to obtain atomic secrets and who refused to cooperate with government investigators was a Russian spy.

Ironically, the Rosenbergs' execution reinforced the national belief in the dangers of Communism that had made their execution possible. Just as the logic of the Cold War demanded a demonized and stereotyped enemy, so too it required an idealized American state, one that, by definition, could not possibly kill innocent people. Psychologically, therefore, if not legally, the execution of the Rosenbergs provided the most persuasive possible evidence that they—and by extension all Communists—had endangered American security. Their case contributed to McCarthyism even as it was shaped by it.

NOTES

1 Ronald Radosh and Joyce Milton, *The Rosenberg File: A Search for the Truth* (New York: Holt, 1983), 451.

2 The most useful books on Hoover's life and work are Richard Gid Powers, *Secrecy and Power: The Life of J. Edgar Hoover* (New York: Free Press, 1987), and Athan Theoharis and John Stuart Cox, *The Boss: J. Edgar Hoover and the Great American Inquisition* (Philadelphia: Temple University Press, 1988).

3 This statement or some variant thereof appears routinely in almost every report the FBI disseminated during the early Cold War years. It soon made its way into the general discourse of federal officials and others who accepted the formulation without question, thus ensuring its wider dissemination. In his important 1946 assessment of the Soviet threat, President Truman's special assistant Clark Clifford simply appropriated the FBI's language about the espionage danger. See Clark Clifford, "American Relations with the Soviet Union," George M. Elsey papers, Box 63, folder, Foreign Relations, Russia (1946 report) (3), and FBI report, "Soviet Activities in the United States," July 25, 1946, Clark M. Clifford papers, Box 15, folder (Russia—Folder 5), both in Harry S. Truman Library, Independence, Missouri (hereafter HSTL).

4 J. Edgar Hoover, *Masters of Deceit* (New York: Holt, 1959), 77.

5 This passage appeared everywhere. It was cited in Hoover's *Masters of Deceit* (201), quoted by prosecution witnesses at the big Smith Act trial of the Communist Party in 1949, and used by the CIO's leadership to justify the expulsion of the Left-led unions in 1950.

6 The case, that of Nicholai Redin, has been largely overlooked by historians. See Daniel Leab, "A Speck on the Turtle's Neck: The Arrest, Trial, and Acquittal by a U.S. Jury of Soviet Naval Lt. N. Redin in 1946," paper delivered at the annual meeting of the Organization of American Historians, Anaheim, California, Apr. 16, 1993.

7 Custodial detention memo, May 27, 1941, in J. Robert Oppenheimer, San Francisco file, no. 1; Hoover to James F. Byrnes, Nov. 15, 1945, Hoover to Harry Hawkins Vaughan, Nov. 15, 1945, Oppenheimer, HQ file, no. 20; Hoover to Vaughan, Feb. 28, 1947, in Harry S. Truman, President's Secretary File, Box 167, Subject File, FBI Atomic Bomb, HSTL. The best single book on Oppenheimer and his case is still Philip M. Stern, *The Oppenheimer Case: Security on Trial* (New York: Harper, 1969). See also Barton J. Bernstein, "The Oppenheimer Loyalty-Security Case Reconsidered," *Stanford Law Review* 42, no. 6 (July 1990): 1383–1484, and the transcript of Oppenheimer's 1954 hearing itself, United States Atomic Energy Commission, *In the Matter of J. Robert Oppenheimer* (Cambridge: MIT Press, 1970).

8 There is almost no scholarship on FAECT apart from Bernard Palmer, "The

Heritage of Architects, Engineers, Chemists, and Technicians (FAECT-CIO)," in *The Cold War against Labor*, ed. Ann Fagan Ginger and David Christiano (Berkeley: Meiklejohn Civil Liberties Institute, 1987), 378–84. I have also relied on two interviews, one with Martin Cooper that Rachel Bernstein conducted in December 1985 and one I did with Beryl Gilman in November 1993.

9 S. V. Constant [G–2] to Assistant Chief of Staff, G–2, May 20, 1941, in FAECT FBI file, no serial number.

10 Henry Stimson, memorandum for the president, Sept. 9, 1943, in File W3, Map Room, 171, Franklin D. Roosevelt Library. (I am not sure this citation is correct, since a xerox of the document was sent to me by a colleague and I do not know its precise location in the records.)

11 N. J. L. Pieper letter to Director, Nov. 26, 1943, FAECT FBI file, no. 172.

12 For a more complete description of the incidents surrounding the Berkeley Radiation Laboratory, see Ellen W. Schrecker, *No Ivory Tower: McCarthyism and the Universities* (New York: Oxford University Press, 1986), 130–38. See also Warren Olney III, Oral History Interview, 351–54, Bancroft Library, University of California, Berkeley.

13 The spy charges against the Berkeley scientists are presented in a widely disseminated FBI report of Mar. 5, 1946, "U.S. [sic] Infiltration of the Radiation Laboratory, University of California, Berkeley, California."

14 Gregg Herken's *The Winning Weapon* (New York: Knopf, 1980) contains a good discussion of the fallacy of the "secret" of the bomb.

15 Alice Kimball Smith, *A Peril and a Hope* (Chicago: University of Chicago Press, 1965), describes the scientists' campaign to avert military control of atomic energy.

16 Hoover to George E. Allen, Nov. 6, 1945, Hoover to Vaughan, Dec. 7, 1945, both in HST-PSF, Subject File, Box 167, FBI, "C," HSTL.

17 A useful summary of the Condon case (though one that does not use FBI materials) is Jessica Wang, "Science, Security, and the Cold War: The Case of E. U. Condon," *Isis* 83, no. 2 (June 1992): 238–69.

18 For the Radiation Laboratory hearings, see House Committee on Un-American Activities, "Excerpts from Hearings Regarding Investigation of Communist Activities in Connection with the Atom Bomb," Sept. 9, 14, 16, 1948, 80th Cong., 2d sess.; "Hearings Regarding Communist Infiltration of Radiation Laboratory and Atomic Bomb Project at the University of California, Berkeley, Calif., vol. 1: Apr. 22, 26, May 25, June 10, 14, 1949; vol. 2 (identification of Scientist X): Aug. 26, 1949, July 1, Sept. 10, 1948, Aug. 14, Sept. 14, 27, 1949, 81st Cong., 1st sess.; vol. 3: Dec. 20–22, 1950, 81st Cong. 2d sess.

19 On the relationship between HUAC and the FBI, see Kenneth O'Reilly, *Hoover and the Un-Americans: The FBI, HUAC, and the Red Menace* (Philadelphia: Temple University Press, 1983). See also HUAC, "Report on

Soviet Espionage Activities in Connection with the Atom Bomb," Sept. 27, 1948; Rep. Burr Harrison, remarks, HUAC, Dec. 20, 1950, 81st Cong., 2d sess., 3422.

20 Schrecker, *No Ivory Tower*, 139–48.

21 The most useful sources on the Gouzenko case are Merrily Weisbord, *The Strangest Dream: Canadian Communists, the Spy Trials, and the Cold War* (Toronto: Lester and Orpen Dennys, 1983); Royal Commission to Investigate the Facts..., *The Report of the Royal Commission* (Ottawa: E. Clothier, 1946); Robert Bothwell and J. L. Granatstein, eds., *The Gouzenko Transcripts* (Ottawa: Deneau, [1983]).

22 Bothwell and Granatstein, *The Gouzenko Transcripts*, 9–10, 136; Hoover to Matthew Connelly, Sept. 12, 18, 27, 1945, in HST-PSF, Box 167, Subject File, FBI Atomic Bomb, HSTL.

23 According to Gregg Herken, who has investigated the leaks about the Gouzenko case, the most likely source of the leak was Major General Leslie Groves, the head of the Manhattan Project. Herken, *The Winning Weapon*, 114–36, 362–63.

24 Hoover to Harry Hawkins Vaughan, Nov. 8, 1945, HST-PSF, Subject File, Box 169, FBI, "S," HSTL.

25 C. W. Evans to G. C. Callan, Nov. 26, 1945, Silvermaster-Bentley HQ file, no. 75; Ladd to E. A. Tamm, Nov. 19, 1945, ibid., no. 37; R. C. Hendon to Tolson, Nov. 19, 1945, ibid., no. 38; H. B. Fletcher to Ladd, Feb. 2, 1950, Harry Dexter White HQ file, no serial number; Guy Hottel, Summary Report, Nov. 16, 1950, ibid., no. 21; "Budget Estimates, Federal Bureau of Investigation, Nov. 30, 1945," HST-PSF, Box 167, Subject File, FBI "B," HSTL.

26 August Raymond Ogden, *The Dies Committee* (1945; reprint, Westport, CT: Greenwood Press, 1984), 244–48; D. M. Ladd, memo, for E. A. Tamm, March 30, 1942, Harry Dexter White, HQ file, no. 3.

27 Ladd, memo, for E. A. Tamm, Mar. 30, 1942, in Harry Dexter White, HQ file, no. 3, Ladd to Hoover, Nov. 27, 1953, ibid., no serial number.

28 Ladd to Director, Nov. 12, 1953, White HQ file, no. 59; L. V. Boardman to Director, Aug. 26, 1954, encl. summary brief on H. D. White, ibid., no. 1245.

29 The Hiss case remains unsolved. For persuasive presentations of the differing sides, see Allen Weinstein, *Perjury: The Hiss-Chambers Case* (New York: Knopf, 1978), and Athan G. Theoharis, ed., *Beyond the Hiss Case: The FBI, Congress, and the Cold War* (Philadelphia: Temple University Press, 1982).

30 There is almost no scholarship on the Coplon case. I have tried unsuccessfully to get her FBI files released. Coplon herself is alive and well and living in Brooklyn but will not talk about the case. Accordingly, I have based most of this narrative on the trial transcript that was microfilmed in the 1950s under the auspices of the Ford Foundation's Fund for the Republic: *Coplon v. United States*, Trial Record, Record on Appeal, microfilm edition.

In his memoir the former FBI special agent Robert Lamphere claims that the Bureau was alerted to Coplon's activities by the deciphering of an intercepted wartime cable from the Russian consulate in New York. See Robert J. Lamphere and Tom Schachtman, *The FBI-KGB War: A Special Agent's Story* (New York: Random House, 1986), 99–125.

31 Lamphere and Schachtman, *The FBI-KGB War*.

32 [Name deleted], New York City, report, Mar. 23, 1945, in FAECT, file no. 289.

Sean Connery as James Bond.
(AP/Wide World Photos)

10

Helplessness and Heartlessness

Irving Howe, James Bond, and the Rosenbergs

Bruce Robbins

In 1953 Irving Howe accepted a teaching job in the English department of Brandeis University. It was also in 1953 that the first James Bond novel, *Casino Royal*, was published.[1] These two events, though not as momentous as the execution of the Rosenbergs in the same year, are linked to it and to each other by a motif of profitable treachery. By May 1953, the first printing of *Casino Royal* had sold out. Forty-odd years later, it is now the baby-boomer, ex-1960s generation of intellectuals that is said to have sold out—especially those of us who teach in English departments rather than doing "real" politics and who teach things like James Bond rather than "real" literature. And these charges have come, with a certain historical irony, from Irving Howe and the generation of New York intellectuals who, like him, eagerly approved the official story of the Rosenbergs' betrayal. What I have to say about the supposed betrayals of intellectuals and spies, reflections in a time that speaks more readily about a supposed "McCarthyism of the Left" than about the McCarthyism that helped kill the Rosenbergs, will be in favor of selling out in both senses.[2]

As Andrew Ross and Virginia Carmichael have suggested, the figure of the "atom spy," a new sort of villain hastily constructed in the postwar period, prepared the ground both for the success of the James Bond novels and for the frame-up of Julius and Ethel Rosenberg. The spy became a compelling figure of the national imagination, in Ross's words, "despite, or perhaps because of the fact that there was no real 'secret' to give away—the bomb had been produced from a fund of international wartime knowledge."[3] By means of the spy, one might say, international knowledge took on the appearance of national secrets. Remembering the Rosenbergs, we should try to recall the full strangeness of this transformation. First, the strangeness of the notion that knowledge can and should be *national*—that it can and should be restricted by a citizen's loyalties to his or her country. And second, the strange parallel between this nationalizing of knowledge and another, more familiar form of monopoly: to create the impression that nationally significant secrets exist, that our national security or welfare depends on maintaining an unequal distribution of knowledge and ignorance is, of course, a founding strategy of professionalism, a process by which, at least in the usual view, would-be professionals including literary critics like Howe and myself—"double agents," in Morris Dickstein's phrase—supply themselves with a quantity of significant knowledge that they can control, thereby claiming the right to a limited but not negligible autonomy.[4]

The suddenness of this linkage between the nationalizing of knowledge and the professionalizing of knowledge can be measured if we think of an event that occurred only five years before the Rosenberg trial in 1951. At the Nuremberg trials of 1946, as everyone knows, the Nazi war criminals claimed that they had been "just doing their job." And just doing your job meant, in effect, not acting on the hypothetical universalist or internationalist dictates of humanity but submitting to what your government presented as the interests of your nation. This position, you will remember, was rejected by the court. The Nazis who tried to affirm a double immunity, professional and national, were, of course, found guilty. You can calculate the moral distance traveled by McCarthyism, therefore, if you consider that the Rosenbergs were executed because they were believed to have done just what the Nazi war criminals were executed for *not* doing, what we were implicitly telling the Nazis they *should* have done. That is, what even the Oak Ridge scientists were saying had to be done in the interests of humanity: "to take [knowledge of the bomb] out of the control of any one nation—including our own."[5]

We have clearly come a long way from such skepticism about the nation, or from the pragmatic cosmopolitanism expressed by Walter Lippmann in October 1945: "to those who contend that we should guard this secret, we must, I believe, reply that on the contrary the safest course is to guard against its being a secret anywhere."[6] Accustomed as we have become to what might be called the national-professional intellectual dedicated to the control of national secrets, we may need to be reminded that, like the "atom spy," this figure had to be created. According to Zygmunt Bauman, the word "intellectual" was coined, during the Dreyfus affair, at a time when professional specialization was already well developed. "The word was thus a rallying call, sounded over the closely guarded frontiers of professions."[7] The analogy between professional and national frontiers is obviously not an arbitrary one. In taking their expertise into the marketplace in defense of a convicted German spy, the Dreyfusards were held by their opponents to be betraying both their discipline and their nation at the same time. Thus Julien Benda's classic statement of the intellectual vocation, *The Treason of the Intellectuals* (1928), which was forged in the battle over Dreyfus, uses the same terms but in reverse. For Benda the betrayal begins when considerable numbers of people "feel that for the sake of the prosperity of their own occupations it is essential for them to belong to a powerful group which can make itself feared"—that is, with "the feeling that from a professional point of view they have an interest in belonging to a powerful nation." "Today," he concludes darkly, "the game is over. Humanity is national. The layman has won…. The man of science, the artist, the philosopher are attached to their nations as much as the day laborer and the merchant."[8]

To say this, of course, was also to enact an exception to it, and (at whatever risk to the logic of his argument) to appeal to others to make themselves exceptional in the same way. If this appeal has been better received among scientists, artists, and philosophers than Benda seemed to judge possible, if it has even become a general creed for intellectuals in all sorts of disciplines and occupations, it is because neither the nation nor the profession has ever exhausted the possibilities within its field—or, more precisely, because each has always required, and has always been open to transformation by, crossings of its own borders that gave the appearance of treasonous intent. In other words, the tightening alliance between nationalism and professionalism has been accompanied at every stage by a cosmopolitan countertradition, if also often an antiprofessional one. Speaking in this tradition, Jean-Paul Sartre defined the intellectual as "someone who concerns himself with what is none of his business." And Sartre's response to what he called the "legal lynching" of the Rosenbergs was consistent with the tradition's obstreperous internationalism: "You thought that the murder of the Rosenbergs was a private settling of scores," he declared the day after the execution. "A hundred thousand voices kept telling you: 'They are innocent.' And you stupidly answered: 'We punish our citizens according to our law. This is none of your business.' Well, actually the Rosenberg affair is our business: when two innocents are sentenced to death, it is the whole world's business.'"[9]

Like Sartre and like the other New York intellectuals, Irving Howe refused to see his intellectual business as shaped or constrained by a discipline or profession.[10] He celebrated "the idea of the intellectual as antispecialist, the writer whose specialty is not to have one."[11] But Howe's response to the Rosenbergs, which differs both from Sartre's and from that of his fellow New Yorkers, shows how the "antispecialist" could be subordinated to the emerging national-professional synthesis. As Andrew Ross has reminded us, New York intellectuals like Robert Warshow and Leslie Fiedler chose to intervene in the case from a strange angle: they mocked the Rosenbergs' prose style. Reviewing the *Death House Letters*, a collection of private-but-public writings published while the Rosenbergs were appealing their sentence, Fiedler and Warshow ridiculed their "secondhand" imitations, whether of Soviet propaganda or of "literary" effects to which the uneducated ought not aspire.[12] There is a hidden logic in this apparent obliqueness. To show what is lacking from the letters is also to show what is *not* lacking from, or indeed what is constitutive of, the professional literary critic: namely, private (that is, apolitical) authenticity and command of genuine, original literariness.

Howe's retrospective comments further this logic while making a discrimination. "Warshow and Fiedler scored points: who, against the Rosenbergs, could not?... Very well, the Rosenbergs were entrapped in Stalinist devices; but surely at the moment what counted much more was that, innocent or guilty, they were waiting to be killed. Was it not heartless to write in this spirit, even if the Rosenbergs were indeed the pure besotted dupes one took them for?... That the Rosenbergs were innocent I very much doubted; that they were helpless anyone could see."[13] As always, Howe chooses his words carefully. He separates off the public guilt of the Rosenbergs, which he does not doubt, from their private helplessness, which demands that one not be "heartless." That is, he does to the Rosenbergs just what they refused to do to themselves: he rests a claim for mercy on private selves, and on a private standard, that are incongruous with their publicly chosen positions. And Howe does so for motives that I would describe as national-professional. The domain of helplessness, helplessness that has its own ambiguous but afflicted innocence and that thus precludes heartlessness, is of course the domain of the *Death House Letters*, but it is also the domain of letters itself, or, one might say, the domain of literature. Literary criticism, according to Howe, was "a surrogate mode of speech for people blocked in public life."[14] For the New York intellectuals, the Rosenbergs helped define this sense of public blockage, which both split the Left and gave one of its tendencies a new channel. Alfred Kazin wrote about the Rosenberg case: "It seemed impossible in public to admit doubts, divisions, nuances, contradictions, hesitations, lost illusions."[15] One wants to add, of course, that there exists a domain in which "doubts, divisions, nuances, contradictions" *can* be expressed, in which it is precisely such things that one is *trained* to express. It is familiar to many of us as the public, professional domain of literary criticism. But I ask you to think of it, more specifically, as the cultural domain that Howe and the New York intellectuals, for all their pugnacious antiprofessional worldliness, were helping to institute as a professional knowledge base—the base for a profession that steadfastly denied that it was a profession, and the base from which they would then go on, thirty years later, to attack multiculturalism and "political correctness" as a supposed "new McCarthyism." Setting themselves off against the spy, who possessed knowledge that was powerful, these antiprofessional professionals would be content with culture, or knowledge that was not powerful but heartfelt. By this self-definition they would make sure that culture remained a site that, faced with the risk of resembling the heartlessness of the Rosenbergs' executioners, could neither accept power from nor bestow power on any social group.[16] Hence knowledge of direct pertinence to women, African Americans, gays and lesbians, or any other constituency— knowledge that participates in a recomposition of cultural capital and thus at the same time, however slowly and frustratingly, in a recomposition of social authority, knowledge of the sort that the academy of the 1990s has begun to take as its mission to propagate—becomes illegitimate: a sellout. And all the more of a sell-out to the extent that, like the antifascist spirit of the Second World War but unlike the national spirit of "just doing your job," this new multicultural knowledge strives to be neither literary nor nationalist, in the usual heartening sense of those terms.[17]

There is something paradoxical about the fact that the trajectory of the New York intellectuals can be described, on the one hand, as a "journey from politics to literature" (Howe's phrase about his own career) and, on the other hand, as a move from cosmopolitanism to national identity, an abandonment of (again in Howe's words) "the sterilities of their earlier 'internationalist' position."[18] Given the overarching narrative of increasing identification with national and institutional power that observers have ascribed to them, one might have imagined their endpoint as a conjunction of the two weightier or more powerful terms, nationalism and politics, at the expense of the two more ethereal terms, cosmopolitanism and literature.[19] What we have instead, I would suggest, is a narrative of literary professionalization that works hard to resolve their contradictions into the new identity of the national-professional intellectual.

The sense of nation, Benedict Anderson writes with a certain lyricism, is a "deep, horizontal comradeship."[20] According to Anderson, the nation takes the place of religion, becomes "the most universally legitimate value in the political life of our time,"[21] because people feel so deeply about it that they are willing to die for it. But the same does not hold, in his view, for the sort of internationalism that shouted its solidarity with the Rosenbergs. "Who," Anderson asks pointedly, "will willingly die for Comecon or the EEC?"[22] With perhaps a trace of self-contempt, Anderson thus disposes of the Abraham Lincoln Brigade, Médecins sans frontières, and Amnesty International, allowing the internationalist or cosmopolitan to become a sub- or inhuman subject unwilling to die for anything—floating in a chilly void, without the warmth of any real emotional attachment.[23] This is the cold that Howe and his generation come in from. But if, as they affirmed, cosmopolitanism could not be sustained on the emotional level of politics, some of it could be salvaged in the diminished, unthreatening form of literature—and with it some of the critical distance it guaranteed from the critic's own society. And if political activity could not be founded on attention to literature, as they also affirmed, some of the self-dramatizing or self-legitimizing that politics seemed to offer could be salvaged by redefining literature as a site of national identity—and with it a usefully heartfelt reconnection to the critic's own society.

The paradox of private helplessness as a source of professional strength is neatly illustrated by a page in Howe's autobiography. On this page we read first of the death of his father and then of the sudden and unexpectedly lucrative success of *World of Our Fathers*. He judged his father to be "weak," Howe says—the quotation marks are Howe's own—and this is why the son could never "speak words of love" to him.[24] The love finally comes out, however, at the point of coincidence when the father dies and *World of Our Fathers*, which is "no more than an extension of what I knew about him," becomes a best-seller. It is hard to avoid the conclusion that the secret of this achievement of loving, reverential expression is the cultural demise that is a sort of collective consummation of the father's weakness. The ultimate helplessness of death, transferred from the father to the father's world, allows the son to take on the superior role of professional rescuer, the chronicler and sustainer of what is otherwise, luckily for him, doomed to nonexistence. The point about the Yiddish culture depicted in *World of Our Fathers*, as Howe himself recognized, was not its new or continuing usefulness for people seeking to "find their roots," but rather the moving prospect of its imminent disappearance. "My book was not a beginning, it was another step to the end."[25] In this sense, the apparent particularity of this Yiddish culture is misleading, for *World of Our Fathers* is a flawless representative of Culture with a capital C, at least as it is envisaged by professionalism's self-legitimizing "salvage paradigm." As T. S. Eliot and the other modernist founders of literary study had discovered, people would pay to contemplate the extinction of helpless cultural species, and the more helpless the better. The professional who uttered a heartfelt lament for what the inhabitants of the wasteland had lost would never be suspected of a profit-making interest in keeping the wasteland as wasted as possible. Working the pathos of survivalism could even make you a celebrity.

The Rosenbergs, who did not survive the larger logic of national self-consolidation of which this is one minor variant, shared with Irving Howe's father a lack of educated nuance, stylistic fluency, and upward mobility. In this sense they define what is necessarily left behind by the narrative of professionalization. (Or perhaps it would be better to say—since it is important to stress the semireverential clinging that is the other side of the profession's proud superiority to them—that they are carried helplessly along in its wake.) But if it is true, as I have been trying to suggest, that criticism in the form the New York intellectuals gave it reproduced Howe's combination of pity and contempt for the Rosenbergs, if their helplessness (again shared with Howe's father) is also the helplessness that Howe projects onto literature, it does not follow that those who turned away from the Rosenbergs to become national-professional intellectuals thereby succumbed to professionalism itself. They only gave professionalism an obnoxiously hypocritical and long-lasting form.[26]

For all the to-do about the supposed sellout of professional academics, selling out in the other sense offers evidence both that professionalism can be popular and at the same time that it can offer an alternative to nationalism. This is evidence that the people who buy all those copies of James Bond novels have never been "poor besotted dupes" of Cold War polarity any more than the Rosenbergs were. The genre of the spy thriller has always served to make transnational knowledge widely available, if not always in optimally reliable forms. And its characteristic repertoire of extreme transnational situations has increasingly come to express in particular the knowledge that in domestic social life, as in the world of nations, conventional oppositions between us and them, good and evil have become irrelevant to the real flows of desire, sympathy, and identification by which we live. This is why, as Michael Denning notes in his 1987 book *Cover Stories*, the genre draws its readers into a "fetishization of professionalism." "The protagonists are consummate professionals, to the point of having no affective life whatsoever," Denning writes, yet they "mobilize the reader's sympathies simply by their position in the foreground, even though they are working for the 'wrong' side."[27] Denning cannot quite bring himself to take the next step, but its direction is clear. It is not merely "their position in the foreground" by which these professional protagonists have enlisted the reader's allegiance but their very refusal of an "affective life" that could not possibly correspond to the amorality of their situation—in other words, their refusal of "right" and "wrong" sides.

Consider *Casino Royale*, whose phenomenal success coincided with the Rosenbergs' last months.[28] The end of the novel, after the suicide of Bond's lover, Vesper Lynd, and the revelation that she had been a double agent, involves Bond's submission to the code of the Cold War, as personified by SMERSH (the Soviet anti-espionage agency in Fleming). The surprise is that he *has* to decide to join the Cold War—in other words, that so much of Fleming's first novel might be seen as an argument against participation in the Cold War. Bond has got his double-0 number by killing two people, he has earlier told Lynd. "Probably quite decent people. They just got caught up in the gale of the world like that Yugoslav that Tito bumped off. It's a confusing business, but if it's one's profession, one does what one's told" (201). Later, recovering from his torture by Le Chiffre, he tells his French confederate, "I've decided to resign.... You see, when one's young, it seems very easy to distinguish between right and wrong, but as one gets older it becomes more difficult" (243). Bond says:

> "The hero kills two villains, but when the hero Le Chiffre starts to kill the villain Bond and the villain Bond knows he isn't a villain at all, you see the other side of the medal. The villains and heroes get all mixed up."
>
> "Of course," he added, as Mathis started to expostulate, "patriotism comes along and makes it seem fairly all right, but this country-right-or-wrong business is getting a little out-of-date. Today we are fighting communism. Okay. If I'd been alive fifty years ago, the brand of conservatism we have today would have been damn near called communism and we should have been told to go fight that. History is moving pretty quickly these days and the heroes and villains keep on changing parts." (244)

This vision clearly owes something to the apparent heartlessness of professionalism: its impulse to recognize that one's antagonists are not morally inferior or morally opposed, and thus monsters to be loathed and destroyed, but only decent people like oneself who use their skills to do a job, who find themselves on the other side only by accident, and who do not deserve any special enmity. Nothing that happens in the novel's last few pages can take away the insidiously internationalist force of Bond's heartfelt post-torture speech.[29] "'He's a good-looking chap, but don't fall for him,'" the heroine has been told: "'I don't think he's got much heart'" (201). What is wrong with Bond's heart is not just a defect in his treatment of women; it is also a spot where excess of professional commitment seems to produce an engaging, politically promising deficiency of national commitment.

It ought not to be a surprise, then, that by 1961 the Cold War villains of the early Bond novels (the SMERSH formula) had already given way to the SPECTRE formula: an "assembly of free-lance villains" who belonged neither to the East nor to the West.[30] Ostentatious worries that the end of the Cold War will mean the end of the spy thriller are therefore historically unwarranted. From quite early on, the pervasive pleasures of reading even the most popular spy stories had come to include a pleasure denied to the nationalist intellectual: the pleasure of seeing through the stupidity and arbitrariness of the Cold War's mobilization of national loyalty. In effect, the genre has offered a sort of popular internationalism. When those novels sell out, therefore, it is not time to withdraw into sniffy professional superiority.

I want to conclude with a word about a case that is much less famous than the Rosenberg case but that has some things in common with it and that deserves equally to be reopened. Mordechai Vanunu, an Israeli engineer kidnapped by the Mossad in Rome in 1986, has been held in solitary confinement (as of this writing) for nine years. Convicted of passing military secrets to the enemy in wartime, his actual crime is to have told the *Sunday Times of London* that Israel has developed nuclear capabilities—hardly a secret, since this was "already well known to scientific and military specialists around the world."[31] In the letters from prison to his girlfriend and brothers, letters that are the only communication with the world he is permitted, Vanunu has argued—with some awkwardness no doubt, as he, too, like the Rosenbergs, tries to combine personal and political expression—"that he was motivated by his conscience and by his concern for peace in the middle east and in the world."[32] For those of us who share his commitment to these well-worn concerns, addresses are available to which wishes and protests can be directed.

NOTES

1 Irving Howe, *A Margin of Hope: An Intellectual Autobiography* (New York: Harcourt, 1982), 127.

2 The phrase "McCarthyism of the Left," reportedly used by Harvard history professor Stephan Thernstrom to describe his treatment by students critical of his teaching, immediately became a slogan in the "culture wars" of the late 1980s. I quote the phrase from Dinesh D'Souza, *Illiberal Education: The Politics of Race and Sex on Campus* (New York: Free Press, 1991), 195. For an eye-opening alternative to D'Souza's view of the Thernstrom case, see Jon Wiener, "What Happened at Harvard" in *Beyond PC: Toward a Politics of Understanding*, Patricia Aufderheide, ed. (St Paul: Greywolf Press, 1992), 97–106. For a general overview of the debate, see Bruce Robbins, "Tenured Radicals, the New McCarthyism, and PC," *New Left Review* 188 (1991): 151–57.

3 Andrew Ross, *No Respect: Intellectuals and Popular Culture* (New York: Routledge, 1989), 19.

4 On the spy as a figure of professionalism, see Bruce Robbins, *Secular Vocations: Intellectuals, Professionalism, Culture* (London: Verso, 1993), 127–141.

5 Oak Ridge scientists quoted in Virginia Carmichael, *Framing History: The Rosenberg Story and the Cold War* (Minneapolis: University of Minnesota Press, 1993), 53–54.

6 Walter Kaufman quoted in ibid., 53–54.

7 Zygmunt Bauman, *Legislators and Interpreters* (Cambridge, U.K.: Polity, 1987), 1. With the coinage, a new sense of the (nonprofessional) public was asserted against, but was also created by, a new sense of the (professional) private.

8 Julien Benda, *The Treason of the Intellectuals*, trans. Richard Aldington (1928; reprint, New York: Norton, 1969), 24, 182.

9 Jean-Paul Sartre quoted in Annie Cohen-Solal, *Sartre: A Life*, trans. Anna Cancogni (New York: Pantheon, 1987), 339–40. "Find out who Sartre is," J. Edgar Hoover is said to have ordered.

10 Alfred Kazin writes in his journal in 1942: "suddenly I realized, and for the first time consciously, that I had a passionate and even professional (sic) interest in American culture and literature." Kazin's parenthetical "sic" is the minimal marker of skepticism to be expected from the group. Quoted in Neil Jumonville, *Critical Crossings: The New York Intellectuals in Postwar America* (Berkeley: University of California Press, 1991), 73.

11 Howe, *Margin*, 161.

12 Ross, *No Respect*, 23–35; and the *Death House Letters of Julius and Ethel Rosenberg* (New York: Jero, 1953).

13 Howe, *Margin*, 216. In Howe's telling, how he got the Brandeis job is not part of the same story as his response to the Rosenberg case. Chronologically, the latter obviously began earlier, but in the autobiography it comes thirty-odd pages later.

14 Howe, *Margin*, 147.

15 Alfred Kazin, *New York Jew* (1978; reprint, New York: Knopf, 1987), 291.

16 Howe saw himself, and is still often seen, as a critic defined by his opposition to New Critical formalism, who (in Morris Dickstein's words) found it "difficult to be concerned with literature for its own sake" but instead "saw literature as an adjunct of morality and right conduct." In fact, as Alan Wald notes, Howe consistently defended literature's autonomy against the demands of politics. He made his debut in *Partisan Review* in 1947 with a defense of Trilling's "The Other Margaret," a piece of antiprogressive polemic, as a "work of art" rather than "a thesis or an argument." In a controversy over Arthur Koestler around the same time, Howe called "for a total separation of literature and politics (Wald, 317). Morris Dickstein, *Double Agent: The Critic and Society* (New

York: Oxford University Press, 1992), 96; Alan M. Wald, *The New York Intellectuals: The Rise and Decline of the Anti-Stalinist Left from the 1930s to the 1980s* (Chapel Hill: University of North Carolina Press, 1987), 237, 317. Of course, Howe's argument "that one must refrain from judging the political content of literature...in the manner in which one judges straight political doctrine" was a valuable contribution at the time, as Wald points out (*The New York Intellectuals*, 318).

17 See Bruce Robbins, "Literature, Localism, and Love," in *Postmodern Occasions*, ed. E. Ann Kaplan (London: Verso, forthcoming).

18 Howe, *Margin*, 118, 257.

19 Francis Mulhern, Introduction to *Teachers, Writers, Celebrities: The Intellectuals of Modern France*, by Regis Debray, trans. David Macey (London: Verso, 1981). "The historical record of the New York intellectuals was one of increasing incorporation and dependence" (xxiii).

20 Benedict Anderson, *Imagined Communities* (London: Verso, 1983), 16.

21 Ibid., 21.

22 Ibid., 55.

23 This is not the first time we will have encountered the irony of a radical constructivism producing a conservative celebration of the status quo—in this case, a nationalist status quo and a nationalist horror of the cosmopolitan.

24 Howe, *Margin*, 339.

25 Ibid., 340, 341.

26 This is obviously a defense of professionals like myself. But my point is not to idealize the contemporary academy. There is no question, for example, that multiculturalism today remains deeply marked by the identification of internationalism with literature (that is, its depoliticizing of internationalism) that is part of the New York intellectuals' heritage.

27 Michael Denning, *Cover Stories* (London: Routledge and Keegan Paul, 1987), 146. According to Denning, in its Golden Age (the 60s and 70s) the spy novel attempts to resolve the split between work and home, public and private: "the world of the spy novel is precisely one where this split has not been made, where public and private are intertwined" (131). The "safe house" offers an image of resolution, "an imaginary space where the contradictions are suspended, and the public and private temporarily united" (134).

28 Ian Fleming, *Casino Royale* (London: Glidrose, 1953); page numbers given parenthetically in the text are from Ian Fleming, *James Bond 007: Five Complete Novels* (New York: Crown/Avenel, 1988).

29 It is in keeping with the internationalist vision that the figure who best embodies Fleming's romance of omniscient omnipotence in the novel is not Bond himself (who does better here as a consumer than as a fighter) but the anonymous representative of SMERSH—who also rescues Bond (when Le Chiffre has tor-

tured him into infantile helplessness) just as Bond himself has tried to rescue the helpless, feminized Vesper. Structurally, hero and villain are indeed almost interchangeable.

30 Tony Bennett and Janet Woollacott, *Bond and Beyond* (New York: Methuen, 1987), 33.

31 Yerach Gover and Ella Shohat, "In Defense of Mordechai Vanunu: Nuclear Threat in the Middle East," *Social Text* 18 (winter 1987/88): 97. Address protest telegrams to the Israeli government and/or the Secretary-General of the U.N. through the Mordechai Vanunu Legal Defense Fund, P.O. Box 45005, Somerville, MA 02145; write to Vanunu at Ashkelon Prison, P.O. Box 17, Ashkelon, Israel.

32 Ibid.

11

The Rosenberg Case
and the New York Intellectuals

David Suchoff

The New York intellectuals—the largely Jewish, anti-Stalinist writers and critics that surrounded *Partisan Review*—vigorously denied that anti-Semitism was at work in the Rosenberg case. The charge of Jewish persecution was poisoned for the anti-Stalinist left when the Communist Party trumpeted the Rosenbergs as victims of American anti-Semitism, while it remained silent as Stalin persecuted and executed Yiddish writers and other Jews in the Soviet Union. American Jewish organizations, on the other hand, noted the trial for its promotion of popular anti-Jewish sentiment. The high-cultural and mass-cultural responses of the American Jewish community thus conflicted with each other, yet both, seeking to defend Jews against the taint of Communism or treason, worked together to minimize the Jewish question as it worked itself out in the Rosenberg case. My essay will address this erasure of the Jewish question in the New York intellectuals' response to the Rosenberg case and consider that erasure as a crucial moment in the treatment of Jewish issues in contemporary cultural theory. For the case not only provides an origin of Stephen Greenblatt's "subversion/containment" model of mass culture that flourished in later American cultural criticism but also illustrates several ways in which the problem of postwar Jewish identity for the New York intellectuals provides a not so absent center of postmodern cultural debates.

For Greenblatt's vocabulary for cultural criticism—centered on "subversion," its containment by mass culture, and a sociologically "fashioned" self—is derived from a Cold War history of ethnic containment of "Jewish" subversion in America. The term "subversion" itself was first popularized by Lionel Trilling, the most influential of the New York intellectuals, and a Jew who broke with the Left.[1] In reacting to the threat of the Rosenbergs as subversive Jews, I am suggesting, the New York intellectuals were able to continue a process of fashioning liberal selves in American life that contained the dangers of leftist Jewish identity in America. With its terminology drawn explicitly from the Cold War, Greenblatt's cultural theory registers the traces of this process. *Renaissance Self-Fashioning*, his major work, argues that the "containment" of a theatrically staged "subversion" was a cultural practice developed in early modern England and that such a theater of false subversion was crucial both to the enterprise of modern self-making and to the exercise of power in the early modern state. Greenblatt's terms speak well to the 1950s, when many intellectuals faced a situation in which "the alien" was "marked for attack" and when the creation of a liberal critical identity meant keeping "alien" attachments to the Jewish Left at bay: "any achieved identity always contain[ed] within itself the signs of its own subversion or loss."[2] Such "self-fashioning" provides a model for the New York intellectuals' general response to the case, to contain the alien Jewishness—and its threat to their public identities—that the Rosenbergs came to portray.

Today's flourishing ethnic criticism, it is worth recalling, was preceded by a fifties liberal "consensus" that valued "complexity," feared ideology, and saw ethnicity as a threat. It is certain that the Rosenbergs' Jewish origins were a source of discomfort for Jewish New York intellectuals who were helping to form that liberal consensus in America. "Subversion," the central term Greenblatt drew from Lionel Trilling, registers the fear of being labeled a Jewish leftist that Trilling quite seriously and later Greenblatt more humorously had to confront as representative (male) Jewish intellectuals of the Cold War period.[3] Trilling's high-cultural concept of "subversion" would break with his own Marxist past in the 1930s, just as Greenblatt's concept of a "contained" subversion, developed to describe English Renaissance drama, would offer a description of the process that Jewish identities in Cold War America would undergo.[4]

For the Rosenbergs were associated with a Jewish past that most New York intellectuals thought they had left far behind. A commitment to a Stalinist, or mass-cultural, aesthetic shaped the youth of the largely Jewish intellectuals of Trilling's milieu: the high-modernist, liberal aesthetic developed by the

Partisan Review circle reacted against the aesthetic but also the political dangers of identification with mass culture. For Jews "mass culture" meant being too radical but also too Jewish, like Hollywood's Jewish writers on the Left, who were among the first "subversives" to draw the HUAC's ire after its formation in the 1930s.[5] The cultural ascent of figures such as Trilling depended, as his 1925 story "Impediments" already suggests, on escaping from Hettner, the "scrubby little Jew" from the working class. Trilling's narrator fears that the Jewish Jew might "break down the convenient barrier I was erecting against men who were too much of my own race, and against men who were not of my own race and hated it."[6]

The Popular Front, Moscow-tinged rhetoric of the Rosenbergs in their *Death House Letters* was therefore a nightmare scenario for the New York intellectuals, and a terror to the American Jewish community as well: assimilation depended on a high-cultural, strictly aesthetic, complex, and well mannered version of "subversion" that Trilling would connect with modernist literature and make central to an ethnically emptied "liberal imagination."[7] The Rosenberg case, on the contrary, foregrounded Jewish names in connection with popular fears of conspiracy and thus built on the mass-cultural fantasies of Jewish subversion that the HUAC investigation of Hollywood had already prominently produced in 1947. Leslie Fiedler's notorious essay of October 1953, as Morris Dickstein points out, condemned the Rosenbergs as specters of the working-class, immigrant Jewish past. After criticizing the Rosenbergs' writing as crude, and expressing the liberal hope they might have been spared, Fiedler, decrying the literary failures of their letters, all but greeted their execution as a kind of exorcism: "what was there left to die?"[8]

Fiedler's staging of an alien, Jewish subversion matches far more hostile Cold War theorizations of American power that accompanied the Rosenberg case. An internal CIA memo dated January 22, 1953, for instance, sees the Rosenberg case's effect on the American Jewish community as an opportunity to dramatize fearful specters of the Rosenbergs as Communist aliens and thereby to secure the loyalty of the American Jewish community in the anti-Communist crusade. For the CIA, the staging of the Rosenbergs as Jews was primary: "*Proposal*: A concerted effort to convince Julius and Ethel Rosenberg, now under sentence of death, that the Soviet Regime they serve is persecuting and ultimately bent on exterminating the Jews under its sovereignty. The action desired of the Rosenbergs is that they appeal to Jews in all countries to get out of the communist movement and seek to destroy it."[9] The anonymous CIA analyst who wrote this memo deployed a Cold War sociology that makes clear the historically specific Jewish meaning of the charge of subversion as it was used in and emerged from the Rosenberg case. In the CIA memo the appeal of the Rosenbergs to the public as signifiers of

Jewish subversion—"atom spies" was the pop newspaper term used to describe the Rosenbergs—calls up real fears of Soviet persecution, and thus encourages Jewish loyalty to the American state. "The [Rosenberg] couple is ideally situated," the memorandum continues, "to serve as leading instruments of a psychological warfare campaign designed to split world communism on the Jewish issue, to create disaffected groups within the memberships of the Parties, to utilize these groups for further infiltration and for intelligence work." The use of the death penalty to extract cooperation and information—a fact about the Rosenbergs' execution now certified by no less an authority than Nathan Glazer—defined the Rosenberg case as a spectacle of defeated revolt, manipulated for coercion to serve the purposes of the state.[10]

The Rosenberg case is thus an important episode in the fashioning of Jewish identity in Cold War America. It is a process whose erasures and unconscious returns still inform contemporary cultural debates. Greenblatt's emphasis on "containment" is useful precisely for its suggestion that ethnic control remains part of the logic of modern political power.[11] But the issue of Jewish identity continues to haunt our reception of the New York intellectuals: A liberal such as Morris Dickstein can heroize Trilling as the last public critic in America—while discounting the ethnic containment that was the price of his critical and public fame.[12] Farther to the left, Russell Jacoby hails Trilling in similar terms as one of the "Last Intellectuals" but produces a similar evacuation of Jewish culture, arguing that there was nothing particularly Jewish about the New York intellectuals at all.[13] Today, in other words, we can return to Trilling as a model of the exemplary public intellectual—the position on which Dickstein and Jacoby agree—but only by limiting the cultural and political importance of his Jewishness, or of his suppression of his Jewish identity. The Rosenberg case, and its effect on the New York intellectuals, remains crucial to our contemporary understanding of what the proper role of ethnic identity in cultural criticism should be.

THE ROSENBERGS AND THE JEWISH QUESTION

The outcome of the Rosenberg trial mobilized Jews in support of the verdict, and in support of the death sentence as well. Figures such as Lucy Dawidowicz, the eminent historian, argued that the Jewish question in the case was nothing but a Communist-inspired fiction, while Jewish organizations feared the popular anti-Semitism it evoked and saw self-censorship as the answer.[14] Daniel Bell, for instance, argued against the charge of anti-Semitism, while American Jewish leaders were fearing and experiencing anti-Jewish fervor. In an internal memo of July 31, 1950, "Public Relations Effects of Activities of Jewish Atom Spies," a staff member of the American Jewish

Committee wrote that the old myth of a Jewish cabal was on the rise: "the non-Jewish public may generalize from these activities and impute to the Jews as a group treasonable motives and activities."[15] Less than two years later, Bell would write in the British journal the *New Statesman and Nation* that the charge of anti-Semitism in the Rosenberg case was nothing more than "a convenient method...of distracting attention from the Soviet anti-Jewish campaign."[16] The statement was correct in a strict geopolitical sense, while false semiotically and domestically: anti-Communism ruled out perceiving the Jewish question in America, while the American Jewish Committee's concerns showed that it had not been solved. The AJC led the way in calling for the Rosenbergs' execution rather than clemency, and the historian of Jews in America, Howard Sachar, notes that the Rosenberg case was part of the "ongoing hunt for subversives" experienced by Jewish America; it resulted in many Jewish endorsements of controls on "subversives" that were actually controls on Jews.[17]

Unlike the New York intellectuals, however, soon to be president Eisenhower recognized and skillfully responded to the American ethnic undertones of the Rosenberg case. In a speech delivered in ceremonies marking his departure from the presidency of Columbia University for the White House, Eisenhower decried "subversion" in the universities: both William Perl and Klaus Fuchs, with their Jewish-sounding names, had worked at Columbia and been mentioned in the trial. Eisenhower's remarks on leaving Columbia are instructive in this regard: before he became Columbia's president, Eisenhower declared, the New York school had been rumored to be a place where "there was subversion...and communism lurking behind every brick...and every blade of grass"; fighting it, he said, meant a "war of light against darkness, freedom against slavery, Godliness against atheism."[18] The American Jewish Committee understood this kind of threat by implication. In response to a *Daily Mirror* editorial praising "good Jews" like Bernard Baruch and Adam Gimbel, Andhill Fineberg wrote: "the *residue* in the mind of the average person is likely to be, 'But why is it all those atomic spies are Jews?'"[19] One reason was the HUAC hearings on Hollywood in 1947, where Senator John Rankin declared it the task of the committee to save "the Christian people of America" and performed it by a kind of identity politics, reading names from a pro-First Amendment petition: "there is one who calls himself Edward Robinson. His real name is Emmanuel Goldberg. There is another one who calls himself Melvyn Douglas, whose real name is Melvyn Hesselberg.... Another one is Eddie Cantor, whose real name is Edward Iskowitz."[20] The Yiddish press and allied organizations expressed sympathy for the Rosenbergs; but no voice among the New York intellectuals publicly spoke the fact that Eisenhower's "darkness" was a coded ethnic threat.

The spectacle of "subversion" as a means of control, moreover, depended on an elision of overt discussions of ethnicity. Even those courageous enough to oppose McCarthyism near its height left the Jewish question unaddressed. Hannah Arendt was unusual among the New York intellectuals for her forthright condemnation of anti-Communist hysteria in an essay that appeared while the Rosenberg appeal was still under way. Like Eisenhower, Arendt made no mention of the Rosenbergs, or of the persecution of Jews as ethnic "aliens" that remained a potent if coded Cold War threat. Two months after Eisenhower made his Columbia speech, however, Arendt addressed its logic in print. The final anti-Communist war of "light against darkness" that Eisenhower evoked was indirectly called to account by Arendt, even if she ignored its ethnic content. Such apocalyptic visions, Arendt argued, were a staple of totalitarian thought: "it belongs to totalitarian thinking to conceive of a final conflict at all. There is no finality in history—the story told by it is a story with many beginnings but no end."[21] Arendt's own story, that of a Jewish immigrant who came to America fleeing Hitler, was just such a different historical beginning, and a telling one where the questions of subversion and Jewishness that lay behind the Rosenberg case are concerned. Opposing anti-Communism from a liberal position, she ran the risk of making herself suspect as a foreign alien as well.

For Arendt was directly threatened: her husband, Heinrich Blücher, was a former German Communist and had lied about his past when he emigrated with Arendt from Nazi Germany, by way of France, in 1940. The "dragon" of anti-Communism she condemned in "The Ex-Communists" was carefully abstract, but the piece appeared less than a month after February 11, 1953, the day Eisenhower denied the Rosenbergs' appeal for executive clemency. The essay, to be sure, mentioned neither the Rosenbergs nor the Jewish question explicitly when it appeared in March 1953, but it spoke to the fears of immigrants and leftists at the very moment when the Rosenberg case placed all alien-appearing Americans under suspicion. It was just prior to the appearance of Arendt's piece that Eisenhower's attorney general, Herbert Brownell, Jr., announced that "12,000 citizens were being investigated for denaturalization, and 12,000 aliens for deportation as 'subversives.'"[22] The government's efforts at controlling subversion were more than a specter for Arendt in early 1953, as she feared her husband would fall victim to the anti-Communist wave: the Subversive Activities Control Board chartered by Congress was investigating the American Committee for the Protection of the Foreign Born.[23]

Whatever her feelings about the Rosenbergs themselves, Arendt would indeed have been courageous to support them publicly. What was nonetheless explicit in her essay was that her opposition to persecutory anti-

Communism grounded itself in the Dreyfus case. Without mentioning anti-Semitism, Arendt used Dreyfus obliquely to call the hysteria that would lead to the Rosenbergs' execution by one of its historical names. "The breach of the law (or for that matter, the risking of civil liberties in order to trap a bad man)," she wrote, "is necessarily the beginning of the end of civil liberties for all."[24] Because of her position as what Daniel Bell has called one of the "elders" of the "New York Jewish Intellectuals," the comparison Arendt drew between European anti-Semitism and American democracy's manipulation of the Rosenberg case had all the more force.[25] At the moment when her *The Origins of Totalitarianism* (1951) could be understood as drawing an absolute Cold War demarcation between liberalism and Nazi and Soviet practice, Arendt warned against the "totalitarian form[s] of domination" that—"no matter what [their] cause or ideological content"—were in fact already under way in the modes in which Jewish Americans and immigrants were being policed.

Arendt's sensitivity to the cultural politics of ethnicity might seem surprising, however, given the liberal emphasis on the public sphere rather than cultural power that informs her political theory as a whole. But Jewishness was never far from her thoughts about politics, particularly in the American phase of her career. Arendt's "The Ex-Communists" understood—without mentioning the Rosenbergs—the coded anti-Semitism that allowed the control of cultural subversion to thrive. Figures farther to the left of Arendt voiced more public support for the Rosenbergs but said much less about the case and American Jews. Michael Harrington, for instance, distinguished himself by opposing the Rosenberg execution, a public stand that was far more direct than Arendt's. But for Harrington, anti-Semitism and its cultural politics were not an American but a Soviet concern. In "The Sin of Anti-Semitism," an article he published in the *Catholic Worker* in February 1953, Harrington thus took the Stalinist persecution of Jews, particularly the Prague trials and attacks on Yiddish writers in Russia, severely to task.[26] But the Rosenberg case was a different affair. It was the Communists, Harrington wrote three months before the execution, who sought to make hay of the fact that the Rosenbergs were Jews: "Communists the world over are guilty of this approach.... it is true that the fact that the Rosenbergs are Jewish insinuated a problem into the deliberations and made them subjective to a certain extent. But there is no evidence of conscious anti-Semitism on the part of the government."[27] It was not so much Communism that erased the Jewish question in America as the kind of public positioning that anti-Communism required: realistic attention to American anti-Semitism in the period of McCarthy looked like agreement with the Soviet line. While Arendt attacked right-wing "Ex-Communists," adverting to the Dreyfus affair, and Harrington mounted a left-wing assault on the East bloc, the role of the case in disciplining the American Jewish community went unaddressed.

Neither Arendt nor Harrington recorded the terroristic effect that the Rosenbergs' prosecution had on American Jews in the Cold War period. In fact, Arendt's later, public-centered theory of political action, with its emphasis on the freedom citizens achieve in the public realm, excludes precisely the fears she experienced in her "private" Jewish life in America. One can only conjecture whether Arendt might have spoken out against the execution, had her own family not been at risk. What is certain is that President Eisenhower, who refused the pardon request, understood that political power was not just a public affair and that he saw his life-and-death power of pardon in theatrical terms.[28] To his cabinet President Eisenhower declared that his intervention in the impending execution could be justified only "where statecraft dictated in the interests of American public opinion or of the reputation of the United States Government in the eyes of the world."[29] In the view of "statecraft," and the public opinion it valued, the Rosenbergs could accurately be said to be Jews, but Jews who cast a blind eye at Soviet anti-Semitism and therefore hardly Jews in the terms of Cold War America at all. The Rosenbergs could thus be feared in the strongest terms native to modern anti-Semitism—as part of an international conspiracy that Eisenhower irrationally believed Ethel to have "master-minded"—while the state that executed them could be absolved of anti-Semitism.[30]

The "statecraft" of the Rosenberg's execution consisted of using subversive Jewishness as a means of containment, without the end of policing ethnic assimilation ever having to be named. That assimilatory hope was expressed in the CIA's memorandum on the Rosenberg case, which explicitly linked Jewishness to ideological anti-Communism. In its plan to bring the Rosenbergs to confess, the CIA hoped to "utilize the Rosenbergs as figures in an effective international psychological warfare campaign against communism primarily on the Jewish issue."[31] The plan depended on getting already politically assimilated American Jews to coerce the Rosenbergs into naming names, thereby saving their lives: "perhaps the ideal emissaries would be highly intelligent rabbis, representing reformed Judaism, with a radical background or sympathetic understanding of radicalism, and with psychiatric knowledge."[32] This hoped-for manipulation based itself on an understanding of American Jewish fears of the charge of double loyalty: for the Jewish prosecutor and judge, as Morton Horwitz notes, the trial was a chance "to show that Jews could be loyal Americans, especially when fellow Jews were being charged with betrayal."[33] Such fears were largely silenced after the case, but there is no better accounting of the overall strategy of containment it made available to assimilated American Jews than Stephen Greenblatt's reading of the theme of betrayal in Shakespeare's *Henry V*: "moral authority,...as the play defines it, is precisely the ability to betray one's friends without stain."[34]

It was Lionel Trilling, however, who first registered the Rosenberg case as an unconscious but shaping force in American cultural criticism. In effect, Trilling's "Freud: Within and beyond Culture," first given as a lecture in 1955, was an apology for an American Jewish community that mounted little effective opposition to the Rosenbergs' execution and whose leading organization sought to bring it about. "In a society like ours," Trilling announced, "...defenses against the domination of the culture grow weaker and weaker... the small separatist group set apart by religious or ethnic difference loses its authority, or uses what authority it has to support the general culture."[35] It was thus not surprising, or a non sequitur, when, in 1955, Trilling discussed Freud's importance, and his Jewishness, by linking both to "the period of McCarthyism." Freud was depicted as a kind of wish fulfillment for Jewish American intellectuals who were silent, assented to the Rosenbergs' conviction, or merely named names. His example, Trilling suggested, showed that the "threats to...jobs" and "social acceptability" that characterized the McCarthy period were compatible with a kind of culturally rebellious Jewishness, albeit one that cut it ties with the Left.

Trilling's Freud was therefore "much concerned with his own cultural commitment and achievement," and a man who "loved fame." But for Trilling, Freud was also a heroic rebel, a Jew who suggested that ethnic authenticity and the acceptance that required assimilation might not be incompatible goals. It was thus to the specific analogy of Freud's Jewishness that Trilling turned. McCarthyism could not be understood solely as a form of terroristic "institutionalized suspiciousness," Trilling insisted, for proof was to be found in the example of Freud's Jewish self. Freud's "ethnic situation" and persecution in Vienna provided a kind of model for the threatened Jewish self in Cold War America. Freudian rebellion made a kind of social dissidence possible, figuring a culturally rebellious but socially acceptable kind of Jew. For just as Freud combined worldwide fame with an adversarial relationship to Vienna, where "hatred of the Jews" unified a country otherwise "torn asunder by the fiercest national and cultural jealousies," so Trilling's ideal of liberal society tried to imagine a tenable "subversive" literature, when anything close to a real Jewish subversive in America lived under constant threat.[36]

Trilling expressed this fear of an ethnic inquisition nowhere more acutely than in his essay on Isaac Babel, which, like his Freud essay, first appeared in 1955. The revolutionary Babel rode with the Cossacks but never enunciated his fears of persecution as a Jew: "we know that he has either suppressed, for political reasons, the denunciations of him as a Jew that were actually made, or, if none were actually made, that he has in heart supposed they were made."[37] Babel's predicament thus echoes, in distanced form, the situation of American Jews with ties to the left, particularly in the aftermath of the Rosenberg case. But Trilling's reading of Freud canceled the recognition of American anti-Semitism the Babel essay revealed. The liberal consensus in America demanded that Jews pay the price of ideological conformity to achieve full assimilation and its rewards; the Cold War made anti-Semitism a charge that could be leveled against the Soviets, but not the Americans. Trilling's Freud was therefore ashamed of his Jewishness—"the culture of another nation intervened between him and what was bad in his own culture"—but only as that Jewishness was magically transformed into a fictionally resistant stance: "enough of the Jewish sub-culture reached him to make a countervailing force against the general culture."[38]

No such "countervailing force," however, kept Trilling from making his own practical contribution to anti-Communism at the Columbia where Eisenhower had served. In 1953 Trilling helped draft a Columbia University policy statement on academic freedom that declared Communism "entirely at variance with the principles of academic competence as we understand them."[39] The statement called loyalty investigations "harmful," however, and thus took the same centrist tack that Trilling's Freud essay would use the idea of Jewishness to construct. Freud—like literature and Jewishness—was subversive for Trilling when he was "ambivalent," silently standing "beyond" the "homogeneity and demandingness" of culture. Highbrow complexity provided an escape from Jewishness that existed, as the Freud essay announced, as a "biological necessity and biological *reason*." Such essentialized Jewishness was hardly threatening, because it excluded every question of Jewish cultural politics that the Rosenberg case and anti-Communism had raised: "there must come to us a certain sense of liberation when we remember our biological selves."[40] It would be up to Leslie Fiedler and Robert Warshow to imply that such biologism tainted the Rosenbergs as lower-class, instinctual Jews: Trilling remained silent, defending a kind of taste and sophisticated modernism that more assimilated Jews could prize.

CODA: THE LEGACIES OF SUBVERSION

Public silence on the Jewish element of the Rosenberg case echoes from the height of the Cold War period to our own. New York intellectuals such as Trilling knew Jewish identity and connections with the Left were a threat and fashioned a literary, universal self that aimed at silencing the dangers which ethnic particularism posed to Cold War success.[41] I have used Stephen

Greenblatt's concept of self-fashioning, and his rethinking of "subversion" in Renaissance literature, to suggest several things: how paradigmatic the New York intellectuals remain—as figures to be contested, or accepted, or whose terms are to be incorporated—for the current generation of postmodern literary intellectuals and how important the social construction of Jewish identity in Cold War America is to the terms of contemporary cultural debate today. In the debate over the canon and in discussions of "political correctness" positions that recall the terms in which the Rosenbergs were attacked are easy to observe. Statements made in our culture wars echo Fiedler and Warshow's charges against the *Death House Letters*: a liberal, properly public culture is often pitted against a supposed leftism that is "ideological," "totalitarian," ethnically marked, and literarily suspect as well.[42] Returning the Jewish question to the Rosenberg case makes it clear that cultural constructions of totalitarian ethnic "subversion" still circulate in subliminal form in the ethnic particularism often made to seem threatening when the reality of our postassimilationist culture is attacked.[43]

Delmore Schwartz, nonetheless, brought the Jewish question in the Rosenberg case powerfully, if subtly, to the surface. In "The Duchess' Red Shoes," his essay of 1952 on Lionel Trilling, Schwartz spoke indirectly, likening Trilling's liberal cultural criticism, with its fixation on manners, to the moment of truth for the Duchess of Guermantes in Proust. When Swann, a Jew, tells her he is soon to die, all she can think of is her anxiety that "she is not wearing the right shoes," and she departs without saying a word.[44] The silence Schwartz mirrored is still telling: the representation of Jews as "subversives" in liberal culture—as a means of censuring their Jewishness as well as an "unmannered" ethnic culture—remains an undiscussed legacy of the New York intellectuals' response to the Rosenberg case. Instead of being granted a place in public debates, the case has largely been banished to the political unconscious of Jewish families, where it is contained. In an era in which signs of ethnic conflict are superabundant and cultural memory is in short supply, we can only hope that cultural criticism's traditional sidestepping of Jewish culture will end and that we will find a new language to discuss the contemporary significance of the Rosenberg's fate.

NOTES

1 I discuss Greenblatt's "subversion/containment" cultural criticism, its debt to Trilling, and its significance for Cold War cultural politics in David Suchoff, *Critical Theory and the Novel: Mass Society and Cultural Criticism in Dickens, Melville, and Kafka* (Madison: University of Wisconsin Press, 1994),

15–25. For an excellent account of Lionel Trilling's Jewishness and its significance for the development of his liberal cultural thought, see Susanne Klingenstein's *Jews in the American Academy, 1900–1940: The Dynamics of Intellectual Assimilation* (New Haven: Yale University Press, 1991), 137–99. For a different perspective on the effect the Rosenberg case has had on contemporary cultural criticism, see Andrew Ross's excellent "Reading the Rosenberg Letters," in his *No Respect: Intellectuals and Popular Culture* (New York: Routledge, 1989), 15–41.

2 Stephen Greenblatt, *Renaissance Self-Fashioning: From More to Shakespeare* (Chicago: University of Chicago Press, 1980), 9.

3 Greenblatt comments on this problem in a comic andecdote he relates about his difficulties in teaching a course about Marxist theory: "In the 1970s I used to teach courses with names like 'Marxist Aesthetics' on the Berkeley Campus. I tended to like those figures who were in troubled relation to Marxism—Walter Benjamin, the early rather than the late Lukacs, and so forth—and I remember someone finally got up and screamed in class, 'You're either a Bolshevik, or a Menshevik—make up your fucking mind.' It was a little unsettling.... after that I started teaching courses with names like 'cultural poetics.'" See Stephen Greenblatt, "Towards a Poetics of Culture," in his *Learning to Curse: Essays in Early Modern Culture* (London: Routledge, 1990), 147.

4 See, for instance, the original version of Stephen Greenblatt, "Invisible Bullets: Renaissance Authority and Its Subversion," *Glyph* 8 (1981): 40–61, an essay whose title emphasizes the Cold War concept of "subversion." Introductions to the New York intellectuals define the importance of Jewishness, their flight from leftist "subversion," and the legacy of their work for American culture quite differently. The best introduction emphasizing the leftist heritage of the group and its general turn to neoconservatism is Alan Wald's *The New York Intellectuals: The Rise and Decline of the Anti-Stalinist Left from the 1930s to the 1980s* (Chapel Hill: University of North Carolina Press, 1987); for another perspective, see Ruth Wisse, "The New York (Jewish) Intellectuals," *Commentary* 34 (Nov. 1987): 28–38. Daniel Bell's discussion and listing of the "New York Jewish Intellectuals" in "The 'Intelligentsia' in American Society," in Daniel Bell, *The Winding Passage: Essays and Sociological Journeys, 1960–1980* (Cambridge, MA: Abt, 1980), 119–37 makes clear that the group was neither all from New York, nor entirely Jewish.

5 For an excellent account of this neglected period, crucial to contemporary American concepts of mass culture, see Neal Gabler, *An Empire of Their Own: How the Jews Invented Hollywood* (New York: Doubleday, 1988); on the persistence of the fears of Jewish Hollywood into the Cold War and blacklist era proper, see See Nora Sayre, *Running Time: Films of the Cold War* (New York: Dial Press, 1982), 17–18.

6 Lionel Trilling, "Impediments," in *Of This Time, of That Place* (New York: Harcourt, 1979), 3.

7 For an excellent analysis of Hofstadter, Trilling, and the "end of ideology" movement of the fifties, see William A. Chace, *Lionel Trilling: Criticism and Politics* (Stanford: Stanford University Press, 1980), 113–14.

8 See Leslie Fiedler, "Afterthoughts on the Rosenbergs," in *An End to Innocence: Essays on Culture and Politics* (Boston: Beacon Press, 1955), 25–45, here 45; for a similar contemporary position, see Robert Warshow, "The 'Idealism' of Julius and Ethel Rosenberg," in Warshow, *The Immediate Experience: Movies, Comics, Theater and other Aspects of Popular Culture* (Garden City, NY: Doubleday, 1962), 69–82. Morris Dickstein responds to both in "Cold War Blues: Politics and Culture in the Fifties," in *Gates of Eden: American Culture in the Sixties* (New York: Basic, 1977), 42–45.

9 CIA memorandum, Jan. 22, 1953, "The Rosenberg Case." This memo was obtained as part of a Freedom of Information request made by Professor Blanche Wiesen Cook. I am grateful to Robert Meerepol for making his copy available to me.

10 Nathan Glazer, "Did We Go Too Far?" *National Interest* 31 (spring 1993): 139. Roy Cohn reports in his memoirs that Judge Kaufman had settled on capital punishment for Julius Rosenberg "*before* the trial." See Sidney Zion, *The Autobiography of Roy Cohn* (Secaucus, NJ: Lyle Stewart, 1988), 77. Much later in the Cold War, Greenblatt would discuss the "representation of rebellion" in the service of social control as an aspect of Renaissance culture. See Stephen Greenblatt, "Murdering Peasants: Status, Genre and the Representation of Rebellion," in *Representing the English Renaissance*, ed. Stephen Grenblatt (Berkeley: University of California Press, 1988), 1–29.

11 See, for instance, Greenblatt's discussion of Jewishness in *The Jew of Malta* in *Renaissance Self-Fashioning*, 203–7.

12 Reverence for Trilling informs Dickstein's criticism of theory-centered approaches to current criticism in Morris Dickstein, *Double Agent: The Critic and Society* (New York: Oxford University Press, 1992).

13 See Russell Jacoby, *The Last Intellectuals: American Culture in the Age of Academe* (New York: Basic, 1987).

14 See Lucy Dawidowicz, "Anti-Semitism and the Rosenberg Case: The Latest Communist Propaganda Trap," *Commentary* 5, no. 14 (July 1952): 41–45.

15 Memo to John B. Slawson, "Public Relations Effects of Activities of Jewish Atom Spies," quoted in James Navasky, *Naming Names* (New York: Viking, 1980), 115–16.

16 Daniel Bell, letter, *New Statesman and Nation*, Jan. 31, 1953, 121.

17 See Howard M. Sachar, "The Rosenberg Affair: Aftermath and Trauma," in his *A History of Jews in America* (New York: Knopf, 1992), 640.

18 *New York Times*, Jan. 17, 1953, "Eisenhower Takes Leave of Columbia," 1.

19 Andhill Fineberg quoted in Navasky, *Naming Names*, 116.

20 John Rankin quoted in the *Congressional Record*, v. 93, pt. 7, Nov. 24, 1947, 10792.

21 Hannah Arendt, "The Ex-Communists," *Commonweal*, Mar. 20, 1953, 598.

22 See Elisabeth Young-Bruehl, *Hannah Arendt: For the Love of the World* (New Haven: Yale University Press, 1982), 274–75.

23 Ibid. On the Subversive Activities Control Board, see Mary Sperling McAuliffe, "A New Liberalism," in *Crisis on the Left: Cold War Politics and American Liberals*, 1947–1954 (Amherst: University of Massachusetts Press, 1978), 133.

24 Arendt, "The Ex-Communists," 598.

25 Bell, "Intelligentsia," 127.

26 Michael Harrington, "The Sin of Anti-Semitism," *Catholic Worker*, Feb. 1953. Harrington's opposition to the anti-Semitism manifest in the Slansky trial in Prague was uncompromising. The charge against Slansky of being a "Cosmopolitan," he wrote, was "a vicious attack on Jews. It has nothing to do with Zionism. It is an attempt to perpetuate a terrible caricature of the 'rootless Jew'" 3, (3, 8).

27 Michael Harrington, "Holy Father Begs Mercy for the Rosenbergs," the *Catholic Worker*, Mar. 1953, 3. The full passage is as follows: "Communists the world over are guilty of this approach…. it is true that the fact that the Rosenbergs are Jewish insinuated a problem into the deliberations and made them subjective to a certain extent. But there is no evidence of conscious anti-Semitism on the part of the government." I am grateful to Maurice Isserman for making these articles available to me.

28 Greenblatt's understanding of the authority of the sovereign to record and discipline "alien voices" is very similar in the revised version of "Invisible Bullets," published in 1988 in Stephen Greenblatt, *Shakespearean Negotiations: The Circulation of Social Energy in Renaissance England* (Berkeley: University of California Press, 1988), 37. The essay's first, shorter version was published with a title that emphasized the 1950s origin of its cultural theory. See Stephen Greenblatt, "Invisible Bullets: Renaissance Authority and Its Subversion," *Glyph* 8 (1981): 40–61.

29 Herbert S. Parmet, *Eisenhower and the American Crusades* (New York: Macmillan, 1972), 259.

30 Jeff Broadwater, *Eisenhower and the Anti-Communist Crusade* (Chapel Hill: University of North Carolina Press, 1992), 81.

31 CIA memorandum, Jan. 22, 1953, 5.

32 Ibid., 3–4.

33 Morton Horwitz, "Jews and McCarthyism: A View from the Bronx," unpublished paper delivered at the conference "Forty Years After: The Rosenberg

Case and the McCarthy Era," 6, Harvard University, May 8–9, 1993.

34 Stephen Greenblatt, "Invisible Bullets," in *Shakespearean Negotiations*, 58.

35 Lionel Trilling, "Freud: Within and beyond Culture," in *Beyond Culture: Essays on Literature and Learning* (New York: Harcourt, 1965), 77–102, here p. 98. The Freud essay was first given as a lecture to the New York Psychoanalytical Institute in 1955, and was published in a different version as *Freud and the Crisis of Our Culture* in that year.

36 Trilling, "Freud," 89, 95–99.

37 Lionel Trilling, "Isaac Babel," in *Beyond Culture*, 122.

38 Trilling, "Freud," 97.

39 Lionel Trilling et al., "Statement on Academic Freedom," 1953, Central Administration files, Columbia University, quoted in Wald, *The New York Intellectuals*, 274.

40 Trilling, "Freud," 99.

41 Trilling himself, as Susanne Klingenstein notes, wrote that "as a Jew, a Marxist, a Freudian," he faced a double barrier to his tenure at Columbia. For her account of this "Taming of the Jew" as represented in Trilling's fiction, see Klingenstein, *Jews in the American Academy*, 160–88, here p. 177.

42 Leslie Fiedler's recent essay on the culture wars, for instance, is startlingly similar in its terms to those Fiedler established in the Rosenberg debate: a teacher who favors ethnic approaches to literature is not only "ideological," he writes—in language that is unmistakably resonant of the the the charge of Stalinism—but may be "perhaps unwittingly…collaborating in the creation of what may well be the most totalitarian of canons." See Leslie Fiedler, "The Canon and the Classroom: A Caveat," in *English Inside and Out: The Places of Literary Criticism*, ed. Susan Gubar and Jonathan Kamholz, (New York: Routledge, 1993), 34.

43 Even more temperate arguments against multiculturalism borrow from the vocabulary of the Rosenberg era, pitting ideas of liberal American culture against threatening forms of ethnic and political assertion. For a more and less measured example, see Arthur Schlesinger, Jr., *The Disuniting of America* (New York: Norton, 1992).

44 Delmore Schwartz, "The Duchess' Red Shoes," in *Selected Essays of Delmore Schwartz*, ed. Donald A. Dike and David H. Zucker, with an appreciation by Dwight Macdonald (Chicago: University of Chicago Press, 1970), 217.

Ethel and Julius Rosenberg, in a prison vehicle
following their conviction in March, 1951.
(AP/Wide World Photos)

12

The Rosenberg Letters

David Thorburn

More than four decades after their execution, Julius and Ethel Rosenberg are irretrievably mythic figures, the subject of journalistic and scholarly studies in many languages, the inspiration for plays, novels, poems and a remarkable range of visual art—heroic martyrs to many on the Left; false-speaking ideologues who betrayed their country, their young sons, and their own humanity to many on the Right. It is impossible now to imagine that all the questions surrounding the Rosenberg case will ever be fully resolved.

But the largely unnoticed publication in 1994 of *The Rosenberg Letters: A Complete Edition of the Prison Correspondence of Julius and Ethel Rosenberg*, edited by Michael Meeropol,[1] the older of the two Rosenberg sons, clarifies and deepens our understanding of them. Revealing something of their contradictory humanity, these letters implicitly challenge mythographers both Left and Right. I take it as beyond argument that whether or not the Rosenbergs were guilty of anything, they were certainly railroaded. One major revelation of the collected letters is that the Rosenbergs were victimized by some of their closest allies and friends as well as by the courts and by their anti-Communist critics.

This conclusion seems inescapable if one compares the new edition of the 568 letters Julius and Ethel actually wrote to the selection of 187 tendentiously edited—revised or rewritten might be more accurate terms—letters compiled by the anonymous editors responsible for their first publication forty-two years ago. *Death House Letters of Ethel and Julius Rosenberg* was first published in June 1953, the very month of their execution. A second printing was produced in July 1953.[2] An enlarged and revised edition, containing thirty-four additional letters as well as the first and second appeals for clemency to then president Eisenhower, appeared in 1954 under the title *The Testament of Ethel and Julius Rosenberg.*[3]

These strange and fascinating texts occupy a unique place in the history of the Rosenberg case and in the larger history of American constructions of the Cold War. They were excoriated at the time of their publication in now notorious essays by Robert Warshow in the *Partisan Review*[4] and by Leslie Fiedler in the inaugural issue of *Encounter*,[5] the journal of the newly established Congress for Cultural Freedom, later exposed as having been heavily funded by the CIA; they were used extensively by the Rosenberg children in their autobiographical book about the case and about their subsequent lives, *We Are Your Sons*;[6] recently they have been thoughtfully and sympathetically treated by Andrew Ross, in his book *No Respect: Intellectuals and Popular Culture.*[7]

Ross is withering in his critique of Fiedler and Warshow, representative "Cold War liberals who sought to exorcise their own pre-war political 'innocence' by demonizing the untidy contradictions of lower middle-class culture."[8] Ross and others such as Harold Rosenberg,[9] Morris Dickstein[10] and Irving Howe[11] have been right, I think, to stress the shameful way in which Fiedler and Warshow exploit the *Death House Letters* to attack the Stalinist Left and, as Ross puts it, to assert "the superiority of the liberal conscience" in "the caste-bound voice of the secular priesthood of intellectuals."[12] But his defense of the *Death House Letters* themselves, as against his exposé of the motives of their critics, is far less persuasive.

Even at this distance in time and even to the eyes of a reader such as myself, raised in an ambience of Popular Front sympathies, convinced that the Rosenbergs were victims of Cold War hysteria and massive official deceit and injustice—even to me, the letters as first published are problematic documents, morally disturbing in ways not intended by their authors or their editorial handlers. And whatever their motives, however inhumane and excessive their demonizing of the Rosenbergs, Fiedler and Warshow were also responding to elements in the *Death House Letters* that were really there.

The radically shortened, edited, and altered fragments of the actual Rosenberg correspondence contained in the *Death House Letters* are manipulative and politically vacuous, psychologically implausible, at times so obviously propagandistic as to insult the intelligence even of friendly readers. And despite all the attention the case has received from scholars and journalists and partisan commentators over the last four decades, these documents have remained our primary source for understanding the Rosenbergs, ostensibly a kind of self-portrait: the Rosenbergs as they themselves would have us see them.

The complete letters show decisively that this portrait is partial and skewed, obliterating nuance and contradiction, distorting sensible or commonplace sentiments by destroying their context, reducing the Rosenbergs to relentless ideologues for whom all topics serve a political agenda. The Rosenbergs *were* deeply committed Popular Front Communists, and their political principles were an essential part of their character. Moreover, they knew at an early point in their imprisonment that their letters might be published, and they understood also that every line they wrote to each other, to their children and to their lawyer Emanuel Bloch would be closely read by prison authorities and by the government.

The contradictions inherent in this situation—the letters are simultaneously personal communication, documents open to their jailers and a public case for their innocence—are apparent even in the complete letters now available. But in the *Death House Letters* these contradictions are intensified —through editorial carelessness, ruthless excision, principles of selection that *are* relentlessly political—to the point of making the Rosenbergs appear to be crudely manipulative and insincere, easy targets for intellectuals such as Warshow and Fiedler.

Warshow's polemic consists primarily of a series of quotations from the *Death House Letters*, fragmentary selections of material already simplified, shortened, fragmented. These quotations lead Warshow to speak of "the awkwardness and falsity of the Rosenbergs' relations to culture, to sports, and to themselves."[13] Warshow's most damaging argument—the point, really, on which his whole case for the mendacity of the Rosenbergs and their politics rests—centers on a letter from Julius to Ethel, written on July 4, 1951. His discussion of this passage confirms Andrew Ross's notion that Warshow, like many other Cold War liberals, was avid to use the Rosenbergs to affirm his own righteous anti-Communism.

One is forced to wonder [Warshow writes] whether the literal truth had not in some way ceased to exist for these people. It is now seventeen years since the Communists told the truth about themselves—the "popular front" was inaugurated during Julius Rosenberg's student days at City College—and enough time has passed for the symbolic language of Communism to have taken on an independent existence. On July 4, 1951, Julius clipped a copy of the Declaration of Independence from the *New York Times* and taped it to the wall of his cell. "It is interesting," he writes to Ethel, "to read these words concerning free speech, freedom of the press and of religion in this setting. These rights our country's patriots died for can't be taken from the people even by Congress or the courts." Does it matter that the Declaration of Independence says nothing about free speech, freedom of the press, or freedom of religion, and that Julius therefore could not have found it "interesting" to read "these words" in that particular document? It does not matter. Julius knew that America is supposed to have freedom of expression and that the Declaration of Independence "stands for" America. Since, therefore, he already "knew" the Declaration, there was no need for him to actually read it in order to find it "interesting," and it could not have occurred to him that he was being untruthful in implying that he had just been reading it when he had not. He could "see himself" reading it, so to speak, and this dramatic image became reality: he *did not know* that he had not read it.

Similarly, when he says "it is obvious that I could never commit the crime I stand convicted of," we cannot assume that he is simply lying. More probably, what he means is something like this: If it were a crime, I could not have done it. Since in the language of the unenlightened what I did is called a crime, and I am forced to speak in that language, the only truthful thing to say is that I did not do it.[14]

I've quoted at such length partly to supply a sense of Warshow's tone; the arrogant ease with which he dismisses the values of the Popular Front and with which he speculates about Julius's powers of self-deception is characteristic of the anti-Communist rhetoric of the 1950s, as Ross and Morris Dickstein rightly remind us. Communists are not in the usual sense human, this argument ran, they live in a falsity and hypocrisy so complete as to be mere automata, ideological robots. "The implicit moral" of both Fiedler's and Warshow's essays, Dickstein writes, is that the Rosenbergs "were so empty, so crude, so bereft of style that there was nothing for the electric chair to kill. It takes Fiedler with his talent for blatant absurdity to announce this message clearly: 'they failed in the end to become martyrs or heroes, or even men. What was there left to die?'"[15]

But Warshow does nonetheless make an apparently devastating point. Who but a blindly careless propagandist, indifferent to truth and contemptuous of the ordinary people for whom his sermon is intended, would claim to have read the Declaration, even to have attached it to the wall of his cell, only to confuse it with the Bill of Rights?

It turns out, however, that the propagandist who committed this howler is not Julius Rosenberg but the anonymous editor who prepared his letter for publication. Julius's version is inelegant and verbose, but it does not mistake the Declaration of Independence for the Bill of Rights. A comparison of the "improved" version with Julius's original will demonstrate in small compass the immense latitude taken by the editors throughout the *Death House Letters*. First, the edited version:

My Dearest Ethel,

Fortified by Ossining Manor's delicious ice cream on this Independence Day, I'm making a celebration of this holiday for freedom. I clipped out a copy of the Declaration of Independence from the *New York Times*. It is interesting to read these words concerning free speech, freedom of the press and of religion in this setting. These rights our country's patriots died for can't be taken from the people even by Congress or the courts.

Certain politicians would use our case to frighten liberal and progressive people, but we are exposing this frame-up and we are not alone. It is a fight for our very lives, but also part of a fight for justice and free thought. (*DHL*, 46)

My Sweetest Precious Girl,

Fortified by Ossining Manors [*sic*] delicious ice cream on the occasion of Independence Day my thoughts naturally go to this memorable holiday of freedom in our country. I clipped out a copy of the Delaration [*sic*] of Independence that appeared in the New York Times. It should be read and studied especially the history surrounding it. The greatness of our country is the heritage of liberty derived from the sacred words of free speech, press and religion. These rights that the forefathers and patriots of our country have fought, bled and died for cannot even by Congress or the courts be taken away from the people. It is a source of encouragement to me that in this spirit and the justice of our position we are fighting for our freedom. Certain politicians have used our case as a wedge to scare liberal and progressive people but we'll continue to expose this black frameup and in this effort we are not alone. At present this is a fight for our very lives but it is also part of the fight for justice and free thought. (*RL*, 155)

Nearly every one of the 187 letters in *Death House Letters* has undergone similar corrective surgery, though this is perhaps the single most disastrous revision if one judges by its impact on the reputation of the Rosenbergs among American intellectuals. For Warshow's essay was widely influential, and his deconstruction of the July Fourth letter was understood to be the linchpin of his argument. Here, for example, is Irving Howe, in a memoir published in 1982, recalling the Fiedler and Warshow articles, which he describes as "perverse overkill":

Warshow and Fiedler scored points: who, against the Rosenbergs could not? Julius had written his wife that he had hung the Declaration of Independence on his cell wall so as to "read these words concerning free speech, freedom of the press, and freedom of religion," whereupon Warshow tartly noted that the Declaration says not a word about any of these matters. Very well, the Rosenbergs were entrapped in Stalinist devices; but surely at the moment what counted much more was that, innocent or guilty, they were waiting to be killed. Was it not heartless to write in this spirit, even if the Rosenbergs were indeed the poor besotted dupes one took them for?[16]

Howe's limited sympathy is creditable, I suppose, but far less instructive than the damaging afterlife of an arrogant editor's careless revision.

Many of the *Death House Letters* have been condensed even more radically than the one just discussed. Words and phrases are routinely altered, long paragraphs are excised or reduced to a few sentences, syntax is regularly smoothed and simplified, and, as the example of the July 4, 1951 letter indicates, even the salutatory endearments are censored by editorial commissars apparently reluctant to allow their heroic martyrs to lapse into sentimentality or idiosyncrasy. This last recurring practice is revealing precisely because the intellectual or psychological stakes are so small. Ethel and Julius are rarely permitted to exceed their allotment of one endearment per letter. Here is a random sampling chosen from dozens of similar repressions: "Darling" disappears from "My Most Precious Darling Ethel" (August 16, 1951), and "Sweetest" from "My Dearest Sweetest Wife" (August 23, 1951), Ethel's "Dearest Darling" (February 29, 1952) becomes merely "Darling," Julius's playful "Hello Bunny" (October 5, 1952) dwindles to "Hello Dear."

The impulse to minimize or suppress oddity, emotional display, simple playfulness or high spirits, even verbal or grammatical complexity in the *Death House Letters* is linked to the volume's governing political motive: to establish the Rosenbergs as political martyrs whose letters will be recognized as "world classics of democratic eloquence and inspiration," as the cover blurb of the second edition asserts. The sad irony, of course, is that in their ruling passion to place the political content of the letters in an unimpeded foreground the Rosenberg editors taint the residue of personal material that has escaped excision. Most of what might be called personal or nonpolitical in the *Death House Letters*—discussions concerning the welfare of the Rosenberg's young sons; reports of books read, songs sung, radio programs enjoyed; exchanges about their shared passion for baseball or the sustenance they find in their Jewish heritage; even the couple's professions of love and longing for one another—all this is so systematically and often heavy-handedly subordinated to the political that it is made to appear not merely secondary but insincere, a set of transparent stratagems aimed at gaining the reader's sympathy.

Here is a representative instance of the pervasive tendency of the *Death House Letters* to simplify, purify, and thus dehumanize the Rosenbergs—a letter from Ethel to her husband, written on October 4, 1951, so ruthlessly altered and "improved" that it obliterates not only a series of mundanely vivifying details, not only her awkward, sometimes florid prose but also her emotional confusion and pain, her very identity as a mother and a wife.

Dearest Julie,

I had never dreamed I could experience such intense hunger and such bitter longing; I glow with aliveness the better to savor the ashes of death. No, what is true is that the threat of death only fans the flame in me more fiercely, creating a renewed striving to triumph and to live.

Oh, darling, what a wave of wanting washes over me for the children and for you; it grows more and more difficult to put off my natural maternal and human desires, to warn myself of the searing destruction of our hopes that yet may be ours.

Only love me, my dear husband, I am your wife. Your loving

Ethel (*DHL*, 68)

Dearest Sweetheart:

Since my last letter to the children in which I described the activities of the trash I have been observing I find it increasingly difficult to sort out my thoughts and feelings concerning them, and to communicate there [sic] with some degree of clarity to myself, let alone to attempt to establish an unbroken line of correspondence with them. There is a commingling of resistance and guilt which is most disconcerting indeed. Perhaps I need the stimulus of a visit from Manny [the Rosenberg lawyer, Emanuel Bloch] and from Dr. [Saul] Miller [her psychiatrist], bringing me news of them and the home situation generally to arouse me out of the stupor into which I seem to have sunk. I am most desirous of seeing one of them at least this week end.

My darling, I had never dreamed I could experience such intense hunger such bitter longing; I glow with aliveness the better to savor the ashes of death. [Yet?] can the acrid taste accomplish aught but a fanning of the flame, a fiercer burning, a renewed striving to triumph and to live.

Sweetheart, I find myself regretting that we were unable to "exchange" our individual visits with Lee [Julius's sister Lena]. Neither of us got around to sharing information the other had received about the kids. For example did she recount for you a certain phone call during which Robby assured her he always gave Michael her regards "but what's the use, he never pays any attention to what I say anyway!" She also mentioned that "Pop" [Ethel's affectionate name for Alexander Bloch, Emanuel's father] had urged her not to forget to tell Ethel that I [that is, "Pop"] am fast becoming acquainted with them and they are very bright children! Incidentally Robby, with that refreshing lack of inhibition common to our emotionally healthy normal child, complained to "POP" about the size of the Hershey bar he had brought him compared it in favorable (and out loud) [terms] to the kind his uncle Dave usually buys!

Oh, darling, what a wave of wanting washes over me for them and for you; it grows more and more difficult for me to put off my natural human desires, to warn myself of the searing destruction of our hopes that may yet be ours to contend with!

Only love me, my dear husband, only love me; I am your wife with all of myself!

Your loving Ethel (*RL*, 235-36)

In their son's edition of the letters the Rosenbergs appear, I think for the first time, as credible human beings. They are not sources of wisdom, not elegant writers (though as the last paragraph of the letter above demonstrates, they achieve at times a genuine, unforced eloquence that is usually undermined by the editors of the *Death House Letters*). Neither monsters nor saints, their deep anguish over the fate of their children, their intense commitment to one another, their identity as Jews no longer seem, as in the inept hagiography of the *Death House Letters*, mere inauthentic facades but essential aspects of their character.

Their politics remains central, of course, the defining moral force in their lives. They are unswerving Communists—though the word they must use instead is "progressives"—and their political and cultural values are shaped by the eclectic simplicities of Popular Front culture.[17] Julius's letters in particular are full of the unrigorous universalism, the vague mingling of religious, patriotic, and Marxist categories embraced by Communists and other Leftists nurtured in Popular Front circles. In a representative letter in March 1953, for example, he asserts that "the lessons of the struggle for freedom of the Jewish people from bondage will continue to serve...as an example of the endless striving for newer and broader horizons by mankind in every sphere of human endeavor, physical, mental, social, political" (*RL*, 638–39). But however vulnerable as history and theory such perspectives are, they operate for both Julius and Ethel as the ground of a humanizing sympathy for the powerless, for racial minorities, for the union movement. "Advocacy of better conditions, social improvements, civil liberties and world peace," Julius asserts defiantly, "are in the best traditions of the forefathers of our country. It is not necessary to conform with the political hacks who are in the saddle today to be a real patriot" (*RL*, 372). In a similar vein Ethel speaks of the "peace and good will and security all decent humanity so bitterly craves," of a common "responsibility to our fellow-beings in the daily struggles for the establishment of social justice. Jew and Gentile, black and white, all must stand together in their might, to win the right!" (*RL*, 231). (The awkwardly rhyming final phrase is, characteristically, excised from the version of this sentence in the *Death House Letters*.) Far more effectively and movingly than the *Death House Letters*, the new collection is a kind of archive of the political and cultural values embraced by many thousands of working-class and lower-middle-class Leftists in the decades before and after World War II.

Those values include a range of specific items with which few would quarrel—civil rights, economic justice, free speech, and the right of political dissent. What is troubling in the letters, especially those of Julius, who clearly sees himself as theoretically and philosophically enlightened, is their unquestioning belief in "progress," "improvement," "social advancement," the imminent triumph of the working class. This naive Marxist teleology is the governing principle both of politics and of personal life for Julius. Through the agency of "the people" we are moving toward "peace and a better world" (*RL*, 640), "the fraternal solidarity of mankind" (*RL*, 644) gives him strength to withstand his imprisonment. These terms operate in the letters as a kind of mantra, their repeated invocation is Julius's form of prayer. Although always disturbing even to a sympathetic reader because they are entirely unanalyzed, mere ritualized expressions of a faith beyond question or rational discussion, these professions of confidence and belief come to seem routinized and desperate as the couple's various legal pleadings and appeals for clemency fail.

"I am encouraged," Julius writes, clinging to hope in a letter to Ethel on March 26, 1953, less than three months before their electrocution, "and feel strong in the unity that binds us with our brothers allover [sic] the world against the tyrants that want to destroy us. Since they have no faith in the people, they fail to understand the elementary historical truth and to recognize the strength of the people" (*RL*, 637). It would be cruel to mock Julius's faith in this god that failed, but it would be intellectually irresponsible not to acknowledge its vacuity and its moral and historical blindness.

Yet whatever the limitations of Julius's simplistic Marxist faith in progress and in the people, his interpretation of the case is remarkably exact and persuasive. In several letters he notes the subtext of anti-Semitism that stains public attitudes toward alleged Communists; again and again he points to the link between the Korean War and the American government's impulse to demonize Communism; his detailed analyses of the trial record power-fully expose the weakness of the evidence against them and the surreal excess in Judge Kaufman's rationale for the death penalty. There is a poignant and terrible power of concentration and will in Julius's obsessive, unflagging, out-raged critique in letter after letter of every detail of the trial record and of the anti-Communist propaganda and innuendo that saturated mainstream press accounts of their arrest and trial.

Ethel, in contrast, falls into near silence during the last nine months of their lives. Though she writes occasionally to their lawyer and to the children, she writes nothing to Julius after October 3, 1952. (They were executed June 19, 1953.) Julius continues to write her two and three times a week, but Ethel never answers. In her thoughtful biography of Ethel, Ilene Philipson sees this near silence as evidence of clinical depression.[18] The letters themselves are unreliable clues in this regard, of course, since all were composed at least partly as public documents. But it is possible to see a change in Ethel's writ-ing. During the first year or so of her imprisonment, Ethel's letters are in part lighthearted, even witty, and some to Julius contain openly passionate expressions of sexual desire. These personal and idiosyncratic elements sub-side over time, and she seems more and more to be addressing posterity, sometimes in tones that hint at suffering and even hysteria. Here too one may say that Ethel was ill-served by her first editors; their changes have a marginally calming effect, but the very excess in what Ethel actually wrote is surely more emotionally truthful and revealing. In the following excerpt, from a letter to Emanuel Bloch on February 9, 1953, the italicized material does not appear in the *Death House Letters*.

> So now my life is to be bargained off against my husband's; I need only grasp the line chivalrously held out to me *by the gallant defenders of hearth and home* and leave him to drown without a backward glance. How diabolical, *how bes-tial, how utterly depraved! Only fiends and perverts could taunt a fastidious woman with so despicable, so degrading a proposition*! A cold fury possesses me and I could retch with horror and revulsion, for these *unctuous* saviors, *these odi-ous swine,* are actually proposing to erect a terrifying sepulchre in which I shall live without living and die without dying! (*RL*, 581)

In her first letter from prison, written August 12, 1950, the day after her incarceration in the Women's House of Detention in New York City, Ethel tells her husband, "Darling, we mustn't lose each other or the children, mustn't lose our identities" (*RL*,19). They did, of course, lose each other and the children. But some part of who they really were, surviving the Cold War and the mythmaking of their friends and enemies, is available now in the words they wrote.

NOTES

1 Michael Meeropol, ed., *The Rosenberg Letters: A Complete Edition of the Prison Correspondence of Julius and Ethel Rosenberg* (New York: Garland Publishing, 1994). Hereafter cited as *RL*.

2 *Death House Letters of Ethel and Julius Rosenberg* (New York: Jero, 1953). Hereafter cited as *DHL*.

3 *The Testament of Ethel and Julius Rosenberg* (New York: Cameron and Kahn, 1954).

4 Robert Warshow, "The 'Idealism' of Julius and Ethel Rosenberg" in *The Immediate Experience: Movies, Comics, Theater, and Other Aspects of Popular Culture* (Garden City, NY: Doubleday, 1962), 69–81; originally published in *Partisan Review*, 1953.

5 Leslie Fiedler, "Afterthoughts on the Rosenbergs," in *An End to Innocence: Essays on Culture and Politics* (Boston: Beacon Press, 1955), 25–45; originally published in the first issue of *Encounter*, 1953.

6 Robert Meeropol and Michael Meeropol, *We Are Your Sons: The Legacy of Ethel and Julius Rosenberg* (Boston: Houghton Mifflin, 1975).

7 Andrew Ross, "Reading the Rosenberg Letters," in *No Respect: Intellectuals and Popular Culture* (New York: Routledge, 1989), 15–41.

8 Ibid., 40–41.

9 Harold Rosenberg, "Couch Liberalism and the Guilty Past," in *The Tradition of the New* (Chicago: University of Chicago Press, 1982), 221–40.

10 Morris Dickstein, *Gates of Eden: American Culture in the Sixties* (New York: Basic, 1977), 41–45.

11 Irving Howe, *A Margin of Hope: An Intellectual Autobiography*, (New York: Harcourt, 1982), 215–16.

12 Ross, "Reading," 37.

13 Warshow, *The Immediate Experience*, 76.

14 Ibid., 73–74.

15 Dickstein, *Gates of Eden*, 44.

16 Howe, *Margin*, 215–16.

17 The "Popular Front" policy of making common cause with socialists and other leftists in the worldwide struggle against fascism became official Communist doctrine at the Seventh World Congress of the Comintern in 1935. The policy was abandoned in August 1939, when Stalin signed a nonaggression pact with Hitler. But as the Rosenberg letters show, the ideals and values of the Popular

Front survived long after their repudiation as officially sanctioned CP policy. In their history of American Communism Irving Howe and Lewis Coser suggest that the "the Popular Front phase...required the creation of a mood of unfocused fraternity mixed with fretful alarm, or perhaps more accurately, it exploited among liberals and 'men of good will' a mood of this kind that had arisen since the victories of fascism in Europe" (332). The Popular Front strategy, they suggest, represented the "overthrow" of what had been the basic principles of the Communist movement: "Instead of the class struggle, cooperation with the bourgeoisie. Instead of the Soviet system, eulogy of democracy. Instead of internationalism, nationalism" (319). See Irving Howe and Lewis Coser, Chapter 8, "The Popular Front: Success and Respectability," in *The American Communist Party: A Critical History (1919–1957)* (Boston: Beacon Press, 1957), 319–86. See also Vivian Gornick, *The Romance of American Communism* (New York: Basic, 1977). On the special appeal of the Popular Front for Jewish leftists, see Irving Howe's *World of Our Fathers* (New York: Harcourt, 1976), 341–47. For a helpful account of the Rosenbergs's immersion in the Popular Front culture of New York's Lower East Side, see Ilene Philipson, *Ethel Rosenberg: Beyond the Myths* (New York: Franklin Watts, 1988), 38–109.

18 Philipson, *Ethel Rosenberg*, 324–25; 337–38.

13

The Suffering Body

Ethel Rosenberg in the Hands of the Writers

Carol Hurd Green

On the week in June 1953 when Ethel and Julius Rosenberg were being executed in Sing Sing, I was graduating from Matignon, a Catholic high school in Cambridge, Massachusetts. My classmates and I had very little sense of the world outside, although we did talk seriously about red vs. dead, knowing that as good Catholics we were obligated to choose dead. I suspect, however, that most, like me, doubted that we would be any good at martyrdom. Nobody talked about the Rosenbergs—or if they did, it was in such horrified whispers that I could/did not hear them.

My education on the Left came, quite surprisingly, at Georgetown University, where I enrolled for a master's degree in English after graduating from a small women's Catholic college. At Georgetown, then a careful and conservative place, I met a British socialist who was also studying there; he and his American wife found my political naïveté almost incomprehensible and set out, in the kindest way, to educate me. I will always be in their debt. It was through them that I began to venture out, though never in a very distinguished way, into the streets of the social movements of the 1960s, and to think about injustice in America.

By the early 1970s, through my admiration for Dorothy Day (who wrote

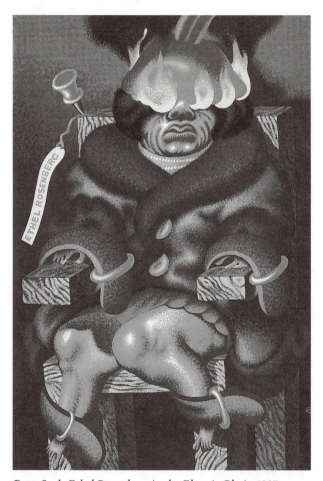

Peter Saul, *Ethel Rosenberg in the Electric Chair*, 1987.
(From *The Rosenbergs: Collected Visions of Artists and Writers*. Courtesy of
Rob A. Okun / Cultural Forecast)

movingly in the *Catholic Worker* about Ethel Rosenberg's death), I had developed a strong interest in the history of radical women. In 1976 I became coeditor of *Notable American Women: The Modern Period* (1980), and our advisory board agreed with me that the volume should include an article on Ethel Rosenberg. When Robert and Michael Meeropol were able to gain the release of the FBI files on their parents' case, I was fortunate enough to be permitted to use the papers. They were then in the New York office of attorney Marshall Perlin, the home also of the nascent Fund for Open Information and Accountability (FOIA). I read to discover everything I could about Ethel Rosenberg, not only about the validity of the charges against her but also about how she maintained her identity within the context of deprivation and death of the prison years.

The NAW article on Ethel Rosenberg appeared in 1980, and although I continued to read the books that came out on the Rosenbergs, I did not pursue any further work on the case until 1990 when a public thirsting for the death penalty became increasingly vocal. In Massachusetts, where former governor Michael Dukakis had made clear his opposition to the death penalty, the next governor, William Weld, made even more clear his enthusiasm for it, declaring in 1990 that fourteen was not too young to be executed. (Under pressure, he later raised the age to eighteen.) The rhetoric that advocates of capital punishment used to urge their case had become increasingly disembodied; their focus was not on the executed body but rather on advances in technology and the development of such "humane" methods of execution as lethal injection, ways in which the state can perform an act of legal homicide without a laying on of hands, in the passive voice, without agency, without body. The shift in discourse permitted a very troubling and bizarre dislocation: both the body of the executed and the body of the executioner were being subsumed under discussions of method.[1]

Having the wrong body (black, poor, housing a brain that is not fully developed) has, as history abundantly demonstrates, regularly made an accused person more liable to capital punishment. Though in American history the executed body has seldom been that of a woman, it seemed crucial to me to begin to tell again the story of the death by electrocution of Ethel Rosenberg: I wanted to make the point that innocent bodies can be made into wrong bodies for the purposes of the state.[2]

THE DEATHS OF ETHEL ROSENBERG

Elaine Scarry says, in *The Body in Pain*: "This body, this intensely—and sometimes, as in pain, obscenely alive tissue, is also the thing that allows...anyone, to be one day dead."[3]

In July 1950, before Ethel Rosenberg's arrest, James McInerney, head of the Justice Department's Criminal Division, said there was not enough evidence to proceed against Mrs. Rosenberg, though he noted that she might be useful as a lever against her husband.[4]

At a February 1951 meeting of the Joint Congressional Committee on Atomic Energy, six months after Ethel Rosenberg's arrest, United States attorney Myles Lane said: "The case is not strong against Mrs. Rosenberg. But for the purpose of acting as a deterrent, I think it is very important that she be convicted, too, and given a stiff sentence."[5]

Judge Irving Kaufman said in 1953: "Instead of deterring him from his ignoble course, she encouraged and assisted the cause. She was a mature woman, almost three years older than her husband and almost seven years older than her younger brother. She was a full-fledged partner in the crime."[6]

Denying clemency, President Dwight Eisenhower explained to his son John: "The woman is the strong and recalcitrant character. The man is the weak one."[7]

On June 19, 1953, the grim-faced official observer of the execution gave his report to the press of what had happened:

> Julius and Ethel Rosenberg have gone to the electric chair. The first to go into the death chamber was Julius Rosenberg.... The first volts of electricity entered his body at 8:04 p.m.... She died a lot harder. When it appeared that she had received enough electricity to kill an ordinary person, and had received the exact amount that had killed her husband, the doctors went over and pulled down the cheap prison dress, a little dark green printed job, and placed the sethe... [he stumbles over the word] I can't say it... stethoscope to her and looked around and looked at each other dumbfounded, and seemed surprised she was not dead.
>
> Believing she was dead, the attendants had taken off the ghastly strapping and electrodes and black belts and so forth. These had to be readjusted again and she was given more electricity which began again the ghastly plume of smoke that rose from her head and went up against the skylight overhead. After two more of those jolts, Ethel Rosenberg had met her maker, and she'll have a lot of explaining to do.[8]

Ethel Rosenberg died twice, terribly. Subjected in death to further indignity, her body became an ironic collaborator in her condemnation. Its unwilled resistance to the multiple volts of electricity sent through it by the executioners has provided evidence to those who sought it of her unseemly will.

Ethel Rosenberg's last two willed acts, a letter and an embrace, had been acts of love and connection. In her final gesture, she reached out for comfort to another woman. Confined in Sing Sing in virtual solitary confinement for two years, the only woman prisoner, Ethel Rosenberg had populated her confined space with conversations and stories of the prison matrons. As she entered the death chamber, she turned, stopped, and embraced the matron who had accompanied her there, expressing a final connectedness, body to body.

Just before going to the execution chamber she sent, through Manny Bloch, a message of "love and honor" to the psychiatrist she had been permitted to see on occasion during the prison years. The writing on her letter was edgy, the physical effort clear: the paper was indented with the force of the pen in the way students nervously grind into the paper of an examination book. She wants to know that "he shares my triumph": her only regret as she goes to death is that "the release from the trap [of her family] was not completely effectuated and the qualities I possessed could not expand to their fullest capacities."[9]

The pathos and poignancy of this letter is obvious. It is also a proud letter, exhibiting at the end that fierce determination that was Ethel Rosenberg's undoing in the eyes of the Justice Department and the public. Despite the evidence that historians have presented of the fear and excruciating psychological anguish that haunted her Sing Sing years, that "unseemly" will has continued to haunt representations of her—particularly by male writers—in books since her death.

THE SUFFERING BODY

Elaine Scarry's profound observation about death and the body comes from a powerful and chilling chapter in *The Body in Pain* on the process of torture. Scarry emphasizes there the constriction, the narrowing of the world that encloses the torturer and the condemned, and the destruction of the voice and thus the humanity of the victim. Excruciating pain obviates everything else: it renders communication, selfhood impossible. Ethel Rosenberg was not subjected to the physical torture Scarry describes, not flogged or subjected to water torture or (until the end) attacked with electric shocks or other instruments of brutality. But her body was tortured in a particularly modern way: by negation, by sexual deprivation, by refusal of the sensate and of connectedness—with her husband, her children, and with her voice, which fell silent many months before it was silenced. Seeing the Rosenbergs' hungry embrace at their first Sing Sing meeting, the shocked authorities put a table between them. Subsequently, at their rare meetings, they were separated by a wire mesh screen, not allowed to touch. Their open sexuality was intolerable to their guards: asserting her body into the political conversation was more proof, if any was needed, of her guilt.

Ethel Rosenberg found physical outlets, for a while: she sang in the prison chapel ("Un Belle Di" was a favorite), she ate (there is a wryly comic letter in the files in which she asks, with some chagrin, for her sister-in-law to send her a larger girdle), and for as long as she could she wrote. Her letters were addressed to Julius, though written in the knowledge that they would be released for publication in an attempt to raise money for their children's support. Julius encouraged her to write with passion and she did: the letters record her torment over the loss of her husband and children, as well as her pride and anger. Ethel Rosenberg's death house letters have been criticized for their overblown prose—as if the situation somehow should have offered a sense of proportion, as if there were a discourse appropriate to the denial of the body in all of its expressiveness.[10]

While she was alive and in prison—refusing to bend to the pressure to confess, refusing the proper womanly roles—and since her death, that body has been subject and source of curiosity, condemnation, sometimes pity, a charred mannequin on which writers have draped cloth woven of their own needs and obsessions. The burned body of Ethel Rosenberg has been a focus for those who believed that too much had been allowed her for too long, for those who are baffled by her refusal to act as she might have been expected to, even—as in the case of Sylvia Plath and Adrienne Rich—as a means to understanding herself.

In a number of texts by male writers Ethel Rosenberg's ordinary woman's body—its very ordinariness seeming an affront—is grotesquely transformed and represented as an act of will. This representation follows a too familiar pattern; when it seems useful (to the state, to power) to do so, the physical being that can feel pain is denied in order to rationalize its expendability.

The fact that it took more electricity to penetrate Ethel Rosenberg's body than that of her husband has had prurient attention from a number of writers. In *The Implosion Conspiracy* (1973), an odd mixture of supposed fact and fantasy that was supposed to be a movie, Louis Nizer says:

> She was only five feet tall and weighed a hundred pounds. Her body was ill-proportioned, her hands small and ungraceful. She looked better seated behind the table where her thick, short legs were not visible. The overall impression of her face was pleasant and just missed being beautiful. She had a condescending look...she spoke deliberately.... One thing was clear. There was enormous determination. Her life and death confirmed an extraordinary will—a will to rise above her environment, a will to become an artist, a will to be a revolutionist.

The final proof that such a will in woman is grotesque came in the body: she had a "superhuman will to live against a current powerful enough to have destroyed two other lives."[11]

Jonathan Root in *The Betrayers* (1966), similarly an essay in gratified condemnation, gives an account of the observer's announcement of the death of this "dumpy, tiny woman with heavy hands and thick ankles," then notes: "The fact [of the discrepancy in the time it took for wife and husband to die] provoked a number of cynical pressroom observations about the comparative hardiness of the female. Unseemly as such comment may have been, it was quite true."[12]

The two major novels based on the Rosenberg case, E. L. Doctorow's *Book of Daniel* (1971) and *The Public Burning* (1977) by Robert Coover, seem, though in a much more complex way, to concur. Though neither novel sets out to condemn the Rosenbergs, in both the physical body of Ethel Rosenberg is transformed into a representation of ferocious will. As wife, mother, lover, prisoner, victim, she is unnatural in her pride and determination, stronger than she has any right to be.[13]

In *The Book of Daniel* we see Rochelle Isaacson, the Ethel Rosenberg figure, through the memories of her son, Daniel. He is an untrustworthy narrator, the "divided and incoherent individual overwhelmed by history," as Virginia Carmichael notes, but Doctorow provides no other perspective on Rochelle. In Daniel's memory, his mother was inappropriate in her behavior and her determination. She was, he recalls, "a sexy woman, despite her austerity, her home-cut hair, her baggy clothes, her no make up except for very red lipstick on her small, prim mouth in the full cheeks.... She was full-breasted and heavy-hocked and wore corsets, which I would see her pull on or off while she said something like, 'Danny, go turn the light out under the coffee.'" There is, we should note, no corresponding physical description of Paul Isaacson (the Julius Rosenberg figure), except as a kind of mannequin whose broad-shouldered suit hangs off of him as he is taken away in handcuffs by the FBI.[14]

What that body adds up to for Daniel is will: Rochelle "had enormous energy. The whole thing with Rochelle was defending herself against the vicious double-crossing trick that life was.... [She] was as unstable as he [Paul] was. In her grim expectations. In her refusal to have illusions. In her cold, dogmatic rage. As if there were some profound missed thing in her life which she could never forget. Some betrayal of promise." She designs their court strategy, "no groveling, no show of emotion." After the conviction, Daniel thought that Paul might crack. But—the image of the jerking body in the death chamber intervenes—"I knew she would take it finally, to the last volt, in absolute selfishness, in unbelievably rigid fury." Not the monster of Nizer, the Rochelle/Ethel of Doctorow is nonetheless one-dimensional, a representation of wrenching will in the body of a woman.[15]

Doctorow's is a modest book in contrast with Robert Coover's *The Public Burning*. Neighing and braying and going on and on like the tall tale it aspires to be, the novel defiantly raises and embraces the specter of bad taste—commenting outrageously on the monstrosity of American society in the 1950s through the presentation of the Rosenberg execution as carnival. The exhibitionist vulgarity of the time is to be symbolized by a public burning, the execution of the Rosenbergs in Times Square before an audience of thousands—a return by a thrill-seeking, voracious public to a spectacle of the kind with which Foucault opens *Discipline and Punish*.[16]

The novel's frame of the last days before the execution is full of grotesquerie and monstrous display (though no more grotesque, perhaps, than the actuality of the lost executioner that the Rosenberg files reveal). The novel veers from melodrama to farce, risking the moral outrage of the reader, daring laughter in the midst of death. It is, as Virginia Carmichael notes in her very useful discussion of the novel in *Framing History*, a "devastating critique of masculinist hegemony" personified in the person and performance of "Dick Nixon."[17]

In *The Public Burning*, Ethel Rosenberg is a figure of the sexual fantasies of Dick Nixon; she is an urban sophisticate to his bottoms-obsessed country bumpkin. He is sweatily clumsy, inarticulate, obsessed with the anal, a schlemiel, a survivor of dead brothers, a kind of quixotic modern hero trying to pull off a rescue of the Rosenbergs. His focus is on the soft, plump, sexy body of the character called Ethel Rosenberg. He forces himself on her in a visit to Sing Sing: then, in the anteroom to the execution platform, as he imagines a rewriting of their lives, we read a lyrical, 1940s movie scene of lovemaking, with the pliant body of Ethel Rosenberg capitulating to Dick's advances, then actively demanding that he take her, "Here! Now!" The scene depends on as well as mocks her passionate body. He can't get his pants off in time, the scene becomes farce, she rubs and pretends to clean his bottom, dragged across the floor in their impatient haste.

Their farewell is tearful, climaxed by Nixon's ponderous summation: "a man who has never lost himself in a cause bigger than himself has missed one of life's mountaintop experiences: only in losing himself does he find himself." When Nixon stumbles onto the stage, his pants down, we find that Ethel has gained a wry victory: she has written "I am a Scamp" on his bare rear, an echo of her youthful days as a union organizer. The comic triumph of her sly trick on "Nixon" is quite at odds, however, with the voice that Coover gives her: when this Ethel Rosenberg speaks, she is neither witty nor dignified, as she talks in the stilted rhetoric of the letters.

The execution scene that follows is told by an unnamed narrator, the voice of the American tall tale for whom exaggeration is the stuff of life and this exaggeration—the public burning—a culmination of the American effort. Ethel appears on the stage defiant, playing Saint Joan, admirable, ready, "plumping herself down in the electric chair as if to a seat in the subway."

Coover extends the execution scene painfully, blending quotations from the Rosenberg letters, memories of their past, glimpses of their sons with the inexorable movement toward their death. Finally we return again to that image:

> With her body half unstrapped from the chair, they all rush forward, led by young Dick Nixon, ...fighting for position as though their very future depended on it, racing for the switch.... The guard...has been frantically trying to belt Ethel up again, but he only gets one of the straps done up when the charge hits, hurling him backwards off the stage.... Ethel Rosenberg's body, held only at head, groin, and one leg, is whipped like a sail in a high wind.... Her body, sizzling and popping like firecrackers, lights up with the force of the current, casting a flickering radiance on all those around her, and so she burns—and burns—and burns—as though held aloft by her own incandescent will and haloed about by all the gleaming great of the nation.

Investing the body of Ethel Rosenberg with agency through the active voice—with her "incandescent will" she "burns—and burns—and burns—" the image swoops the reader away from the fact that gets left out—that the body is dead and can will nothing.[18]

For Sylvia Plath and Adrienne Rich, young women in the 1950s, the death of Ethel Rosenberg became a piece of their emerging female consciousness. Unlike Coover and Doctorow, they try to absorb rather than distance her, to find in her some explanation of themselves. Plath's Esther Greenwood in *The Bell Jar* walks into her awareness of the tension between choosing life and choosing death in the context of Ethel Rosenberg's ambiguously unchosen death. Rich married in June 1953, one week after the execution. Then, she recalls ("For Ethel Rosenberg"), Ethel's family story reminded her of her own: "a bad daughter a bad mother." In her self-absorbed anxiety, Rich pushed her aside, her "life and death the possible / ranges of disloyalty / so painful, so unfathomable." Later, in the wake of the revelations of the Rosenberg files and the books in their defense, she tries to imagine who Ethel Rosenberg might have become: "would you / have marched to take back the night / collected signatures / for battered women who kill / What would you have to tell us?" Like Holden Caulfield, Rich wants to "call her up / to console my pain," but finally she must cease to appropriate the dead woman's pain as her own and allow her "to be at last / political in her ways not in mine."[19]

There was a neatness to the wrongful deaths of the saints and martyrs we learned about in religion class in the 1950s: they died for what they believed and offered models of resistance for us. For most of us the models were unusable: we did not have the strength of their faith. Ethel Rosenberg had the

191

strength of hers, and it killed her: "We are innocent.... This is the whole truth. To forsake this truth is to pay too high a price even for the priceless gift of life—for life thus purchased we could not live out in dignity and self-respect."[20]

Wrongful death—on the city streets, in Sarajevo, in the electric chair—makes us uncomfortable in our living bodies. We want to contain it, explain it, forget it. With even hostile critics finding it difficult to find proof of her guilt for the crime with which she was charged, the historical Ethel Rosenberg does not allow that containment and dismissal. The fictional Ethel Rosenbergs, transformed from sentient body to act of will, are attempts to limit that discomfort. "After her death," Adrienne Rich says, "she became a natural prey for pornographers / her death itself a scene/her body *sizzling half-strapped whipped like a sail* / She becomes the extremest victim / described nonetheless as *rigid of will*."[21]

NOTES

1 In June 1994 Governor Weld succeeded in getting the state senate to vote for the restoration of the death penalty, attaching the bill as a rider to the budget. Fortunately, the state house of representatives refused to go along. He persists, however, in his efforts to restore the death penalty in Massachusetts. The "humane" methods are ill-named: In November 1992, in Arkansas, Rickey Ray Rector, a retarded man, was executed for murder by lethal injection. He weighed three hundred pounds and the executioners had to search for forty-five minutes for a vein for the IV tube. The medical administrator said, "We were lucky to find a vein at all.... Rickey Ray Rector...helped." Quoted by James Carroll, "Let's Get Real about Execution in America," *Boston Globe*, May 31, 1994, 15.

2 A 1987 study published in the *Stanford Law Review* notes that between 1900 and 1985 there were 349 individuals wrongly convicted in capital cases. Twenty-three were executed. Cited in Amnesty International, *When the State Kills: The Death Penalty, a Human Rights Issue* (New York: Amnesty International USA, 1989), 14. See also Ian Gray and Moira Stanley, eds., *A Punishment in Search of a Crime* (New York: Avon, 1989). In May 1993, on the eve of the CLCS conference on the Rosenbergs, "Forty Years After," a 1:00 a.m. news broadcast announced, "The two hundreth person to be put to death since the resumption of the death penalty in 1976 will die tonight by lethal injection."

3. Elaine Scarry, *The Body in Pain: The Making and Unmaking of the World* (New York: Oxford University Press, 1985), 31.

4 JR Headquarters File, vol. 3, no. 188, Julius and Ethel Rosenberg papers, FOIA.

5 FBI Headquarters Files, vol. 5, Julius and Ethel Rosenberg papers. See also

National Committee to Re-open the Rosenberg Case, *The Kaufman Papers* (1976), in author's collection, and Ronald Radosh and Joyce Milton, *The Rosenberg File: A Search for Truth* (New York: Holt, 1983), 163–69.

6 Transcript of Record, *United States of America v. Julius Rosenberg, Ethel Rosenberg, Anatoli A. Yakovlev, David Greenglass, and Morton Sobell*, U.S. District Court, Southern District of New York, C.134–245, Mar. 6–Apr. 6, 1951, 1614, quoted in National Committee, *Kaufman Papers* and Radosh and Milton, *The Rosenberg File*, 283–84.

7 Dwight Eisenhower quoted in Stephen Ambrose with Richard Immerman, *Ike's Spies* (New York: Doubleday, 1981), quoted in Radosh and Milton, *The Rosenberg File*, 379.

8 Transcribed from a segment in *Atomic Cafe*, produced and directed by Kevin Rafferty, Jayne Loader, and Pierce Rafferty (Los Angeles: Thorn EMI Video, 1982).

9 The original of Ethel's letter with its postscript message to her psychiatrist was in the files when I saw them. For a full text of the letter, see Michael Meeropol, ed., *The Rosenberg Letters: A Complete Edition of the Prison Correspondence of Julius and Ethel Rosenberg* (New York: Garland, 1994), 702–3, and Michael Meeropol and Robert Meeropol, *We Are Your Sons: The Legacy of Ethel and Julius Rosenberg* (Boston: Houghton Mifflin, 1975), 265–66.

10 See Andrew Ross, "Reading the Rosenberg Letters," in *No Respect: Intellectuals and Popular Culture* (New York: Routledge, 1989), 15–41, for further comment on Ethel's letters.

11 Louis Nizer, *The Implosion Conspiracy* (New York: Doubleday, 1973), 209.

12 Jonathan Root, *The Betrayers: The Rosenberg Case—A Reappraisal of an American Crisis* (New York: Coward McCann, 1963), 277, 279.

13 The more recent novel, *Ethel: The Fictional Autobiography*, by Tema Nason (New York: Delacorte, 1990) is a well-researched book that attempts to recreate the historical Ethel Rosenberg rather than to transform her into a symbol. There is also a full-length biography by Ilene Philipson, odd in its criticism of Ethel Rosenberg for her reliance on her psychiatrist but mostly irritable at the Rosenberg sons for their disapproval of her interpretation. Ilene Philipson, *Ethel Rosenberg: Beyond the Myths* (New York: Franklin Watts, 1988).

14 Virginia Carmichael, *Framing History: The Rosenberg Story and the Cold War* (Minneapolis: University of Minnesota Press, 1993), 137. E. L. Doctorow, *The Book of Daniel* (New York: Vintage, 1971), 52. In the film *Daniel*, based on Doctorow's novel, Rochelle's willfulness is almost totally suppressed. Lindsay Crouse is a blond, gentle, and lovingly anxious Rochelle: only once, in a conversation at a beach, is she "political."

15 Doctorow, *The Book of Daniel*, 76.

16 Foucault opens his study of penology and punishment with a portrayal of the

execution of Damiens the regicide, "'taken and conveyed in a cart, wearing nothing but a shirt,... to the place de Grève, where on a scaffold,... the flesh will be torn from his breasts, arms, thighs, and calves with red-hot pincers, his right hand, holding the knife with which he committed the said parricide, burnt with sulphur, and, on those places where the flesh will be torn away, poured molten lead, boiling oil, burning resin, wax and sulphur melted together and then his body drawn and quartered by four horses and his limbs and body consumed by fire....'" In modern times, Foucault notes, torture has disappeared as a public spectacle: "the body as a major target of penal repression disappeared.... Punishment [tends] to become the most hidden part of the penal process.... As a result, justice no longer takes public responsibility for the violence that is bound up with its practice.... [T]he punishment-body relation is not the same as it was in the torture during public executions.... Physical pain, the pain of the body itself, is no longer the constituent element of the penalty. From being an art of unbearable sensations punishment has become an economy of suspended rights. If it is still necessary for the law to reach and manipulate the body of the convict, it will be at a distance, in the proper way, according to strict rules, and with a much 'higher' aim. As a result of this new restraint, a whole army of technicians took over from the executioner.... by their very presence near the prisoner, they sing the praises that the law needs: they reassure it that the body and pain are not the ultimate objects of its punitive action." Michel Foucault, *Discipline and Punish*, trans. Alan Sheridan (New York: Vintage, 1979), 3, 8, 9, 11.

17 Carmichael, *Framing History*, 139. Carmichael warns against a too literalist reading of the novel that would see it as "pornographic and sexist." In pointing to Robert Coover's continuation of the representation of the body of Ethel Rosenberg as will incarnate, I risk that reading.

18 Robert Coover, *The Public Burning* (New York: Viking, 1976), 640–41. The image comes at the top of an otherwise blank page.

19 See elsewhere in this volume Marie Ashe, "*The Bell Jar* and the Ghost of Ethel Rosenberg" for a discussion of Esther Greenwood/Ethel Greenglass. Adrienne Rich, "For Ethel Rosenberg," in *The Fact of a Doorframe: Poems Selected and New* (New York: Norton, 1984), 286–90. In a recent fictional incarnation, in Part 1 of Tony Kushner's *Angels in America*, Ethel Rosenberg is a ghostly visitor to Roy Cohn, who is dying of AIDS. Just before her appearance he has brayed of his triumph in convincing Judge Kaufman to send her to the electric chair: "my greatest accomplishment,... what I am able to look back on and be proudest of." She gets the last word here, calling an ambulance for him in stage Jewish dialect and then turning to warn: "History is about to crack wide open. Millennium approaches." Tony Kushner, *Angels in America, a Gay Fantasia on National Themes: Part I: Millennium Approaches* (New York: Theater

Communications Group, 1993), 107–12. Ethel returns in *Perestroika*, Part 2 of *Angels in America* (New York: Theater Communications Group, 1994), to tell Roy Cohn of his disbarment and to watch him die; in the 1995 touring production he greets her as "Mrs. Reddy Kilowatt." "I came to forgive," she tells him, "but all I can do is take pleasure in your misery…. You're dying in shit, Roy, defeated. And you could kill me, but you couldn't ever defeat me (114)." Tricked by Cohn into singing a lullaby just before he dies, she says Kaddish over his body and then vanishes (125–26).

20 Ethel Rosenberg, clemency petition to President Harry S. Truman, January 9, 1953, quoted in Miriam Schneir and Walter Schneir, *Invitation to an Inquest: A New Look at the Rosenberg-Sobell Case* (New York: Dell, 1968), 186. On hostile critics, see especially Radosh and Milton, *The Rosenberg File.*

21 Rich, "For Ethel Rosenberg," 288; emphasis in the original; Rich is quoting Robert Coover.

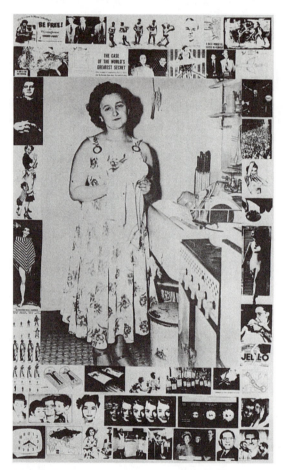

Martha Rosler, *Unknown Secrets*, 1988, detail.
(From *The Rosenbergs: Collected Visions of Artists and Writers*.
Courtesy of Rob A. Okun / Cultural Forecast.)

14

A Bond of Sisterhood

Ethel Rosenberg, Molly Goldberg, and Radical Jewish Women of the 1950s

Joyce Antler

Ethel Rosenberg was not the most famous Jewish woman of the early 1950s, though she came close. That honor must go to Molly Goldberg, the Yiddish-accented immigrant heroine of the long-running hit radio and TV series *The Goldbergs*. Although a fictional character, Molly was played with such verisimilitude by Gertrude Berg—in fact an American-born middle-class Jew—that the public easily confused the mythical Molly with her real-life impersonator. As we shall see, Berg, who created the character of Molly Goldberg as well as acted it, lived a very different life from that of her character. Yet Molly/Gertrude was powerful in popular culture precisely because she ostensibly represented—and existed in—reality. Molly's character, tied to Gertrude Berg, not only mobilized the cultural power of a historical, "real" person but in some senses, became a real person.

In much the same way that Molly Goldberg enjoyed a reality independent of Gertrude Berg, although closely linked to her, so the media representations of Ethel Rosenberg came to dominate public perceptions of the real Ethel. Yet the flesh-and-blood Ethel Rosenberg differed as much from the media's "Ethel" as Molly did from Gertrude.

Second-generation daughters of East European immigrant families,

Gertrude Edelstein Berg and Ethel Greenglass Rosenberg illuminate the changing aspirations of Jewish women in the mid-twentieth century. Sixteen years older than Rosenberg, Gertrude Berg, born in 1899 in an up-and-coming lower-class area of Harlem, attended high school in New York City and took several courses at Columbia University. As a child, she created and acted in amateur theatricals and hoped for a career as a writer or performer. Ethel Rosenberg, born in 1915 on the Lower East Side, where she lived most of her life, graduated from high school with honors, expecting to attend college. A veteran of school plays and musicals, she, too, looked forward to a career as an actress or singer. Unlike their mothers, both saw themselves as full Americans and as modern, educated women; with the right opportunities, they believed they could overcome any possible disadvantages wrought by their gender, ethnicity, or class and propel themselves, by dint only of their talents, into public careers in the arts.

In their mature years, both women defied convention: Gertrude, by building a media career and directing and producing a long-running hit series, all the while managing her own household and family life; Ethel, by combining a staunch commitment to radical ideology with a conscientious, even obsessive motherhood. For a generation or more, however, the cultural construction of the images of Molly and "Ethel" has left little room for imagining the full historical matrix in which Gertrude and Ethel lived their lives. Ultimately both women were vulnerable to the fashionings of fictionality—to the impositions of values and judgments wrought by American popular culture. The potent alliance between media and politics that characterized the postwar "red scare" years obliterated all but the masks of Molly and "Ethel"; the multi-sided women who inhabited their characters are harder to find.

The constructions of "Ethel" in the popular media were not, however, the only myths created about her. For a small group of American radicals, Ethel Rosenberg became a heroine, admired for the strength of her convictions, her courage, and her defiance. For one particular organization of Jewish women on the Left—the Emma Lazarus Federation of Jewish Women's Clubs—Rosenberg became a symbol of democratic protest and dissent. Her name was frequently linked to that of the group's most potent cultural symbol, Emma Lazarus.

Although more than forty years have passed since the execution of the Rosenbergs, the stories of Julius and Ethel as a couple and as individuals remain as controversial as the trial itself. Ethel's story is particularly elusive. The first complete biography of Ethel has been denounced by the Rosenberg sons as biased; Michael Meeropol, the eldest son, has recently published a compete edition of his parents' jailhouse correspondence, which he believes presents a more accurate portrait. Another attempt to have Ethel Rosenberg speak for herself comes from Tema Nason, author of a "fictional autobiography" in which Nason invents Ethel Rosenberg's voice on the basis of material from the historical record. In Virginia Carmichael's analysis, the continued retelling of the Rosenbergs' story in fiction, biography, history, and the performing arts is itself an indication of how deeply embedded the Rosenberg stories have become in Cold War and post-Cold War political and popular culture.[1]

One way to "know" Ethel Rosenberg is to separate the facts from the fictions of her life, placing her within the context of the domestic images and realities of her era; Molly Goldberg, because she sprang from the same immigrant milieu as the real Rosenberg and became the standard by which Jewish mothers were measured, is a particularly appropriate benchmark with which to gauge representations of Ethel Rosenberg. The juxtaposition of Ethel/"Ethel" and Gertrude/Molly tells us a great deal about public perceptions of American women—especially Jewish women—in the 1950s. While we may not recover the "true" Ethel Rosenberg, such an exploration, along with the alternative pairing of Ethel with Emma Lazarus and her 1950s self-styled radical successors, may bring a more fully rounded Ethel into view.

MOLLY GOLDBERG, "SO BASICALLY TRUE A CHARACTER"

The Rise of the Goldbergs was one of the most popular serials of radio's golden era, running from 1929 to 1946, and then from 1949–1950. After 1931 the show aired nightly, for some years carried by both the CBS and NBC networks. In 1948 the show, then known as *The Goldbergs*, made the transition to television, running through 1955. It was revived in the early 1960s as *Mrs. G*, a new series about Molly at college. Along the way came a comic strip, a syndicated column (*Mamatalks*), a published version of the show's early scripts, a cookbook, a hit Broadway play (*Me and Molly*), two films, and Berg's biography, *Molly and Me*. So identified was Gertrude Berg with Molly Goldberg that she was frequently greeted as "Molly" and signed autographs in Molly's name as well as her own. Yet it was Berg, the consummate professional, who wrote, directed, and produced the show's more than five thousand radio scripts as well as the later television programs.[2]

During the second quarter of the twentieth century, Molly Goldberg became the quintessential representation of the American Jewish mother in popular culture. "Kindhearted," "humane," "gentle," "gracious," "sympathetic," and "tender"—words typically used in advertisements about the show—Molly Goldberg, like her creator, Gertrude Berg, was nonetheless a woman of force and dominance; her co-stars considered Berg a "Napoleon" on the set. Berg's brilliance was to wed the iron qualities of traditional East European Jewish women with a charm and humor that counteracted the threatening aspect of their power. During the depression, when a negative stereotype of the Jewish mother as materialistic, pushy, and soulless began to appear in the works of Clifford Odets and other Jewish male writers, Berg's Molly demonstrated a more positive appeal.[3]

Molly's qualities of compassion and the comic elements in her character diverted attention from potentially troublesome traits. At best, meddlesome and at worst, nagging and controlling, Molly got her way in almost every show, but always for the purpose of helping others. Molly's speech, full of malapropisms, represented her status as an immigrant whose eagerness to adapt to American usages outweighed her knowledge: "Come sit on the table, dinner is ready…. I'll spill you in the soup…. Cut yourself a piece of the cake…. Please, Jake, don't disturb my faculties, please…. You'll swallow a cup, darling?…."[4] Molly's generosity and the quaintness of her language—including the famous opening lines of the show, "Yoo, hoo, Mrs. Bloom," which she yelled out her window to her tenement neighbor—endeared her to audiences.

No matter how exaggerated, caricatured, or sentimental were the show's characters, to audiences, they seemed believable and realistic. Writing in 1951, novelist Charles Angoff praised the show for its realistic representation of "virtually the whole panorama of middle-class Jewish-American life":

> There are the neighbors who borrow from and lend to one another, and who offer advice, whether asked or not…. there are the sisters and cousins and aunts, with all their jealousies and bickerings and generosities and meddlings…the young folks who sometimes think they have "outgrown" their parents but who find that for comfort and counsel there are no substitutes for these same parents…the widowed cousin or aunt with an only daughter who is still unmarried…the widower uncle who is obsessively proud of his son the doctor or the lawyer or the accountant, but in whose house he cannot live happily…. the miserly relatives who are not at all aware of their miserliness… the teen-age daughter, blossoming out into young womanhood, and who sorely needs grown-up advice, which she rejects as soon as it is given…the perpetually complaining mother-in-law… and there is Molly herself, whose heart bleeds for every unmarried girl and starving butcher and lonely grocer, and who is as quick as the proverbial lightning in concocting ideas to get the "right" girl and the "right" man together, to straighten out family squabbles, to help out a reformed thief, to get her own son to invite her to a college affair—in short, Molly the Mixer and the Fixer.

Together they presented "neurotic tension, despair, ecstasy, conniving, kindliness, back-biting—in short, the normal life of Bronx and Brooklyn and Manhattan and Chicago and Boston and Philadelphia and San Francisco Jews." Angoff concluded: "I have never heard anyone who knows Jewish life say that 'The Goldbergs' are not true to that life. Molly Goldberg, indeed, is so basically true a character that I sometimes think she may become an enduring name in the national literature. She is the prototype of the Jewish mother during the past twenty-five years."[5]

A good part of the praise for *The Goldbergs* came from its uplifting message about American family life and moral values. Berg once described the show to a reporter, using Molly's lines, "Jake wants the children to have everything money can buy, and I want them to have everything money can't buy."[6] Such a philosophical difference formed the core of the show's dramatic conflict, and despite the Goldberg's upward mobility, it was always resolved in Molly's favor. Listeners found *The Goldbergs'* message inspirational: ministers composed sermons around the program, and at least one Orthodox rabbi instructed congregants not to turn their radios off on Friday afternoon, so that they could listen to Molly on Shabbos evening "without breaking the law."[7] During wartime, especially, the show received accolades as "a force for decency and the democratic way of life."[8]

Three elements stand out in the Molly Goldberg character. First, Molly as a Jewish mother was an odd but lovable, generous woman who solved all the problems of her family, neighborhood, and community through her skillful "mixing-in." She as a voluble, talkative busybody, a *balabuster* with a loving heart who could always be trusted to do the right thing.

The second point is that in spite of her ethnicity, which was always prominent (even when the use of dialect subsided substantially), Molly and her children espoused assimilationist values. Over the decades the audience saw the family leave their Bronx neighborhood and move to the suburbs and send the children off to college. In this respect the Molly Goldberg show was an accurate representation of the Jewish middle class's rise to mainstream prosperity and to fundamental Americanism. Despite the family's economic transformation, Molly herself changed very little. Even in the mid-1950s, she looked and sounded like a newly arrived immigrant; according to a contemporary commentator, the series exhibited a "comicstrip changelessness …weirdly mating th[e] past and the present."[9]

The third point is that as the Goldbergs became America's surrogate family, Molly became everybody's mother, a woman who *because* of her ethnicity (that is, her difference) represented the American idea of "brotherly" love and interreligious cooperation. This point was emphasized in the huge amount of fan mail Berg received and in accolades from non-Jewish as well as Jewish organizations.

In order to achieve such wide acceptance in both the mainstream and Jewish audiences, Berg made a conscious decision, as she told one reporter, not to bring up "anything that will bother people…unions, politics, fund-raising, Zionism, socialism, intergroup relations, I don't stress them. And after all, aren't such things secondary to daily family living? The Goldbergs are not defensive about their Jewishness, or especially aware of it.... I keep things average. I don't want to lose friends."[10]

Like other situation comedies of the 1950s, *The Goldbergs* portrayed the family as a sea of domestic tranquility—a "suburban middle landscape," according to one critic—isolated from problems in the larger society. Sitcoms became "Cold War comedies of reassurance" in which politics, "by its telling absence... was a contaminating force to be kept beyond the threshold of the private household."[11] In shows like *Leave It to Beaver, Father Knows Best, The Adventures of Ozzie and Harriet, The Donna Reed Show, I Love Mama*, and *Make Room for Daddy/The Danny Thomas Show*, television reinforced values of family togetherness—responsibility, maturity, adjustment, and "enlightened permissiveness."[12] In most of these comedies, it was not the maternal figure but the benevolent patriarch who navigated his family through the shoals of neighborhood life. Yet Molly Goldberg's affable, homespun wisdom, like that of the Norwegian mother in *I Love Mama* (played by Peggy Wood), was no less authoritative than that of her male counterparts. As women in command of a vast repository of folk wisdom, Berg and Wood steered their families' adjustment to the special challenges of modern American life while demonstrating for the television audience that conflict could be easily managed and contained if "normal" family values were followed.

But this is not the whole story. Gertrude Berg could eliminate controversy from her show, but not from her life. Philip Loeb, who played Molly's husband, Jake, on radio in the late forties and took the character to its TV beginnings in 1949, was a victim of the blacklist in 1950. After a debate with her sponsors (who eventually pulled out) Gertrude Berg succumbed and fired Loeb in 1952; he committed suicide three years later. According to Donald Weber, Gertrude Berg might herself have been the target of a blacklist. Berg belonged to an actors group which included many well-known Left artists, including Paul Robeson. Comedian Milton Berle reveals in his memoirs that his sponsors and NBC would not permit Berg to appear on his show, even though she had her own.[13]

The portrait of Molly Goldberg as an ideal image of the Jewish mother in the 1950s may thus have clashed with the reality of Gertrude Berg's own politics; it certainly contrasted with Berg's professionalism. Married and the mother of two children, Berg had grown up writing skits to amuse the guests at her parents' summer hotel in the Catskills. Even after marriage and motherhood, she determined to pursue her career as a writer, but the short stories she submitted to popular magazines all came back with rejection slips.

Then came her breakthrough, with a trial run of *Goldberg* scripts, written for radio. Almost immediately, Berg became a highly successful media entrepreneur. She was no Molly Goldberg, stay-at-home housewife, though she prided herself on her "normal" family life.

ETHEL ROSENBERG: "NOT A GOOD MOTHER AFTER ALL"

Ethel Rosenberg also aspired to an artistic career, although it was as a singer and actress rather than a writer that she hoped to make her mark. An excellent student at Seward Park High School, on Manhattan's Lower East Side, Ethel planned to attend college and took college preparatory courses. Graduating in 1931, at the height of the depression, however, she felt herself lucky to obtain a clerical job with the National New York Shipping and Packing Company. But it was the Clark House Players, an amateur theater group sponsored by a settlement house around the corner from her home, that attracted her greatest enthusiasm over the next few years; she also took acting classes at the Henry Street Settlement and attended lectures given by members of several experimental theater companies, including the notable Group Theater. At the age of nineteen, Ethel was accepted into the prestigious Schola Cantorum, becoming the choir's youngest member; the group occasionally sang at the Metropolitan Opera House. The following year, singing an operatic solo at a benefit for the International Seamen's Union, Ethel met Julius Rosenberg, who claimed she had the most beautiful voice he had ever heard. They were married three years later.

Ethel pursued her singing and acting interests only sporadically after her marriage. Her independent involvement in political action also declined. Before she met Julius, she had helped to organize the Ladies Apparel Shipping Clerks Union at her company and served as the only woman on a four-person strike committee that called a citywide action in which over ten thousand workers participated. Fired for her role in this strike, Ethel instigated a complaint with the newly formed National Labor Relations Board; the case was later decided in her favor. By this time she had secured employment as a stenographer with Bell Textile Company. She left this job after Julius found work with the United States Signal Corps, and turned to volunteer activities. Among the groups she joined were the women's auxiliary of her husband's union—the Federation of Architects, Engineers, Chemists, and Technicians (FAECT)—and, after the outset of World War II, the Lower East Side Defense Council.[14]

After the births of her sons, Michael, in 1943, and Robert, four years later, Ethel became increasingly absorbed in family matters. According to one neighbor, she was "literally a mother 24 hours out of 24."[15] But motherhood did not come as easily to Ethel as it did to either Molly Goldberg or

Gertrude Berg. Beset by physical ailments resulting from her chronic scoliosis and the emotional strain of dealing with young children, she grew increasingly concerned about her parenting skills. Setting limits for her children and responding to them with both the generosity and the authority she felt good parenting entailed were especially problematic; such parental capacities emanated from the pages of *Parents* magazine, which Ethel read religiously, and from the vastly popular performances and pen of Gertrude Berg. Seeking help, Ethel took a course on child psychology at the New School for Social Research, and enlisted the assistance of a social worker at the Jewish Board of Guardians and, soon afterward, a private psychiatrist. Though she deeply loved and respected Julius, he could not alleviate her anxieties about raising their sons. Despite their political radicalism, both accepted gender role divisions that allotted breadwinning responsibilities to the husband while bestowing the wife with complete responsibility for childrearing. "The good mother is the key to proper child rearing," Ethel wrote to her lawyer, Manny Bloch, after she had been arrested and imprisoned, along with Julius, on the charge of conspiracy to commit espionage.[16]

In view of Ethel's faith in Communism, her resort to psychoanalysis and social work may seem surprising. But Ethel's worries as a mother apparently overshadowed any doubts she might have had at succumbing to such opiates of capitalist adjustment. In the emphasis she placed on childrearing, Ethel was in fact not far removed from the Molly Goldberg ideal. We don't know whether Ethel read Gertrude Berg's advice column in the 1930s, or listened to any of the *Goldberg* shows on radio or TV, but her ideal of the "good" mother overlapped with Berg's portrayal of Molly as understanding, tolerant, generous, everything her own mother—Tessie Greenglass—had not been.

According to Ethel Rosenberg's biographer, Ilene Philipson, Tessie Greenglass was an unhappy, troubled woman, disappointed with her husband's lack of ambition and inability to move the family out of poverty. Unlike the Goldbergs or the Bergs, the Greenglasses never realized their dream of American success; Tessie's frustrations with this failure were apparently visited on her only daughter. Favoring her three sons, especially the youngest, David (Davey or Doovey), she treated Ethel with a disrespect bordering on cruelty; Ethel was abused emotionally (and perhaps physically, since Tessie apparently used corporal punishment on all the children). Despite (or because of) Ethel's excellence at school and her good-girl demeanor at home, she also became the butt of her brothers' jealousy; according to Philipson, she was very much the "scapegoat" of the entire family.[17]

When, years later, David Greenglass accused Ethel and Julius of masterminding the spy ring in which he was allegedly involved at Los Alamos, Ethel was not surprised that her mother accepted her brother's story rather than her own. But the extent of her mother's lack of support for her, and her children, hurt her enormously. When Tessie at first visited Ethel in prison, it was only to scream at her for harming Davey and to call her daughter a "dirty Communist."[18] After Ethel was transferred to solitary confinement at Sing Sing, Tessie did not visit her at all for two years; when she eventually came it was only to urge her daughter to confess. Ethel responded angrily, but she admitted to her lawyer that she would "still give anything in the world for one kind word from her." Tessie returned two months before Ethel's execution to insist again that she affirm her brother's account and admit her guilt. According to the prison official present, Ethel, enraged, called her mother a "witch" and "yelled and raved to such an extent, that she was cautioned by the guard that the interview would be terminated unless she quieted down."[19] That was the last time Ethel saw Tessie.

No doubt the troubled relationship Ethel had with her mother accounted in good part for her concerns about her own parenting. But Ethel's anxieties about her performance as mother and her children's emotional well-being came also in part from cultural messages that she, like others of her background and aspirations, absorbed from the era. Under the growing influence of child guidance specialists and behavioral psychologists, parenting in the late forties and early fifties became more than ever a matter of expert counseling and knowledge rather than innate capability. During these years, the notion of motherhood as "pathology" became a staple of both the popular and scientific press, with all manner of experts holding mothers accountable for creating withdrawn, destructive, disturbed, and "deviant" children.[20] If Ethel Rosenberg blamed herself for childrearing problems within the Rosenberg family—however normal—she was merely reflecting accepted wisdom. So too was her exaggerated faith in the science of childrearing a mirror of popular tastes. Ethel's belief in professional child guidance in fact illuminates why Molly Goldberg became so popular a figure in the postwar period. In representing an earlier time when parents dominated their children's lives and truly "knew best," sitcoms like The Goldbergs—with Molly and other parental figures in indisputable if kindly command—provided nostalgic reassurance to a generation increasingly troubled about the viability of family life in modern society. Ethel's alarm about her own family, and her resort to therapy for herself in addition to counseling for the children, suggests how deeply a part of her generation she was.

In spite of her intense concerns about her children, Ethel Rosenberg's behavior during her trial convinced the American public—and jurors—that she was guilty precisely because she lacked maternal feeling. That Ethel was arrested and tried as a "lever" to force her husband to talk is now well documented. Depending wholly on the testimony of her brother, David

Greenglass, and his wife, Ruth, the case was "not too strong against Mrs. Rosenberg," as one prosecutor acknowledged privately. Such doubts continued even after Ethel's conviction: "Was your wife cognizant of your activities?" prosecutors asked Julius Rosenberg in a questionnaire submitted to him at Sing-Sing Death House.[21] In light of the paucity of evidence about Ethel's active participation in the conspiracy, her presentation at the trial became all-important.

Ethel's failure to break down under the pressure of her arrest and trial gave rise to the widespread belief that she cared more about ideology than her offspring and was therefore guilty. Her own denial of guilt, along with her repeated reliance on the Fifth Amendment, created the impression, according to one legal scholar, of a "cold, well-composed woman lacking 'normal' feminine characteristics."[22] Because of her failure to lose her composure on the witness stand (her husband and codefendant Morton Sobell appeared much more uneasy), Ethel appeared to be enigmatic, "unnatural." To the jury foreman she as a "steely, stony, tight-lipped woman. She was the mastermind. Julius would have spoken if she would have permitted him. He was more human. She was more disciplined."[23] According to another juror, she was certainly guilty—of being a bad mother: "I had two daughters at the time, and it bothered me how they would subject their children to such a thing. I just couldn't understand it."[24]

After the Rosenbergs were convicted and sentenced to death, the image of Ethel as an "unnatural" woman and mother blocked appeals for clemency. FBI director J. Edgar Hoover used the fact of Ethel's failure to talk with her own mother for two years as evidence of her evil nature; when Douglas Dillon, then ambassador to France, protested the severity of her sentence compared to that inflicted on convicted British spies Klaus Fuchs and Allan Nunn May, who received fourteen- and ten-year terms respectively, Hoover reported that when Tessie Greenglass urged Ethel to confess to spare her children, Ethel had rebuked her with the words, "Don't mention the children. Children are born every day of the week." Although he had previously opposed the execution of Ethel as well as Julius on the grounds that it would leave two young children orphaned, Hoover changed his mind after receiving the FBI's report that "Ethel was not a good mother after all."[25] In his denial of clemency, President Eisenhower used similar gender-based reasoning: "In this instance, it is the woman who is the strong and recalcitrant character, the man who is the weak one." He believed that as the unquestioned "leader in the spy ring," Ethel Rosenberg had renounced all rights for special treatment as a woman and mother of two young children.[26] She was the first American woman to be executed for the crime of conspiracy to commit espionage.

No greater contrast could be drawn between the Molly Goldberg motherhood ideal of the 1950s—friendly, garrulous, kindhearted, family-oriented, noncontroversial, and nonpolitical—and the public image of Ethel Rosenberg: silent and mysterious, conspiratorial and political, dominating and evil. Blindly loyal to her husband at the cost of abandoning her own children, she seemed, above all—and perhaps most dangerously—a neglectful, uncaring mother.[27] Many Americans who loved Molly Goldberg were deeply shocked by Ethel Rosenberg.

This portrait of Ethel Rosenberg, elaborated by the media, was especially troubling to Jews. Rather than the seamless adjustment to American society made by the Goldbergs, the Rosenbergs presented themselves as an alien couple, actually linked to a foreign power; their rejection of mainstream American values, such as those espoused by the Goldbergs and other TV sitcom families, spoke to the dark underside of the American dream and enhanced the presumption of guilt. Moreover, in contrast to the seemingly realistic Goldberg family and its image of wholesomeness, the Rosenbergs were a family fatally divided between brothers and sister, mother and daughter. In the early 1950s, such a family was not yet labeled "dysfunctional," the 1990s term of choice; in postwar America, the Rosenbergs seemed not only abnormal but un-American. For Jews who prided themselves on the closeness of their family ties, the portrait was a devastating reminder—and one that all of America could witness at first hand—that despite the warmth and folk wisdom of such characters as Molly Goldberg, they could not escape the centrifugal forces pulling apart modern family life.

That the Molly Goldberg ideal of mothering coincided with the behavior and aspirations of the real Ethel Rosenberg was no more ironic than the fact that Ethel, intensely, excessively concerned about mothering, was portrayed by government officials and the media as a cold, uncaring "monster" mother. Ethel's convincing portrait of stoicism in the face of her most enormous loss—that of her children—may have been her finest performance.

DEFENDING ETHEL ROSENBERG: CLARA LEMLICH SHAVELSON AND THE EMMA LAZARUS FEDERATION OF JEWISH WOMEN'S CLUBS

It was not, however, Ethel Rosenberg's mothering, or apparently lack of it, that made her a cause célèbre among a small, dedicated group of Jewish women. The Jewish community as a whole distanced itself from the Rosenberg case, fearing that the alleged connection between Jews and Communism could unleash a powerful anti-Semitic backlash. Even Jewish groups on the Left, including groups affiliated with the Communist Party, remained unusually silent on the subject of the Rosenbergs' guilt or innocence. After the death penalties were handed down, Jewish organizations came out strongly in favor of the sentence. The American Jewish Committee, for example, issued much propaganda in favor of the verdict; staff member Rabbi S. Andhill Fineberg supported all aspects of the government prosecution in his book *The Rosenberg Case: Fact and Fiction*, while alleging that the major group supporting the Rosenbergs, the Committee to Secure Justice in the Rosenberg Case, had been infiltrated by Communists. Organizations in which Jews were influential, like the American Civil Liberties Union, likewise defended the government's handling of the case, and denied that any civil liberties issues were involved.[28]

The Emma Lazarus Federation of Jewish Women's Clubs was one of the few Jewish organizations to challenge the government case. The ELF was a national organization with approximately seventy local chapters at its peak, including a strong representation in Brooklyn, the Bronx, and Manhattan; given its many Communist members, it was not surprising that the group sympathized with the Rosenbergs. Many "Emmas," as they called themselves, felt that the Rosenbergs were being prosecuted for their pro-Communist political views, not because they had committed acts of conspiracy; while most of America assumed the Rosenbergs' guilt, these groups just as naturally assumed their innocence. They were particularly supportive of Ethel, sympathizing with her plight as a mother and as a concerned Jewish radical. Ethel's silence on the witness stand and her "cold-hearted" demeanor appeared to them not as evasions but as principled demonstrations of dissent. Many agreed with her decision to deny her Communist associations in the belief that in the "red scare" McCarthy era, these would automatically be interpreted as evidence of treason or conspiracy. In any event, they considered Ethel Rosenberg not as a liar or a spy or even a misguided wife defending her husband, but as a patriot serving in the battle for social justice and convinced of her right, as an American, to defy the authorities and speak out on behalf of her convictions. In their study guides, they likened her to the women protesters who had established America's tradition of dissent: Anne Hutchinson, the seventeenth-century midwife and religious leader who challenged New England's clerical and secular authorities; the mill girls of Lowell, who fought attempts to speed up the conditions of work in nineteenth-century Massachusetts; and Jewish women garment workers, who led the battle for the fair treatment of laborers in the early twentieth century.

One of the women most drawn to Ethel Rosenberg's defense was Clara Lemlich Shavelson, a founder of the Emma Lazarus Federation of Jewish Women's Clubs and a labor heroine in her own right.[29] Shavelson was the young woman, barely out of her teens, who on November 22, 1909, at Cooper Union in New York, came to the floor to urge thousands of union workers to call a general strike. Already having been arrested seventeen times, Clara Lemlich was then recovering from a beating she had received two days earlier. Her speech, in Yiddish, led to pandemonium, and, after an oath to the Jewish faith, the assembly passed a general strike resolution. By the next night twenty thousand workers had gone out on strike. When the strike ended fourteen weeks later, hundreds of shirtwaist shop owners had signed union agreements. Although not all the workers' demands were met, the strike helped shape the course of labor organizing in the twentieth century and dispelled the myth that women wage earners could not be organized.

Although Clara Lemlich's activities after the strike have largely dropped from the historical record, she was one of a number of Jewish immigrant women whose activism never faded. She became a delegate to union conventions, an activist with the Women's Trade Union League, an outspoken socialist and suffragist, and a tireless organizer of women workers. After marrying Joseph Shavelson, a printer and union activist, and having three children, she helped organize tenants in her Brooklyn neighborhood and during the depression led hunger marches and bread, meat, and milk strikes. In the 1920s, she and several women members of the newly organized American Communist Party founded the United Council of Working-Class Women, which focused on organizing wives of workers around such issues as food, housing, clothing and schools.

In the 1930s, Shavelson attended the first International Women's Congress against War and Racism in Paris, traveling afterward to the Soviet Union. After her return she lectured on the Soviet Union to the Progressive Women's Council, the successor to the Housewives Council, which she served then as educational director. She became a familiar figure on Brighton Beach street corners, rallying workers against Hitlerism. In 1934 she ran for state senate on the Communist Party line, the only woman candidate.

At the time of World War II, the Progressive Women's Council, of which Shavelson was then president, merged with the women's clubs of the International Workers Order (IWO), a fraternal benefit insurance company formed after a split in the Workmen's Circle (the Arbeiter Ring) between the centrist "Forward Socialists" and the left-wing "progressive" radicals (who became the new IWO group) in 1929. Shavelson became New York City secretary of the IWO's Women's Division and was also active in the Jewish Peoples Fraternal Order (JPFO) of IWO.

In 1944 this Jewish order spawned an Emma Lazarus Division, attracting a membership of left-wing, largely Yiddish-speaking women, many of them of the immigrant generation. Motivated by the Holocaust, the division determined to fight against anti-Semitism and to nurture positive Jewish identification through a broad program of Jewish culture. Beginning in 1945 it offered fellowships for works of fiction and history on Jewish themes; it also supported a home for French war orphans and established a day nursery of children of working mothers in Israel. The division also supported a broad range of progressive women's issues: full employment for men and women; equal pay for equal work; maternity, unemployment, old-age, health and housing benefits, day nurseries and after-school care; the inclusion of greater numbers of women in government; support for black women's rights.

In 1951 the division became an autonomous Emma Lazarus Federation of Jewish Women's Clubs. This transition was influenced by attacks on the Communist Party and left-wing organizations like the IWO. At about this time New York State's Department of Insurance, aided by Joseph McCarthy and J. Edgar Hoover, initiated a campaign to liquidate the IWO as a subversive institution formed and directed "under the auspices of the Communist Party of America"; despite what are now recognized as questionable tactics, the IWO was forced to liquidate in 1954. Several IWO constituencies reorganized as independent entities; the Emma Lazarus Division had been moving away from the JPFO-IWO link in the late 1940s as it became more women-centered in any event; the Cold War attack on the IWO consolidated its autonomy as a women's group.

Because they were identified with the IWO and the Communist Party, several leaders of the Emma Lazarus Federation suffered from harassment during the McCarthy years. The government tried unsuccessfully to deport ELF executive director June Gordon, who had come to United States from Canada at age three; Clara Lemlich Shavelson had her passport taken away; other Emmas who were radical activists or Communist Party members were also harassed by the FBI. Under assault, ELF leaders protested McCarthyism, including the HUAC investigations.

The terrors of McCarthyism, which stigmatized many Jewish radicals as "un-American" Communists, contributed to the Emmas' desire to claim their own Jewish identity by promoting a progressive, secular Jewish heritage. Though its program was multifaceted, the federation's primary work in its first decade lay in writing and promulgating the neglected history of Jewish women. Like Gertrude Berg, who masterfully built the image of Molly Goldberg into a popular cultural icon, the immigrant leaders of the ELF also understood cultural symbols. They chose the poet and essayist Emma Lazarus—in their reading, a powerful and pioneering Jewish-identified feminist and human rights activist—as the emblem of a committed Jewish feminism. In the early 1950s, the ELF commissioned biographies of Emma Lazarus and Ernestine Rose, another nineteenth-century Jewish feminist committed to goals of social justice. They also wrote study guides about such other Jewish women activists as Rebecca Gratz and Lillian Wald and developed curricula on the role of America's working women in the Lowell mills, garment factories, and sweatshops. It was in this context that they highlighted Ethel Rosenberg as a symbol of forcefulness and dissent.

In the purposeful creation of such cultural heroines—especially Emma Lazarus—the ELF offered Jewish women symbols in which they could locate their hopes for a social movement that was radical, oppositional, and deeply imbued with the American values of civil liberties and social justice. Unlike Molly Goldberg as cultural heroine, however, Emma Lazarus, Ernestine Rose, and Ethel Rosenberg, were overtly, and proudly, political.

In Ethel Rosenberg's former union activism and the experience of her left-wing past, Clara Lemlich Shavelson recognized her own life story and the tradition of Jewish activism. She believed that Ethel's persecution could have happened to any one of her colleagues who had been active in radical politics, particularly those who joined the Communist Party. In defending Ethel from the charges against her, which she believed false, Shavelson affirmed the right of radical women to pursue political causes on the Left without compromising their Americanism. She devoted several years to working for the Rosenberg defense; although not many Emmas shared her commitment, many protested the death sentence and the "witch-hunt" hysteria they believed had caused it as political persecutions veiled over with anti-Semitism.

Shavelson did not acknowledge Rosenberg's growing isolation from the political and labor associations that had sustained her before her marriage and the birth of her children, probably because Ethel's family dilemmas were unknown to the ELF. To these women Ethel Rosenberg appeared not as an unnatural, uncaring mother—the flip side of the idealized, sanitized Molly Goldberg—but as the symbol of an activist, committed Jewish woman working on behalf of the wider interests of mothers and children all over the world as well as for her own family.

Had not she been arrested and convicted, it is possible to imagine that Ethel might well have emerged from the isolation she experienced in the late 1940s and early 1950s and connected with a community of radical women activists. She might, indeed, have found her way into the Emma Lazarus Federation, identifying herself not only with the progressive causes of the working class but as a Jewish woman concerned with anti-Semitism and antiracism. Ann Meeropol, the Westchester teacher who was the adoptive mother of the Rosenberg children, was in fact an active member of the Federation.[30]

In image if not in reality, Ethel Rosenberg did indeed find a place within the Emma Lazarus community. In Los Angeles, where a few ELF groups survived after the national organization disbanded in 1989, some Emmas participated in a project of the Hamish Amish quilters of Southern California which depicted 42 significant women in American history. The quilt they made became a poster produced by the National Women's History Project in 1992, one of its most popular artworks. As the Emma Lazarus Federation had earlier tried to place Ethel Rosenberg within a tradition of women's activism, she now found a place in a visual pastiche of the historical lives of diverse American women created by a group which included a number of former "Emmas."

But because one of the panels of the quilt contained Ethel's portrait, the poster created a brouhaha when it was hung in the Department of Justice in honor of National Women's Month.[31] While some posters remained in the halls of Justice, at least one copy was taken down. At another location in the department, Ethel's image—in the top left corner of the poster—was covered up. As much as the affable, benevolent image of Molly Goldberg, quintessential Jewish and American mother, stands for the experience of postwar American women, Ethel Rosenberg's somber portrait on the National Women's History poster—and the controversy it created—frames another, ironically related chapter in American women's history.

NOTES

1 Ilene Philipson, *Ethel Rosenberg: Beyond the Myths* (New York: Franklin Watts, 1988); Michael Meeropol, ed., *The Rosenberg Letters: A Complete Edition of the Prison Correspondence of Julius and Ethel Rosenberg* (New York: Garland Publishing Co., 1994); Tema Nason, *Ethel: The Fictional Autobiography* (New York: Delacorte Press, 1990); and Virginia Carmichael, *Framing History: The Rosenberg Story and the Cold War* (Minneapolis: University of Minnesota Press, 1993).

2 For information on Gertrude Berg, see Gertrude Berg (with Cherney Berg) *Molly and Me* (New York: McGraw-Hill, 1961); Joan Jacobs Brumberg, "Gertrude Berg," *Notable American Women: The Modern Period*, ed. Barbara Sicherman and Carol Green Hurd (Cambridge: Harvard University Press, 1980), 73–74; and Stephen J. Whitfield, "Gertrude Berg," in *Jewish-American History and Culture: An Encyclopedia*, ed. Jack Fischel and Sanford Pinsker (New York: Garland, 1992), 59–60.

3 See, for example, Beverly Gray Bienstock, "The Changing Image of the American Jewish Mother," in *Changing Image of the Family*, ed. Virginia Tufte and Barbara Myerhoff (New Haven: Yale University Press, 1979).

4 Charles Angoff, "'The Goldbergs' and Jewish Humor," *Congress Weekly* 18 (Mar. 5, 1951): 13; "The Goldbergs March On," *Life*, Apr. 25, 1949, 59; *The*

Goldbergs, script, Oct. 3, 1949, Gertrude Berg Papers, George Arents Research Library, Syracuse University.

5 Angoff, "'The Goldbergs,'" 12–13; undated scripts, Berg Papers.

6 Molly Goldberg cited in Jack Long, "Her Family is Her Fortune," *The American*, n.d., 111, Berg Papers.

7 Joan Jacobs Brumberg, "Gertrude Berg"; "Gertrude Berg," *The American Hebrew*, Oct. 8, 1943, 14. Sulamith Isk-Kishor, "Interesting People: Gertrude Berg," *The Jewish Tribune*, Oct. 10, 1930, 7.

8 See Louis Berg, "Entertainment Programs and Wartime Morale: Radio's Ten Best Morale-Building Programs," address at Regional Conference of the Association for Education by Radio, Stephens College, Columbia, Missouri, Nov. 5, 1942, Berg Papers.

9 Morris Freedman, "The Real Molly Goldberg," *Commentary*, 21 (Apr. 1954), 364; see also Donald Weber, "Popular Culture and Middle-Class Imagination: The Figure of Gertrude Berg in Radio and Television, 1930–1962," unpublished paper. Donald Weber's nuanced reading of Berg's career in radio and television as a benchmark of changing representations of ethnic identity was especially helpful to this analysis.

10 Freedman, "The Real Molly Goldberg," 360.

11 Hal Himmelstein, *Television Myth and the American Mind* (New York: Praeger, 1984), 84–97; David Marc, *Comic Visions: Television Comedy and American Culture* (Boston: Unwin Hyman, 1989), 65; Darrell Y. Hamamoto, *Nervous Laughter: Television Situation Comedy and Liberal Democratic Ideology*, New York: Praeger, 1989, 25. For a discussion of television's role as mediator between changing consumer roles and family life, see George Lipsitz, *Time Passages: Collective Memory and American Popular Culture* (Minneapolis: University of Minnesota Press, 1990), 39–75.

12 Hamamoto, *Nervous Laughter*, 24.

13 Weber, "Popular Culture."

14 For details of Ethel Rosenberg's life, see Carol Hurd Green, "Ethel Rosenberg," *Notable American Women: The Modern Period—A Biographical Dictionary* (Cambridge: Harvard University Press, 1980), pp. 601–4, and Philipson, *Ethel Rosenberg: Beyond the Myths*, passim.

15 Virginia Gardner, *The Rosenberg Story* (New York: Masses and Mainstream, 1954), 67, cited in Sheila M. Brennan, "Popular Images of American Women in the 1950s and Their Impact on Ethel Rosenberg's Trial and Conviction," *Women's Rights Law Reporter* 14, no. 1 (winter 1992): 47.

16 Ethel Rosenberg to Emanuel Bloch, Aug. 31, 1951–Sept. 6, 1951, in Robert Meeropol and Michael Meeropol, *We Are Your Sons: The Legacy of Ethel and Julius Rosenberg* (Boston: Houghton Mifflin, 1975), 101.

17 Philipson, *Ethel Rosenberg*, 28.

18 Ibid., 258.

19 Ibid., 345.

20 See, for example, Barbara Ehrenreich and Deirdre English, *For Her Own Good: 150 Years of the Experts' Advice to Women* (New York: Doubleday, 1978), Chap. 7.

21 Ronald Radosh and Joyce Milton, *The Rosenberg File: A Search for the Truth* (New York: Holt, Rhinehart, and Winston, 1973), 417.

22 Sheila M. Brennan, "Popular Images of American Women," 56.

23 Ted Morgan, "The Rosenberg Jury," *Esquire*, May 1979, 127, cited in Brennan, "Popular Images," 58.

24 Morgan, ibid., 131, in Brennan, "Popular Images," 59.

25 Brennan, "Popular Images," 60. David Oshinsky calls the FBI report "preposterous." See Oshinsky, "The Rosenberg Case," in *Jewish-American History and Culture: An Encyclopedia*, ed. Jack Fischel and Sanford Pinsker (New York: Garland, 1992), 553–54.

26 Brennan, "Popular Images," 60.

27 On women's images in the Cold War era, see Elaine Tyler May, *Homeward Bound: American Families in the Cold War Era* (New York: Basic, 1988), and Joanne Meyerowitz, ed., *Not June Cleaver: Women and Gender in Postwar America, 1945–1960* (Philadelphia: Temple University Press, 1994).

28 Benjamin Ginsberg, *The Fatal Embrace: The Politics of Anti-Semitism in the United States* (Chicago: University of Chicago Press, 1993), 121–22.

29 The following discussion of Clara Lemlich Shavelson and the Emma Lazarus Federation of Jewish Women's Clubs is adapted from Joyce Antler, "Between Culture and Politics: The Emma Lazarus Federation of Jewish Women's Clubs and the Promulgation of Women's History, 1944–1989," in *U.S. History as Women's History*, ed. Linda Kerber, Alice Kessler-Harris, and Kathryn Kish Sklar (Durham, NC: University of North Carolina Press, 1995), 267–95.

30 Conversation with Robert Meeropol, June 11, 1994.

31 Ibid; conversation with Lisl Smith, National Women's History Project, May 3, 1995.

15

The Bell Jar and the Ghost of Ethel Rosenberg

Marie Ashe

It was a queer, sultry summer, the summer they executed the Rosenbergs.

—Sylvia Plath, *The Bell Jar*

On the evening of June 19, 1953, Ethel Rosenberg and Julius Rosenberg were executed by electrocution at Sing Sing Prison. It has often been noted that Sylvia Plath's novel *The Bell Jar* takes the Rosenberg execution as its point of departure. Little attention, however, has been given to the nature and scope of the novel's particular involvement with the life and death of Ethel Rosenberg.

Upon her death in England in February 1963, Sylvia Plath was buried in Yorkshire. Her grave site was marked with a stone bearing the name "Sylvia Plath Hughes." By 1968, Plath's gravestone had on four separate occasions been altered by unknown persons who had prised off from the stone the marking of the name "Hughes," which was, of course, the surname of Ted Hughes, Sylvia Plath's estranged husband at the time of her suicide. These acts of alteration were generally taken to have been the work of feminists attempting to restore to Plath "her own name."[1]

The act of excision and/or excerpting performed repeatedly on Plath's gravestone reproduces an act that she herself performed in her writing of *The Bell Jar*. The name by which Plath identifies her protagonist, Esther Greenwood, is, with only slight variation, extractable from the full name of

Esther Ethel Greenglass Rosenberg.[2]

Sylvia Plath's naming of Esther Greenwood can be read as resembling, in its purpose or effect, that of her feminist interpreters. Her naming of Esther Greenwood can be seen as corresponding to their valorization of certain features of a woman's complex identity and their repudiation of others. In her naming of Esther Greenwood, Plath selected, isolated, distinguished, and reproduced the names that marked Ethel Rosenberg as a "private" person. She erased and repudiated the elements that identified Ethel Rosenberg in terms of her marital status: the surname of her husband, Julius; her motherhood: the surname she shared conventionally with her sons; and her "public" identity as political activist and as "spy." Indeed, the "Greenwood" variation of "Greenglass" can be read as preserving only those features of Ethel Rosenberg that are most purely "private" in that it erases the connection by common surname that publicly marked her "motherly" relationship to her younger brother, David Greenglass, a crucial witness against both Rosenbergs at their trial.[3] "Esther Greenwood" is an untainted and uncorrupted face of Ethel Rosenberg.

The Bell Jar is in part a story of struggle with familial relationship. It can be read as a young person's attempt to construct an identity separated from problematic parenting. It can be read in standard psychological-developmental terms as an account of separation from a bad mother or of emergence from a family in which parents had—as Louis Nizer says the Rosenbergs themselves had—"failed their children" and denied them a happy home.[4] The erasure, by Plath's naming in *The Bell Jar*, of all the mother-names of Ethel Rosenberg may reflect Plath's own preoccupation with having "permission to hate [her] mother," a permission, she noted following her own "breakdown" of 1953, that she believed essential to her own survival.[5]

That mother hating was fully implicated in the mother idealization of "how America lived" in the 1950s continues to be elaborated.[6] Recent work has provided detailed accounts of the public and private silencing of women in American families during the postwar period. The story of Ethel Rosenberg's prosecution, sentencing, and execution instances the most dramatic real-life penalizing of a woman of that era for reasons that relate specifically to her marriage and her motherhood. The consequences of what is often called "the problematic of motherhood" could hardly present themselves more dramatically and with greater power than they did in the execution of Ethel Rosenberg. That act evidenced the way in which law may be bowed, bent, and profoundly distorted by the power of a prevalent cultural construct.

Commentators have consistently noted that the decision to prosecute Ethel Rosenberg was directly attributable to her marital relationship with Julius Rosenberg. Ronald Radosh and Joyce Milton, for example, have pointed out that "from the very first, the government's interest in Ethel was based less on her own alleged complicity than on the possibility that the threat of prosecuting her could be used to pressure her husband into a full confession."[7]

Radosh and Milton cite a memorandum of July 1950 in which J.Edgar Hoover noted, "There is no question [but that] if Julius Rosenberg would furnish details of his extensive espionage activities it would be possible to proceed against other individuals...proceeding against his wife might serve as a lever in this matter."[8]

If her relationship to Julius Rosenberg, one in which she played the roles of wife and secretary, was the motivation of her prosecution, Ethel Rosenberg's maternal status, and an interpretation of her performance as failing to satisfy 1950s models of motherhood, worked to justify the imposition of the death penalty. Interestingly, J. Edgar Hoover himself became "genuinely appalled" at the reality that the attempt to use the prosecution of Ethel Rosenberg as a "lever" had failed but was likely to result in her execution. Hoover directed the preparation of a memo concerning FBI recommendations about the sentencing of the Rosenbergs, stressing Ethel's situation as the mother of two small children as a mitigating factor. Radosh and Milton point out that Hoover never changed his mind about the inappropriateness of the death penalty for Ethel Rosenberg until "...much later, when secret FBI reports gave him an excuse for convincing himself that Ethel was not a good mother after all."[9]

The need to construct Ethel Rosenberg as a "bad mother" was not limited to Hoover. And if it took some time for Hoover to achieve that construction, it took none at all for Judge Irving Kaufman to formulate it for himself and for the public. Thus Kaufman observed in his remarks at the time of sentencing, offering public assurance that the parental status of the Rosenbergs was peculiarly demonic, "Love for their cause dominated their lives—it was even greater than their love for their children."[10]

The degree of resonance that these comments had not only for the public in general but also for careful reviewers of the Rosenberg case is evident in Louis Nizer's ready acceptance and expansion of their import. Suggesting that the Rosenbergs' subsequent hatred of Judge Kaufman was attributable less to his imposing the death sentence than to his characterization of them as "sacrificing their children," Nizer proposes a "reason" for that "reality":

> The reason was that they knew subconsciously, at least, that there was some validity to the accusation. They had failed their children even before their arrest. Although brimming with love, they had not communicated it sufficiently to Michael and Bobby to prevent their neurotic behavior. Hadn't their intense activity for a better Communist world deprived their children of a better home? A

happy home, so goes a proverb, is an early heaven. The Rosenbergs may have begun to suspect that in searching for a heaven for society they had denied their children a heaven at home.[11]

Dwight Eisenhower, in justifying his denial of the Rosenbergs' request for presidential clemency, felt a need to construct Ethel Rosenberg as particularly "bad." Responding to a friend's suggestion that the execution of a young mother might seem inhuman, Eisenhower noted that Ethel was "the more strong-minded and the apparent leader of the two."[12] Further, contradicting the beliefs of the prosecutors and relying on false speculations about her particular role, Eisenhower wrote to his son, John, concerning Ethel Rosenberg that "it is the woman who is the strong and recalcitrant character, the man who is the weak one. She has obviously been the leader in everything they did in the spy ring."[13]

Ilene Philipson has suggested that Ethel Rosenberg's own acceptance of the powerful cultural mandate of "perfect motherhood" may have contributed to her declining to "cooperate" in ways that might have mitigated her own sentence. Philipson suggests that Ethel Rosenberg both accepted what most Americans of the 1950s understood "good motherhood" to be— "a full-time, isolated, all-consuming occupation that demanded perfection, a thorough knowledge of the most modern advice literature, and complete emotional equilibrium"—and recognized her own incapacity to achieve that standard. Philipson suggests that Ethel Rosenberg may well have believed, following her sentencing, that there remained only two mutually exclusive roles available to her: that of the "inadequate and contemptible mother," whom she actually believed herself to be; and that of the "stoic heroine" whom, by facing death, she might become.[14]

If Ethel Rosenberg embodied in the most powerful way imaginable the operation of the problematic of motherhood in American culture during the 1950s, that problematic operated in similar, if more symbolic ways for Esther Greenwood in *The Bell Jar*. It has already been suggested that the naming of Esther Greenwood produces a separation and repudiation of "Ethel" as public figure and stoic heroine, along with attempted resuscitation of the private, premarital, and nonmaternal "Esther."

The commentary on marriage and family life during the 1950s in both sociology and fiction readily discloses circumstances that would motivate Esther Greenwood's frequent declarations in *The Bell Jar* that she "would never get married." But, *The Bell Jar* cannot be read as a simple rejection of the marital and maternal roles assigned to women of the 1950s. For, indeed, Plath makes clear very early in the novel that Esther Greenwood's experience will record a successful navigation through constraints and challenges, culminating in a "recovery," a restoration to well-being, that involves the assumption of marriage and motherhood.Our deepening appreciation of the constraints of 1950s life for women makes puzzling Plath's reassurance or promise of recovery. In order to uncover the workings of Ethel Rosenberg as "ghost" in *The Bell Jar*, it will be helpful to follow Esther Greenwood through her summer of 1953. The text of *The Bell Jar* abounds with expressions of profound struggle and eruption, of allure and recoil that are not susceptible of containment—for Esther Greenwood, for Sylvia Plath, or for us—in the resolving simplicity of the postelectroshock, "all right again" 1950s mother.

The Bell Jar records an interchange between Esther Greenwood, the novel's protagonist-narrator, and Hilda, a student editor of Ladies' Day, at the Amazon Hotel on the day of the Rosenberg execution:

> The night before I'd seen a play where the heroine was possessed by a dybbuk, and when the dybbuk spoke from her mouth it sounded so cavernous and deep *you couldn't tell whether it was a man or a woman*. Well, Hilda's voice sounded just like the voice of that dybbuk....
>
> So I said, "Isn't it awful about the Rosenbergs?"
>
> The Rosenbergs were to be executed late that night.
>
> "Yes!" Hilda said, and at last I felt I had touched a human string in the cat's cradle of her heart. It was only as the two of us waited for the others in the tomb-like morning gloom of the conference room that Hilda amplified that Yes of hers.
>
> "It's awful such people should be alive."
>
> She yawned then, and...I stared at the blind cave behind her face until the two lips met and moved and the dybbuk spoke out of its hiding place, "I'm so glad they're going to die." (118–19; emphasis added)

Hilda's naming the execution as good is experienced by Greenwood as a horrifying enunciation.[15] It emerges from a place of darkness that is particularly disturbing because of its defiance of gender categorization. To read that passage as a simple statement of political protest relative to the execution would be to greatly minimize its textual power and its apparent meaning for Greenwood. The posture of Greenwood with regard to the execution is far more complex and ambivalent than can be summed up by or reduced to political positioning. *The Bell Jar* suggests the operation of intimate familial and sexual impulses within Greenwood's preoccupation with the Rosenbergs. The execution of Ethel Rosenberg was not simply horrifying to Esther Greenwood: it was also attractive and seductive.

The Bell Jar opens with evocations of sexuality and of heat: "It was a queer and sultry summer...." The first sentence suggests a conjunction of "queerness" and "sultriness."[16] *The Bell Jar* can clearly be read as a coming-of-age novel of the 1950s, as its protagonist's construction of sexual as well as social identity. Throughout the novel Esther Greenwood distinguishes persistently and consistently between sexualities: hetero- (problematic but eventually embraced) and homo- (strongly repudiated). But the construction of "sultry queerness" or "queer sultriness" of the first sentence repeatedly ruptures the surface of the text, threatening to subvert the simplicity and finality of the protagonist's ultimate "choice" or commitment.

The last phrase of the opening sentence refers to a major political event: "...the summer they executed the Rosenbergs." This phrase, too, marks a site—of the play of electricity and the proximity of death—about which the protagonist purports unitary feelings while betraying ambivalent ones. Esther Greenwood reflects: "I'm stupid about executions. The idea of being electrocuted makes me sick, and that's all there was to read about in the papers—goggle-eyed headlines staring up at me on every street corner and at the fusty, peanut-smelling mouth of every subway"(1).

She assumes a position of distance from the execution: "It had nothing to do with me" (1), she comments. But the execution-to-come, so repugnant that it "made her sick," at the same time represents some fascination. "I couldn't help wondering what it would be like" (1), she notes. And she proposes a preliminary account, that it would be like "being burned alive all along your nerves" (1).

Esther Greenwood resolves the ambivalent tension of attraction and repugnance by simplification: "I thought it must be the worst thing in the world" (1). But that summing-up did not undo the persistent and intrusively looming advance of the execution. Greenwood is surrounded by its imminence, unable to escape it, imagining the meaning of death by execution as entailing stench and decay. "I kept hearing about the Rosenbergs over the radio and at the office until I couldn't get them out of my mind. It was like the first time I saw a cadaver. For weeks afterward, the cadaver's head—or what there was left of it—floated up behind my eggs and bacon at breakfast and behind the face of Buddy Willard, who was responsible for my seeing it in the first place, and pretty soon I felt as though I were carrying that cadaver's head around with me on a string, like some black, noseless balloon stinking of vinegar" (2).

The persistence of these images tells her that something is wrong: "I knew something was wrong with me that summer, because all I could think about was the Rosenbergs" (2).

In a summer of opposing forces, heat produced intense dryness, burning, sizzling: "By nine in the morning the fake, country-wet freshness that somehow seeped in overnight evaporated like the tail end of a sweet dream. Mirage-gray at the bottom of their granite canyons, the hot streets wavered in the sun, the car tops sizzled and glittered, and the dry, cindery dust blew into my eyes and down my throat" (1). And it produced, as well, dampness, fizzling: "How stupid I'd been to buy all those uncomfortable, expensive clothes, hanging limp as fish in my closet, and how all the little successes I'd totted up so happily at college fizzled to nothing outside the slick marble and plate-glass fronts along Madison Avenue" (2). Greenwood moves or is propelled without agency through the city's summer, "like a numb trolley-bus" (3), she tells us. She replicates the city's surfaces by day (walking the sidewalks in "size-seven patent leather shoes, …black patent leather belt and black patent leather pocketbook to match" [2]) and by night ("skimpy, imitation silver-lame bodice…on some Starlight Roof" [2]). She does not "steer New York like her own private car" (3). She is not steering anything, she says, not even herself. In the queer and sultry time, in the "heat and humidity," preoccupied by the execution of the Rosenbergs, "I felt very still and very empty, the way the eye of a tornado must feel moving dully along in the middle of the surrounding hullabaloo" (3).

After providing this account of affliction and anxiety, Greenwood moves immediately to offer reassurance and promise. She shifts, in her first-person voice, to assure us that 1953 is a time remembered, not the present time of her remembering. The present time, she assures, is a time of well-being. The present is a place from which she is able to look back, resummoning in fine detail the summer of 1953 but escaped from the numbness and anxiety produced by that summer's associations of death. The summer of 1953 has had a happy sequel, she assures, in which the narrator occupies a different stage with a different interior state, in which figures of wellness and of life displace the eruptions of death and decay that troubled the New York summer. The novel is written, the narrator assures, from a position and a time in which she is "all right again" (4).

In this new and better place, she has retained from the summer experience what was of value, letting go of the rest. She has retrieved what "for a long time afterward" she had hidden away. She has become a woman integrating an appropriate occasional sexual glamour into the well being of attentive motherhood.

Esther Greenwood describes the "make-up kits" given the student editors by the magazine. She enumerates the small tools for self-construction that her needy former self had accepted as gifts while recognizing that they were not quite so. Salvaged from the troubling summer, those instruments adapt, with only minor modification, to her new life of motherhood and well-being:

I still have the make-up kit they gave me, fitted out for a person with brown eyes and brown hair: an oblong of brown mascara with a tiny brush, and a round basin of blue eyeshadow just big enough to dab the tip of your finger in, and three lipsticks ranging from red to pink , all cased in the same little gilt box with a mirror on one side. I also have a white plastic sunglasses case with colored shells and sequins and a green plastic starfish sewed onto it.

I realized we kept piling up these presents because it was as good as free advertising for the firms involved, but I couldn't be cynical. I got such a kick out of all those free gifts showering on to us. For a long time afterward I hid them away, but later, when I was all right again, I brought them out, and I still have them around the house. I use the lipsticks now and then, and last week I cut the plastic starfish off the sunglasses case for the baby to play with. (4)

"Using the lipsticks" marks—for Esther Greenwood and for Ethel Rosenberg, 1950s women—mental health, emotional stability, spiritual resourcefulness, hero(ine)ism. Louis Nizer has "reported" the remarks of lawyer Manny Bloch to Ethel Rosenberg when Bloch visited her following her transfer to Sing Sing: "The real purpose of my visit is to cheer you up a bit. Look at you—no lipstick, hair all over the place. Come on, you have had so much courage up to now. Don't let up."[17]

Ethel Rosenberg in Sing Sing had been removed from the possibility of actively mothering her two young children. But she continued to conform to prescriptions for sexual attractiveness in marriage that were not inconsistent with her "stoic heroine" role. Nizer has Ethel responding to Bloch's exhortation to use her lipstick: "Wait till Julius gets here. I'll doll up to kill."[18] Similarly, Esther Greenwood defines her state of wellness, the particular "integration" of motherhood and sexualized wifehood she has accomplished, as one of "us[ing] the lipsticks" "now and then," while providing for the baby's play.

Clearly, *The Bell Jar* cannot be read as reporting a journey toward well-being corresponding to the full course of Plath's own life. It can, however, I think, be read as a figurative "killing" of Ethel Rosenberg, and a haunting return of what I will call the "ghost" of Ethel Rosenberg. By the killing of Ethel Rosenberg, I refer to the distancing, displacement, and banishment—through the construction of Esther Greenwood—of a troubling model of 1950s public woman, a model of disturbingly unsuccessful marriage and motherhood culminating in destruction. By the haunting of Ethel Rosenberg, I refer to the resurfacing and return of what is banished in Esther Greenwood—a return that insists on the reality of imperfection, the inadequacy of an "identity" based on a simplicity located on one face of binarism. Beyond that, the "haunting" marked by Esther Greenwood's preoccupation with the Rosenberg execution itself, with the reality of death, marks a surfacing that signals something "other"—something less definable than the figures of "Esther" and of "Ethel" taken singly or in conjunction.

The text of *The Bell Jar* abounds with images expressing Esther Greenwood's efforts to resolve issues of sexual identity, efforts occurring on the surface of a depth of conflicting and confusing desires. Greenwood renders electrocution-execution as horrifying, sickening, and lethal. She renders electrocution-electroshock as curative, restorative, and life-giving. This deviating parallel bespeaks an attempt to resist by containment, limitation, and restructuring the deathward attraction embodied for Esther Greenwood in Ethel Rosenberg. *The Bell Jar* can be read, in its broad ambivalences about sexuality and about death, as in its particular rejection of parts of Ethel Rosenberg's identity/name, as recording an attempt to achieve "integration" or "identity" on the basis of a limited exposure to electrocution different from Ethel Rosenberg's, on the basis of an embodiment of wifehood and motherhood likewise different from hers.

The Bell Jar purports to record the passage of Esther Greenwood from an unsatisfactory relationship with a boyfriend (Buddy Willard) through a series of attempted and missed connections with young men and women ("boys" and "girls") whom Greenwood encounters in the city, in her hometown, and in the mental hospitals' wards. Somehow, this passage culminates in a resolution consisting of marriage and maternity. Paralleling and supporting Greenwood's exploration of possible relationships with men is a determined rejection of the seductive possibilities of connections to women. Both these kinds of movements occur within a context of persistent and recurring suggestions of undecidable gender.

The pursuit of satisfactory heterosexual relationship against a backdrop of interesting or seductive lesbian possibilities is apparent throughout the novel. An examination of the subtext of other-than-heterosexual possibility that recurs throughout *The Bell Jar* is evident in the novel's elaboration of the relationship between Esther Greenwood and another of the student editors, Doreen.

Esther's relationship with Doreen proves to be "troubling" because Doreen attracts her and invites her to share experiences into which, it proves, Esther is unable to enter fully.

> I guess one of my troubles was Doreen.
>
> I'd never known a girl like Doreen before. Doreen came from a society girls' college down South and had bright white hair standing out in a cotton candy fluff round her head and blue eyes like transparent agate marbles, hard and polished and just about indestructible and a mouth set in a sort of perpetual sneer. I don't mean a nasty sneer, but an amused mysterious sneer, as if all the people around

her were pretty silly and she could tell some good jokes on them if she wanted to. Doreen singled me out right way. She made me feel I was that much sharper than the others, and she really was wonderfully funny. She used to sit next to me at the conference table, and when the visiting celebrities were talking she'd whisper witty sarcastic remarks to me under her breath. (5)

Doreen is attractive to Esther. Her ways of being suggested "a whole life of marvelous elaborate decadence that attracted me like a magnet" (6). And Doreen's attractiveness is sexual. She lounges on Esther's bed in a silk-dressing gown while Esther works dutifully at her editorial tasks. Unlike the other student editors, Doreen "wore these full-length nylon and lace jobs you could half see through and dressing gowns the color of skin, that stuck to her by some kind of electricity. She had an interesting slightly sweaty smell that reminded me of those scallopy leaves of sweet fern you break off and crush between your fingers for the musk of them" (6).

Together Doreen and Esther discuss Jay Cee, Esther's boss. Esther has admired Jay Cee, who "had brains," so that the "plug-ugly looks" that Doreen ridicules have not troubled Esther. Esther tries to imagine Jay Cee in some integration of intelligence and sex, but the attempt fails. "I tried to imagine Jay Cee out of her strict office suit and luncheon-duty hat and in bed with her fat husband, but I just couldn't do it. I always had a terribly hard time trying to imagine people in bed together" (7).

Esther determines that perhaps what she needs to know will not be learnable from Jay Cee. "Jay Cee wanted to teach me something, all the old ladies I ever knew wanted to teach me something, but I suddenly didn't think they had anything to teach me. I fitted the lid on my typewriter and clicked it shut." Esther determines to look to Doreen's teaching instead. "Doreen grinned. 'Smart girl'" (7).

Doreen is different from "the other girls" at the Amazon in her overt sexuality and especially, Esther notes, in her intuition. In this respect she differs not only from the other girls but also from the Yalies who will be invited to the evening's dance, and especially from Buddy Willard who went to Yale and had good marks but "didn't have one speck of intuition. Doreen had intuition. Everything she said was like a secret voice speaking straight out of my own bones" (8).

When Esther and Doreen travel together by cab across the city, Doreen wears a "strapless white lace dress zipped up over a snug corset affair that curved her in at the middle and bulged her out again spectacularly above and below" (8). Esther, by contrast, "wore a black shantung sheath," a dress that, she says was cut "queerly"—so much so that "I couldn't wear any sort of bra under it, but that didn't matter much as I was skinny as a boy and barely rippled, and I liked feeling almost naked on the hot summer nights" (9).

When their cab sits wedged between cabs carrying some of the "other girls," a "man in a blue lumber shirt and black chinos and tooled leather cowboy boots" approaches Doreen and Esther, to ask the question that gives rise to 1990s jokes: "And what, may I ask, are two nice girls like you doing all alone in a cab on a nice night like this?" (9). The two exit the cab to accompany the man—Lenny—Doreen in her bridelike outfit, leaving behind the "other girls," who resemble "a wedding party with nothing but bridesmaids" (11).

For Esther, accompanying Doreen into the world of heterosexual activity framed in 1950s style marks no escape from the morbidity of cadavers and anticipated execution that she has already disclosed. She is paired up with a "short, scrunty fellow" who makes her feel "gawky and morbid." She finds herself cast as voyeur to the stylized heterosexual performance of Doreen and Lenny. When Doreen returns, drunk, to the Amazon Hotel, knocking at Esther's door, Esther makes a decision, rejecting both the confidently assertive heterosexuality that Doreen models and also the figure of Doreen-as-bride:

> I felt if I carried Doreen across the threshold into my room and helped her onto my bed I would never get rid of her again.
>
> Her body was warm and soft as a pile of pillows against my arm where she leaned her weight, and her feet, in their high, spiked heels, dragged foolishly....
>
> I made a decision about Doreen that night. I decided I would watch her and listen to what she said, but deep down I would have nothing at all to do with her. Deep down, I would be loyal to Betsy and her innocent friends. It was Betsy I resembled at heart. (26–27)

The nonheterosexual allusions of *The Bell Jar* surface early in the novel in the note that its major site, the Amazon Hotel, is an "improper" place, a site of nonheterosexual living arrangements: "It wasn't a proper hotel—I mean a hotel where there are both men and women mixed about here and there on the same floor" (4). *The Bell Jar* suggests that, for Esther Greenwood, heterosexuality can be dangerously violent (for example, in the encounter with Marco)[19] as well as unsatisfactory. It also suggests that a relationship between a woman and a man that does not follow the expected and prescribed scenario can be surprising and disappointing (as Greenwood's encounter with Constantin).[20] But beyond raising possibilities that there exist alternative homosexual possibilities, *The Bell Jar* raises insistently the reality of undecidability against which both prescribed and alternative structures emerge. Such undecidability is most to be feared and most horrifying—as is evident in the speech that emerges from Hilda's mouth—from a source about which "...you couldn't tell whether it was a man or a woman" (118). This undecidability operates to evoke horror. And it demands a resolution into the kind of simplicity that will permit escape from horror.

The simplifying resolution surrounding sexual issues is repeated in Greenwood's resolution of the ambivalence she experiences with regard to the execution of the Rosenbergs. The prospect of the execution at one and the same time "makes her sick" and invites and receives her lingering thoughts. It seems, in its burning, "the worst thing there is." But, among the turns of *The Bell Jar* occurs the turn through which Esther Greenwood redefines electrocution. Electroshock treatment—a preferred "therapy" for women of the 1950s[21]—ultimately is experienced not as deathly but as saving. Greenwood ultimately defines that experience of "blue volts and noise" (246) as redemptive.

Her New York sojourn being followed by deepening depression and dissociation, Greenwood undergoes a first experience of electroshock. The description of the preparations for that procedure are reminiscent of the details of preparation of the bodies of Julius and Ethel Rosenberg for execution. The preparation takes place in a "bare room at the back of the house," a room with barred windows, in which "everything that opened and shut was fitted with a keyhole so it could be locked up" (170).

> Doctor Gordon was unlocking the closet. He dragged out a table on wheels with a machine on it and rolled it behind the head of the bed. The nurse started swabbing my temples with a smelly grease....
>
> Doctor Gordon was fitting two metal plates on either side of my head. He buckled them into place with a strap that dented my forehead, and gave me a wire to bite.
>
> I shut my eyes.
>
> There was a brief silence, like an indrawn breath.
>
> Then something bent down and took hold of me and shook me like the end of the world. Whee-ee-ee-ee-ee, it shrilled, through an air crackling with blue light, and with each flash a great jolt drubbed me till I thought my bones would break and the sap fly out of me like a split plant.
>
> I wondered what terrible thing it was that I had done. (171)

When the procedure is completed, someone asks Greenwood, "How do you feel?"

> An old metal floor lamp surfaced in my mind. One of the few relics of my father's study, it was surmounted by a copper bell which held the light bulb, and from which a frayed, tiger-colored cord ran down the length of the metal stand to a socket in the wall.
>
> One day I decided to move this lamp from the side of my mother's bed to my

desk at the other end of the room....I closed both hands around the lamp and the fuzzy cord and gripped them tight.

Then something leapt out of the lamp in a blue flash and shook me till my teeth rattled, and I tried to pull my hands off, but they were stuck, and I screamed, or a scream was torn from my throat, for I didn't recognize it, but heard it soar and quaver in the air like a violently disembodied spirit.

Then my hands jerked free, and I fell back onto my mother's bed. A small hole, blackened as if with pencil lead, pitted the center of my right palm.

"How do you feel?"

"All right."

But I didn't. (172)

The first shock treatment is followed by Greenwood's nearly successful attempt at suicide and her subsequent hospitalization. Emerging from her near-death state, she requests a mirror in which to examine herself:

At first I didn't see what the trouble was. It wasn't a mirror at all, but a picture.

You couldn't tell whether the person in the picture was a man or a woman, because their hair was shaved off and sprouted in bristly chicken-feather tufts all over their head. One side of the person's face was purple, and bulged out in a shapeless way, shading to green along the edges, and then to a sallow yellow. The person's mouth was pale brown, with a rose-colored sore at either corner.

The most startling thing about the face was its supernatural conglomeration of bright colors.

I smiled.

The mouth in the mirror cracked into a grin. (208)

The mirror recognition of gender undecidability is succeeded by a second set of electroshock treatments. Greenwood learns that the electroshock will be administered on a particular morning when, like the Death Row occupant awaiting his—or her—last meal, she waits for her breakfast tray. The tray is not delivered and she inquires about it:

"What's the name?"

"Greenwood. Esther Greenwood."

"Greenwood, Greenwood, Greenwood." The maid's warty index finger slid down the list of names of the patients in Belsize tacked up on the kitchen wall. "Greenwood, no breakfast today."

"...There must be a mistake. Are you sure it's Greenwood?"

"Greenwood," the maid said decisively as the nurse came in. (p. 253)

Given this information, Greenwood hides away in an alcove, feeling betrayed by the psychiatrist who has not warned her ahead of time about the shock treatment. Had she been warned in advance, she would have "gone down the hall...with dignity, like a person cooly resigned to execution" (253). Had she been warned, she would have summoned up the dignity and courage of Ethel Rosenberg.

The administration of this electroshock, like that of the earlier one, occurs within an environment whose depiction reminds the reader of death-chamber descriptions, and, significantly, against the haunting backdrop of gender undecidability: "Through the slits of my eyes, which I didn't dare open too far, lest the full view strike me dead, I saw the high bed with its white, drumtight sheet, and the machine behind the bed, and the masked person— I couldn't tell whether it was a man or a woman—behind the machine, and other masked people flanking the bed on both sides" (256). The rituals preparatory to death by electrocution are performed. The attendant began "smoothing the salve on my temples and fitting the small electric buttons on either side of my head" (256). And then, for Greenwood, electricity delivers not death but relief, the lifting of the "bell jar": "All the heat and fear had purged itself. I felt surprisingly at peace. The bell jar hung, suspended, a few feet above my head. I was open to the circulating air" (257).

The electroshock experience is succeeded by a series of similar ones—"a brief series of five" (258)—which accomplish for Greenwood "the sweetness of recovery" (258) and the effect of "rebirth." Electricity, the "being burned along the nerves" (1), has been tried and found not lethal but rebirthing. It is to the electroshock experiences that Greenwood attributes her ultimate departure from "the asylum." Attending the funeral of a copatient (a "seductive lesbian" who has killed herself),[22] Greenwood recognizes her own "recovery" and her firmed "identity":

> I took a deep breath and listened to the old brag of my heart.
> I am, I am, I am. (289)

Having achieved that identity, Esther Greenwood has truly become the partiality that her name names. As *The Bell Jar* concludes, Esther Greenwood believes herself able to "reenter" the world. The formerly uncategorizable faces of the electroshock attendants, the "cadaverous" face of the nurse, have all become, in the aftermath of electroshock, clearer and beneficent. Greenwood herself stands comfortably in the black shoes of the New York summer, ready for restoration:

> My stocking seams were straight, my black shoes cracked, but polished, and my red wool suit flamboyant as my plans. Something old, something new....
> But I wasn't getting married. There ought, I thought, to be a ritual for being born twice—patched, retreaded and approved for the road....

Pausing, for a brief breath, on the threshold, I saw...the pocked, cadaverous face of Miss Huey, and eyes I thought I had recognized over white masks.

The eyes and faces all turned themselves toward me, and guiding myself by them, as by a magical thread, I stepped into the room. (275)

So *The Bell Jar* ends, leaving a gap between the moment of Greeenwood's "recovery" and the later scene of her writing while her baby plays. *The Bell Jar* ends with Esther Greenwood's having seemingly extinguished the troubling gendered reality of Ethel Rosenberg. Having escaped the fate of the woman found "deserving" of death, Esther Greenwood has "magically" passed through the experience of electrocution redeemed and reborn.

The ironies attaching to that resolution are, of course, chilling, when we recall that the publication of *The Bell Jar* in January 1963 was followed by Sylvia Plath's death by suicide in February 1963. Those ironies invite our speculation about the range of possible "identities" afforded by female experience during the 1950s. They suggest the incapacity of such "identities" to withstand the deathward pull of undifferentiated forces—what Julia Kristeva might call "powers of horror"—that "float up," like the head of the cadaver (2), through the cultural forms within which they are produced.

NOTES

This article was suggested by Anna Mollow's reminding me of the connections between Sylvia Plath and the Rosenbergs.

Thanks to Kathleen Marotta, Marjorie Garber, and Rebecca L. Walkowitz for helpful readings.

Epigraph from Sylvia Plath, *The Bell Jar* (New York: Harper, 1971), 1. Subsequent page refernces in *The Bell Jar* will be indicated in the text.

1 Jacqueline Rose, *The Haunting of Sylvia Plath* (Cambridge: Harvard University Press, 1992), Chap. 3, 65–113.

2 Ilene Philipson, in *Ethel Rosenberg: Beyond the Myths* (New York: Franklin Watts, 1988), distinguishes the periods of Ethel Rosenberg's life with reference to her self-identifications as "Ethel Greenglass," "Ethel Rosenberg," and "Saint Joan."

3 Ethel Rosenberg cared, as a kind of "second mother," for her younger brother, David Greenglass, whom she called "Doovey." David Greenglass was born when Ethel was six and a half years old. Philipson, *Ethel Rosenberg*, 27; Louis Nizer, *The Implosion Conspiracy* (New York: Doubleday, 1973), 5, 18.

4 Nizer, *The Implosion Conspiracy*, 367.

5 Sylvia Plath, *The Journals*, ed. Frances McCulloch and Ted Hughes (New York: Dial Press, 1982), 265–85.

6 Stephanie Coontz, *The Way We Never Were: American Families and the Nostalgia Trap* (New York: Basic, 1992).

7 Ronald Radosh and Joyce Milton, *The Rosenberg File: A Search for the Truth* (New York: Holt, 1983), 98.

8 J. Edgar Hoover cited in ibid., 99.

9 Radosh and Milton, *The Rosenberg File*, 281, 386.

10 Judge Irving Kaufman cited in Nizer, *The Implosion Conspiracy*, 357.

11 L. Nizer, *The Implosion Conspiracy*, 367.

12 Dwight Eisenhower cited in Radosh and Milton, 378.

13 Ibid., 379.

14 Philipson, *Ethel Rosenberg*, 149–65, 310–13.

15 The importance of the Rosenberg execution to Plath is reflected in her journal writing as well as in *The Bell Jar*. See *Journals*, 81–82. The *Journals* editors note that the single surviving journal entry made by Plath concerning her "Guest Editor" experience at *Mademoiselle* is the following:

> June 19, 1953. All right, so the headlines blare the two of them [the Rosenbergs] are going to be killed at eleven o'clock tonight. So I am sick at the stomach. I remember the journalist's report, sickeningly factual, of the electrocution of a condemned man, of the unconcealed fascination of the faces of the onlookers, of the details, the shocking physical facts about the death, the scream, the smoke, the bare honest unemotional reporting that gripped the guts because of the things it didn't say.
>
> The tall beautiful catlike girl who wore an original hat to work every day rose to one elbow from where she had been napping on the divan in the conference room, yawned, and said with beautiful bored nastiness: "I'm so glad they are going to die." She gazed vaguely and very smugly around the room, closed her enormous green eyes, and went back to sleep.
>
> The phones are ringing as usual, and the people planning to leave for the country over the long weekend, and everybody is lackadaisical and rather glad and nobody very much thinks about how big a human life is, with all the nerves and sinews and reactions and responses that it took centuries and centuries to evolve.
>
> They were going to kill people with those atomic secrets. It is good for them to die. So that we can have the priority of killing people with those atomic secrets which are so very jealously and specially and inhumanly ours.
>
> There is no yelling, no horror, no great rebellion. That is the appalling thing. The execution will take place tonight; it is too bad that it could not

be televised…so much more realistic and beneficial than the run-of-the-mill crime program. Two real people being executed. No matter. The largest emotional reaction over the United States will be a rather large, democratic, infinitely bored and casual and complacent yawn."

16 For discussion of the historicity of the term "queer," see Judith Butler, *Bodies That Matter* (New York: Routledge, 1993), 176.

17 Nizer, *The Implosion Conspiracy*, 370.

18 Ibid.

19 Marco is a man whom Esther Greenwood defines as a "woman-hater": "I could tell that Marco was a woman-hater because in spite of all the models and TV starlets in the room that night he paid attention to nobody but me. Not out of kindness or even curiosity, but because I'd happened to be dealt to him, like a playing card in a pack of identical cards" (*The Bell Jar*, 87). Marco beats Esther up at the end of their evening together; see *The Bell Jar*, Chap. 9.

20 Esther Greenwood finds that the time she spends with Constantin, who is a Russian interpreter at the United Nations, reminds her of the "purely happy" times she spent in childhood with her father. She decides to let Constantin "seduce" her. But Constantin proves to have no interest in so doing; see *The Bell Jar*, Chap. 7.

21 Carol Warren, *Madwives: Schizophrenic Women in the 1950s* (New Brunswick, NJ: Rutgers University Press, 1987). Coontz, *The Way We Never Were*, 32.

22 *The Bell Jar*'s character Joan Gilling was referred to as a "seductive lesbian" by Irving Kaufman, the trial judge and sentencer of the Rosenbergs. See Irving R. Kaufman, "The Creative Process and Libel," *New York Times Magazine*, Apr. 5, 1987, 28–36. Kaufman's article addresses issues of libel law presented by the assertions of Jane Anderson, who claimed damages incident to the release of the film version of *The Bell Jar*. Anderson had been a McLean Hospital copatient of Sylvia Plath and claimed to have been the "real-life" model for Joan Gilling. Anderson asserted that she had been libeled by *The Bell Jar*'s false representations that she had committed suicide and that she had attempted to seduce Plath. In discussing that claim, Kaufman made no comment on connections between *The Bell Jar* and the execution of the Rosenbergs.

PART THREE

Testimonies

Julius and Ethel Rosenberg, surrounded
by U.S. Marshalls.

(AP/Wide World Photos)

Michael Rosenberg, 9, and Robert
Rosenberg, 5, (from left to right) leave
Sing Sing Prison after a two-hour visit
with their parents in February 1953.
They are with their parent's attorney,
Emanuel H. Bloch (far left).

(AP/Wide World Photos)

16

Rosenberg Realities

Robert Meeropol

Throughout my adult life hundreds of people have asked me in one way or another why I'm not bitter or dysfunctional. After all, for the first three years of my life I was raised by Ethel and Julius Rosenberg, and then I suffered through their trial and execution, family rejection, institutionalization, police seizure, and custody battles. Even without the latter, how could a child not be irretrievably damaged by a mother and father who it is widely believed attempted to mix two seemingly irreconcilable activities: high-risk Communist politics and parenting during the McCarthy period. But perhaps these roles were not mutually exclusive. Certainly, the public personas imposed on my family during the years 1950 to 1954 stand in sharp contrast with my memories of that time. Is it possible to be progressive activists while remaining sensitive and caring parents and people?

It is not my purpose here to argue my belief that my parents were framed. I feel compelled, however, to state briefly my position. There is overwhelming evidence that my parents were not guilty as charged. That is, that they did not conspire with David and Ruth Greenglass, Harry Gold, and Anatoly Yakovlev to steal critical information about the atomic bomb. But I can't prove that they never had any contact with Soviet agents. I do not know all that they did between 1939 and 1950. But it is indisputable that two people were executed for *conspiracy* on the say–so of three others (David and Ruth Greenglass and Harry Gold). These informants were repeatedly shown to have perjured themselves with the connivance of government agents, and two of them also faced the death penalty if they did not testify as they did. In our country one is presumed innocent until convicted. If the evidence necessary to support a guilty verdict is fraudulent, the conviction cannot stand. If the conviction is discarded, the defendants must once again be presumed innocent. The government's files demonstrate that the guilty verdict in my parents' case was based on perjured testimony and fraudulent evidence. In other words, my parents were framed and are, therefore, entitled to be presumed innocent.

What is known about my parents is that until 1950, they were a left–wing working–class Jewish couple with two children living on New York City's Lower East Side. They were people with their share of familial problems, personal limitations and future aspirations. The rest is "controversial." The remainder of this article will focus on my memories of my parents and upbringing, how the media developed their public personas, and the conclusions I draw from the difference between the former and the latter.

MEMORIES

Perhaps my memories of a warm and functional family are merely childhood fantasies of a pretempest era of golden tranquillity. Looking back on that period over forty years later, however, I believe our family must have been functional for two reasons. First, from as early as I can remember such thoughts, I have never put the principal blame for my parents' disappearance from my life on them but have rather blamed the government for taking them away from me. While I may merely have idealized them, in failing to blame my parents I believe I drew on the reservoir of good feeling I unconsciously retained from before their arrest. Second, given the terrible experiences I endured from the time I was three until almost my seventh birthday, it is not likely the Meeropols could have helped me to recover so quickly if I did not have a firm base during the first three years of my life on which they could build.

I was only two months past my third birthday when my father was arrested and consequently remember very little of the family life in the Rosenberg household. Our apartment must have been tiny because it seemed quite small even to a three year–old. I have a vague memory of feeling protected and happy. I remember that my brother was a somewhat spoiled child, prone to throwing tantrums if he did not get his way.

It is a laughable understatement to say that the years between 1950 and

1954 were difficult for my brother and me. After our father's arrest we lived with our mother for several weeks. One day in August she left us with a neighbor because she had been subpoenaed to testify before the grand jury that was still investigating the charges against our father. When she completed her testimony, she, too, was arrested, and the only times Michael and I ever saw either of them again were during visits at the Death House in Sing Sing Prison.

The neighbor had no choice but to take us to our maternal grandmother's house, which was only a few blocks away on the Lower East Side of Manhattan. Once under arrest my parents were told that they faced the death penalty and that their children would be orphaned if they did not cooperate. However, "cooperation" in this case meant admitting that they had helped steal the secret of the atomic bomb so it could be transmitted to the Soviet Union, naming the others they had worked with to accomplish this feat and joining the FBI team in the battle against Communism. In the words of one CIA analyst, writing in early 1953, they would be given "a generous commutation" if they agreed.[1] David Greenglass, my mother's younger brother, and his wife, Ruth, were told that they and their two children faced the same fate, and they took the deal. Thus Ruth Greenglass, who swore at the trial that she had helped steal the secret of the atomic bomb, was neither indicted nor imprisoned, while my mother, who testified that she was not involved, was executed.

Tessie Greenglass, my mother's mother, supported her son David. She reprimanded my mother for not "back[ing] up David's story."[2] I remember my life at Tessie Greenglass's house as grim and viewed her as a nasty woman who was mean to Michael and me. She threatened to leave Michael and me in a children's shelter if my mother did not cooperate with the FBI and then carried out her threat in the fall of 1950. One of my first memories is Tessie explaining that we could not live in her apartment because it was a cold-water flat and the toilet froze in the winter. I went into the bathroom and peered down the toilet to see the ice. Winter was still months away and there was none.

Sophie Rosenberg, my father's mother, was hospitalized suffering from high blood pressure at that time, and my father's siblings were too frightened to shelter us in their homes. So we stayed at the shelter for seven months until Sophie was well enough to take us in. My father's family came to visit us on Sundays, and we would get to leave the "home," as we called it. I remember feeling that I was imprisoned just like my parents were during those days. Michael and I lived with Grandma Sophie until the summer of 1952, but it was not an easy time. There was a great deal of publicity about the case and my brother, who was nine by the end of this period, was harassed in the neighborhood. I was more fortunate. I was too young to start school and spent most of my time either playing fantasy games with little metal cars at home or watching television. Grandma Sophie was still grieving for her husband, who had died in 1946, and was distraught over what was happening to her son and slightly infirm. She was incapable of controlling two active boys despite the presence of a day nurse hired to help her.[3] Michael was becoming more wild and unruly and I was increasingly withdrawn.

We were sent to live with friends of my parents in Toms River, New Jersey, that summer. We lived in semi secrecy. That is, for a while the local people did not know who we were and the press stayed away. I remember being reasonably happy. I started kindergarten at Toms River elementary school that fall. I don't believe the other students and teachers knew who I was, but I felt there was something strange about my circumstances and so was not at ease. Michael and I visited with our parents in prison about once every two months during this time. I can't sort out one visit from another, but I remember them as relatively calm affairs.

I remember going to one demonstration in front of the White House at the beginning of the last week of my parents' lives. I have no memory of any adult telling me what the demonstration was about, but I had some idea that it was to save my parents' lives. Michael delivered a letter to a guard at the White House, but we were protected and even surrounded by supportive adults while we were there.[4] The people in charge of our care during this period were not insensitive to our needs.

After my parents' execution the publicity surrounding the execution alerted the local school board about who we were. I attended first grade for a few months in Toms River before we were suddenly removed from school and sent back to Grandma Sophie's in New York City. I was not told why this happened, but I later found out that the school board had declared that since we were not New Jersey residents, we couldn't attend public school there. We spent a short time at Grandma's house. She was in dreadful shape after the executions, and other relatives were still unwilling to adopt us. Emanuel Bloch, our parents' chief attorney and legal guardian, ultimately placed us with Abel and Anne Meeropol. They were progressive people who I now believe only left the Communist Party to increase their chances of successfully adopting us.

My brother and I started living with the Meeropols during the last days of December 1953, but anti–Communist forces took one more shot at us. This time the Society for the Prevention of Cruelty to Children, the Jewish Child Care Agency, and the New York City Welfare Department were the agents of the attack. The former with the cooperation of the latter filed a petition alleging neglect in New York Family Court just a few weeks after we started living with Abel and Anne Meeropol.[5] The petition claimed we were being abused for political purposes and were being exploited by those who were raising a trust fund for our benefit. These were false claims, but the judge issued the order and we were taken from the Meeropols and placed, once again, in an orphanage. In effect the Jewish Child Care Agency argued that, because the Meeropols were political supporters of the Rosenbergs, they could not be good parents.

But ultimately the Meeropols won the ensuing custody battle. We returned to live permanently with them in the fall of 1954, our names were changed to Meeropol and we dropped from public sight for twenty years.[6] Those who filed the petition were not content with killing our parents, they wanted to kill their legacy as well! They wanted us to forget our parents or grow up reviling them. But the Meeropols and others in the movement that tried to save my parents nurtured and protected Michael and me for many years afterward.[7] This was a critical factor that enabled us to grow up with a positive attitude toward our parents, toward those who fought to save them, and toward life in general.

POLITICS AND PARENTING

As I have said above, my parents were ordinary people who had family problems even before their arrest. They were trying to follow the methods preached by Dr. Spock without imposing sufficient limits. My mother did seek counseling with a social worker, Dr. Elisabeth Phillips, to help her manage my brother, Michael. My mother also sought help from a psychiatrist, Dr. Saul Miller, so there can be little doubt that she had serious emotional problems. These were certainly exacerbated by spending over two years in solitary confinement as the only woman on death row in Sing Sing Prison.

But the pedestrian nature of their problems did not jibe with the extreme nature of the charges against them. It was particularly important to cast my parents in a bad light, because the public might otherwise come to feel sympathy for a young married couple with small children and recoil at the government's act of killing them. The McCarthy period assault on domestic left-wingers, both within and outside of the Communist Party, was predominantly political, but the ad hominem attacks on my parents demonstrate the accompanying social and personal components of that assault. Such attacks appear to have been viewed as necessary copartners by the opinion makers in American society in the 1950s. They "proved" to many Americans that leftists not only had bad ideas but were also bad people. They would short-circuit the possibility that some might first see American leftists as decent human beings and next come to consider their political views in a more positive light. This made my parents' demonization inevitable.

Judge Irving R. Kaufman in sentencing my parents to death said: "Indeed the defendants Julius and Ethel Rosenberg placed their devotion to their cause above their own personal safety and were conscious that they were sacrificing their own children, should their misdeeds be detected—all of which did not deter them from pursuing their course. Love for their cause dominated their lives—it was even greater than their love for their children."[8]

In Judge Kaufman's opinion Ethel and Julius Rosenberg were not only spies but bad parents as well. Perhaps he even believed that by sentencing them to death he was doing my brother and me a favor by making sure that we did not grow up in their household. There is little mystery about why Judge Kaufman spoke as he did when he sentenced my parents. He sought to absolve himself and the government for orphaning Michael and me by blaming my parents for what happened to us. Kaufman even wondered to the FBI "whether he ought to send for the [Rosenberg] boys and talk with them,"[9] because he heard that the "older boy...allegedly stated that he was going to devote his life to avenging his parents."[10]

In 1973 the renowned trial lawyer Louis Nizer wrote *The Implosion Conspiracy*, a book about my parents' case. While rejecting Judge Kaufman's death sentence as unduly harsh, he nevertheless joined in condemning my parents' parenting: "Even [Judge Kaufman's] death sentence did not make them hate him as much as his slur upon them as parents. The reason was that they knew subconsciously, at least, that there was some validity to the accusation. They had failed their children even before their arrest. Although brimming with love, they had not communicated it sufficiently to Michael and Bobby [sic] to prevent their neurotic behavior."[11] He further noted that while each legal defeat brought their execution closer and

they might have collapsed from the harsh blows that beat upon them from all directions—their children, her mother and the judges—were it not for one saving grace.

They were scoring triumph after triumph in another arena. Those victories freed their spirits if not their bodies. Their misery turned to the elation of martyrdom.[12]

I do not remember feeling unloved as Nizer would have the public believe. Family members and others report that my brother was troublesome, not because my parents had difficulty communicating their love to him but rather because they doted on him and had trouble setting limits. There is no evidence that I was "neurotic" before my parents' arrest, as Nizer claimed. According to Dr. Phillips, my mother had some trouble getting me to eat but solved that problem by pretending that the spoon was an airplane and my mouth the hangar.[13]

Nizer is not the only one to state that he was privy to my parents' psyches and conclude that they courted martyrdom. As Yacov Luria wrote, "The Rosenbergs gladdened the hearts of those who wanted them to burn. They seemed to court death. By their martyrdom, they would testify to their devotion to the cause of communism and expose the hollow pretensions of capitalist democracy."[14] The same author proclaims that they "mounted the electric chair on schedule, defiantly singing 'The Battle Hymn of the Republic.'"[15] This latter assertion is pure nonsense. As those who witnessed the executions attested, both my parents went to their deaths quietly.

No evidence supports the charge of Nizer and others that my parents courted martyrdom. Their lawyers, at their direction, did everything they could think of to forestall that event. They were ecstatic when Justice Douglas stayed the execution on June 17, 1953, because they believed it might never take place.[16] Their letters, both those apparently written for public consumption and those that they never expected to be published, reflect their love for each other, their children, and for life in general. Nizer believes my parents were guilty and so dismisses their claim that they went to their deaths because they were innocent and would not place others in the same position the Greenglasses had placed them in. But this is a circular argument that presumes because they were guilty that their refusal to confess proved that they sought martyrdom.

The fonts of conventional wisdom also helped popularize the characterization of my mother as dominant and my father as submissive. Such a relationship was widely viewed as "unnatural" in the 1950s. Morris Ernst, cocounsel for the American Civil Liberties Union, first offered to represent my parents if they would confess, and then offered the FBI his analysis of the dynamics of my parents' relationship. Ernst, the amateur psychologist who had never met my parents, concluded that "Julius is the slave and his wife, Ethel, is the master."[17] President Eisenhower, who may have been privy to Ernst's analysis, also chimed in. He explained his refusal to grant my parents' pleas for clemency in a letter to his son. "It goes against the grain to avoid interfering in the case where a woman is to receive capital punishment. Over against this, however, must be placed one of two facts that have greater significance. The first of these is that in this instance it is the woman who is the strong and recalcitrant character, the man is the weak one. She has obviously been the leader in everything they did in the spy ring."[18]

The press frequently echoed this strong woman—weak man theme. Commentator Bob Considine, who witnessed the execution wrote, "As in life…Ethel Rosenberg was the stronger of the two." He described her as: "the plump *deceptively gentle looking* Lower East Side housewife."[19] A *Time* magazine article, published on June 29, 1953, described my parents' final appeals in the following terms: "For the sixth time the mousy little engineer and his wife had petitioned the highest tribunal."[20]

There is no evidence that my mother was the dominant force in my parents' personal relationship or political activities other than the words of those who propounded that characterization. In fact, there is evidence to the contrary. At a secret meeting with the Joint Congressional Commission on Atomic Energy only a month before the trial government prosecutors stated that they had almost no evidence of my mother's participation but wanted to involve her anyway so they could coerce my father into confessing. One file contains a very revealing passage: "if we can convict [Julius's] wife, too, and get her a stiff sentence of 25 to 30 years, that combination may serve to make this fellow disgorge...."[21] Not long before Eisenhower wrote that he would not grant my mother clemency because "she was obviously the leader in everything they did in the spy ring,"[22] government operatives developed a list of questions to ask my father if he made an eleventh-hour decision to "cooperate." Question six read: "Was your wife cognizant of your activities?"[23] Evidently the government agents close to the case believed my father was the dominant political force in the family. These government agents apparently felt that my mother was so unimportant that they did not even bother to create a similar list of questions to ask her.

That is not to say that my mother merely followed my father's lead. My parents' letters indicate that they both had strongly developed opinions and often interacted as equals. There is also little doubt that they accepted the Communist Party's positions. They stayed in the party despite the Hitler–Stalin pact of 1939, and they probably believed Stalin was a great leader until the day they died. That does not necessarily mean that they supported the purges. It is more likely that, like so many fellow Communist Party members, they believed the horror stories about mass slaughter to be disinformation spread by the capitalist press. We will, of course, never know what positions they would have taken after 1953.

Extreme characterizations of my parents' marriage and parenting are not confined to those who attacked them. Virginia Gardner, in *The Rosenberg Story*, a laudatory biography published in 1954, described my parents as paragons of virtue who never did anything wrong and had a kind word for everyone. "Ethel was literally a mother 24 hours out of 24." "All their spare time was spent with...Robby and Michael." Ethel would "buy a very inexpensive fish for herself and Julie, then spend 50 [cents] on cherries for Michael." Ethel and Julius were "absolutely contented together, absorbed in the children and their future." Julius "idolized Ethel," "consulted her on everything," and "neither cared anything for their own personal comfort."[24] These quotes are taken from just two pages of Gardner's book, and there are dozens more like them sprinkled liberally throughout its 126 pages.

Contrast this with Ilene Philipson's more recent *Ethel Rosenberg: Beyond the Myths,* which focused on my mother's psychological makeup. Philipson argues that my mother's public demeanor was an act designed to cover for the fact that my mother felt rejected by her mother and viewed herself as an "inadequate and contemptible mother."[25] Philipson writes of the "utter indifference with which Ethel Rosenberg was regarded by her own family,"[26] adding that my brother, Michael, her first child, was such a total terror "that she had begun to think of giving him up to foster care."[27] I do not remember Michael's behavior in such extreme terms, and Dr. Phillips flatly denies that my mother ever considered putting my brother in foster care. Dr. Phillips further states that Philipson's characterization does not accurately portray the woman she knew.[28]

Philipson describes the facets of what she calls my mother's "act." In her trial testimony "Ethel played her new role on the witness stand with great composure."[29] Much of what my mother wrote in her letters was "studied and rehearsed."[30] No displays of courage were genuine. In response to each legal defeat, "she would emerge from enveloping depression, experience anger or outrage, and write letters that reflected great courage and strength,"[31] but "with Julie, however, she could not be heroic; with him she wanted only to indulge her misery."[32] According to Dr. Miller, however, this evaluation more accurately describes her problems before her imprisonment. When he visited my mother in prison after a one-year absence, Dr. Miller found that her self–hatred and misery had vanished and that she had become a "resolute person."[33] I have always found it ironic that only my mother's imprisonment gave her the "freedom" to develop as a writer. Such a state of affairs speaks volumes about the "imprisonment" of many women by traditional sex roles and poverty.

Few question that my parents discussed in advance how they would act when they testified at trial. But Philipson displays little understanding of the motivation behind my mother's demeanor. Philipson's analysis of my mother's "act" makes no allowances for the circumstances of the trial, in which presentation was a matter of life and death: my mother's demeanor was not false bravado at a cocktail party but studied composure for a trial in which appearances and insinuation meant everything. Moreover, as the children of immigrants who grew up in poverty, both my parents sought to preserve their dignity. The theme of behaving in a dignified manner echoes repeatedly throughout their letters.[34] It was their attempt to demonstrate that they were not inferior to their middle- and upper-class judges and tormentors. That meant being formal when they testified, to prove that they, too, could conduct themselves in a civilized manner. My father carried this to the extreme by implacably addressing Chief Prosecutor Irving Saypol as "Mr. Saypol" or "sir" even under grueling cross–examination.[35]

In fact, some of my mother's letters expressed outrage and showed an indomitable will to resist, while others bespoke abject depression.[36] Philipson concludes that the latter documents reveal the real Ethel while dismissing the former as phony posturing. Naturally, only the letters of outrage and determination were published by those in charge of rallying the growing movement to save them. My parents' attorney, Emanuel Bloch, reported that at one of his last meetings my mother said she "shivered from head to foot" when she thought of getting into "that chair" and having the current run through her, but "I will die with dignity."[37] Moments before she left her cell to be executed, she wrote the following note to her lawyer. "All my heart I send to all who hold me dear. I am not alone—and I die with honor and with dignity—knowing my husband and I must be vindicated by history."[38] At what point does keeping up a courageous front in the face of electrocution in itself become an act of courage? Is it possible that both types of letters written by my mother reflected the complex personality of someone under extreme stress?

ART AND FANTASY

The U.S. government did and still does portray my parents as dangerous people. This was not because they helped steal vital atomic–bomb secrets. As General Leslie Groves, the army commander of the Los Alamos facility where the first bombs were built and a fervent believer in my parents' guilt, privately said after they were killed: "I think that the data that went out in the case of the Rosenbergs was of minor value. I would never say that publicly. Again…it should be kept very quiet, because irrespective of the value of that in the overall picture, the Rosenbergs deserved to hang."[39]

They were dangerous and deserved death because they refused to succumb to the government's attack, in spite of the forced abandonment of their children, imprisonment, and death. The resistance of ordinary loving, caring and proud people is inspirational to oppressed people and those who identify with oppressed people. But most Americans, living in relative comfort and conformity, had a difficult time identifying with such force of will and easily accepted fantasies to explain or understand such commitment.

My parents were ordinary people, but once charged with such a dramatic, earth-shattering political crime as stealing the secret of the atomic bomb, they became extraordinary. Few were or are able to mesh the "facts" of their private lives with the public figures they became. Irreconcilable images, such as "housewife" and "master spy," coupled with their resistance left a vast void that artists, composers, writers, poets, and filmmakers have attempted to fill with fantasy and artistic inspiration for over forty years.

Mainstream efforts often merely translated the popular myths visually. My mother's presumed dominance, for instance, might be "subtly" demonstrated by making her taller than my father. Thus in Stanley Kramer's dramatization of the trial for the ABC television network in January 1974, my mother, who was played by Brenda Vacarro, appeared to be taller than Alan Arbus, the actor who played Julius. Many of the artistic images collected by the Rosenberg Era Art Project, although sympathetic to their plight, unconsciously echo this theme by either emphasizing my mother's power,[40] depicting only my parent's heads in a manner that increases my mother's relative size,[41] or even portraying my mother as larger than my father.[42]

On the other side, my father, too, became larger than life. Those who were close to the defense knew my father was taller than my mother and even exaggerated his height. Author John Wexley described my father as tall.[43] I have often been told by people who knew my parents that my father was six feet tall and, until recently, accepted it. For the record, the full-length "mug shots" taken by the FBI when my parents were arrested show my mother barely clearing five feet in high heels and my father to be five feet nine inches tall.

The most famous fictionalization of my parents' case, E.L. Doctorow's *The Book of Daniel*,[44] suggests that the movement that worked to save them was, while attempting to do so, insensitive to the needs of the accused couple's children. This insensitivity is powerfully dramatized in one of the scenes from Paramount Pictures' 1983 film version of the book, entitled *Daniel*. In it the two small children of the couple who have been condemned to death for stealing the secret of the atomic bomb are brought to a huge clemency rally. The throng is so tightly packed that the children can't be brought to the front. So they are lifted up and passed from person to person over the crowd and deposited on stage while thousands chant "the children," "the children." The children are, of course, traumatized!

Nothing like the scene depicted in the movie *Daniel* ever happened to us. *The Book of Daniel* is fiction, and Doctorow is entitled to his artistic creation. But it is difficult for me, given the obvious parallels between the story he tells and my own, not to bristle at what I perceive as his undeserved attack on people who did everything in their power to protect us. It is especially galling because that attack mimics trite mainstream stereotypes about the insensitive nature of politically committed people.

While I readily understand Judge Kaufman's motivations for attacking my parents' parenting, it is more difficult to understand why E.L. Doctorow would lead readers to a somewhat similar conclusion, by writing, in effect, that both the government and those that worked to save our parents must share the blame for the nightmare we endured. Maybe his work reflected the new conventional wisdom of liberal circles that viewed both government repression and the Old Left with an equally jaundiced eye. But the hell visited on Michael and me between 1950 and 1954 must be laid firmly at the feet of the government and the forces of reaction.[45]

MY REALITY NOW

The tension between political activism and successful parenting has been the central force of my life. I grew up with a positive connection to my parents and those who worked to save them, because I was nurtured and protected by politically active parents and progressive community members who were excellent parents and sensitive to the needs of children. Of course I became involved in the civil rights and antiwar movements of the 1960s, and it was only natural to get married and have children even during a time when such activity was viewed as too conservative by some of my peers. My oldest daughter was two when my brother and I began our effort to reopen our parents' case in 1974. My wife and I were concerned that this would have a negative impact on our family, but we decided to go ahead. I gave up the pursuit of an academic career in anthropology and made reopening my parents' case and parenting my full–time work for five years. After two more years working for a progressive journal, I curtailed my political involvement, went to law school, and after graduation joined a mainstream law firm. But I found the latter unsatisfying and felt that somehow I was not doing justice to my legacy.

I have a profound respect for all socially conscious people who are willing to act on their beliefs. Many who worked to save my parents do not realize that they had one final victory. They saved Michael and me. Without their support I doubt we would have become happy and productive adults or been able to spearhead the effort to reopen our parents' case in the 1970s. Nor, in 1990 would I have been able to fulfill my legacy by leaving the practice of law to start the Rosenberg Fund for Children (RFC). The RFC is a public foundation that provides for the educational and emotional needs of children in this country who are enduring today what Michael and I survived in the 1950s.

Devoting a significant amount of time to progressive activism while attempting to raise children is a difficult task. Attempting to swim against the current in a public manner strains family relationships. Children of activists can easily grow to resent their parents and their activism. Children usually do not like having parents who are "different." Activists can easily give too much to the greater human good and not enough of themselves to their children. My experience provides clues about how both children and

Michael and Robert Rosenberg, aged 9 and 5, (from
left to right) depart Sing Sing Prison after a visit with
their parents in February 1953.
(AP/Wide World Photos)

Recent photo of Michael and Robert Meeropol
(from left to right).
(Paul H. Schnaittacher)

parents can meet these special challenges. Founding and building the RFC is, in part, my effort to utilize this experience. The RFC helps children in the same way I was helped, by channeling the resources of a supportive community to nurture the children of progressive activists who have been attacked.

This is not to say that all or most progressive activists are good parents. It does, however, refute the presumption that it is impossible to simultaneously be good parents and progressive activists. I am living proof of this. I am the son of Ethel and Julius Rosenberg. I survived their incarceration and execution. I was protected, nurtured, and healed by my adoptive parents and the community that fought to save the Rosenbergs. I have shared the last 27 years of my life with Elli, my wife and fellow activist. We've raised two happy and productive daughters, now 22 and 19, who are also proud of their heritage. I strongly believe that it is possible not only to raise children *and* work to make this world a better place but that these are complementary activities. My parents shared this belief. I am building the Rosenberg Fund for Children to make this conviction—my own and my parents'—a reality. This is why I'm not bitter.

NOTES

This article is based upon a keynote address I gave at a conference sponsored by the Center for Literary and Cultural Studies at Harvard University on May 8, 1993. Many of the ideas presented in it were developed through discussion with Ellen Meeropol, who has also provided valuable editorial suggestions. Special thanks also to Gilda Zwerman for providing important structural and editorial suggestions, and to Michael Meeropol for factual corrections and footnote information. Katherine Conway, Jenn Meeropol, Nancy Meyer, Bruce Miller, Jane Miller, William Newman, Rob Okun, Elisabeth Phillips, David Rosner, Arlene Tyner and Marc Weiss read the initial draft and made helpful suggestions. Finally, thanks to coeditors Majorie Garber and Rebecca L. Walkowitz for their careful consideration of and useful suggestions for my manuscript. The mistakes it contains are my own.

1 In 1953 the CIA made a detailed proposal to the FBI for my parents to be used in a psychological warfare campaign to split world Communism on the "Jewish issue." In exchange they would be granted a "generous commutation." See the CIA memorandum, Jan. 22, 1953, prepared by an unidentified CIA employee, enclosed in Keay to Belmont, Feb. 2, 1953, JR HQ 1772. All references to FBI documents related to my parents' case are by file name, file location, and document number. JR is Julius Rosenberg, HQ is FBI Headquarters. The documents are available in the FBI reading room in Washington, D.C. My brother's and

my personal collection is currently temporarily housed at Columbia University Law School and is available in that library.

2 As quoted in Robert Meeropol and Michael Meeropol, *We Are Your Sons: The Legacy of Ethel and Julius Rosenberg*, 2d ed. (Urbana and Chicago: University of Illinois Press, 1986), 184.

3 In fact, Grandma disagreed with the limits the nurse tried to impose on us, a state of affairs that precipitated arguments leading to her dismissal. See Meeropol and Meeropol, *We Are Your Sons*, 108.

4 Michael remembers going to two other events. He insisted on dragging me up on stage over the protests of the adults in charge of us to wave to the crowd at a meeting at Friendship Farms Camp in New Jersey in the summer of 1952. We also attended a clemency rally in Downing Stadium in New York City in April 1953, but our presence was not publicly acknowledged, and those who attended did not even know we were there.

5 For a recent account of these proceedings, see Evelyn Williams, *Inadmissible Evidence*, (New York: Lawrence Hill, 1993), 31–36. The author was the probation officer of the New York City Children's Court assigned to make factual findings and recommendations about who should get custody of my brother and me. She reports that the family court judge threatened to have her fired if she did not find against the Meeropols but that she resisted this improper and illegal pressure. See also Meeropol and Meeropol, *We Are Your Sons*, 246–52.

6 We used the name Meeropol from the day we started living with our adoptive parents, but our names were not officially changed until 1956.

7 For instance, once we were released from the orphanage in February 1954 into the custody of Grandma Sophie, several supporters, at some personal risk, arranged to transport us daily from her house to the public school we were attending near the Meeropols'. This enabled us to attend the same school and spend afternoons with the Meeropols in the spring of 1954.

8 *U.S. v. Rosenbergs, Sobell, Yakovlev, and Greenglass*, CR 124–245. The full trial transcript was reprinted from the submission to the United States Supreme Court for a writ of certiorari on June 7, 1952. Reprints are available from many libraries, especially law school libraries. The pagination of the reprinted version is commonly used by researchers. I will refer to the transcript as "Record." The quote from Judge Kaufman is on p. 1616.

9 Sheidt to file, JR NY 1890, Jan. 28, 1952.

10 Ibid.

11 Louis Nizer, *The Implosion Conspiracy* (New York: Doubleday, 1973), 367.

12 Ibid., 415.

13 From a personal conversation with Dr. Elisabeth Phillips, June 5, 1993.

14 Yaccov Luria, "A Haunting Yahrzeit," *The Jewish Exponent*, supplement, July 2, 1993, 1X, 6X, 16X.

15 Ibid., 16X.

16 Meeropol and Meeropol, *We Are Your Sons*, 235.

17 Morris Ernst quoted in L.B. Nichols to Clyde Tolson, JR HQ 1453, Jan. 9, 1953. See also L.B. Nichols to Clyde Tolson, JR HQ 1390, Dec. 20, 1952.

18 Dwight Eisenhower, *White House Years: Mandate for Change, 1953–1956*, (New York: Doubleday, 1963), 225.

19 Alvin H. Goldstein, *The Unquiet Death of Julius and Ethel Rosenberg* (New York: Lawrence Hill, 1975), (emphasis added).

20 *Time* magazine, June 29, 1953.

21 U.S. Joint Congressional Committee on Atomic Energy, Feb. 8, 1951, 6 (AEC documents).

22 Eisenhower, *White House Years*, 225.

23 Government agents quoted in Ronald Radosh and Joyce Milton, *The Rosenberg File: A Search for the Truth* (New York: Holt, 1983), 417.

24 Virginia Gardner, *The Rosenberg Story* (New York: Masses and Mainstream, 1954), 67–68.

25 Ilene Philipson, *Ethel Rosenberg: Beyond the Myths* (New York: Franklin Watts, 1988), 313.

26 Philipson, *Ethel Rosenberg*, 236.

27 Ibid., 188.

28 From a personal conversation with Dr. Elisabeth Phillips, June 5, 1993.

29 Philipson, *Ethel Rosenberg*, 247.

30 Ibid., 235.

31 Ibid., 338.

32 Ibid., 341.

33 Meeropol and Meeropol, *We Are Your Sons*, 71.

34 See, e.g. "Ethel my darling you are truly a great, dignified and sweet person." JR, letter to ER, Apr. 10, 1951. "Manny Bloch was here Saturday, and his Dad turned up today... how can we fail with such precious, dignified human beings in our corner!" ER, letter to JR, May 27, 1951.

35 See Record, 1163–1231, passim.

36 For the only complete collection of my parents' letters, see Michael Meeropol, ed., *The Rosenberg Letters: A Complete Edition of the Prison Correspondence of Julius and Ethel Rosenberg* (New York: Garland, 1994).

37 Meeropol and Meeropol, *We Are Your Sons*, 237.

38 ER, letter to Emanuel H. Bloch, June 17, 1953.

39 This section of the transcript was classified and deleted from the published transcript. The deleted section was released to my brother and me as a result of our FOIA lawsuit and enclosed in a letter, Richard G. Hewlett to Marshall Perlin, Feb. 23, 1979. Leslie Groves quoted in Gerald E. Markowitz and Michael Meeropol, "The 'Crime of the Century' Revisited: David Greenglass's Scientific

Evidence in the Rosenberg Case," *Science and Society* 44 (1980): 1.

40   See, e.g., Cook Glassgold, "Ethel and Julius Rosenberg: The Atom Spy Hoax," in *The Rosenbergs: Collected Visions of Artists and Writers,* ed. Rob. A. Okun (Montague, MA: Cultural Forecast, 1993), plate 55.

41   Juan Sanchez, "The Rosenbergs: Framed Conspiracy," plate 36, and Angel Bracho and Celia Calderon, "We Have Not Forgotten The Rosenbergs," plate 6, in Okun, *The Rosenbergs.*

42   Louis Monza, "The Couple That Paid," plate 43, in Okun, *The Rosenbergs.*

43   John Wexley, *The Judgment of Julius and Ethel Rosenberg* (New York: Cameron and Kahn, 1955), 108.

44   E.L. Doctorow, *The Book of Daniel* (New York: Vintage, 1971). This is not an exhaustive review of the fiction inspired by my parents' case. For excellent examples of such works, see Tema Nason, *Ethel: The Fictional Autobiography* (New York: Delacorte, 1990). See also Robert Coover, *The Public Burning* (New York: Viking, 1976).

45   This is not to say that the National Committee to Secure Justice in the Rosenberg Case was above public manipulation. For instance, it produced a phonograph for public distribution in which one of the guards at Sing Sing maliciously taunts my brother by asking him if he wants to see the electric chair, causing him to cry. In reality, my brother asked a guard if he could see the electric chair and did not cry.

17

Some Remarks about Trials

David Kennedy

I was reluctant to address the Rosenberg trial because it has never been a significant event for me, historically, politically, nostalgically. Still, I have no desire to estrange myself from those for whom it was and is deeply significant, and having floated about in left-leaning academic culture on the East Coast for twenty years, I know that includes a lot of my closest friends.

In part my disengagement from the case is simply a matter of geography and timing. I was six when the fifties ended and JFK became president, and I grew up in the heartland. I am fairly sure I had never heard of the Rosenbergs until I came East, had rarely, for that matter, met a Jew or a person of color except our housekeeper. I think I absorbed the name "Rosenberg" like the name "Phillips Exeter"—Eastern arcana, sodden with vague associations. The Rosenberg trial—a fifties tawdriness, a historic injustice, something anyone on the left should always already know about, something very important to older people, city people, Jews, and ex-Communists.

Two aspects of the case stuck with me. First, it apparently involved a trial, public and political—a show trial from our past like the Nuremberg trials or the Stalin trials or the Salem witch trials. Second, it was freighted with clarity—a matter about which one spoke softly, earnestly, with convictions and commitment.

I thought I might comment on these combinations —trials and clarity, trials and earnestness, trials and conviction[s].

There is a view of trials as scenes of clarity and decision, of law as a formalizer of differences, consequentialist. Culture—and politics and history—swims all around, ebbing and flowing and flexing and fluctuating and then hits the channel of law, rushing between two banks toward the falls, the trial, decision, judgment.

And then there is a result, a fact, a rock around which little eddies of interpretation can begin to swirl. The trial renders readable, cultural differences become legal distinctions.

And the trial is also a last stronghold of binary logic, win/lose, good/evil, either/or. Right to life or *not*, insane or *not*, speech free or *not*, treason or *not*. Cultural ambiguity become legal choice.

However much we may think of trials as theater, television, spectacle, participants become characters spoken by their roles, still there is the fascination of their reality—in law we might touch the fabulous real, a theater staged on a field of pain, death, and the recovery of damages. These twelve men *are* angry, and with reason. Faith, justice, vindication. Where people swear oaths, rely on their peers, recover large sums, get angry, get even, get convicted, killed. We place the trial there, where the rubber meets the road.

The political trial all the more so—the McCarthy hearings, unabashed spectacle, symbolic collision of forces in a national culture war, but always the power and powerlessness of one, client and victim and judge. People with personality, gladiators in a pit, swords beaten into argument, death rendered as judgment and verdict.

So it is not surprising that we should remember trials with earnestness—when everything is interpretation, here something happened, can be witnessed, however much we might resist, resent, revile the outcome, there's something reassuring about the clarity of trials, particularly perhaps trials past—perhaps we're right to preserve them as moments of clear choice, perhaps we are grateful to law for these intermittent but spectacular demonstrations of virtue, venality, and judgment. Favorite tunes, familiar smells, oh infamous iniquity!

Alas, the law betrays us, our outrage misfires. For inside the law, the trial, all is vague, ambivalent, at once lengthened and foreshortened. Differences between become differences within, and reverse, and forward, and switch, and fight, and one and two and three and four. All now allegory, prevarication: choices refracted, distinctions merged, mediated, reshuffled. Property just a bundle of rights, rights just so many remedies, remedies procedure, process substance.... The law a lazy, looping narrative of cases, knit together, unwoven, sewn up, set aside.

Binary choices become differences split—from Solomon to Rodney King, one trial becomes two becomes four, one crime now a dozen counts, juries hung, restrung, judgments appealed, remanded, quashed. Law as culture, multiple and shifting, wishing, projecting its own fantasies about a choice, clarity, fact and judgment.

My hope for cultural studies revisiting a legal trial, archaeologists puttering about the sacred sites of the American Left, is that we might recapture ambivalence, confusion, complexity, not burden law with our heavy nostalgia for earnest days and clear nights.

18

Jews and McCarthyism

A View from the Bronx

Morton J. Horwitz

MY JEWISH NEIGHBORHOOD IN THE BRONX

My family lived in the Hunts Point section of the East Bronx, a then still largely Jewish, working- and lower-middle-class enclave in a larger neighborhood that was in the process of absorbing two of the great postwar migrations—of blacks moving north and of Puerto Ricans leaving their island for the isle of Manhattan and, eventually, the Bronx. Hunts Point was contiguous with two "red" electoral precincts in Bronx Park East whose nucleus was a workers' cooperative apartment house built in 1927. "Intended as a Communist heaven on this capitalist earth,"[1] the project had gone bankrupt twice and was eventually privatized. These two "red" precincts, along with eight others in East Harlem, continued to show an American Labor Party (Wallace) majority as late as the 1950 elections. In the twenty other precincts that Wallace had carried in 1948, by contrast, the ALP received only a small vote in 1950, "indicating," Samuel Lubell speculated, "that their vote for Wallace was not Communist-inspired, but primarily a protest against Truman's stand on Palestine." Lubell estimates that of the 1,150,000 votes Wallace received in the entire country "probably three fourths of Wallace's vote came from Negroes and Jews."[2]

Hunts Point, along with the neighboring "red" precincts, were included in a larger congressional district. As Lubell observed: "In February, 1948, something of a national sensation was created by an obscure, young Bronx lawyer, named Leo Isaacson. Running for Congress under the Wallace banner, Isaacson trounced his Democratic opponent in staunchly Democratic territory by a two-to-one majority. The incident, which ruined the Florida vacation of Democratic boss Ed Flynn, was generally explained away as a protest against Truman's Palestine policy, the district being about 40 percent Jewish. What this explanation overlooked was that the East Bronx where Isaacson swept to victory—and where Wallace [seven months] later got one of every five [presidential] votes cast—is a dying Jewish neighborhood where the chill of being trapped penetrates everywhere."[3] "By 1948," Lubell concluded in a more upbeat tone, "the East Bronx had become an almost perfect example of the new zone of political insurgency developing in our larger cities."[4]

MY FAMILY'S POLITICS

The range of my family's politics can most quickly be captured by observing that my paternal grandfather read the mildly socialist Yiddish newspaper, the *Forward*, while my maternal grandfather read the Communist Yiddish newspaper, the *Freiheit*. Both of my grandmothers had already died by the time I was born. My father's politics were liberal, pro-union, and anti-Communist, especially after 1948, when, in New York, the Liberal Party split off from the American Labor Party, charging the latter with being Communist-dominated. In 1948, when I was ten years old, my father voted for Truman, my mother for Wallace.

My mother's father, the rebellious son of a rabbi, was a devout Communist until the day he died in 1962, unaffected either by Khruschev's secret speech or the invasion of Hungary. Both events, in 1956, had devastated the American party, causing a decline in membership equaled only by the reaction to the Hitler-Stalin Pact of 1939. One of his sons, my mother's brother and my uncle, had remained an active Communist, serving as treasurer of the Manhattan party during the McCarthy era. Our families were very close, providing regular opportunities for passionate political argument when we came together, as we often did. From the time I was ten or eleven years old, I read the *New York Times* thoroughly in order to participate in family political argument. By the time I was a teenager I could debate learnedly about the Hitler-Stalin Pact, the Stalin purge trials, or the Stalin-Trotsky split. On the Friday night the Rosenbergs were executed, I drove past Sing Sing with my Communist relatives on the way from New York City to Peekskill. I remember that night as if it were yesterday.

Many summers were spent in Peekskill, N.Y., where my aunt and uncle, along with many of their comrades, had bought land, pitched tents, and eventually, after World War II, built summer homes. In our particular summer colony, the newspaper boy delivered only two newspapers, the *Daily Worker* and the *Freiheit*. Peekskill was the site of the terrible assault of Westchester county hoodlums and American legionnaires on those who attended a Paul Robeson concert in Peekskill in August of 1949. My aunt and uncle often described the terrors of fleeing from the concert in trucks, while thugs stood overhead showering them with rocks and torches. One of the scenes in E.L. Doctorow's *The Book of Daniel* brilliantly imagines Julius and Ethel Rosenberg encountering those terrors as they flee from the Robeson concert. Howard Fast's *Peekskill, USA* compellingly captures the moment for history.[5]

AMERICAN JEWS AND MCCARTHYISM

For American Jews, the years between the end of the Second World War in 1945 and the execution of the Rosenbergs on June 19, 1953, were particularly traumatic. One might have thought that the defeat of Hitler would have produced unmitigated joy or at least relief from the terrors associated with what was, only a short time before, a real possibility that Hitler would rule the world. Hitler did make anti-Semitism unfashionable for a time in America. Earlier, during the few years before Pearl Harbor, anti-Semitism had grown in volume and virulence, as Hitler's appeal to such figures as the hero Charles Lindberg and the radio priest Father Coughlin suggested the complicity of both the American Establishment and the Catholic Church in anti-Semitism.

For most ordinary American Jews, not tuned in to either the Jewish press or organizational networks, the full realization of the horrifying dimensions of the Holocaust only began to sink in slowly after 1945, as *Life* magazine published pictures of the liberation of the death camps, of the crematoria, of the stacks of skeltons and of the emaciated and barely living survivors. American Jews, as a result, entered the postwar world burdened down with survivor guilt and forced to recognize that while they had been leading quite safe and prosperous lives during the war, a third of all the world's Jews were being murdered by Hitler. McCarthyism and, in particular, the Rosenberg case touched every raw nerve, every terror of renewed genocidal anti-Semitism, every nightmare that Nazism had embodied.

Among Jewish intellectuals, McCarthyism was regularly interpreted as the spread of populist fascism in America. One of the most striking features of postwar American historiography is the negative reinterpretation of the history of American populism as xenophobic and anti-Semitic. As Peter Novick shows, virtually all of these postwar reinterpretations of American populism were the work of Jewish American historians.[6] Non-Jewish historians continued to treat populism much more favorably.

259

A neglected aspect of the relation of Jews to McCarthyism involves the fact that a large number of American Communists were Jews. One would never learn from reading Irving Howe's *World of Our Fathers* that there was a sizable number of Jewish Communists and sympathizers. While Howe gives a very rich account of Jewish socialists, he ignores the substantial number of Jews who were either members of the Communist Party or fellow travelers.[7] One also needs to realize that the success of the United Nations Resolution of May 1948 recognizing the State of Israel was possible only within a two-year "window of opportunity" provided by a temporarily fickle Soviet foreign policy, before it began its unwavering forty-year support for the Arab cause. Were there many Jewish American Communists who felt betrayed by the abrupt Soviet turn against Israel? Had most of those Jews who felt any conflict between their Communism and their Jewishness already jumped ship after the Hitler-Stalin Pact? After the outbreak of the Korean War in 1950, Israel, which for two years had sought to stay neutral in the emerging great power split, finally sided with the West. As Russia began to arm Egypt after Nasser seized power in 1951, Soviet policy became hostile to Israel. Even the pro-Soviet but Zionist part of the Israeli kibbutz movement, once proud of the Soviet role in the creation of the state, turned against the Soviet Union as the 1952 Slansky trial in Czechoslovakia revealed the depth and extent of Stalin's anti-Semitic obsessions.

DUAL LOYALTY

There were two varieties of "dual loyalty" that American Jews had to face during the years between 1945 and 1953. The question of whether there should be a Jewish state in Palestine divided the American Jewish Community between Zionists and anti-Zionists and raised new doubts about whether, in Louis Brandeis's comforting words, "Zionism is Americanism." This was especially true in the anguished months leading up to the end of the British Mandate and the Israeli Declaration of Independence on May 15, 1948. President Truman's own ambivalence and his resentment of Zionist pressures for a time dominated American policy-making. The efforts of Undersecretary of State Robert Lovett, the person in charge of the Palestine question in the U.S. Government, to influence President Truman against a Jewish state included a threat to publicly expose the existence of a Jewish Lobby for Israel. Whether President Truman's decision to extend recognition to Israel was influenced by the forthcoming election or by sympathy for the Jewish people after the holocaust, by the time election day rolled around Truman had done almost everything that a Zionist could have hoped for. If the election of Leo Isaacson as a congressman in February can be plausibly related to Jewish displeasure over Truman's Palestine policy, it seems difficult to believe that the sizable Jewish vote for Wallace in November can be similarly explained as primarily caused by displeasure with Truman's Israel stand.

The Truman-Wallace split triggered the second charge of dual loyalty for Jewish leftists. Throughout the war years the Soviet-American alliance nurtured the view that there was no incompatibility between being a loyal American and being pro-Communist. And despite the quick shift in the focus of the House Un-American Activities Committee from fascism and Nazism to Communism after its creation in 1938, American Communists, like French and Italian Communists, emerged from World War II with the Popular Front belief that Communism was an advanced form of democracy and that the Soviet Union was the most democratic and progressive place on earth.

As the Cold War set in, American Communists were finally forced to choose. Churchill's "Iron Curtain" speech was delivered in March 1946. The Communist coup in Czechoslovakia took place in February 1948. The Berlin Blockade (and eventual airlift) began in June 1948, raising a real possibility of war with the Soviet Union. In August Whittaker Chambers denounced Alger Hiss, a leading member of the foreign policy elite, as a Soviet spy. In December, after denying under oath that he knew Chambers, Hiss was indicted for perjury.

The Truman-Wallace split in 1948 was primarily over the direction of American foreign policy and, in particular, over Truman's responsibility for the growing rift with the Soviet Union. Between 1948 and 1950 there were splits everywhere on the Left—in the union movement, in Hollywood, between New York newspapers (*New York Post* v. *P.M.*), and between the Liberal and American Labor parties in New York. In all of these cases, as in the Progressive (Wallace) Party in 1948, there were well-founded accusations of Communist domination.

By the time Senator Joseph McCarthy delivered his notorious Wheeling, West Virginia speech on February 9, 1950, loyalty to the Soviet Union had increasingly come to be regarded as disloyalty to the United States. During the previous year, Judith Coplon was arrested for passing twenty-eight FBI documents to a Soviet national, NATO was created, and the Soviet Union exploded an atomic bomb years before anyone had predicted. In October 1949 China fell to the Communists and, one month later, the second Hiss trial—the first had ended in a hung jury—resulted in his conviction for perjury. Six months after McCarthy's speech the Korean War began, and *one month later*, as the North Korean army was driven northward to the Chinese border, the Chinese Communists entered the Korean War, routing the U.S.-led army and driving it far down the Korean peninsula until the U.N. counterattack began in January 1951.

Between 1948 and 1950, then, terrors associated with the triumph and expansion of Communism and the threat of a nuclear holocaust dominated public perceptions.

THE ROSENBERG CASE

The Rosenbergs were indicted together with Morton Sobell on March 6, 1951, at a time when the defeat of the U.S.-led army in Korea remained a real possibility. Until the beginning of the allied counteroffensive on January 25, it appeared that the Chinese invasion force might succeed in imposing total defeat on the U.N. led army. The search for spies and scapegoats was on.

For American Jews the Rosenberg case became a major test of loyalty. For anti-Communists, who had grown more strident since 1948, it meant dissociation with Jewish Communists and denial that the Rosenberg case had anything to do with anti-Semitism. Within the Jewish Community, the years after 1948 spurred an effort to isolate, denounce, and marginalize Jewish Communists and fellow travelers, to insist that Jewish loyalty was never in doubt. For the Jewish prosecutor and judge in the Rosenberg case, it presented an opportunity to show that Jews could be loyal Americans, especially when fellow Jews were being charged with betrayal. Most Jews ran for cover during the Rosenberg case, feeling not only that it was a major test of their loyalty but also that it might be turned into another orgy of anti-Semitism. At the deepest levels, I suspect, it triggered all sorts of holocaust fears that had never been acknowledged or dealt with.

CONCLUSION

How much influence did McCarthyism and the Rosenberg case have on the subsequent course of American Jewish culture? Did they significantly contribute to the collapse of a Jewish Left or to the rise of Jewish neoconservatism as embodied in, for example, *Commentary* magazine? After Stalin's death in 1953, the Soviet leader's insane anti-Semitic delusions, resulting in the Jewish doctors' plot as well as a widespread purge of leading Eastern bloc Jewish intellectuals, began to be discussed. But it was only Khruschev's 1956 revelations, including documentation of the doctors' plot, combined with the invasion of Hungary that decimated the American Communist Party.

But what was the effect of McCarthyism on the Jewish non-Communist Left? By 1960, the children of parents who had wept at the death of Stalin turned to the civil rights movement; by 1965 to anti-Vietnam War protest. Marxist thinkers shifted from "scientific" to "cultural" Marxism, from Old to New Left. In Israel, after 1967, the powerful socialist idealism of Labor Zionism began to fade amid conquest and unrivaled prosperity, degenerating into varieties of statism and bureaucratic socialism that were far removed from the decentralized utopian socialism of the kibbutz movement. Whether what had been distinctly Jewish about American Jewish leftism had began to fade or to change, American Jewish leftists did increasingly become universalists and assimilationists, even to the extent of accepting the Third World denunciation of Israel as an agent of imperialism. Yet perhaps there was a closer connection between between the alienated, diaspora Jewish intellectual so criticized in Zionist literature and critical leftist Jewish intellectuals like Marx, Freud, Einstein, and Lévi-Strauss. And perhaps Stalin's grandchildren were just being Jewish once again.

NOTES

1 Samuel Lubell, *The Future of American Politics* (New York: Harper, 1952), 207.
2 Ibid., 207, 208.
3 Ibid., 85–86.
4 Ibid.,
5 E.L. Doctorow, *The Book of Daniel: A Novel* (New York: Random House, 1971); Howard Fast, *Peekskill, U.S.A.: A Personal Experience* (New York: Civil Rights Congress, 1951).
6 Peter Novick, *That Noble Dream: The "Objectivity Question" and the American Historical Profession* (New York: Cambridge University Press, 1988).
7 Irving Howe, *World of Our Fathers* (New York: Harcourt, 1976).

19

Contrasting Fates of Repression

A Comment on *Gibson v. Florida Legislative Investigation Committee*

Randall Kennedy

In this essay I recall a revealing episode of the 1950s that sheds light on two campaigns of repression that significantly affected modern American life. In one, every level of government mobilized the entire society in a concerted effort to destroy the Communist Party. No event more vividly illustrates the ferocity of this campaign than the execution of Julius and Ethel Rosenberg on June 19, 1953. In the other campaign, white supremacists used the power of state governments in the South to attack the National Association for the Advancement of Colored People (NAACP). While the campaign against the Communist Party largely succeeded, that against the NAACP largely failed. The two overlapped on many occasions, one of which involved an effort by the State of Florida to damage the NAACP by investigating it, purportedly to determine whether the Miami branch of the organization had been infiltrated by Communists. Florida's harassment provoked protracted litigation that began in 1956 and ended in 1963 in a Supreme Court decision, *Gibson v. Florida Legislative Investigation Committee.*[1]

BACKGROUND

In 1956 the Florida legislature formed a committee to investigate groups that, in its view, endangered "the well being and orderly pursuit of...personal and business activities by the majority of the citizens of [the] state."[2] Although the legislature did not expressly single out the NAACP, that was its principal target. White supremacist politicians were outraged by the Supreme Court's 1954 decision in *Brown v. Board of Education*, which invalidated segregation in public schooling, and they sought revenge on the civil rights organization most responsible for that ruling. Moreover, these politicians recognized that the NAACP would not limit itself to winning judicial decrees but would seek to effectuate these rulings in day-to-day life, thereby changing the fabric of the South's Jim Crow pigmentocracy. Therefore, Florida, along with other segregationist states, tried to crush or at least cripple the NAACP by scrutinizing and otherwise inhibiting the practices of its attorneys, disseminating derogatory propaganda, and seeking to compel disclosure of membership lists. It was this third tactic—compelling disclosure of membership—that most concerned the NAACP. Because the NAACP was widely viewed in white southern society as a dangerous, extremist organization, public knowledge of membership in it could have disastrous consequences for individuals who might be subjected to loss of employment, credit, or, indeed, basic protection against violence. If states succeeded in obtaining membership lists, not only would present members be endangered but fear of disclosure would also dissuade individuals from joining in the future.

In 1959, after a series of skirmishes, the Florida Legislative Investigation Committee (FLIC) ordered Father Theodore R. Gibson, an Episcopalian clergyman who was president of the Miami branch of the NAACP, to appear before it and to bring with him the organization's membership records. The FLIC stated that it needed to pursue the question of Communist influence on the basis of information supplied by one of its own investigators and a former official of the NAACP. The investigator identified by name some fourteen persons whom he claimed had an affiliation with the NAACP and were either active or former members of Communist or Communist front organizations. The former NAACP official corroborated some of what the investigator claimed.

At a hearing before the FLIC, Gibson acknowledged that he was the custodian of the Miami NAACP's membership files. He also volunteered to answer questions on the basis of his own personal knowledge. When given the names and shown photographs of fourteen persons identified as Communists or members of Communist front organizations, Gibson stated that to his knowledge, none were affiliated with the NAACP. He refused, however, to consult the NAACP membership files. He maintained that acquiescing to any compulsion with respect to the files, even merely to consult them for the purpose of informing his own personal testimony, would interfere with the constitutionally protected associational rights of current and prospective members of the NAACP.

At the behest of the FLIC, Gibson was brought before a state court, adjudged to be in contempt of the legislature, and sentenced to six months of imprisonment and a twelve hundred dollar fine, a decision subsequently affirmed by the Supreme Court of Florida.

THE SUPREME COURT

The NAACP'S executive secretary, Roy Wilkins, viewed the prosecution of Father Gibson with considerable alarm. Writing to Harry Belafonte, Wilkins stated that the case "is of strategic importance to the survival of the civil rights movement in Florida and the entire southeast."[3] The NAACP petitioned the Supreme Court to review the judgment of the Florida courts. The Supreme Court granted the NAACP's petition and proceeded to adjudicate the dispute. The case was initially argued on December 5, 1961. It was reargued on October 10-11, 1962. At first, a bare five-to-four majority of the justices held in favor of Florida. But one member of that majority, Justice Felix Frankfurter, fell seriously ill in April 1962. Deadlocked in the absence of Frankfurter, the Court decided to hear a reargument of the case. That summer Frankfurter retired and was replaced by Arthur Goldberg who voted differently upon hearing the reargument. Hence a bare five-to-four majority ultimately ruled in favor of the NAACP.

The close vote reflected several vexing difficulties posed by the case. The first had to do with the existing state of the law regarding freedom of association. When the Supreme Court reviewed the prosecution of Father Gibson, there existed two lines of unstable precedent. The first emphasized that "compelled disclosure of affiliation with groups engaged in advocacy may constitute [an]…effective restraint on freedom of association," that there exists a "vital relationship between freedom to associate and privacy in one's associations," that "inviolability of privacy in group association may in many circumstances be indispensable to preservation of freedom of association, particularly where a group espouses dissident beliefs."[4] These sentiments militating in favor of protecting associational freedom arose from cases in which southern states attempted to stifle the NAACP by exposing its members to the glare of hostile opinion in the South, making them vulnerable to social ostracism if not violent retribution. In *NAACP v. Alabama* (1958) the Court reversed a state court judgment for contempt of court when NAACP officials refused to surrender membership lists to state judicial officers. In *Bates v. City of Little Rock* (1960) the Court reversed the conviction of NAACP officials who violated ordinances that required organizations operating within given municipalities to make public the identities of officers, members, and contributors. In *Shelton v. Tucker* (1960) the Court invalidated an Arkansas statute that required every public school teacher to file an annual affidavit listing every organization to which he or she had belonged or regularly contributed during the preceding five years.

At the same time that the Supreme Court protected the associational freedom of the NAACP from attack, it subordinated the associational freedom of the Communist Party to the asserted need of state and federal legislatures to investigate "subversive" organizations. The Court issued a series of rulings emphasizing that rights to associational freedom are limited, that the power to conduct investigations is a broad power inherent in the legislative process, and that with respect to the Communist Party or persons or organizations affiliated with it the balance between associational privacy and governmental power tilts decisively in favor of the latter. Thus in *Barenblatt v. United States* (1959) the Court sustained the conviction for contempt of Congress of a former graduate student and teaching fellow at a university who refused to answer on First Amendment grounds questions put to him by the infamous House of Representatives Committee on Un-American Activities. Similarly, in *Uphaus v. Wyman* (1959) the Court sustained the conviction of an official of an organization who refused to produce documents demanded of him by the attorney general of New Hampshire pursuant to an investigation of possible violations of the state's Subversive Activities Act. In these and other cases the Court permitted investigations of feared Communist penetration into education, basic industries, and journalism. Now, in *Gibson*, the FLIC claimed that it simply sought to follow up on information suggesting that Communists might have penetrated the NAACP.

Apart from the difficulty posed by two lines of precedent that were in strong tension with one another, the Supreme Court's resolution of Father Gibson's case was also encumbered by facts peculiar to Gibson's situation. First, the Florida courts and legislature had had the benefit of observing the deficiencies of previous local efforts to thwart the NAACP. Florida authorities were considerably more guarded, refined, and moderate than their candid, direct, and obstreperous segregationist counterparts in other states. Because of this, the Supreme Court found it much more difficult to rule against the Florida authorities. Several of the justices were made quite uneasy by the perception, and the evident fact, that whether or not the Court ruled for or against a given party in cases involving federally guaranteed rights to freedom of expression and association turned on the identity of the litigants before it. This constituted an embarrassment to notions of judicial neutrality and impartiality. Out of a desire to escape the charge that the Supreme Court played favorites and to show that the Court treated race cases, like any other disputes, according to neutral principles of law, the dissenting justices shut their eyes to the real motives animating Florida's effort to investigate the possibility of Communist infiltration of the NAACP and instead credited with good faith the asserted justifications articulated by the Florida authorities. Florida eased the way for this delusion. The Florida courts, for instance, did not demand that the Miami NAACP disclose its entire membership list to the legislature. Rather, deferring to previous United States Supreme Court rulings on the subject of associational freedom, the Florida Supreme Court demanded only that Father Gibson make use of membership lists as a testimonial aid in answering the legislature's questions about Communists in the NAACP. The Florida court ruled, in other words, that the NAACP could maintain the privacy of the vast majority of members but that it would have to divulge whether the names of asserted Communists were found on the organization's membership lists. Whatever one's view of this ruling, it was undeniably less intrusive and provocative than the earlier repressive actions undertaken by segregationist officials in Alabama, Louisiana, and Arkansas.

A second complication that burdened the defense of the NAACP and Father Gibson was the fact that the latter was willing to testify freely about what he knew personally regarding alleged Communists, especially their relationship to the NAACP, yet unwilling to consult membership lists for the purpose of verifying or refreshing his personal recollection. In a dissent joined by three other justices, John M. Harlan declared that Father Gibson's willingness to testify without benefit of the membership lists made it difficult for him to see how the legislature's demand that Father Gibson simply consult the lists presented "any serious question as to interference with freedom of association."[5] "In effect," Justice Harlan complained, "we are asked to hold...that [Father Gibson] had a constitutional right to give only partial or inaccurate testimony."[6]

Notwithstanding these problems, the Court sided with the NAACP. Justices Hugo L. Black and William O. Douglas disapproved of Florida's action on grounds that would have granted protection to the Communist Party as well as the NAACP. Black declared that in his view

> the constitutional right of association includes the privilege of any person to associate with Communists or anti-Communists, Socialists or anti-Socialists, or, for that matter, with people of all kinds of beliefs, popular or unpopular.... Since as, I believe , the National Association for the Advancement of Colored People and its members have a constitutional right to choose their own associates, I cannot

understand by what constitutional authority Florida can compel answers to questions which abridge that right.[7]

Similarly broad was Douglas's view that "government is not only powerless to legislate with respect to membership in a lawful organization; it is also precluded from probing the intimacies of spiritual and intellectual relationships in the myriad of such societies and groups that exist in this country, regardless of the legislative purpose sought to be served."[8]

By contrast, the principal opinion for the Court, written by its newest member, Arthur J. Goldberg, reversed the Florida courts on two narrow, fact-bound grounds. First, reviewing in detail the evidence on which the Florida legislature predicated its investigation of Communist influence within the Miami NAACP, the Court merely concluded that "the record in this case is insufficient to show a substantial connection between the Miami Branch of the NAACP and Communist *activities* which...is an essential prerequisite to demonstrating the immediate, substantial, and subordinating state interest necessary to sustain [the State's] right of inquiry into the membership lists of the association."[9] Although the Court held that "the strong associational interest in maintaining the privacy of membership lists of groups engaged in the constitutionally protected free trade in ideas and belief may not be substantially infringed upon such a slender showing as here made [by the State of Florida],"[10] it clearly, albeit implicitly, left open the door that future investigations of organizations like the NAACP based on stronger evidence of Communist influence might be found to be permissible.

Second, in contrast to the willed naïveté of the dissenting justices, the majority recognized that at least part of the NAACP's conflict with Florida stemmed from the state's effort to use the methods of anti-Communism against what segregationists perceived as the *other* great domestic conspiracy threatening "the American way of life." "We cannot close our eyes," Justice Goldberg declared on behalf of the Court, "to the fact that the militant Negro civil rights movement has engendered the intense resentment and opposition of the politically dominant white community."[11]

LESSONS

Gibson is a fascinating case that highlights several points that are too often forgotten or ignored. One has to do with the hostile relationship that existed between the NAACP and the Communist Party. This relationship exemplifies the ideological diversity that has always been part of African American political culture. It also illustrates the fact that reactionary demagogues and their gullible followers were not the only ones who condemned and ostracized Communists; many intelligent, bighearted progressives did so as well, including such leading figures in the struggle for racial justice as Roy Wilkins and Thurgood Marshall.

To be sure, as a general rule, there was "less antipathy to the [Communist Party] among Negroes than elsewhere in American society."[12] More than any other predominantly white political party, the Communist Party attempted to recruit African Americans into every level of its operation. It showed itself to be "the one element in American life that demanded the goal that even Negro political organizations hesitated to put forward: the complete merging of Negro and white in a common society."[13] Some of the most courageous attempts at interracial political activism in American history involved black and white Communists in the thirties and forties, particularly those who participated in the organization of unions in the Deep South.[14] Moreover, two of the most famous and respected African American cultural icons of the twentieth century—W.E.B. Du Bois and Paul Robeson—were closely affiliated with the Communist movement; the Soviet Union awarded Du Bois the Lenin Prize and Robeson the Stalin Prize.

Many African American artists, intellectuals, and political activists, by contrast, were profoundly anti-Communist; one thinks here of Richard Wright, Ralph Ellison, and Bayard Rustin, among others. Anti-Communist, too, was the NAACP. Indeed, the NAACP was militantly anti-Communist, promulgating in 1950 a resolution pursuant to which it appointed a committee to investigate and study the ideological composition and trends of its membership and pledged to take action to prevent, and, if need be, eradicate Communist influence within its ranks. The NAACP purged and excluded Communists for a variety of reasons. It did so primarily to protect itself against the whirlwind of anti-Communist sentiment that swept the nation during the early years of the Cold War. *Gibson* reflects the prudence of the NAACP's actions. The Supreme Court favorably commented on the fact that the NAACP had "demonstrated its antipathy to Communism."[15] By taking stern measures against Communists, the NAACP leadership successfully insulated the organization against charges of "subversion."

But there were also other considerations behind the NAACP's aggressive anti-Communism. One was a sense of bitter, rancorous organizational competition; it had long competed against the party for the hearts and minds of African Americans. Another was a belief that Communists would have been willing to penetrate and wreck the NAACP if party leaders perceived that doing so would redound to the benefit of their movement. Yet another was a deep-seated antagonism toward the authoritarian, relentlessly secular, anti-capitalist ethos of the Communist movement. Unlike the Communists, the leaders of the NAACP were not revolutionaries seeking to overturn the political economy of the United States; they were moderate reformers seeking simply to make the status quo accessible to African Americans.

A second point highlighted by *Gibson* has to with certain realities of constitutional adjudication. One reality is that, notwithstanding the endlessly repeated slogans regarding apolitical judicial neutrality that form the civil religion of American constitutionalism, the fact is, as *Gibson* shows, that judicial choice—which is to say, *politics*—is inescapably part of any ruling made by justices (or any other decision maker). When Felix Frankfurter was on the Court, *Gibson* was decided in favor of the State of Florida. When Arthur Goldberg succeeded him—bringing to bear on the same law and set of facts a different set of sensibilities and commitments—the ruling went the other way.

Another reality is the significance of a litigant's reputation in the process of decision making. The Supreme Court protected the associational privacy of the NAACP in large part because a majority of the justices considered it an unquestionably "legitimate and nonsubversive" organization. At the same time, this same majority treated as virtual outlaws the Communist Party and other "subversive" groups, even though the party and its allies were never expressly banned outright. Sympathetic to the aims, methods, and personnel of the NAACP, the Supreme Court extended to the nation's leading civil rights organization a measure of protection against legislative harassment that it declined to grant to the Communist Party. Legal doctrine did not compel such disparate treatment. A political judgment did—one that cautiously embraced the NAACP and fearfully rejected the Communist Party.

NOTES

1 See *Gibson v. Florida Legislative Investigation Committee*, 372 U.S. 539, 541 (1963). For excellent analyses of *Gibson*, on which I have relied heavily, see Harry Kalven, "Anonymity, Privacy, and Freedom of Association," in *The Negro and the First Amendment* (Chicago: University of Chicago Press, 1965), pp. 65–121, and Steven F. Lawson, "The Florida Legislative Investigation Committee and the Constitutional Readjustment of Race Relations, 1956–1963," in *An Uncertain Tradition: Constitutionalism and the History of the South*, ed. Kermit L. Hall and James W. Ely, Jr. (Athens: University of Georgia Press, 1989).

2 *Gibson v. Florida Legislative Investigation Committee* at 541.

3 Roy Wilkins quoted in Lawson, "The Florida Legislative Investigation Committee," 311.

4 See *NAACP v. Alabama*, 357 U.S. 449, 462 (1958).

5 *Gibson v. Florida Legislative Investigation Committee* at 582.

6 Ibid.

7 Ibid. at 559.

8 Ibid. at 565.

9 Ibid. at 551.

10 Ibid. at 555–56.

11 Ibid. at 557.

12 Nathan Glazer, *The Social Basis of American Communism* (New York: Harcourt, 1961), 180.

13 Ibid., 170.

14 See, e.g., Robin D.G. Kelley, *Hammer and Hoe: Alabama Communists during the Great Depression* (Chapel Hill: University of North Carolina Press, 1990).

15 *Gibson v. Florida Legislative Investigation Committee* at 554.

20

Arbitrary Convictions?

The Rosenberg Case, the Death Penalty, and Democratic Culture

Karl E. Klare

INTRODUCTION

This essay seeks to draw connections between the Rosenberg case and contemporary political issues and concerns. The title phrase "arbitrary convictions" has two meanings, each of which signals a type of linkage I want to establish between the case and the present. "Convictions" refers, first, to successful criminal prosecutions, and, in this context, "arbitrary" calls to mind the disregard for fairness and due process exhibited by various levels of the United States government in its trial, sentencing, and execution of Ethel and Julius Rosenberg. The linkage to the present, I argue, is that the very existence of death as a criminal punishment continues to distort the legal process, diminish government officials' respect for human life, and promote sentencing outcomes skewed by racial and class hierarchy. "Convictions" also refers to beliefs. In that regard, the essay explores the *quality* of the beliefs underlying contemporary opposition to the death penalty, particularly those held by progressives and social change activists in the United States. Is their opposition to the death penalty an ad hoc, arbitrary political position, or does it reflect a grounded moral commitment that is part of some broader vision of democratic culture? If the latter, is there any link between the Rosenberg case and the ideals of contemporary social justice advocates, or at least those whose lives were touched and transformed by the case?

The Rosenberg case was a massive, brutal act of political terrorism carried out by the government in order, among other things, to frighten the Left of the early 1950s into submission. The government's initiative was highly successful in the short run. As a result, many connections between political generations have been lost or obscured. But in the long view the government failed. With the civil rights movement, the Vietnam peace movement, the resurgence of feminism, and other social-change efforts, came new waves of social-justice activism. Contemporary activists would do well to look back on the Rosenberg case. The case itself and the brave and creative effort to reopen it led by Robert and Michael Meeropol, the children of the Rosenbergs, have important lessons to teach. As I will argue, the Rosenberg case can be a source of insight and inspiration for renewed activism and political commitment in our time.

THE DEATH PENALTY AND DEMOCRATIC LAW

To focus on the first of the two 1950s-1990s connections, consider the Rosenberg case not only as a political trial but also as a death-penalty case. The Rosenberg case was used not only to demonize Communism and Jews and to promote Cold War militarism but also quite specifically to sell the American people on the death penalty. Since World War II, many of the so-called advanced democracies have abolished the death penalty. Slowly but steadily, abolition is coming to be seen as one of the minimum criteria according to which nations are deemed civilized. Even the apartheid regime in South Africa suspended executions during the period of constitutional negotiations leading to the first free elections, understanding this to be an essential precondition of a peaceful transition to democracy.[1] Yet the United States retains killing as punishment despite, or perhaps partly because of, its racially biased aspects.

A very important function of the Rosenberg case, which we sometimes overlook when we focus on its more overtly political aspects, is that it legitimated and to some extent still legitimates the death penalty and all of its perverse effects on our culture. The case fostered a pro-death political climate or at least forestalled any nascent momentum toward abolition. As we know, thousands of people who were unsure about the Rosenbergs' guilt or innocence nonetheless rallied to their cause because they were appalled by the harsh sentence. But for many Americans who actually believed that the Rosenbergs gave the secret of the atom bomb to the Russians the awesome penalty of death seemed an appropriate sanction, perhaps the only adequate one, to punish such a heinous megacrime. Ironically, part of the drama of the

Rosenberg case was to conjure up the very archenemy suitable to receive this ultimate punishment. In the closed, circular logic of the Rosenberg case, the crime and the death penalty justified each other. Moreover, many Americans no doubt believed that the Rosenbergs' puzzling and inexplicable refusal to confess their obvious guilt confirmed the government's message that actually the couple had only themselves to blame for getting the chair.

The death sentence was celebrated in the popular culture of the time as an essential feature of an ordinary, democratic society. Many cowboy and gangster movies ended with an execution scene portrayed as an inevitable and fitting outcome that sets things right. The FBI used to sponsor a mobile exhibit on its achievements built into a custom-modeled trailer truck complete with an authentic replica of a death chamber containing an electric chair. The exhibit was rolled out to shopping malls—perfect family entertainment for Sunday afternoons.[2]

We should recall, however, that opposition to the death penalty played an important role in the awakening of the New Left. In 1960, only a few years after the Rosenberg execution and the height of McCarthyism, California's execution of Caryl Chessman prompted stirrings of protest by college students and a new call for abolition. The gifted African American artist and activist Bill McAdoo wrote a song about the Chessman case, which he recorded with Pete Seeger, linking death penalty opposition to civil rights concerns. The NAACP Legal Defense Fund and other legal-activist organizations across the country began riveting attention to the race and class dimensions of the death penalty and launched a series of brilliant Eighth and Fourteenth Amendment challenges that continue to this day.

As in the Rosenberg case, the death penalty today is associated with debasement of the legal process and subordination of individual rights to the interests of governmental power. The grisly rituals of capital punishment breed cynicism and disregard for the value of life among public officials and encourage them to treat human beings as mere instruments for accomplishing their political objectives. For government to teach that taking life is an appropriate way to achieve social objectives breeds arrogance and the abuse of power.

The following are early-1990s decisions of the United States Supreme Court that illustrate this degradation of American law, one brought on, in part, by the conservative justices' death-penalty agenda. Each case received notice in the press, but the general public does not know the depths to which law has sunk under pressure from judicial partisans of capital punishment or the degree to which the law has been drained of compassion.

1. *Coleman v. Thompson.*[3] The defendant, Robert Keith Coleman, claimed both that he was innocent and that the procedures used to convict him were

illegal. However, many legal questions he raised were not reviewed by higher courts or the Supreme Court because, at one early stage, Coleman's attorney filed an appeal paper three days too late. In an opinion by Justice Sandra Day O'Connor, the Supreme Court ruled that Virginia could kill Coleman without hearing his legal arguments because of the "procedural default" committed by his attorney. Coleman died in the electric chair on May 20, 1992.

2. *Herrera v. Collins*.[4] Here the Supreme Court granted review in a death-penalty case but expressly declined to enter a stay postponing the execution until after the hearing. State court judges had the decency to stay the execution so that the defendant would still be alive on the day the Supreme Court decided his case. Then, when it issued its ruling on the merits,[5] the Court made additional atrocious law. Leonel Torres Herrera claimed that he was factually innocent of the crime for which he was sentenced to death. He said that certain evidence discovered after his trial, including an eyewitness statement implicating his brother and affidavits indicating that the brother had confessed to the crime, would prove his innocence. The courts refused to hear the newly acquired evidence. The Supreme Court ruled that nothing in the Constitution prevented Texas from executing Herrera without providing a hearing at which he could present his postconviction evidence of actual innocence. On May 12, 1993, Texas killed Herrera; he died protesting his innocence.

3. *Vasquez v. Harris*.[6] The gruesomely prolonged execution of Robert Alton Harris in California's gas chamber on April 21, 1992, drew considerable media attention. Journalists and commentators around the world heaped scorn on the American criminal justice system. But one particularly alarming aspect of the case has received surprisingly little attention in the press. In its final order granting California permission to proceed with the execution,[7] the Supreme Court barred all lower federal courts from thereafter entering any further stays of execution in the case without Supreme Court authorization.[8] This seemingly innocuous and buried technicality embodies an abuse of power that should be frightening to the American people. Under the separation-of-powers principle central to American constitutionalism, the Supreme Court simply does not have the authority to order other courts to ignore or refuse to hear colorable claims properly placed before them. The final order in *Harris* has no legal basis but the naked fact that the Court's majority commanded it. This is known to lawyers as "ipse dixit," which literally means "he himself has said it," or more roughly translates as "it is so because he [the judge] says so." The Court simply arrogated to itself a power it cannot rightfully exercise in order to further the conservative agenda of promoting the death penalty.[9]

These appalling decisions, devoid of humane sensibility, are typical of contemporary American death-penalty law and of the type of jurisprudence that the existence of the death penalty invites.[10] They illustate a particular kind of arbitrary and abusive power that consists of making bad laws. The judicial and prosecutorial misconduct exhibited in the Rosenberg case exemplifies a distinct but related form of arbitrariness, in which the powerful ignore and violate the laws and rules that they impose on others. The case record, as supplemented by government documents recovered in 1976 under the Freedom of Information Act (FOIA), strongly suggests numerous instances of misconduct by the prosecution and of prejudgment and misconduct by the trial judge, Irving R. Kaufman.

Questions concerning the fairness and legal propriety of the trial and post-conviction process have long been aired and analyzed in the Rosenberg literature and need not be recounted here. By way of example, I will discuss only one particularly disturbing but surprisingly little-remarked episode. The particular incident deserves emphasis because of the identity of the participants and the enormity of the misconduct in which, it appears likely, they so casually engaged.

The episode concerns Supreme Court activity during the frantic days just prior to the execution on June 19, 1953. The conferences and other inner workings of the Court are ordinarily shrouded in secrecy. However, aided by FBI documents obtained under FOIA and the private papers and journals of now-deceased justices who were on the Court in 1953, historians have been able to reconstruct in some detail what transpired during those fateful days.[11]

The available evidence strongly suggests that on June 16, 1953, Chief Justice Fred M. Vinson and Attorney General Herbert W. Brownell, acting on the recommendation of Associate Justice Robert H. Jackson, met secretly to discuss the Rosenberg case. At the time, Justice William O. Douglas was considering a petition for a stay of execution filed on behalf of the Rosenbergs. The apparent purpose of the meeting was to develop a plan of action in the event that Douglas granted the stay. The Supreme Court had recessed for the summer; in the ordinary course of things, a stay granted by Douglas would have been effective until the Court reconvened the following October, allowing considerable time for Rosenberg activists, who were already gaining ground, to mobilize further support and sympathy in the United States and abroad. Vinson, Jackson, and Brownell keenly opposed further delay. The evidence suggests that at the secret meeting Vinson and Brownell agreed that if Douglas stayed the execution, the government would immediately move for, and the chief justice would grant, the convening of the Court for a highly unusual special session. As it happened, Douglas did grant the stay, whereupon, without notice to the Rosenbergs' lawyers, the Department of Justice moved for and the chief justice granted the convening of a special session to consider the Rosenberg matter. After hearing argument the reconvened Court vacated Douglas's stay on the afternoon of June 19. The Rosenbergs were executed a few hours later.

The most important piece of evidence pointing to this scenario of a secret meeting is an internal FBI memorandum released in the Meeropols' FOIA suit (see next page). The document recites that a member of the prosecution team, Assistant United States Attorney James Kilsheimer III, informed Judge Kaufman of the meeting, and that Kaufman relayed the information to the New York FBI headquarters. Kaufman's report included his understanding that if Douglas stayed the execution, Vinson would reconvene the full Court for the purpose of vacating the stay. Because the document contains second- or thirdhand information, we cannot be certain of its accuracy. Nonetheless, most commentators on the Rosenberg case, regardless of their differences on other questions, appear to have concluded that the meeting occurred more or less as described in the FBI letter.[12] There are some other fragments of supporting documentary evidence.[13] Apart from the postulate that the alleged participants would have known that such a meeting was highly improper, no evidence or argument to rebut the FBI memorandum has surfaced. The document became available to the public in 1976. So far as I have been able to determine, Brownell, who celebrated his ninetieth birthday in 1994,[14] has never issued a denial or any statement about the FBI report or the books and articles that discuss the meeting.[15] Further confirmation of the FBI report may be found in the fact that the plan of action (for Vinson to reconvene the full Court) was actually carried out essentially as predicted in the FBI document.[16] We may never know for sure, but the most plausible conclusion in light of the available evidence is that the secret meeting did indeed take place, and for the purpose of considering further steps to ensure a conclusion to the case by the prompt execution of the Rosenbergs.

Assuming this to be so, and assuming the participants could offer no special justification for their conduct (it is hard to imagine what justification there might have been), both the mere fact of the meeting and the specific matters discussed were highly improper[17] and possibly criminal. Communications between the judge and one of the parties regarding a pending adversary proceeding, outside the presence of any representative of the adverse party, are called "ex parte." Except under special circumstances not relevant here, ex parte contacts constitute serious misconduct that is forbidden by the ethical canons governing the legal profession. It is easy to see why. If ex parte contacts were permitted, the judge's impartiality could succumb to the influences of attorneys the judge knows or favors; false or ambiguous evidence could be presented to judges in secret without an opportunity for rebuttal

Office Memorandum • UNITED STATES GOVERNMENT

TO   MR. LADD   DATE: June 17, 1953

FROM   MR. BELMONT

SUBJECT: JULIUS ROSENBERG, ET AL
           ESPIONAGE - R

         We checked with the Washington Field Office at 10:45 A.M. this morning on the status of the motion before Justice Douglas of the Supreme Court by attorney Fyke Farmer. The Agent who was in the Court building advised that Justice Douglas and Justice Jackson went to their respective offices at 9:40 A.M. today and have not come out. The attorneys are standing by.

         At 10:50 A.M. Supervisor Tom McAndrews of New York called to advise that Judge Kaufman had called the New York Office. Judge Kaufman said he learned from AUSA Kilsheimer that last night, on the recommendation of Justice Jackson, the Attorney General and Chief Justice Vinson met at 11:00 P.M. to determine whether to call the complete Court into session to dispose of Fyke Farmer's motion. Judge Kaufman advised that as of 7:30 P.M., Douglas was disposed to grant the writ. However, after he came back from dinner, he was wavering and undecided. Judge Kaufman said that even if Douglas does throw out the motion, Justice Frankfurter will hear it. Judge Kaufman said that Justice Jackson was very upset about the indecision of Douglas. Jackson felt that the whole theory of listening to Farmer's motion was ridiculous and Douglas should have turned it down yesterday.

ACTION:

         For your information.

ADDENDUM: AHB:ner 6-17-53

         At 11:15 A.M. Supervisor McAndrews called back to advise that Judge Kaufman had very confidentially advised that at the meeting between the Attorney General and Chief Justice Vinson last night, Justice Vinson said that if a stay is granted he will call the full Court into session Thursday morning to vacate it.

Facsimile of FBI internal memorandum released in Freedom of Information Act case brought by Michael and Robert Meeropol; distributed, with other documents obtained in the suit, by the National Committee to Reopen the Rosenberg Case.

or clarification by the other side; and judges might be led to prejudge the matters before them. The ban on ex parte contact is therefore a fundamental premise of the adversary system of justice in the United States To put it simply, ex parte communication is cheating, and ethical lawyers recognize it as such.

True, the model ethical codes prepared by the American Bar Association are not specifically enacted as rules of the Supreme Court and therefore are not directly binding on the justices. Moreover, other incidents of ex parte contact between the Department of Justice and the Court are known to have occurred in the era of the Rosenberg case.[18] Nonetheless, I believe that most legal ethics experts, then and now, would regard an ex parte meeting between the attorney general and the chief justice to discuss a federal prosecution then pending before the Court as violating fundamental norms of our legal order that should and do constrain even our highest prosecutors and judges; as subjecting those involved to disciplinary action and censure; and as tainting the prosecution of the Rosenbergs. Moreover, the evidence, if accurate, is consistent with, although by itself insufficient to establish, the conclusion that a crime of obstruction of justice (or perhaps a crime of conspiracy to obstruct justice) occurred in connection with the ex parte discussions between the attorney general and the chief justice.[19]

Because there is no adjudicated precedent for this type of misconduct, we do not know to what remedies, if any, the Rosenbergs might have been entitled had the facts of the incident come to light before the execution. (The question of possible remedies for the Rosenbergs is distinct from the issue of disciplinary, contempt, and/or criminal sanctions against the participants.) Not all judicial and prosecutorial misconduct automatically results in a mistrial or in the disqualification of the judge. Unprofessional conduct might be sanctioned as such yet deemed to be "harmless" so far as the underlying trial is concerned. But in this particular instance, again assuming the accuracy of the FBI memorandum and related evidence, we have the chief judge of the court in which the matter was then pending acting in the case pursuant to an ex parte agreement with the prosecution's top lawyer as to how to move it along toward a certain result (prompt closure by execution of the Rosenbergs). There is good reason to believe that the misconduct directly and substantially prejudiced the defendants in their final legal efforts to avoid execution. Had the facts surfaced immediately, surely the Rosenbergs would have had a weighty argument for a stay of execution pending reconsideration, with Justices Vinson and Jackson disqualified. We can only speculate as to whether such a procedure might have saved their lives.

We do not ordinarily think of contemporary death-penalty cases of the type described above as linked or in any way comparable to the Rosenberg case. The contemporary cases are not "political trials" in the ordinary sense of the term, and they involve people charged with common crimes, not political offenses. Yet I think there is an affinity or indirect connection. In their haste to assure that the Rosenbergs would die on schedule and to preempt the growing popular movement to save them, government officials at the highest levels appear to have completely disregarded basic legal principles of fair play and due process. The available evidence also suggests troubling incidents of judicial and prosecutorial misconduct at the trial court level. Power was abused, and individual rights were ignored or prejudiced. Similarly, abuse of power and disregard for individual rights characterize contemporary death penalty jurisprudence (although typically in the contemporary cases the operative mechanism is the making of bad law rather than misconduct).

THE DEATH PENALTY AND DEMOCRATIC POLITICAL CULTURE

I turn now to a second point of connection, one that might link the nature of at least some contemporary opposition to the death penalty with aspects of the Rosenberg case.

In fairness to readers, I need before proceeding to insert a personal reference that bears on this branch of my argument. I was a six-year-old New York City child of leftist parents when the Rosenbergs were executed. I did not really understand at the time what was happening. My parents were reluctant to tell their children about the case and related matters of the day, or about their own political activities, for fear that we might say something damaging at school or on the playground. Although I was too young really to understand, it was obvious to me that whatever was happening was a great catastrophe in my parents' lives. The level of fear they unwittingly conveyed and that we children internalized was so great that I still experience release and exhiliration even today, over forty years later, simply to discuss these matters openly. After the execution, the Rosenbergs' bodies were laid in rest at a funeral home in New York City. I have an imprecise but vivid image of my parents taking us by car to the streets adjacent to the funeral home, where large crowds of mourners came to pay their respects. This was a central experience of my childhood. Although the image still arouses feelings of terror in me, I will always be grateful to my parents for including me in this expression of respect for the Rosenbergs. Subsequently, I befriended Robert and Michael Meeropol and learned about the case and the meaning of what I had seen as a kid that day in June 1953. Given this background, I doubt whether I have ever been capable of seriously considering arguments in favor of the death penalty. Nevertheless, I believe my background situates me to draw some useful connections between past and present that are not so bound up in my personal experience.

283

I have never done a poll, but I assume that there is widespread opposition to the death penalty among today's diverse, if very fragmented, American Left. This was not always so. New Leftists often enthusiastically supported revolutions in Cuba, China, and elsewhere, without questioning these regimes' implementation of the death penalty in both criminal and political cases. Earlier generations on the Left, including those in the Rosenbergs' political milieu, approved or remained silent in the face of political terror in the Soviet Union. I may be quite wrong, but I think that for most progressives in the United States today, opposition to the death penalty has become an article of faith. Moreover, despite the important influence of the philosophy of nonviolence on the 1960s civil rights movement, I think most contemporary opposition to the death penalty does *not* derive from a consistent pacifist position. For example, many death penalty opponents, myself included, believe that the use of force in self-defense or pursuant to multilateral peacekeeping and security efforts can be morally justifiable, depending on the circumstances.

If I am correct that there is widespread opposition to the death penalty among today's diffuse Left, I want to make a further claim about the quality of this opposition. Abolitionist opinion does not follow from any unified or totalizing political philosophy. Rather, death-penalty opposition reflects deeply felt but somewhat intuitive and not fully theorized moral and political commitments and sensibilities, which are in turn informed by a historical sense of how the death-penalty has functioned in American power relations and social hierarchies. Perhaps the most important historical or functional concern underlying death-penalty opposition is that the application of the death penalty in the United States is intimately connected to and reflective of practices of racial domination and discrimination. The death penalty has become a bizarre surrogate for lynching. An example of a more abstract moral or political intuition driving contemporary opposition is the felt sense that, besides killing people, the death penalty corrupts democratic life. The irreversibility of the death sentence violates a postulate central to the development of democratic political culture: that all people have the capacity for learning and self-transformation.

If I am right, contemporary opposition to capital punishment emerges out of deeply felt commitments about the preciousness and transformability of human life combined with an awareness of the specific social evils associated with the implementation of the death penalty. I think this kind of political commitment—grounded in democratic and egalitarian values, and informed by an understanding of social context—exemplifies something good in contemporary radicalism.

There is an affinity between this type or quality of political belief and an aspect of the Rosenberg case. Much has been said about the orthodox and perhaps simplistic nature of the Rosenberg's Popular Front or even Stalinist beliefs and rhetoric.[20] We should attend carefully to this facet of the Rosenberg case and avoid transforming the couple into something they were not: saints or political visionaries.

Nonetheless, in retrospect, there are some aspects of the Rosenbergs' politics and ordeal that foreshadow a more contemporary kind of radicalism. I think we can see this more clearly if we focus on what the Rosenbergs actually *did* during their prison years, rather than on what they wrote or on the ideological lenses through which they might have interpreted their own experience. From the time of their arrest onward, in nearly total isolation and, of course, under the compulsion of tragic circumstances, the Rosenbergs were propelled into and accepted and fashioned certain roles as political activists. They not only struggled to vindicate their own cause but, inevitably, also fought against the death penalty and all its baneful and corroding influence on American life. They became living advocates for abolition.

The Rosenbergs were placed in this situation because they would not buy mercy by confession and cooperation. Their "political practice," if it is not inappropriate to label their ordeal as such, taught an important lesson. One should not harm others—for instance, by naming names—for instrumental reasons and in order to advance one's own interests. To put it simply, people are ends, not simply means with which to accomplish one's projects in the world.

Moreover, the Rosenbergs' courage, as it played out in the unique circumstances of the case, led them simultaneously to embody two truths: both that the death penalty is wrong as a matter of principle—and regardless of guilt or innocence—and that the death-penalty question concerns not just philosophical and ethical abstractions but concrete questions about power, social hierarchy, and political repression. That is, the Rosenbergs' death-house struggle merged a foundational moral intuition with an understanding of social context. Because of the way the case unfolded, the Rosenbergs did not fall easily into a familiar category of political martyrdom, but neither is it accurate to see them as mere bystanders who got caught up in a political trial by mistake. In fact, they were not just ordinary people. They were singled out because they were working-class Jews and members of the radical, probably Communist Left. And there was an overt political dimension to their struggle in their last years because, as Robert Meeropol explains elsewhere in this volume, they resisted and refused to submit to illegitimate authority. Their ordeal created an example of a politics founded on an inner sense of integrity and commitment; a politics that eschewed the instrumental treatment of others for personal gain; an exalted merger of the personal and the political, one forced on them by circumstances but nonetheless bravely embraced. There is in this political example something important, vital, and timely from which contemporary activists can still draw inspiration.

NOTES

© Copyright 1995 by Karl E. Klare. I am grateful for the assistance of Robert Meeropol, Michael Meltsner, Marshall Perlin, and Deborah Ramirez. Responsibility for error is mine alone.

1 In February 1995, the new South African Constitutional Court heard its first case, which will determine the constitutionality of the death penalty under the fundamental rights provisions of the new, democratic constitution.

2 As a kid, I once saw the FBI's exhibit on display at the Cross County Shopping Center in Westchester, New York. My parents would not allow me to enter the truck to see the display; I was quickly pulled away. This was, I imagine, a few years after the execution.

3 111 S.Ct. 2546 (1991).

4 112 S.Ct. 1074 (1992).

5 *Herrera v. Collins*, 113 S.Ct. 853 (1993).

6 112 S.Ct. 1713 (1992)(no. 5). Stephen Reinhardt, a participating judge of the U.S. Court of Appeals for the Ninth Circuit, has written an extraordinary, harrowing description of the final days of the *Harris* case, "The Supreme Court, The Death Penalty, and The *Harris* Case," *Yale Law Journal* 102 (1992): 205–223. Judge Reinhardt writes: "The *Harris* case was a nightmare. It served no one well. The process was ugly, cruel, injudicious. At a critical time in its history, the American legal system failed to function fairly or well…. The saddest part of all this is that *Harris* did not just happen. It was no accident. It was inevitable. It was the logical culmination of a series of Supreme Court decisions subordinating individual liberties to the less-than-compelling interests of the state and stripping lower federal courts of the ability to protect individual rights" (205, citations omitted).

7 *Vasquez v. Harris*, 112 S.Ct. 1713 (1992)(no. 5).

8 "No further stays of Robert Alton Harris' execution shall be entered by the federal courts except upon order of this Court." Ibid.

9 For an excellent analysis of the Supreme Court's performance in the Harris case, see Evan Caminker and Erwin Chemerinsky, "The Lawless Execution of Robert Alton Harris," *Yale Law Journal* 102 (1992): 225–54. The authors conclude: "Out of a desire to achieve a result—Harris's execution—the [Supreme] Court mischaracterized the issue, applied the wrong legal standard, and arrogated to itself a power of superintendence over all federal courts that it simply

does not possess" (226).

In response, Steven G. Calabresi and Gary Lawson, in "Equity and Hierarchy: Reflections on the Harris Execution," *Yale Law Journal* 102 (1992): 255–79, challenge the Caminker and Chemerinsky analysis on many points. However, regarding the question of the Supreme Court's purported bar to further lower federal court stays in the case, they conclude: "We agree generally with Professors Caminker and Chemerinsky's excellent argument that this order is very troubling and, if taken at face value, was issued without authority" (257).

10 As this book entered production, the Supreme Court's death penalty jurisprudence reached a new low. Jesse Dewayne Jacobs was convicted of capital murder by the State of Texas, principally on the basis of a confession made at the time of his arrest. But Jacobs recanted the confession and testified that his sister was responsible for the murder. The sister was later prosecuted and received a prison sentence. At her trial, the same prosecutor who had tried Jacobs' case disavowed the original confession and called Jacobs as a witness against his sister, announcing that he now believed Jacobs' version that she pulled the trigger. By inexorable implication, the prosecutor thus conceded that Jacobs could not be guilty of capital murder. Texas prosecutors declined, however, to reopen his case. After the Supreme Court denied his petition for a stay, Jacobs v. Scott, 115 S.Ct. 711 (1995), Texas killed Jacobs on January 4, 1995.

11 Accounts of Supreme Court activity immediately prior to the Rosenbergs' execution appear in Michael E. Parrish, "Cold War Justice: The Supreme Court and the Rosenbergs," *American Historical Review* 82 (1977): 805–842; Joseph H. Sharlitt, *Fatal Error: The Miscarriage of Justice that Sealed the Rosenbergs' Fate* (New York: Scribner's, 1989); and James F. Simon, *Independent Journey: The Life of William O. Douglas* (New York: Harper, 1980), 304–313.

12 See, for example, Parrish, "Cold War Justice," 835; Sharlitt, *Fatal Error*, 4–5, 66–67; Simon, *Independent Journey*, 308–10; Ronald Radosh and Joyce Milton, *The Rosenberg File: A Search for the Truth* (New York: Holt, 1983), 403–404.

13 See, for example, a memorandum of a telephone conversation with Brownell that has been located in the papers of John Foster Dulles (cited in Radosh and Milton, *The Rosenberg File*, 566) and some notes in the papers of Justice Felix Frankfurter (cited, e.g., in Parrish, "Cold War Justice," 834, and Sharlitt, *Fatal Error*, 75–76).

14 See the *New York Times*, Feb. 15, 1994, late edition-final, B4.

15 In his lengthy memoirs, Brownell discusses the Rosenberg case only in passing. See Herbert Brownell, with John P. Burke, *Advising Ike: The Memoirs of Attorney General Herbert Brownell*, (Lawrence, KA: University Press of Kansas, 1993), 230, 244–45, 250nn. Brownell notes that, after Justice Douglas had granted the stay, he "instructed the Justice Department to petition Chief Justice Vinson to call an unprecedented special meeting of the Court to review

the stay," ibid. at 244, but he neither mentions nor denies an ex parte contact with Vinson.

Chief Justice Vinson and Justice Jackson died a short time after the Rosenbergs' execution and long before release of the FBI documents on the case. Vinson died on September 8, 1953, before the Court reconvened for the new term. In his memoirs, Justice Douglas claimed that in August 1953, shortly before Vinson's death, the chief justice confided to Douglas's brother that he regretted his actions in the Rosenberg case and that he thought Douglas had been right about the stay. William O. Douglas, *The Court Years: 1939–1975* (New York: Random House, 1980), 84–85.

Vinson was replaced as chief justice by Earl Warren, who led the Court in a more liberal direction. The appointment of Warren as chief justice is one of several reasons (including the end of the Korean War) why a stay of execution and reconsideration in the following term might have aided the Rosenbergs.

Jackson died on October 9, 1954.

16 See Sharlitt, *Fatal Error*, 4–5, 68; Simon, *Independent Journey*, 308–310.

17 See, generally, Sharlitt, *Fatal Error*. Sharlitt concludes that irrespective of whether the Rosenbergs were guilty or innocent in the factual sense of having engaged in the crimes alleged, their execution was illegal (ix). He bases this conclusion, among other things, on the meeting between Brownell and Vinson and their subsequent conduct in arranging for the full court to vacate Justice Douglas's stay.

18 Philip Elman was a law clerk for Justice Felix Frankfurter in the early 1940s. Subsequently he had a lengthy career in the Office of the Solicitor General, whose attorneys appear before the Supreme Court on behalf of the U.S. government. In an interview he gave to the Columbia Oral History Project, Elman reveals that Frankfurter confided information to Elman about the inner workings of the Court for a period of many years while Elman was with the Solicitor General. See Philip Elman (interviewed by Norman Silber), "The Solicitor General's Office, Justice Frankfurter, and Civil Rights Litigation, 1946–1960: An Oral History," *Harvard Law Review* 100 (1987): 817–52. These conversations included discussions of cases involving the United States as a party that were pending or likely to go before the Supreme Court. Elman noted that "there were certain unspoken restrictions. We never discussed a case that I had argued" (844). However, the discussions did include some matters in which Elman's office was involved and even some cases, notably the school desegregation cases, in which Mr. Elman himself participated. He remarks: "*Brown v. Board of Education*, which we fully discussed, was an extraordinary case, and the ordinary rules didn't apply. In that case I knew everything, or at least [Frankfurter] gave me the impression that I knew everything, that was going on in the Court. He told me about what was said in conference and who said it" (844).

Several experts on legal ethics interviewed by the *New York Times*, including a leading academic authority on the subject, the then-current solicitor general, and two past solicitors general, opined that the reported communications about pending cases in which Elman was involved were clearly improper. See the *New York Times*, Mar. 22, 1987, late city final edition, sec. 1, part 1, 1.

19 Whether criminal activity in fact occurred would depend, among other things, on exactly what was said at the meeting, and with what intent. For example, if it could be shown that the attorney general attempted to sway or influence the chief justice, with the specific intention to set in motion a process that he knew would deprive the Rosenbergs of legal rights they had before the Court, without any justification, this might be enough to constitute an obstruction offense. Obviously, determining whether a crime occurred would require a legal analyst to possess information that is now virtually impossible to acquire. And, as noted in the text, we cannot be absolutely certain the meeting occurred.

20 For example, see David Thorburn's discussion of the *Death House Letters* elsewhere in this volume.

21

The Work of the State

Andrew Ross

The trial of the month. A large part of political culture in the United States revolves obsessively around public discussion of and commentary on such spectacles—Amy Fisher, Laurence Powell et al, Woody Allen, Mike Tyson, Baby M, Rodney King, Charles Stuart, William Kennedy Smith, Glen Ridge, Central Park, Crown Heights, Howard Beach, the Menendez Brothers, Lorena Bobbitt, O.J. Simpson, and so on. Civil society here is a cumbersome body politic stumbling like some great dorky Gulliver from one trial to the next. There's no one pulling the strings—in the long run it does not serve us well to view the state as a puppetmaster—but there's also nothing random or witless about this kind of behavior. While only a tiny percentage of legal cases ever come to court, an even smaller number qualifies for nomination as full-blown media spectacles whose critical impact on the civil life of the nation is held to be definitive by the armada of media spin merchants wheeled out to "focus" discussion on the ultimate meaning of the proceedings. Sure, everyone loves a good trial, there are still many people who like a good hanging, and there's no doubt that the entertainment quotient of today's heat-seeking trials helps to make such events a primary channel of consent or normalization in national political life. And yet who could deny that the work of the judiciary is the last line of defense for the state's elite interests? One need only consider the vast numbers of political prisoners—choose any definition—held in U.S. penitentiaries, the even greater number of immigrants and "excludable aliens" being kept in INS detention centers around the country, and the incarceration of immense populations of people of color to gauge the penal culture's strategic role in a socially advanced corporate state.

Every so often a case comes to trial in which the interests of the state itself are particularly self-evident. Readers of *Secret Agents* will recognize that such interests were preeminent in the Rosenberg trial of 1953. So were they, too, in the 1994 trial involving the World Trade Center bombers, a trial that served us a lesson in what was to be considered "American" and what was not. This lesson was unfolding against the backdrop of considerable changes in the immigrant composition of the U.S. national population. Beginning in the late 1970s, huge amounts of foreign investment poured into the USA, partly to debt finance Reagan's military buildup, partly to secure access to a large, unified consumer market, relatively unprotected by national trade policies. The USA became the world's largest debtor nation, its regional economies unable any longer to respond to the lead of U.S. capital and the U.S. state. Correspondingly, the new global economy's international division of labor generated vast migration streams, bringing many new arrivals from Asia, the Caribbean, the Middle East, and Latin America to New York City to work in the informal and the service-sector economies. Combining the labor streams with refugees from wars and disasters, the World Bank estimated that the South-North flow across national borders in 1992 amounted to one hundred million people.[1]

New York, the city of global finance, had become home to the cultures of the globe in ways that were quite different from patterns of immigration and acculturation in the earlier, monopoly-capitalist era of the Golden Door. While the rate of immigration came nowhere near the figures achieved at the turn of the century, the new immigration produced multicultural communities that, unlike the previous wave of mostly European immigrants, had no common Western traditions. What ramifications did these developments have for the political and cultural coherence of the U.S. state? No event could have provided a more public focus for this question than the bombing of the World Trade Center, the subsequent bomb plot, and the trials of the suspected ring of bombers. The nets of intrigue and conspiracy publicly projected onto these suspects multiplied and mutated like a nuclear chain reaction in the months following the World Trade Center bombing and the later suspected plot to blow up the U.N., Federal Building, and the Port Authority's Hudson River tunnels. When the long list of likely sponsoring "terrorist states" and "organizations" had run its course in the media—Iran, Iraq, Syria, Libya, Sudan, Pakistan, Nicaragua, the Serbs, the Croats, Hezbollah, Hamas, the Colombian drug cartels (the late Pablo Escobar wrote to the U.S. ambassador, "They can take me off the list, because if I had done it, I would be saying why and I would be saying what I want"), the Sendero Luminoso, the IRA—one thing was clear. The suspects were very much in residence, which is to say that, far from being "hitmen" dispatched from overseas, they had roots and family in the new immigrant communities ringing the metropolitan area. Many of the suspects were also products of the aftermath of the Cold War, recruited and trained under U.S. auspices for the largest covert war of the Reagan years: the Afghan jihad, which was the ideological equivalent of the Spanish Civil War for many of the international volunteers who flocked to Peshawar for the cause in the 1980s. American Muslim radicals who had gone to fight with the Afghan mujahideen, with the aid of billions of dollars in CIA money and weapons, were now bringing the jihad home. Nothing, not even evidence of a monstrous international terrorist network, could have presented more of a nightmare, or a godsend, to the national security bloodhounds. Like the "red spies" omnipresent on our home turf at the height of Cold War paranoia preceding the Rosenberg trial—they could be *your* neighbors—the new terrorist was no longer recognizably alien, at least not for those accustomed, in their communities, to the presence of Muslims, members of the fastest growing religion in the USA.

Over twenty years earlier, media commentary on the New Left bombings of 1969/70 reflected the sense of a family quarrel; generational differences about U.S. policy were being expressed by the sons and daughters of America's white elite, and this view extended as far as white radical chic could be stretched in espousing minority causes like the Panthers and the Young Lords. Media commentary on the "Islamic" bombings of 1993, by contrast, initially treated the affair as a foreign threat for the most part, with coverage of Islamic affairs making the distinction usually drawn between the traditional kinds of Islamic states: those which are friends of the West, basically, like Saudi Arabia, and the new, radical Islamic states like Iran by whom the United States is still demonized as the Great Satan. In addition, distinctions were drawn between the older generation of fundamentalists from the Muslim Brotherhood (founded in Egypt in 1928 by Hassan al-Banna) and the younger, more "impatient" extremists, among whom is counted Sheik Abdel Rahman, Jersey City's exiled leader of Egypt's Islamic Group (Gama'a al-Islamiya), Gulbuddin Hekmatyar, the leader of Hezb-i-Islami in Afghanistan, along with the Sudanese Hassan al-Turabi, the Tunisian exile Rashid Ghanoushi, and the Algerian head of the Islamic Salvation Front, Abassi Madani. This media coverage had little to do with the actual Islamic world—a billion diverse people living in diverse kinds of societies, from theocratic kingdoms to secular democracies. Rather than informing Westerners about the complex struggles (between secular and religious movements) within the Islamic world itself, it was purely a reflection of Western interests in defining that world.

In August the government finally indicted Sheik Abdel Rahman and fifteen others under a seditious conspiracy act broad enough to allow prosecutors to link together a series of events from the assassination of militant rabbi Meir Kahane in 1989 to the 1993 plots. Under this rarely used law, the suspects were charged with "conspiring to overthrow, put down, or destroy by force the Government" by "levying a war of urban terrorism against the United States." Since the law measured guilt simply by the evidence of plotting rather than by any attempt to carry out an insurrection, it was judged by many to come close to threatening freedom of speech and belief. Defense lawyer Ron Kuby argued that the government had created a "vast mythical Islamic conspiracy" in order to cover up its own botching of its manipulation of the World Trade Center circle through the activities of inside informant Emad Salem. Journalists like Robert Friedman asked more pointed questions about the extensive cover-up of the roles played in the whole history of events from Afghanistan to the bombings by "bungling FBI agents, Mossad moles, and CIA officials as zealous as the sheik's holy warriors."[2]

Despite the possibility of disclosures embarrassing to the state's security agencies (none of which surfaced during the trial itself), the pre-judicial publicity generated by the press in the months leading up to the trial of the World Trade Center bombers not only succeeded in affixing a high ratio of guilt on the suspects but also created a national climate of suspicion regarding all Middle Eastern immigrants, especially Muslims from Arab countries. Armed terrorist cells were plotting away again in the heartlands! Anti-immigrant sentiment rose precipitously in the months following the bombing; resident aliens were encouraged by the White House to seek citizenship to ease hostilities. Pat philosophizing about the post-Cold War order quickly placed the World Trade Center incident in the context of theories about the resurgence of premodern conflicts. The new barbarians were familiar stereotypes from early European history. After a century of crude attempts to scare up the socialist specter of collective man, the West was now returning to its more dependable, and racially evocative, non-Western enemy; an "orientalist" Islam. Suddenly "ancient" conflicts were considered to be more legitimate and therefore more dangerous than modern, capitalist ones. This thesis was repeated by many a policy hack in the early 1990s, following the lead of academics like Harvard's Samuel Huntington who pontificated about the essential clash between the civilizations of Islam and the West. A tide of commentators and soundbiters worked overtime to define a post-Cold War order in which "Muslim fundamentalists" are increasingly assumed to be the world's number one enemy of democratic life. It hardly went without saying that two years earlier in the Persian Gulf, the Western allies had fought a war to liberate a nation that is more "Muslim fundamentalist" than virtually any other despite the fact that the term "Muslim fundamentalist" was enjoying a diabolic life in public consciousness as a byword for all things deemed alien to decency and reason. In the flak surrounding the World Trade Center trial, the relationship of Sheik Abdel Rahman's circle to the activities of U.S.-sponsored fundamentalists like Gulbuddin Hekmatyar and Abdur Rafool Sayyaf in Afghanistan was selectively noted in the press, further complicating the equation of the "Muslim fundamentalist" with the State Department's own selective definition of "terrorist." In general, however, this relationship was suppressed, and given a wide berth during the trial itself. Clearly, "Muslim fundamentalists" had been serviceable to U.S. interests abroad as subversives at large, most notably as thorns in the flesh of secular Arab nationalists, even, and especially, when they vigorously mouthed anti-Americanism, as Hekmatyar and his fanatical CIA-bankrolled followers had done all through the 1980s. The World Trade Center trials marked the first phase of the domestic version of this new orientalist narrative. Despite all the public attempts to dissociate the alleged activities of the suspects from the life of the majority of American Muslims and from Arab Americans, secular and Christian as well as Muslim, many used the World Trade Center and the conspiracy trials to reinforce the image of this emergent post-Soviet threat as the new "enemy within."

Forty years before, Ethel and Julius Rosenberg, Communist "enemies within," were put to death after a trial that served to define the present and future state of the Cold War. The serviceablity to the FBI and other state agencies of the existence of pinko "subversives" at home has been well documented in the Cold War era. The hegemonic moment, in the 1950s and 1960s, of the postwar American state would have been impossible, politically, economically, and culturally, without the creation of such subversives. Leaving aside the issue of the Rosenbergs' alleged involvement in espionage, few would deny that the Rosenberg trial was used, expediently, to justify the establishment of a national security state that, to this day, has denied its citizenry access to information not only about public affairs but also about the surveillance of their private activities. Such a trial was "required" by the ideological conditions of the moment, and could therefore draw on the full support of the highest offices of the state.

But the Rosenberg trial was not simply a political trial, required in order to demonize the designs of the Soviet Union and to crack down on the domestic Left. It was also a case allegedly involving technology transfer, the very essence of industrial espionage, and the engine of economic warfare. Indeed, the primary effect of the Rosenberg trial may have been more economic than political. For in many ways, the anxieties it generated about atomic warfare served as the raison d'être for the permanent war economy that has underpinned U.S. policy, both foreign and domestic, ever since. (In 1993 President Clinton's first projected military budget was higher in constant dollars than average spending during the Cold War, confirming that the defense industry is still the most efficient way of providing a 100 percent public subsidy for researching and developing new technologies for American corporations.)

Just as important, however, the Rosenberg trial was arguably the first public postwar event to trouble popular faith in the fledgling national security apparatus. Today, it is second nature among most Americans to distrust the intelligence activities of institutions like the FBI, the CIA, and the NSA. Elites from the White House down undoubtedly selected the Rosenbergs to serve as punitive examples, but the trial ultimately came to function as a publicly tolerated "limit" to the state's repressive activities, a limit set largely as a result of the undying attachment of the American Left to the Rosenberg case. Today, as the extent of the Atomic Energy Commission and the Department of Defense's insolent atomic experimentation with U.S. and Pacific Islander subjects is being officially disclosed, the treatment of the Rosenbergs will increasingly be seen on a continuum with such activities, as one more act of terrorism visited by the state on its own citizens in the atomic age.

What will continue to make the trial exceptional, however, is the role it has played in the history of the American Left. Today, it poses some difficult questions indeed. At the time, anti-Communist liberals referred to the trial as the end of an age of innocence (code for Stalinism) for the Left. Over forty years later, we might be tempted to think of the "innocence" of the Rosenberg moment in much larger historical terms, not restricted to leftist circles alone. To begin with, the broad Left rallied in support of the Rosenbergs in ways it could not and would not during the World Trade Center affair. Some might have sympathized with the anti-imperialist rhetoric imputed to a "Liberation Army Fifth Battalion" that claimed responsibility for the bombing in a letter to the *New York Times* (received four days after the incident) lambasting U.S. policies in support of Israel and other (secular Arab) "dictator countries" in the Middle East: "The American people must know that their civilians who got killed are not better than those who are getting killed by the American weapons and support.... The American people are responsible for the actions of their government and they must question all of the crimes that their government is committing against other people." But the ultimate basis of the letter's appeal was religious, and thus the argument made little headway with liberals/leftists committed to Third Worldist struggles for modern, secular states threatened daily by fundamentalist movements all over the world. There was no end of ambivalence among those who suspected a frame-up and were prepared to put the FBI under immediate suspicion and who, at the same time, thoroughly abhorred the letter and spirit of fundamentalist practices. This ambivalence has a deeper historical dimension, however.

At the dawn of the Cold War, the dominant contest in political ideology in the West had been over the soul and shape of modernity itself—what was it going to look like? Fritz Lang's Metropolis? Auschwitz? Levittown? Disneyland? a kibbutz? a Communist youth summer camp in the Catskills? The Rosenbergs and their supporters believed we would soon be living in either a fascist or, at the very least, a social democratic state—none would have believed we could have endured and survived a Ronald Reagan/Donald Duck presidency. Today, it is not so easy to take *modernity* for granted in quite the same way. The rise of Muslim fundamentalism is often taken to be one symptom of the widespread resurgence of ethnic particularism, tribalistic nationalism, and religious chauvinism in a world that was supposed to have been claimed in advance by secular modernity. Because they all took modernity itself for granted, none of modernity's ideologies—neither liberalism nor Marxism nor free-market libertarianism—foresaw a future in which religio-moral conviction would be playing such a major role in our political culture, locally and globally. The future was not supposed to play host to such "regressive" tendencies. Modernity was supposed to have subsumed cultural and religious differences in the name of the universality of rights and the righteousness of reason. By 1993, it was assumed, Satan would surely have been consigned to the flames of history, and yet right now his is the name on many tongues, Muslim and Christian, in the United States and abroad.

Again, in the early 1950s, the social milieu of the Rosenberg trial was marked by demands made on first- and second-generation immigrants—assimilation, patriotism, consumerism. The Rosenbergs themselves had lived among Popular Front Communists who claimed direct descent from Jefferson and Lincoln, and whose strategic patriotism was trumpeted by their friends and supporters as loudly as it was called into doubt by the government's case against them. By contrast, the backdrop to the World Trade Center trials was the mode of material existence among the new postcolonial migrant communities, for whom melting pot assimilation had long been rejected as an ideology of the past. Indeed, it is in part on the basis of their experience and history that cultural *difference* has been proposed, if far from accepted, as an integral part of a new kind of democratic state. Tolerance of cultural differences within such communities, not the old demand for cultural assimilation, is the challenge for liberal pluralism today. As always, the challenges for radicals are quite distinct, based on enfranchisement and empowerment, and rooted in analyses of institutional racism as a complex and evolved set of beliefs and practices. Following the Second World War, the assimilationist North American state used the Rosenberg trial to define its boundaries. From a less paranoid view, it could be said that the trial marked one of the limits to state power in the Cold War period. To this day the Rosenbergs are invoked for reasons that far transcend the often scholastic debates about details of their trial. Their names are summoned to remind legal authorities of the embarrassing excesses of the Cold War, with a view to averting more of the same. Although it is periodically revived by the nativist Right, official suspicion of Jewish fifth columnist loyalties (like those imputed to the Rosenbergs) has abated somewhat as the likely recipient of those loyalties shifted over the years from the international socialist cause to the "friendly" state of Israel. As Jewish American identity has become *less* alien because of the USA's international political interests, the case of the Muslim in North America has become more visible and more complex.

If only because of U.S. interests in the Islamic world, there has been considerable pressure to avoid another kind of cultural Cold War in which Westerners nurse their images of some stereotypical Muslim enemy, as hot-tempered and fanatical as the Soviet version was cold-blooded and self-denying. But there is little evidence that American citizens learned anything lasting about Islam or the Arab peoples from the extensive media commentary during the Gulf War, and, given the grisly fate of the Bosnian Muslims, there appears to be little political will in Washington to address the human rights of an oil-less people of Islam. The trials of the alleged bombers and conspirators were not only set up as tests of legal justice; they were also bound to turn into tests of cultural, even economic justice. As the first trial came to a close, the Senate had just passed a resolution condemning the anti-Semitic speeches generated by members of the Nation of Islam. Branch Davidians from the Waco trial were being acquitted in a case that embarrassed the FBI from beginning to end. The Christian Right was winning as many legal contests as it was losing. Israel was on the verge of success in creating a Palestinian Vichy-style government in the Occupied Territories. The massacre of Hebron had been "paid back," in the eyes of some, by the shooting of Lubavitchers on the Brooklyn Bridge. The World Trade Center was back to pre-1992 levels of occupancy, but it was surrounded, in the Wall Street area, by twenty million square feet of vacant office space—a grim legacy of the speculation boom and bust of the 1980s. Security in government and corporate buildings had been stepped up tenfold, increasing the degree of high-tech employee surveillance to penitentiarylike levels. The meaning of the trial could have resonated against any of the above.[3]

Was the World Trade Center trial "required" by the state to consolidate some new shift in the definition of the U.S. nation state? Twenty years from now, historians may well be making this argument, as many did in the case of the Rosenbergs. As historians of the present, however, we have a different vantage point. We are witnesses to history's nomination process, the busy milieu of potentiality in which are put forward a whole range of available ideas, values, judgments, victims, scapegoats, penalties, and theories to be tried, tested, and tailored to fit the ideological bill. The story that emerges is "elected" into the realm of official explanation, whence it begins its journey into the congealed state of common sense. The meanings of the events surrounding the World Trade Center bombing were serviceable to a multitude of closely related interests, all appertaining to U.S. global economic policy in the early 1990s. Whether the alleged perpetrators were framed or not (or whether they were guilty and were still being framed), we ought to be able to see how versions of these events were contoured to the shape of the New World Order, just as the ordeal of Ethel and Julius was molded forty years before.

NOTES

1 "The Seekers," *Nation*, July 26, 1993, 124.

2 Robert I. Friedman, "The Four Questions," *Village Voice*, Mar. 8, 1994, 23.

3 Almost one year later, the meaning of the World Trade Center bombing was itself being used to frame discussion of the Federal Building bombing in Oklahoma City. This second bombing incident was, in many ways, a perfect complement to the first, releasing into the public consciousness a complex set of anxieties about a homegrown, internal threat to the state that was as American in its appeal to constitutional rights as the earlier set of bombers had been un-American in their appeals. Henceforth, attempts to define the nation's domestic security interests would have both a Scylla and a Charybdis through which to steer the ship of the state.

Index

Contributors

Joyce Antler is Associate Professor of American Studies at Brandeis University. She is the author, among other works, of *Lucy Sprague Mitchell: The Making of a Modern Woman* (1987); editor of *America and I: Short Stories by American Jewish Women Writers* (1990); and coeditor of *The Challenge of Feminist Biography: Writing the Lives of Modern American Women* (1992). She is currently completing a book entitled *Journey Home: A History of Twentieth-Century American Jewish Women and the Struggle for Identity*.

Marie Ashe is Professor of Law at Suffolk University Law School in Boston. She teaches criminal law, constitutional law, and jurisprudence.

Michael Cadden, Director of the Program in Theater and Dance at Princeton University, is the coeditor of *Engendering Men: The Question of Male Feminist Criticism* and the author of a forthcoming study on contemporary theater, *The Body Theatrical: Essays on the Contemporary Stage*.

Blanche Wiesen Cook is Professor of History and Women's Studies at the John Jay College and the Graduate Center of the City University of New York. Her recent biography, *Eleanor Roosevelt: Volume One*, received the 1992 Biography Prize from the *Los Angeles Times*. She is also the author of *Crystal Eastman on Women and Revolution* and *The Declassified Eisenhower*, which the *New York Times Book Review* listed as one of the notable books of 1981, among other works. She is currently working on volume two of *Eleanor Roosevelt*.

Thomas L. Dumm is Associate Professor of Political Science at Amherst College. He is the author most recently of a study of the American political unconscious entitled *united states* (1994). His *Michel Foucault and the Politics of Freedom* is forthcoming.

Marjorie Garber is William R. Kenan Jr. Professor of English and Director of the Center for Literary and Cultural Studies at Harvard. She is the author of *Vested Interests: Cross-Dressing and Cultural Anxiety* (1992) and three books on Shakespeare: *Shakespeare's Ghost Writers: Literature as Uncanny Causality* (1987), *Coming of Age in Shakespeare* (1981), and *Dream in Shakespeare: From Metaphor to Metamorphosis* (1974). Her most recent book is *Vice Versa: Bisexuality and the Eroticism of Everday Life* (1995).

Stanley Goldberg has taught at Antioch College, the University of Zambia, and Hampshire College. He has written numerous articles on the history of late-nineteenth- and early-twentieth-century physics and its relationship to changing cultural fashions and values. He is the author of *Understanding Relativity: Origins and Impact of a Scientific Revolution* (1984), and he is currently completing a biography of General Leslie Groves, the military head of the Manhattan Project.

Carol Hurd Green is Associate Dean of the College of Arts and Sciences at Boston College, where she also teaches in the American Studies and Women's Studies Programs. She is coauthor of *American Women in the 1960s: Changing the Future* (1993) and coeditor of *Notable American Women: The Modern Period* (1980).

Morton J. Horwitz is Charles Warren Professor of American Legal History at Harvard Law School. He has published two volumes entitled *The Transformation of American Law*. He is one of the editors (with William W. Fisher III and Thomas A. Read) of *American Legal Realism*.

Alice Jardine teaches literary and cultural theory at Harvard University. She is the author of *Gynesis: Configurations of Woman and Modernity* and, most recently, coeditor of *Shifting Scenes: Interviews on Women, Writing, and Politics in Post-68 France*. She is currently writing on the American 1950s and on women and technology.

David Kennedy joined the Harvard Law School faculty in 1980, where he is currently the Henry Shattuck Professor of Law and Director of Graduate and International Legal Studies. He teaches and writes about international law, international trade, the law of the European Union, and legal theory.

Randall Kennedy is Professor of Law at Harvard University, where he teaches courses on race relations and the law, McCarthyism, and contracts.

Karl E. Klare teaches at Northeastern University School of Law, where he is George J. and Kathleen Waters Matthews Distinguished University Professor.

Robert Meeropol received undergraduate and graduate degrees in Anthropology from the University of Michigan and a law degree from Western New England College School of Law. He is founder and Executive Director of the Rosenberg Fund for Children, a public foundation that provides for the emotional and educational needs of children in the United States whose parents have been targeted in the course of their progressive activities. He is married, has two grown children, and lives in Springfield, Massachusetts.

Joyce Nelson taught in the Film Studies Department at Queen's University in Canada before becoming a full-time freelance writer in 1976. She is the author of six books, including *The Perfect Machine: TV in the Nuclear Age* (1987), *The Colonized Eye: Rethinking the Grierson Legend* (1988), *Sultans of Sleaze: PR & the Media* (1989), and *Sign Crimes/Road Kill: From Mediascape to Landscape* (1992).

Robert N. Proctor is Professor of the History of Science at Pennsylvania State University. He is the author of *Racial Hygiene: Medicine under the Nazis* (1988), *Value-Free Science?* (1991), and *Cancer Wars: How Politics Shapes What We Know and Don't Know About Cancer* (1995). His research interests coalesce around the political history and philosophy of science; he has also written on environmental policy, bioethics, and the history of German and American anthropology.

Bruce Robbins teaches in the English Department at Rutgers University. He is the author of *Secular Vocations: Intellectuals, Professionalism, and Culture* (1993) and the editor of *The Phantom Public Sphere* (1993). *The Servant's Hand: English Fiction from Below* was reissued last year. He is also a coeditor of *Social Text*.

Andrew Ross is Professor and Director of the American Studies Program at New York University. His books include *The Chicago Gangster Theory of Life: Nature's Debt to Society* (1994), *Strange Weather: Culture, Science, and Technology in the Age of Limits* (1991), and *No Respect: Intellectuals and Popular Culture* (1989). He is also the editor of *Universal Abandon?* (1988) and the coeditor of *Microphone Fiends* (1994) and *Technoculture* (1990).

Ellen Schrecker teaches American history at Yeshiva University. She has written *The Age of McCarthyism: A Brief History with Documents* (1994) and *No Ivory Tower: McCarthyism and the Universities* (1986) and is currently working on a general study of the anti-Communist political repression of the 1940s and 1950s.

David Suchoff is Associate Professor of English at Colby College and author of *Critical Theory and the Novel: Mass Society and Cultural Criticism in Dickens, Melville, and Kafka* (1994). He is also cotranslator and author of the introduction to Alain Finkielkraut's *The Imaginary Jew* (1994).

David Thorburn is Professor of Literature and Director of the Cultural Studies Project at the Massachusetts Institute of Technology. The author of *Conrad's Romanticism* and many essays and reviews on literary and cultural topics, he is currently writing a book about American television, to be called *Story Machine*.

Rebecca L. Walkowitz is a doctoral candidate in the Department of English and American Literature and Language at Harvard University. She is an editor of *Media Spectacles* (1993), and the forthcoming *Field Work*.